I0120707

Magic's
Translations

Djimatnja Koes

Reality
Politics in
Colonial
Indonesia

Magic's Translations

MARGARET J. WIENER

with an afterword by ISABELLE STENGERS

Duke University Press
Durham and London / 2025

© 2025 DUKE UNIVERSITY PRESS. All rights reserved
Project Editor: Bird Williams
Designed by Courtney Leigh Richardson
Typeset in Merlo and Canela by Westchester Publishing Services

Library of Congress Cataloging-in-Publication Data
Names: Wiener, Margaret J., author.
Title: Magic's translations : reality politics in colonial Indonesia /
Margaret J. Wiener.
Description: Durham : Duke University Press, 2025. | Includes
bibliographical references and index.
Identifiers: LCCN 2024033415 (print)
LCCN 2024033416 (ebook)
ISBN 9781478031734 (paperback)
ISBN 9781478028505 (hardcover)
ISBN 9781478060710 (ebook)
Subjects: LCSH: Occultism—Political aspects—Indonesia—History. |
Witches—Indonesia—Public opinion—History. | Indonesia—
Colonization. | Netherlands—Colonies—Asia—Administration.
Classification: LCC BF1434.I5 W54 2025 (print)
LCC BF1434.I5 (ebook)
DCC 130.9598—dc23/eng/20250106
LC record available at https://lccn.loc.gov/2024033415
LC ebook record available at https://lccn.loc.gov/2024033416

Cover art: Tree and Background. Courtesy contributors
Phuwadon and Aleksandra Konoplya/Adobe Stock #823602411 and
#4885638112f4.

Contents

Acknowledgments

I'll be frank. If I had had any idea where my curiosity about the word *magic* would lead me, I never would have started this book. It all seemed innocent enough. I envisioned thinking about magic through Foucault's power-knowledge. I went up to Cornell and over to the Netherlands over a summer break to create an archive. I started at the card catalogues in Cornell's Echols Library and at the Koninklijk Instituut voor Taal-, Land- en Volkenkunde (now folded into Leiden University's library), looking for anything with even a remote connection. The next summer I branched out to other libraries and archives. Reader, I photocopied everything, an entire file cabinet of paper, all of it in Dutch.

What was I thinking? I loved fieldwork—hanging out, looking, listening, joking, asking annoying questions, trying to explain why the United States on TV wasn't like the United States of lived experience, conversing about what I was discovering and discovering how much I had missed. Learning was living, and vice versa. I knew from archival research for my dissertation that I did not enjoy plowing through documents. Why did I think I could carry out a project based entirely on texts, with no chance to chat about them? My antiquated references to "card catalogues" and "photocopies" reveal how badly I judged the time this project would take: to figure out key categories, to translate (major chunks of text, when I feared missing something important), and especially to think about it all.

And that's the other thing. Foucault went out the window almost immediately. My then colleague Judy Farquhar invited Bruno Latour to give a talk; before I knew it, I was gobbling up books in science studies, often by assigning them in graduate seminars (thank you to all the students who joined me on those journeys!). It wasn't enough to read, though. Happily, for a while Matthew Hull was my colleague at UNC. Not only did we teach a seminar together on actor-network theory, but he read what I was writing, gently pointing out where I remained stuck in habits of thought I had learned in graduate school that were at odds with the approach I was trying to adopt. Like struggling to maneuver a massive container ship, I slowly turned myself around. In a very different way than fieldwork (it was a much more cerebral process), I unlearned and reassembled my conceptual practices on the scaffold built through ethnography. Whew! That was hard.

I have already begun to mention some of the debts accumulated over the many years it has taken to finish this book. Given our long-standing reciprocity over many, many years, I am sure I am not done thanking Chris Nelson, who patiently read every piece of this book, some multiple times. I benefited not only from his kindness and encouragement, but from offhand comments about matters beyond my experience that opened unexpected paths. To Anjana Mebane-Cruz, on whose refrigerator I saw the cartoon with which I begin the book, deep and joyful thanks for her steadfast sisterhood, with just the right mix of support and admonishment, as well as for her astute insights into colonial processes. To Anne Cunningham, for her always practical advice and support and for actual help when I was mired in the morass of my references (above and beyond, Anne, as always!). Molly Mullin is not only a cherished friend but has an acute editorial eye; much gratitude for casting it my way. For perspicacious comments on early drafts of specific chapters, I owe much to Judy Farquhar, Jim Hevia, and Brad Weiss (who also has often provided sustenance for body as well as mind). My debts to Ida Bagus Kakiang and Dayu Niang cannot be paid; this book has kept me away from them, which makes me sad.

It is impossible to adequately thank Marisol de la Cadena for her numerous gifts. Teaching together at UNC many years ago galvanized an intellectually vibrant and warm sisterhood, filled with humorous and challenging exchanges. She read the entire manuscript, offering generous, perceptive, and comprehensive comments, prodding me to greater nuance and care. Her spur to produce ethnographic concepts has inspired me.

My warmest thanks to Isabelle Stengers for her thoughtful afterword, a rich reading that extends the notion of reality politics, subtly bringing it back to Science versus the sciences and elaborating on our shared interest in the capacity of the reclaiming witches to spark thinking.

Who would have thought that at UNC I would discover not only a Dutch librarian, but also a colleague who teaches Dutch, whom I troubled periodically when unsure of my translation of some bit of weird colonial prose? I can't express how much I appreciated the help of Joanneke Fleischauer, who showed me just how remarkable a research librarian can be; she even enlisted her son, Thomas Elliott, an indefatigable researcher, in locating materials on the lives of several figures important to chapter 5. Nor can I thank Dan Thornton enough for his willingness to provide input as I tried to render an archaic and sometimes exotic form of Dutch into readable English. However, as all translations are mine (unless otherwise indicated), so are any errors.

Laurie Maffly-Kipp first introduced me to the phenomenon of writing groups by inviting me to participate (with Sylvia Hoffert and Sarah Shields) in the first of many, often sponsored by UNC's Center for Faculty Excellence. All were wonderful in different ways. The most recent lasted for years. To Emily Bagaranawath, Herica Valladares, Tricia Sullivan, and Meenu Tewari: thank you, comrades, for your company on this journey!

While it is impossible to thank all of the colleagues and friends who contributed to this project, I want to acknowledge the following for stimulating conversation, intellectual inspiration, critical feedback, or just cheering me on: Coen Ackers, Misty Bastian, Peter Boomgaard, Kathryn Burns, Nancy Florida, Richard Fox, and Patricia Sawin. Sadly, three friends did not live to see the final product: Michael Billig, Hilly Geertz, and Roy Wagner (with whom I chatted years ago about the hapless Herr Muller). Thanks too to Charley Siegel, Daniel De Vries, and Hettie Krol for research assistance.

At Duke University Press, Ken Wissoker has been steadfast in his patience and encouragement. Ryan Kendall has deftly handled all editorial details. My wonderful experience with the press continued as Bird Williams ushered the book through production, and Courtney Leigh Richardson took charge of its design. I am humbled and honored by the attentive readings and suggestions of the book's reviewers. Stephen Muecke identified himself to me; so lovely to make your acquaintance, even if long-distant and virtual, given many shared interests.

Much gratitude to the following for research funding, institutional support, and/or research leaves: the National Endowment for the Humanities; the Southeast Asia Council of the Association of Asian Studies for a Luce Foundation Small Grant for Isolated Scholars; the International Institute for Asian Studies in Leiden; Cornell University's Southeast Asia Program; the University of North Carolina at Chapel Hill for funding from the University Research Council, a Junior Faculty Development Grant, an R. J. Reynolds Competitive Research Leave, and a Spray-Randleigh Fellowship; and to the Institute for the Arts and Humanities at UNC for enabling three semesters of sharing this project with colleagues from many disciplines and for a Schwab Academic Excellence Award. I also thank Tricia McAnany, who as chair of my department not only nominated me for the Schwab Award but found funds to support the costs of having a rough draft read by Anitra Grisales. (Thank you too, Anitra, for your deep insights; you were right, of course!)

I was invited to present sections of this work in many venues where I benefited greatly from feedback: the University of California at Davis, the University of Chicago, the University of Michigan, and the University of Wisconsin–Madison. Thanks too to organizers, participants, and audience members at numerous panels and roundtables. Special appreciation is due to the convenors of two conferences in Amsterdam: Birgit Meyer and Peter Pels, whose invitation resulted in the volume *Magic and Modernity*, where I first pondered Nang Mukanis's arrest; and Pieter ter Keurs, who provided an occasion not only to put keris together with magic (in *Colonial Collections Revisited*) but also to meet a bevy of congenial curators, including Harm Stevens and Pim Westerkamp, who spent time showing me and conversing about their collections on a return visit to the Netherlands. Warmest thanks as well to my colleague Francine Brinkgreve, who set up and joined me in an interview with a keris collector and on a jaunt to Bronbeek, and took time out of her busy schedule to respond to long-distance queries.

As some of these appreciations suggest, portions of this book have previously appeared in journal articles and book chapters. In particular, I began writing about Klungkung's heirloom keris in my very first publication; as they have continued their journey, they have continually provoked me to return to them. Guna-guna also prompted revisits. I thank editors (especially David Akin) and peer reviewers for their invaluable feedback.

Last, but never least, I thank my daughter Sophie, who grew with this book from infancy to adulthood, and managed, despite my distraction, to turn into an extraordinary person.

Some years ago, when I first began to think about the genealogy and check-ered politics of magic, a classic anthropological category, I saw a cartoon featuring two famous magical figures on a friend's refrigerator door (see figure I.1).

Her hooked nose, black pointy hat, and broomstick allow us to instantly identify the woman in the hospital bed as a witch. The witch doctor, who is the witch's doctor, is nearly as instantly recognizable by his immense carved mask with feathers, armbands, shell necklace, and grass skirt. While the witch springs from the imaginary of American popular culture—think Margaret Hamilton in *The Wizard of Oz*—she originated across the Atlan-tic. She emerged in an allegedly enlightened Europe where the embers and lingering odor of smoke from the witch trials belonged to a safely distant past, even as a frisson of menace could be repurposed to scare or enter-tain children.[1] The witch serves as shorthand for processes that sutured to-gether a host of practices, forms of life, and ontologies as "magic" and then spat them out as relics of a time gone by in forming the two vast networks called "religion" and "science." No wonder the witch is in a hospital!

Some of the same developments condensed in the figure of the witch also contributed to making the second figure, including his hybrid name *witch doctor*, which simultaneously marks his role as a specialist in undoing the effects of malevolent magic and recognizes his ambiguous powers to harm and heal. He is a figure not from Europe's past, but from the eternal present

FIGURE I.1: JackZiegler/CartoonStock.com, www.CartoonCollections.com.

of some vaguely tropical place, a member of the obscure tribe nineteenth-century anthropologists called the primitives. Blasted out of time to embody humanity's ancient history, no wonder he wears chrono-tech on his wrist. His presence at the ailing witch's bedside is also fitting. For it was by scholarly necromancy, conjuring up humanity's past through living persons, that Europeans revived the witch, bringing a figure that was supposed to be dead back to life.

The witch and witch doctor emerged as entangled products of unholy alliances in the making of modern onto-political formations. The witch materialized as a threatening object across Europe and over the Atlantic as dead cows and blighted crops, inquisitors with a growing expertise on pacts with the devil, printing presses that proliferated such knowledge, technologies to extract confessions, and competing polities and theologies allied against persons (often elderly women) with few supporters among their neighbors or kin. For nearly three hundred years, as Europeans embarked on voyages of exploration and trade, these associations continued to gain traction. But then networks were reshuffled; the witch ceased to be an object around which powerful collectives mobilized. She found herself transmuted into a symbol of modern reason's routing of illusory belief, still lingering, perhaps, in isolated rural pockets and folklore, and eventually finding a place in new cultural spheres growing up around the modern child.

And then she was translated to Africa, where (among other alterations) she underwent a partial sex change to morph into the stereotypical witch doctor. As he coalesced through the reports of explorers, missionaries, and administrators, the witch doctor fueled native superstition, perpetrated fraud, and threatened social order. Travel literature, colonial rule, and fiction secured the witch doctor and the witch as matters of concern in Africa and in anthropology. As noted, however, the cartoon witch doctor does not heal the witch's victims, but the moribund figure herself. And where do they meet but in the biomedical hospital, a sanitary space emblematic of the triumph of enlightened European science over superstition.

This cartoon illustrates magic's life in translation. I argue that magic is not a transhistorical and transcultural phenomenon. Carried by Europeans around the world, it formed an essential ingredient of colonizing projects, differentiating Europeans from others, and strengthening the reality of some worlds (particularly those summarized and ideologically rendered as Science) at the expense of others. My goal in this book is to track some of magic's travels across time and space, looking at what it gathers and the friction it generates as it moves. I take current concepts and the figures of popular fantasies to be the accreted sediments not only of creative and intellectual labor, but also of relations of power and tricky commensurations. That we now use *magic*, a concept with deep roots in Europe's past, to refer to congeries of practices and phenomena across the globe raises questions about the work of making equivalent, and about the making and unmaking of realities.

ISABELLE STENGERS, ADDRESSING Whitehead's concept of adventure, offers a significant elaboration: "'Adventure' . . . implies that all continuity is questionable, and that no principle of economy should prevail that allows us to forget that the resumption of a seemingly similar theme takes place in circumstances that are different every time, and with stakes that are always different. The question 'what has happened to us?' is . . . a resource for telling our stories in another way, in a way that situates us otherwise—not as defined by the past, but as able, perhaps, to inherit from it in another way" (2011b: 14). I treat this inquiry into magic as such an adventure. Rather than proposing a new theory of magic, I attend to how the concept operates. Drawing inspiration from Stengers's (2005a) injunction to slow things down to avoid lazy thinking, and Latour's call for a slow-ciology (2005b), I also take heed of the productivity that resulted when Gramsci found himself forced to avoid language from the Marxist canon (Hoare and Smith 1971: xi). Rather than deploying or extending the familiar vocabulary of terms magical, I aim to decelerate the all too fast work of translation, putting tacks in the road to burst the tires of speeding thought-vehicles, and putting up barricades to divert travel from speedways to back roads. Being slow is not always a virtue. But it offers a way to reconsider, some helpful resistance to traditions and structures of feeling that have both political and ontological consequences, beginning as they do with a problematic judgment that existing categories and analytic procedures are adequate to all worlds. While I visit some classic anthropology of magic, I do not rehearse that vast literature systematically. For anthropologists, magic involves not only a body of theory and adroit analysis but tacit habits and unexamined assumptions. By imposing constraints, I aim to open up room for invention.

How, then, did a host of disparate activities and statements come to be treated as fundamentally alike? Through what extensions and modifications did magic emerge as a descriptor of specific practices, relationships, and experiences, and with what consequences? How was magic made *between* the West and the rest, and how did it even produce that *between*? What *reals* gain and lose strength by diffracting practices and entities through magic? What subjects and objects does magic bring into existence?

To answer these questions, I track Dutch invocations of magic in late nineteenth- and early twentieth-century Indonesia, then a colony of the Netherlands known as the Dutch East Indies, and one of many places shaping images of "the mysterious East." I follow the work magic did when Europeans transported it to a place where such concepts did not exist in order to make sense of subject populations and of their own experiences living there. Traffic in magic, however, hardly moved in only one direction. The practices made into magic in the Indies traveled back to Europe, through anecdotes, objects, expert knowledge, practices, and books, fueling fantasies and adding strength and solidity to scholarly projects, occultist movements, and tourist itineraries.

Moving and Commensurating

> Translation is the mechanism by which the social and natural worlds progressively take form.
> —Michel Callon

We usually understand translation as a semiotic act, a rendering of what is expressed in one language in the terms of another. Such everyday word magic is certainly relevant to this book. By translation, however, I do not refer only to a semiotic process but also to practices of transportation, commensuration, and connection (Callon 1986; Latour 1988, 1993, 2005). The *Oxford English Dictionary* (OED) provides three definitions for *translate*. The first has nothing to do with language.[2] In keeping with its Latin origins, to carry or bring across (an etymology that suggests passage over a boundary, border, or chasm), to translate is to "bear, convey, or remove from one person, place or condition to another," "to transfer, transport."[3] But transference doesn't simply mean taking something from one place and plopping it down in another. *Translate*'s third meaning highlights what such movement entails: "to change in form, appearance or substance; to transmute; to transform, alter." Concepts are not, in short, merely brought to new places. They mutate as they travel. Deployed in new situations, to address new experiences, concepts are bent and reworked, and modify in turn those situations and experiences. To translate is to convey something across space, time, and circumstance, with unpredictable outcomes.

As these entries highlight, translation involves more than the treacherous activity of commensuration. Semiotic technologies are only some of the means by which terms, concepts, and the practices associated with them *moved* around the globe, materializing new objects, and generating unanticipated effects.[4] Europeans deployed magic in part to make unfamiliar situations and experiences more familiarly unfamiliar. Such movements built magic into a category with apparently universal and transhistorical reach.

By emphasizing movement and alteration, however, I by no means intend to dismiss the OED's second definition of *translate*, its "chief current sense": "To turn from one language into another; 'to change into another language retaining the sense' (Johnson); to render; also, to express in other words, to paraphrase." Not only is this the commonsense understanding, but such processes are critical to any investigation of magic's modern making, to the origins of my own interest in the topic, and, more broadly, to processes of commensuration and clashes among worlds.

This project took shape when I started to question both the vocabulary of magic and the long anthropological tradition of theoretical analysis in which it is embedded. The impetus came when my colleague Mark Hobart wondered why, in my first book, I rendered the Balinese and Indonesian word *sakti* as *magical power*.[5] That translation was neither unusual nor original. Quite the contrary: bilingual dictionaries (Balinese-Indonesian,

Balinese-English, and Indonesian-English) commonly gloss sakti by modifying *power* with words such as *magical, supernatural,* or *sacred.*[6] Consulting such dictionaries had shaped my understanding of the term. But the question led me to reflect upon the work that magic does in such definitions, as well as in anthropology (including my own) and in past and current imaginaries.

Much literature on translation examines its operation as both a specialized and mundane semiotic practice.[7] Many have challenged the notion that translation simply communicates information or meaning, or that translators shuttle seamlessly between (bounded, distinct) languages. Translators intervene by the choices they make, deciding to what degree the structures or modes of expression of the "source"—the material being translated— will shape the "target." Selecting along a spectrum that runs from loose paraphrase, aimed at making (common) sense, to word-for-word rendering, a translator may strive to sound idiomatic in the target language (domesticating strategies) or capture some flavor of the source (foreignizing strategies).

If domesticating strategies erase evidence of friction, favoring smooth locutions that keep others from sounding like idiots, foreignizing ones highlight limitations of the target language, stretching the experience of readers and auditors (Venuti 2002 [1995]). Advocates of foreignizing invariably return to Benjamin's "Task of the Translator"—mainly to requote Rudolf Pannwitz's withering critique of domesticators: "They want to turn Hindi, Greek, English into German instead of turning German into Hindi, Greek, English. . . . The basic error of the translator is that he preserves the state in which his own language happens to be instead of allowing his language to be powerfully affected by the foreign tongue" (quoted in Benjamin 1969: 80–81). This position originated with efforts by German romantics to contest dominant translation practices in France and England that were, in turn, influenced by a Roman text (Venuti 2012). As Venuti stresses, domesticating is an imperial strategy, useful for assimilating and dominating territories. To cram unfamiliar practices into the language and categories of dominant societies is never neutral. Those categories domesticate other worlds, rather than foreignizing their own.[8] German intellectuals also rejected the theory such strategies imply, in which language merely expresses ideas rather than constructing them.

To think of translation as shuttling between languages involves more than treating language as primarily a system of referents; it also assumes a common world, a domain of things-in-themselves to which languages refer.[9] But this also falls short in addressing how language operates. As

Silverstein (2003) highlights, translation is never only a matter of matching up words with common referents in a single unitary world. Words are a tiny part of language. Not only does syntax differ among languages, but so does pragmatics, the situations indexed and implied in language use. Translation always extends forms of life, situated in time and space. Any translator worth her salt must know more than the meanings of words or felicitous syntax; language is embedded in modes of life—what anthropologists commonly call culture.

Translating discourse therefore inherently bleeds into what Wagner (1975) calls the invention of culture, processing the material and signifying practices encountered during fieldwork through professional and ambient concepts and categories. In fact, beginning in the 1950s British social anthropologists presented as their goal the "translation of cultures" or "cultural translation," which aimed to convey "modes of thought," the logic or idioms through which others made sense of the world (Asad 1986). It cast the anthropologist as a translator of (non-European, marginalized, and dominated) forms of life for "modern" readers, in dominant languages, especially English. Anthropological texts extended dialogic feelers not only toward the source language/culture, but also to at least two target languages/ cultures: those of professional anthropology and those of the anthropologist's native tongue and world.

But translating an (always inferred) culture through dominant categories impedes the project's envisioned goals. Eduardo Viveiros de Castro argues that cultural translation rests on "uncontrolled equivocation." As he explains it, uncontrolled equivocation "concerns the process involved in the translations of the 'native's' practical and discursive concepts into the terms of anthropology's conceptual apparatus," a process usually "implicit and automatic (and hence uncontrolled)" (2004b: 4). This habitual practice establishes equivalence without attending to the commonsense—and the world—built into professional categories.

Viveiros de Castro (2004a) actually raised another question about culture that explicitly addresses that world. The concept of culture brings with it a presumptive ontology: a single nature, on which there are many perspectives. The world may be multicultural, but it is mono- or uninatural. This dramatically limits relativist claims. On the one hand, we all have different ways of thinking about, viewing, or speaking about a common world. But science's account of that common world is more than merely one among many—and scholars typically presume that science informs their own society's common sense (Latour 1993). As I elaborate below, some work in science studies proposes that there is no nature and no culture, but rather naturecultures, collectives, or worlds, that take shape through practices.

To return to the problem of equivalence in translation: to make something unfamiliar familiar involves finding similarities. But what does it mean to say two things are similar? Or different? As poets know, any two things may be made similar: hence the disruptive wonder of metaphor. In the provocative aphorisms he termed irreductions, Latour highlights translation as the fundamental problematic of knowledge: "Nothing is, by itself the same as or different from anything else. . . . There are no equivalents, only translations. If there are identities . . . this is because they have been constructed at great expense" (1988: 162). Equivalence, in short, is never simply given; things are not naturally "the same" or "different" but must be established as such. This involves work, and even conflict: such judgments "are the consequences of trials of strength, defeats and victories" (1988: 162).

In this light, consider Latour's apparently odd equation of the "work of translation" with networks (1993: 11). Here Latour engages in the very work of translation he is elaborating, by making a surprising connection that simultaneously alters what is meant by translation and by networks. The "work of translation" refers to the labor of relating one phenomenon to another, as opposed to distinguishing and dividing them—what he calls "the work of purification" (which includes analysis and critique). To translate is to associate, to forge a link.

Translation, whether as a semiotic practice for rendering languages and cultures comprehensible, an analytic technique for categorizing unfamiliar phenomena, or a mode of transport, is built on differences. Equivalences do not simply exist. They must be made, through assemblage and power. Ultimately, translation is a process of bringing things together, with all the tension and reshuffling this entails. What translation does, in short, is make relations.

I call translation a knotting technology. If "the work of translation" is synonymous with networks, networks themselves are arrangements of intersecting lines. Knots mark points of intersection, the binding together of different trajectories. Of course, more than two trajectories may be knotted together to make thicker nodes, some so thick that unknotting to see what they are made of becomes a daunting task. As knotwork, translation braids worlds together.

This book involves translation in these multiple senses. In tracking the movement of concepts and things, words count. I trace shifts, for example, from Indonesian vernaculars to Dutch terms in colonial texts, as well as the replacement of older by newer Dutch terms in accounts of Indonesian practices. In the most prosaic sense, this is also a book based on my own translations of Dutch sources into English. Those sources, written in forms of Dutch that, due to changes to the language over time and hybridities peculiar to colonial Dutch, themselves appear odd to current Dutch readers and speakers. I draw on both concepts and my field experiences in Indonesia to complicate what Viveiros de Castro terms equivocations. In the process I aim to knot Indonesian practices into different networks, to extend and strengthen other possibilities for world-making.

Translating Magic and the Problem of Reality

The issues addressed so far would be relevant to any commonplace conceptual device used to aggregate far-flung practices from across the planet. Translation is a feature of all acts of commensuration, of finding equivalence, a condition of inter/intra-collective engagements. But not all translations have the same political or ontological effects. Magic differs from other instruments that stock the anthropological tool kit or pervade popular imaginaries. If translation in general entails knotwork, we might call translating magic (k)not-work, to highlight the simultaneous *not*-work its knots involve. While in other instances as well forging links may occasion decoupling, *nots* are built into magic's modern construction.

Consider, for instance, how familiar anthropological accounts of magic define it in opposition to other categories, as similar to but *not* something else. Early works in anthropology, for example, contrasted magic to religion, science, or both. For Durkheim (1995 [1912]), magic was to religion as the individual was to society. "There is no Church of magic," Durkheim famously declared, and Mauss (1972) argued that the power of magicians stemmed from their position outside of social institutions. For Frazer (1922), magic served as humanity's first stumbling attempt to know and control the world, no longer adequate given the sciences of the nineteenth century.

Such *nots* reiterate and amplify prior ones. Hildred Geertz, commenting on the work of historian Keith Thomas, highlights how they operated: "The attack on certain beliefs as 'magical,' in the senses of 'not-religious' or 'not-reasonable' or 'not-practical' [terms taken from Thomas's book], was a constant part of English religious rhetoric from at least the fourteenth century on. The common core of meaning was always disapproval, but what was not so stable, from person to person and from era to era, were the grounds upon which these beliefs were to be dismissed" (1975: 75). Magic truly appears to be a "floating signifier," attaching itself to an attitude rather than to specific contents (Lévi-Strauss 1987 [1950]: 63). Serving as an offensive weapon, a strategy to array forces in battles over reality, it judges and finds an absence: of piety, of reason, of good sense.

"Not-religious" speaks for itself as a continuous theme, though for anthropologists, religion refers to a theoretical construct rather than, as it did in England, to Christianity. In many parts of the world magic remains the antithesis of proper, pious religion, especially, but not only, monotheistic religions (Davies 2012: 5–8; Van der Veer 2014). As for reason and practicality, they are laminated into commonsense understandings of science. And among the *nots* that magic invokes must be added not scientific, not modern, and, crucially, not real.

Magic does not contrast with reality in all of the knots that it makes. When some Christians or Muslims speak of magic, often in the mode of attack, they consider it very real—and very dangerous. Consider Geertz again, who ended up questioning whether anthropologists should indeed treat magic as a stable transhistorical and transcultural object: "[T]he construct 'magic' as used in much of today's thinking about exotic belief systems draws its aura of factualness from its place in our own culture and its legitimacy from the social prestige of the cultivated groups who employed the construct as an ideological weapon in the past" (1975: 88). Magic here is hardly a neutral descriptor with universal reach, a fact about human societies. Instead, it is an instrument of power. "Its aura of factualness," as well as the accumulation of *nots*, is the outcome of historical struggles "in our own culture." Both the witch hunt and its rejection made magic a problem for shared good realities for European elites—even as neopagans now deploy it to propose (and make) different good realities. But in contrast to Geertz, I urge that these struggles were not internal to North Atlantic societies; instead, they emerged in relations with others.

Definitions of magic as *not* something else are intimately entwined with the production of modern reality, with what John Law (2015) calls the one-world world. The modern making of magic is caught up with hegemonies of the real. Magic and its cognates, in short, did more than render the meaning of a phrase or categorize a practice. Their movement always entailed what I call *reality politics*: fostering some entities, transmuting others, and making still others—and the relations and practices in which they are embedded—vanish from public view.[10]

Drawing matters under the capacious umbrella of magic, of course, has many effects, depending on what, who, when, and where, why, and how. In contemporary metropolitan discussions, for instance, magic has largely positive associations. It forms a major component of the popular genre of speculative fiction, especially in the subgenre of fantasy. No surprise that university students in the United States flock to courses with magic in their titles, associating the word with Harry Potter, Narnia, and *The Lord of the Rings*. Tell acquaintances you are writing about it and pupils dilate. Its aura of mystery, hint of hidden ancient knowledges, and promise of transformation increasingly add seductive glamor to accounts of my own field area of Bali (Abram 1997 ; Stuart-Fox 2015).

This magic does more than attract; it inspires. It summons dreams of metamorphosis, of another world that may be not only possible but achieved without painful struggle. The magic that works in the vein of hope even feeds academic work. It was surely not only anthropology and dictionaries but also my taste for fantasy that informed my use of *magic* to translate what I learned from interlocutors in Bali. But it is worth noting what *fantasy* implies. Imaginary worlds speak to what During (2004) terms "fictionality," a historical emergence of experiences that temporarily suspend a hegemonic real. Fantasy, in short, is *not* real, even if imagination constitutes a potent component of and spur to world-making.

This book tracks some of the complex effects of translating magic, which include magic's allures. But in the one-world world of a host of dominant institutions, including the academy, diffracting the practices and statements of others through magic embroils and embroiled them especially in a particular kind of real: a preexistent, singular, external, and objective nature. The truths of that nature were discoverable through Science, the capital S marking the proper name of a revered entity. Conjuring Science worked to index the general superiority of a European culture engaged in mastering nature (or Nature), thus justifying the "West's" role as master over those—"not reasonable" and clearly "not practical"—ignorant of nature's implacable laws. Even the most sophisticated relativist claims presume multiple perspectives on this single reality, the nature that only Science knows.

Empirical studies of science have complicated this story in profound ways. Drawing attention to the practices that make facts and stabilize objects of knowledge, such work also shifts its focus from epistemological concerns about the adequacy of representation to ontology, the emergence or continuity of phenomena.[11] Multiple sciences rather than Science high-light practices that do not describe reals but bring them into being. Neither subjects nor material entities preexist, nor is anything static. Indeed, matter itself "is always already an ongoing historicity," "not a thing, but a doing" (Barad 2003: 821, 822). How do the myriad acts Europeans translated and translate as magic appear from the perspective of this account of science?

Ironically, anthropological studies of magic, by raising disturbing questions about the relativity of truth, helped to bring science studies into being. Innovators such as David Bloor insisted that any sociology of knowledge worth its salt had to be symmetrical, treating claims we judge true by the same methods as those typically judged false—such as magic. Latour (1993) generalized that principle of symmetry well beyond this. Along with a variety of concepts and methods I borrow from science studies, Latour's promotion of a symmetrical anthropology, which dovetails with efforts to provincialize Europe (Chakrabarty 2000) and decolonize anthropology, inspires my interest in unraveling some of the (k)nots through which magic emerged—and my efforts to reinterpret Indonesian practices as making different realities, which such (k)nots partially connect to the reality of the one-world world.

The Making of a Category

It is no accident that the cartoon witch and witch doctor encounter each other in a scientific space, for they originally met through claims about Science. More specifically, they met at the birth of the once aspiring science of anthropology, which made magic a defining feature of the object elaborated as primitive society. Metropolitan ethnologists enlisted magic as one device to bring together observations made by "men on the spot" as sociomaterial worlds came into relation through exploration, conquest, resource extraction, missionization, and colonial rule. It is easy to fall under the spell of those ethnologists. Dazzled by their dexterity in explaining magic and asserting its significance in the history of humanity—including, for British theorists, its role in declaring a massive gap between the spectacularly successful sciences and technologies of their era and the tentative but failed knowledges of those still purportedly mired in the evolutionary past—we fail to notice the work it takes to bring all of these practices together in a single argument. We are encouraged to accept that theorists of magic merely identify a self-evident similarity and that their contribution lies in elaborating some of its most distinctive features: analogy and contiguity, say, or the notion of force. In short, we assume that the reality preexisted the intellectual work, which merely felicitously represents it.

As noted, I seek to introduce some hesitancy, a conceptual hiccup, to this intellectual habit. The conditions of possibility for the cartoon's visual pun include the labors of a host of actors who produced magic as their common currency. I attend to some of the processes of assembly through which that occurred, treating magic as a sedimented product of global history, movement, and partial connection.

Without paying attention to such matters, the work of translation itself becomes a kind of magic, entailing illicit practices of conjuring—in the dual sense of performing sleight of hand and trafficking with the spirits of intellectual forebears—and a wondrous but inexplicable transformation of existing realities. Anthropology's founders inserted magic into a speculative account of human history, involving the slow but steady advance of reason, culminating in the scientific discovery of laws governing a preexistent nature. In that narrative, magic forms an early stage in the development of human understanding or a cognitive or emotional tendency never fully overcome. But if magic plays a part in humanity's history, it is, I contend, as a product of colonial relations and disciplinary ambitions. Rather than conjectures about human nature or evolution, I advocate exploring the worldly engagements that transported magic across the planet. To trace such movements is to track the making and unmaking of worlds.

What processes, then, turned magic into an all-terrain vehicle, apparently able to go anywhere in the world even if the journey is a bit bumpy? Here I offer some broad statements in anticipation of the specific ones that follow in the body of this book.

First, magic could never have been made into a phenomenon transcending time and space without empire. Colonial agents brought magic to bear on a host of novel situations. In concrete encounters with subject populations, on specific occasions, Europeans called upon magic to mediate unfamiliarity, build divides, and buttress hierarchies.

But these moments would have been transient and fragile without the help of particular nonhumans. New communication and transportation technologies made it possible for official reports, newspaper and magazine articles, and artifacts to travel not only across colonized territories but also back to Europe. They allowed specific actions, comments, or objects in distant places to be brought together, and through the generalizing labor of ethnologists, purveyors of popular culture, and museum curators to circulate further. Such articulations simultaneously disarticulated. Pulling particular practices into magic's gravitational field, they winked out of view all or part of the collective of other-than-humans, things, technologies, forces, concerns, and people to which they had been connected, making the practices appear even more magical.

Second, the magic that European exploration, conquest, and rule transported around the planet brought with it an accumulated history of prior articulations, particularly relatively recent ones equating magic with illusion and delusion. In an important sense, magic always has been in translation, passing between and transforming semiotic-material formations. As a lexical item, *magic*, for instance, came into English (and, as *magie*, into Dutch) via a chain of transmission from Persian to Greek to Latin to French. Similar travels, involving particular transmutations and associations, saturate other terms in the lexicon of matters magical. Over the long span of this history, magic mutated from a species of wisdom from afar (specifically, from places east of Greece) into a concept enlisted to distribute reality, might, and truth. In its passage across time and space, magic always has promoted some entities and groups and marginalized others.

Parsing activities and ideas as magic, for instance, constituted a front line of advancing Christian theologies, legal systems, and commercial relations as the Church spread out from Rome. It formed one of many tools through which the Church could splice existing and alternative collectives into its fold, offering a way to envelop entities and practices (potent places and rites, and the other-than-human and more-than-human entities these made real) posing theological, moral, and political challenges to its claim to be truly catholic.

Voyages of discovery and mercantile transactions began the process of translating magic to the worlds beyond Europe—and translating those worlds through magic. Magic acquired new valences, molding realities and regimes of truth as it began to journey back and forth on ships and in documents between North Atlantic cities and an expanding web of entrepôts, Inquisitions, courtrooms, and mission fields—and later learned societies, administrative offices, plantations, construction sites, schools, doctors' consulting rooms, and laboratories. Europeans brought with them world-producing frames and practices that found themselves both reinforced and stretched through novel applications.

The development in Europe of a highly skilled performance art of sleight-of-hand entertainment added further strength to positions treating magic as a matter of deft manipulation, on the one hand, and naïve gullibility, on the other. Theatrical illusionism was in turn tied to two other cultural developments: the rapid proliferation of fiction, a different modality for producing simulated worlds; and movements reviving interest in occult knowledges, while adding novel technologies and fields of expertise, such as psychology.[12] Thus when colonial agents translated magic and affiliated concepts to describe, analyze, deplore, and intervene in situations in Africa, Asia, and the Americas, they engaged in reality politics.

Both colonial rule and magic's accumulated articulations nourished anthropological theorizations of magic as a defining feature of primitive society in the late nineteenth century. But anthropologists also elaborated magic in dialog with developments in popular culture that both amplified and countered dominant positions. A series of new movements rekindled magic's association with esoteric wisdom or dangerous mysterious powers (sometimes both). Some of these—such as spiritualism, theosophy, and parapsychology, all of which counted prominent public figures, including scientists, among their numbers—aimed to establish the reality of entities challenging divisions between living and nonliving or spirit and matter. These movements also forged unruly connections between North Atlantic and colonized worlds. Madame Blavatsky's theosophists, for instance, constructed associations between esoteric wisdom, mysticism, and the East, especially Tibet. In addition, spirit guides mediating contact with the domestic dead in London parlors commonly were Asian or Native American, as if the only paths Europeans could take to the afterlife intersected with roads built through corvée labor to transport tea in conquered territories.

It was British anthropologist Edward Burnet Tylor, however, who brought novel practices such as speaking to the dead at séances into conjunction with the witch and the witch doctor by claiming spiritualism constituted a revival of the magical thinking fundamental to primitive culture (1958 [1871]). Through such associations, anthropologists helped to shunt these movements beyond the purview of Science. In general, distaste for both the occult and popular culture molded the structures of feeling that became characteristic of anthropological accounts of magic.

In short, the possibility that ethnologists could situate a host of highly diverse activities, people, and things under the broad rubric of magic depended on prior translations and formations, even as it lent strength to particular projects of world-making, including those of colonialism and occultism.

Anthropology solidified in the late nineteenth and early twentieth centuries as a body of concepts, institutionalized practices, and structures of feeling to understand the "primitive." Magic emerged as an object of conceptual elaboration—as the most titillating and challenging feature of Hildred Geertz's "exotic belief systems"—under specific political conditions. Asad's assertion that "the structure of power certainly affected the theoretical choice and treatment of what social anthropology objectified" is particularly pertinent here (1973: 17).

As the discipline coalesced around the figure of the "primitive" in the late nineteenth century, armchair ethnologists re-*cognized* magic—both naming and rethinking it—in reports streaming back from outposts of empire, penned by travelers, merchants, missionaries, colonial officials, and other men on the spot. Making magic a phenomenon with worldwide distribution, they declared accounts depicted forms of life unchanged from a distant past that only the West had overcome. As anthropologists turned from speculative human history to ethnographic description, with some (Gluckman 1963) even arguing magic might itself alter in response to changing circumstances, treatment became resolutely local, a feature of particular peoples and places.[13] Hence, as anthropology developed, it provided a major conduit for magic's spread. But as I argue in this book, magic emerged through mediations of concrete engagements rather than merely as an object of abstract speculation.

Going Dutch

At first glance, a Dutch colony would appear to be an unlikely place to learn about the making of magic, or about its entanglements with colonialism, anthropology, and popular imaginaries. There are no famous Dutch contributions to the canon of the anthropology of magic; in fact, Dutch ethnologists largely modified concepts developed by British, French, and German theorists rather than developing their own. Moreover, although Indonesia, especially Bali, has a growing reputation as a place of magic, it barely registers in academic work on that topic. If any place is linked to magic in both scholarly literatures (fetishism, witchcraft, and witch doctors) and popular culture (as the "dark continent" in, for example, H. Rider Haggard), it is Africa (Pels 1998). Moreover, in Africa, colonial anti-witchcraft legislation not only played a crucial role in shaping key texts (such as Evans-Pritchard's) but still affects African lives and foments debate.

By contrast, the Dutch appear marginal not only to anthropologies of magic but also to the literature on colonialism. Indeed, in his landmark *Orientalism* Said (1978) ignored the Dutch, even what they wrote about the Middle East, despite the fact that Snouck Hurgronje, one of the foremost Orientalists and one of the first Europeans to visit Mecca, was Dutch. While excellent work has appeared on the Dutch in Indonesia, some of the best of it by anthropologists (Keane 2007; Stoler 2002; Stoler and Cooper 1997), such materials have not had the cross-disciplinary impact of studies of former British colonies in Africa and India, or of Latin America.

In a sense, this is unsurprising. Not only did the "sun never set on the British Empire," which extended across oceans and touched every continent, but its replacement by the United States ensured that English remains the dominant language of scholarship. France also had a transcontinental impact; the use of French as a colonizing language and the ascendency of French intellectuals in late twentieth- and early twenty-first-century theory make that empire equally relevant across academic fields. And Latin America, united by a shared experience of Iberian imperialism and primarily Spanish-speaking, has generated a host of analyses of the ongoing "coloniality of power" (Quijano 2000). By contrast, by the twentieth century, the geographic reach of Dutch influence had shrunk mainly to the Indies. It formed a marginal empire, colonialism in a minor key.

Language policy cemented that position. Unlike English, French, and Spanish, Dutch never served as the language of command; instead, the Dutch made Malay—one of hundreds of archipelago languages but, in simplified form, long used in interisland trade—their medium of rule, reserving Dutch for communicating among themselves.[14] As a result, anti-colonial nationalists adopted Malay (renaming it Indonesian) as the national language. Only highly educated Indonesians (such as Engineer Sukarno, Indonesia's first president) mastered Dutch. That colonial documents, however, were written in Dutch means that archival and other historical materials are as well, obstructing projects akin to South Asian or Latin American subaltern studies.

Why, then, write a book analyzing magic's invocation in colonial Indonesia?[15]

In part, of course, because fieldwork in Indonesia led me to ruminate on what magic does as a translation. But in working on this book, I discovered myriad reasons why the particularities and peculiarities of colonial Indonesia clarify magic's contradictory effects as an object of expert and popular concern. It turns out there is much to learn from this marginal anthropology and minor colonialism.

I begin with this: the relation between colonialism and anthropology is exceptionally strong and clear in the Netherlands. It is not only much more overt than in other imperial formations (Ellen 1976; Fasseur

1993; Vermeulen 2008); it is parasitic. While much work has brought out the obscured colonial relations shaping Victorian and structural-functional anthropology (Asad 1973; Pels and Salemink 1994), in the Netherlands they are explicit.

Dutch ethnology focused almost exclusively on the Indies. Little distinction existed between the man on the spot in the colonies and the scholar working up raw data in his cozy metropolitan armchair, without enduring distasteful interactions with primitives, a division of labor characterizing Victorian and French theorists of magic (Stocking 1987). Key texts in Dutch ethnology were written by men engaged in routine work in the Indies (such as Kruyt, a missionary, and Van Ossenbruggen, a jurist), mainly in the employ of the colonial state. Many colonial officials not only penned reports to their superiors, but also contributed to learned journals. Almost all of the Netherlands' first chairs in ethnology were former officials or military officers. And mainly they taught men aspiring to enter the Indies civil service, who increasingly took degrees in Indology or ethnology. Hence it is hardly surprising to find congruence between the conceptual apparatus of colonial officials and academic authors. To recall Asad (1973), what scholars found theoretically interesting was shaped not only by a developing discipline, but by Indies experiences. In turn, officials not only drew on categories developed in Dutch ethnology, but on the premises laminated within them.

Certainly its empirical focus on the archipelago rather than on bits and pieces of description from across the globe made Dutch ethnology more provincial. At the same time, it was remarkably cosmopolitan. In Dutch publications, terms from archipelago languages mingle promiscuously with passages in English, French, German, and Italian. Through such work magic took shape across many worlds.

Apart from anthropology, Indies phenomena translated through magic are intimately bound up with Dutch culture. Louis Couperus's 1900 novel *The Hidden Force*, for example, is one of the great works of Dutch literature (see chapter 5). Stories and artifacts that made their way back to the Netherlands continue to spawn new experiences and ignite associations between Indonesia and magic, often in the form of mystery or mysticism. Even people with no direct connection to Indonesia have some familiarity with *keris* (Indonesian daggers, chapter 3), *guna-guna* (Indonesian "black magic," chapter 4), and hidden forces (chapter 5) from ambient culture such as television serials, novels, movies, and museums.

But the Dutch are not only of interest for exploring the nexus of colonialism, anthropology, and popular culture emerging in nineteenth- and twentieth-century Indonesia. They also played a role in the development of modern institutions, including the supposed ontological transformation that Max Weber famously summed up as the disenchantment (literally *demagification*, as Davies [2012: 46] points out) of reality.

Let's return to the ailing witch in her hospital bed and recall the witches who made pacts with Satan. The moderns crossed out not only God (Latour 1993) but also Satan, demons, and witches, replacing them with the new category of nature. Witches and witch hunts became an embarrassing history, something now *over*. And those who write that history do not themselves treat witches as real, having internalized the commandment "thou shalt not regress!" (Stengers 2018a).

Judicial prosecution of witches ended earlier in the Netherlands than in most of Europe: Dutch magistrates stopped imposing the death penalty for witchcraft by 1608, and the last witch trial in the province of Holland occurred in 1659. Jurists and doctors became increasingly disinclined to attribute illness to the activities of witches, and clerics ignored accusations by parishioners (De Waardt 1991; Gijswijt-Hofstra 1999). In addition to these changes in practice, however, another Dutch development contributed to undermining witchcraft prosecutions elsewhere in Europe: a four-volume treatise entitled *The Bewitched World* (*De betoverde wereld*) that Balthasar Bekker, a minister in the Dutch Reformed Church published in 1691–93.

Some historians credit Bekker with being the first to pose a significant theological and philosophical challenge to the premises of the witch hunt (Levack 1999; Porter 1999; Stronks 1991). Bekker shook up the ontological settlement that undergirded claims that witches made pacts with Satan and trafficked with demons. Drawing on the growing corpus of descriptions of Africa, Asia, and the Americas emerging from commercial ventures and voyages of exploration, his knowledge of scripture and the classics, and Cartesian dualism, he addressed the role that spiritual beings could play in worldly affairs. After surveying societies past and present, and analyzing biblical passages mentioning spirits and their activities, he concluded that from a Christian perspective no noncorporeal beings (other than God) could act in the material world, which had its own regularities.[16] Views to the contrary were the legacy of paganism, as indicated by their ubiquity among existing heathens. Thus, Bekker knotted Cartesian and Calvinist purifications of matter and spirit, divisions between Christian Europe and "heathens," and reason versus mere belief into a new account of the real.

The impact of Bekker's controversial thesis (church leaders accused him of blasphemy) resonated far beyond the Netherlands. Almost immediately, translations appeared in German, French, and English. But the Dutch contributed more to shaping a new ontological settlement than making witches vanish. That voyage literature played a part in Bekker's inquiry indexes the emergence of a global political economy based on mercantile and finance capitalism. And that, in turn, rested on the beginnings of Dutch involvement in the Indies.

Dutch merchants reached the islands now part of the nation-state of Indonesia at the end of the sixteenth century, following Portuguese predecessors. Of the four ships that headed "east" in 1595, the three that returned two years later had managed to reach Banten in West Java, then the center of the global black pepper trade, and had traveled up Java's north coast. Having cracked the secret of the sea route to the Indies, Dutch merchants quickly outpaced the Portuguese in meeting Europe's insatiable taste for spices, reaching the famous Spice Islands (now Maluku) by 1599 and soon ousting Portuguese competitors from everywhere but the island of Timor.

As with many lucrative ventures, these entailed considerable financial risk. To reduce it, investors banded together to form a cartel: the Dutch East India Company (de Vereenigde Oost-Indische Compagnie, literally the United East Indies Company; hereafter the VOC or the Company). The VOC was the world's second multinational corporation; the British East India Company preceded it by a mere two years. In these first corporations a group of investors pooled their capital and sought a government charter. At this time the Netherlands consisted of seven provinces that in 1581 had revolted against Spanish rule and formed a republic; that arrangement lasted until Napoleon's occupation of the Low Countries in 1795. In 1602 the States-General of the Dutch Republic granted the "seventeen gentlemen" who made up the VOC's board a monopoly on all trade east of the Cape of Good Hope; six months later the Company began to issue stock and established the world's first stock exchange in Amsterdam. Unlike multinational corporations now, its charter granted the VOC sovereign powers: the authority to make treaties, form an army and wage war, and administer any territories such activities brought under its purview.

That these events began a process eventuating in the establishment of the Netherlands Indies (and later Indonesia) makes them pertinent to this book. But they were also momentous for the world-shaping processes we sum up with words like modernity. However marginal the Netherlands may now appear, it was once at the forefront of global history.

What is now called the Dutch Golden Age grew out of the spectacular success of the VOC and Dutch sea-based trade.[17] The basis for wealth and power shifted from inherited land to merchants and financiers in Holland's port cities, especially Amsterdam. Mercantilism spawned a host of industries, from shipbuilding (facilitated by the Dutch invention of the windpowered sawmill, which made it possible to build ships more quickly and at less cost) to cartography (many key innovators were Dutch, and Amsterdam became the center for the production of maps and atlases). New economic opportunities, along with the Dutch Republic's toleration of dissent (while Calvinism formed the official religion, rejection of Spain's suzerainty led to a distaste for orthodoxy), attracted people to Dutch cities not only from the countryside but from all over Europe, including philosophers such as Locke and Descartes. (It was not by happenstance that Bekker drew on Cartesian ideas; Descartes had a wide following among Dutch intellectuals.) These processes led to the increasing importance of a new class: the bourgeoisie.

Maritime commerce also fueled dazzling innovations in science, technology, and art. Apart from technologies with direct applications to a mercantile economy, the Republic became known for optics and medicine. And, best remembered now, Dutch painters invented new genres of art: still lifes, landscapes (and seascapes), group portraiture, and scenes from everyday life, scenes containing their own traces of the trade enriching this new class.[18]

These developments shed light on magic's modern reality politics in two ways. One has to do with voyage literature; the other, with assessments of Golden Age art.

Dutch merchants on West Africa's coast played a decisive role in the genesis of concepts and attitudes vital to analytics of magic. The central figure was the fetish, though what was said about this hybrid object also helped to position Africa as the heart of magical darkness in European imaginations. Although *fetish* comes from a Portuguese translation, it was Dutch Protestant merchants who elaborated the concept and propelled it across Europe. There it came to the attention of Charles de Brosse, an Enlightenment intellectual who proposed fetishism (*fétichisme*) as a stage in the development of human mentality.

Bekker actually drew on one of these texts, by Pieter de Marees.[19] The latter's report of his visit to Africa's Gold Coast in 1602 transported the word *fetish* into northern European languages. But Willem Bosman (who had read Bekker) had a more lasting impact. His 1703 book, *A New and Accurate Description of the Coast of Guinea*, made the idea of the fetish go viral. That he had spent many years living and trading in Guinea, moving from a mere apprentice to chief merchant for the Dutch West India Company, gave his text an authority it retained for over a century.[20]

Bosman's lively account of his experiences on the Gold Coast laid the groundwork for subsequent discussions of the fetish as both a type of magical object and as a form of thought.[21] I will have more to say about both Bosman and fetishes in the pages to come. Here suffice it to say that both what he said and the way he said it affected not only what Europeans did with the idea of the fetish, but all manner of things, people, and acts translated through the language of magic. Bosman, emboldened by Bekker's rejection of the devil's agency, ridiculed African practices as ignorant and irrational. In particular, they showed a fanciful understanding of causality, not recognizing the operation of nature's impersonal laws.[22] Such claims began to thicken not only the knots judging non-Europeans as irrational, but also those to reshape what could count as real, and consequently as rational. Bosman writes with an assurance that his assessments of value, virtue, and veracity represent common sense.

Bosman's attitude might have been described with a word late colonial Dutchmen in the Indies used to describe themselves, particularly in contrast with Indonesians. They proudly avowed they were *nuchter*: sensible, sober, down to earth, and unimaginative. It implied they were grounded in the really real, resisting flights of fancy (let alone Deleuzian witches' flights). This is strikingly reminiscent of the way art critics and art historians retrospectively talk of Golden Age Dutch painting. In the mid-nineteenth century, a French study branded that art *realistic* (Yeazell 2005). But that label and those paintings, like being nuchter, index an ontological transformation: the dwindling of one world and the coalescence and *real-ing* of a different one.

Plan of the Book

The temporal and spatial specifications of my title—colonial and Indonesia—are both crucial and misleading. Crucial, because translation always is grounded in particular situations. What concerns me is how practices found themselves enrolled in the conceptual field of magic through encounters between Europeans and those they colonized. Misleading, because these constitute a mere fraction of the encounters sedimented in *magic's* current dense and contradictory uses, including its uptake (a concept I learned from Susan Gal, personal communication) as a domain of anthropological description and theorizing. Hence, this book addresses magic's formation contrapuntally. The chapters focus on specific objects and practices that nineteenth- and twentieth-century Dutch authors diffract through the category magic. I punctuate these chapters, however, with interludes beyond the Indies. These speak to the formation of familiar anthropological structures of feeling and analytical habits, especially (but by no means exclusively) in Anglophone anthropology.

I organize each chapter around Dutch transformations of an Indonesian practice or Indies experience into a species of magic: witch doctors, fetishes (amulets and heirloom weapons with "magical powers"), black magic, and occult forces or legerdemain.[23] Specific incidents, experiences, and entities become occasions for translational (k)notwork. Although Dutch authors ultimately coordinate all as magic, distinct issues were at stake for each, involving different political and ontological labor.

I start from the perspective of the colonial state and move from there to popular culture, both in the Indies and in the Netherlands. In the first three chapters, Indonesian "magic" is a target of colonial governance—and governmentality, as administrators sought to secure "peace and order" (*rust en orde*) by suppressing rebellions and establishing laws and procedures. Changes in policy at the turn of the twentieth century added to this imperative a resolve to "develop" Indonesians; for some, this included addressing the pernicious effects of superstition. These chapters analyze magic's translation in relation to such priorities through specific responses, policies, and regulations. In each case, authorities drew on pedagogies of disenchantment: performances accompanied by confident claims that a particular colonial response would teach Indonesians the "truth" about what was and was not real, and about the deception of trusted local experts. Resembling what Latour (1987) termed trials of strength, they had odd outcomes, strengthening rather than undermining Indonesian realities.

In these initial chapters magic takes shape as a tool to erect confident distinctions between rational Europeans and irrational natives. Throughout all of the chapters magic appears enmeshed with efforts to secure racial and ontological distinctions, as Dutch skepticism repeatedly was contrasted with Indonesian credulity, and Indonesians were charged with confusing nature and culture, agents and objects. But residing in the Indies could result in experiences that disrupted such divides. If the state saw its task as disciplining or transforming backward populations, more intimate relations led to unexpected conversions in the opposite direction: Europeans (including some officials) who became convinced that Indonesians wielded mysterious powers. Such shifts begin to emerge in chapter 3, but the last two chapters pursue these processes further, tracking magic's crystallization in popular culture through anecdotes, popular books, and journalism.

The book makes several larger arguments, and chapters share a number of analytic strategies. As Haraway notes, "'objects' do not pre-exist as such. Objects are boundary projects" (1991: 201). Magic is such a boundary project. It is the "X" that marks the spot where male, bourgeois, Enlightened reason ends and improper (female, rural, uneducated, Indicized, and definitely *native*) unreason begins.

To call something magic may strengthen or weaken it, while strengthening or weakening those using the label as well. On the one hand, magic allies a practice with lots of other phenomena, as well as with proclamations of universality. (Such proclamations inherently involve sleight of hand; like any phenomenon, magic exists only within networks, such as anthropological texts or neopagan rites.) On the other hand, it not only relegates that practice to a subordinate position in projects of making a single world, but also cuts it off from the capillary practices that nourish it and that it, in turn, nourishes in making plural different worlds.[24] If comparisons are knotting technologies, then we need to ask who and what is strengthened or weakened by the knots magic's translations tie. What makes a comparison "good" is inherently political and ontological. I argue that those that address the making of (partly) different worlds make us more careful than those that reinforce the one-world world.

Magic is a technology of bifurcation. It is used to erect or fortify divisions: between humans, with their culture, beliefs, ideas, and words, and all other beings; between culture or society and nature; between subjects and objects, or mind and matter; between modern and backward and the West and the rest. In *We Have Never Been Modern*, Bruno Latour analyzes the interrelation between two Great Divides (1993). He argues persuasively that the distinction between nature—or more precisely a single Nature, the secrets of which are progressively revealed by Science—and society grounds the division between the West and the rest. Despite cultural relativism's pious proclamations of equality among all cultures, each of which has a perspective on the world as it really is (a philosophical bifurcation elaborated by Locke as a distinction between primary and secondary qualities, or by Kant as the gap between the world of phenomena knowable by humans and an unknowable noumenal reality of things-in-themselves), one perspective is actually true: that of the West. I find Latour's Great Divides immensely useful for attending to how magic operates. As my list of divisions indicates, however, there are many more than two at work. Both separately and together, they erect and fortify a Great Wall. Its effects are both ontological—real-ing some entities through an array of practices—and political, deliberately or inadvertently destroying or weakening others. But just as China's Great Wall is built of stone at some locations and of wood or earth at others, some of the divides that magic erects are more vulnerable to assault than others. Nonetheless, all require human and nonhuman labor to maintain, and none are impervious.

These chapters deploy several strategies to open magic's "black box" and defamiliarize its uses. The first is genealogical. Genealogy entails following the processes through which a practice or entity came to colonial attention, the controversies that gathered around it, and its induction into the magical pantheon. Several practices and entities initially were firmly attached to vernacular words, marking them as elements of Indonesian worlds—though many such "vernaculars" are themselves products of earlier connections across the Indian Ocean. European use of vernaculars signals a potential site of unfamiliar connection. Vernaculars, and the practices with which they are imbricated, could in theory become the basis for new concepts or acts, as happened for the Polynesian terms *mana* and *tabu*, Tungus *shaman*, and Ojibwe *totem*. With the exception of keris (rendered in English as *kris*), this did not, however, occur. Instead, as practices began to appear troublesome, they found themselves enlisted in the manufacture of generalities, with Dutch descriptors.

Making such new knots entailed some unraveling of existing ones. Inserting a practice or entity into a new assemblage as a species of magic (or magical thought) meant simultaneously wresting it out of its ecological niche in a nexus of practices. As Dutch experts (administrators, ethnologists, doctors, jurists) hammered Indonesian practices into magical phenomena, they bent them into new shapes. They not only isolated them from the ongoing relations and events to which they contributed, but also simplified them, often dematerializing them into specimens of primitive mentality, local culture, or individual pathology. To counter such work, I not only reinsert practices into local collectives (in Latour's [1999: 304] sense of a gathering of humans and other-than-humans) but also emphasize their materiality.

In addition, I propose alternative commensurations to those in magic's conceptual constellation. Practices may be made legible through analogies that avoid familiar shortcuts, shortcuts that include not only magic but *belief* or *the supernatural*, and even culture or idiom. Instead of reinforcing the Great Wall as magic does, methodological austerities such as avoiding the language of magic analytically yield other connections and slighter differences. Some alternatives come from overlooked or underconceptualized North Atlantic artifacts and routines.

Diffracting practices through magic also entails constant efforts to establish sharp borders: between properly disenchanted Europeans and hopelessly naïve or skillfully fraudulent Indonesians; between science and superstition, or knowledge and belief; and between nature and culture. Practices inscribed through magic commonly appear as so many instances of the rift between European reason and Indonesian credulity, and evidence of non-European failures to grasp a universal reality known to European Science. But examining what colonizers did rather than only what they said undermines such confident divisions. Not only did colonial counter-magic often reinforce or mimic what it aimed to undo, but Indonesian realities infiltrated colonizer lives—and even psyches. On the whole, through colonial rule certain practices Europeans denigrated gained in strength, becoming elements of partly shared worlds. Another strategy I have found helpful, following such phenomena into the present, shows this.

As the arc of this book indicates, I do not treat magic as a North Atlantic category projected onto the blank slate of a terra incognita. Magic materialized through relations, and translations yielded unanticipated fusions. Inevitably, colonizers sought to turn the unfamiliar into the more familiar. But in the process, the familiar mutated. At the same time, although this book is about colonial Indonesia, it mainly addresses Indonesian claims and practices to point out where networks were cut and to suggest alternate connections.[25] Indonesian practices and lexicons do not map easily onto *magic*.

My familiarity with Bali, the site of my ethnographic research, afforded partial insight into some of the practices I address. I draw several incidents from colonial archives I consulted when researching Bali's past, and came across another in a travel book I picked up because Bali was among the places its author had visited. During fieldwork, I encountered the practices, entities, and experts I discuss as well, and talked about them with Balinese friends. But much of the material on which I draw was forged by colonial experiences on the island of Java, a place far more central to colonial history. With the exception of the Spice Islands, Java—especially West Java or Sunda—had the longest and deepest involvement with the Dutch; when nationalists rejected 350 years of colonialism, they mainly spoke from a Sundanese and Javanese perspective. More Europeans lived on Java than in the rest of the archipelago combined. Much Dutch scholarship, and key colonial and scholarly institutions, developed there as well: administrative routines and relations between European and indigenous authorities, commodity production, learned societies, and museums are just some of these.

I lack the kinds of insight in Sunda and Java that fieldwork yields but have done my best to read carefully and cautiously.

A thorough discussion of magic's manufacture in the Indies would attend to many more times and places than addressed here. For millennia before European ships docked, the congeries of people yoked together as subjects of the Netherlands Indies (and, later, as citizens of Indonesia) had trafficked in words and concepts, cosmologies and gods, plants and animals, genes and goods, architecture and performances—not only with each other but with visitors and settlers from regions now called India, the Middle East, and China. The vernaculars and practices the Dutch found were products of prior translation; I note some of these as I proceed. Magic also knots together more than specific colonial assemblages. It ties Indonesians to other collectives, including British colonies in Africa and European naturecultures. While I gesture toward such connections, their story is by no means exhausted.

I envision this book as a contribution to empirical philosophy, one that brings anthropological and science studies insights to bear on specific relations. It is not in any conventional sense a history, insofar as it does not develop its argument chronologically, moving from distant past to recent past, or from the past to the present. On the contrary: not only does each chapter begin and end in the present or near present before tracing, starting from a particular past incident, the formation of the judgment "magic," but the sequence of incidents making up the book's trajectory in chapter 1 begins almost a hundred years after the incident with which it ends in chapter 5. Nor does it propose, as anthropologists might anticipate, a new theory of magic; I hope that by its end it will be clear why I would find the generality such a theory implies problematic. Instead, my main goal is to interrupt business as usual, by attending to emergences and effects and by proposing alternatives to familiar habits.

FINALLY, A NOTE on grammar and orthography. In Indonesian and Balinese, nouns are not marked for plural (except for emphasis), leaving this to context, and I have followed that convention throughout this book (even in quotes from translated Dutch). In addition, both Dutch and Indonesian/Malay orthography have undergone several changes since the nineteenth century. For simplicity's sake, I have used current spelling for both languages throughout.

INTERLUDE 1 ⌄ WITCH DOCTORS

In his magisterial ethnography *Witchcraft, Oracles, and Magic among the Azande* (1937), Evans-Pritchard devotes an entire section to what he terms the witch-doctor. He identifies witch-doctors as specialists who function as "both diviner and magician," that is, who both discover the source of a problem, in dramatic public performances, and remove the affliction, in more intimate settings. No single Zande term exists for such men, however. Azande call someone who dances to reveal the cause of a client's suffering *ira avure* and someone who takes away illness a *binza*. While the same person may have expertise in both skills—hence Evans-Pritchard's decision to treat them as one—he does not explain why he chose the label witch-doctor. Neither does he discuss diviner and magician.

Evans-Pritchard clearly felt no pressure to explain these translations, which drew on existing precedents. Even more than *witch*, inscribed in anti-witchcraft ordinances across British colonial Africa before Evans-Pritchard set foot in Zande society, *witch doctor* had long been etched into European imaginaries of Africa.[1] A glance at the *Oxford English Dictionary* reveals its Enlightened and colonial genealogy. It came into use in the early eighteenth century, with the meaning "[o]ne who professes to cure disease and to counteract witchcraft by magic arts." From the start, the witch doctor not only was a purveyor of questionable claims who could only profess to heal, but also deployed "magic arts"—against witchcraft, a phenomenon elite Europeans no longer found plausible. By 1836, witch doctor had taken to the road, acquiring a crucial second meaning: "a magician among African tribes, whose business it is to detect witches, and to counteract the effects of magic."[2] No wonder the term came so easily to Evans-Pritchard. He had moved into a vibrantly inhabited verbal terrain with familiar landmarks for talking of African practices.

What, however, of *magician*, which Evans-Pritchard restricts to those who remove odd things, sent by witches to harm, from human bodies?[3] Evans-Pritchard's discussion of that practice, which recounts his own tricks in revealing the tricks of the witch doctor's trade, suggests he may have had illusionists in mind. After paying two experts, Badobo and Bögwözu, to instruct his servant Kamanga, he discovered they were holding back in explaining to Kamanga their use of legerdemain to reveal the stuff that caused a client's discomfort. Evans-Pritchard literally took matters into his own hands. Placing himself between teacher and pupil during a session in his home, he casually palmed the charcoal Bögwözu had inserted into a poultice before passing it to Kamanga.

Note the fast translational slides: for Evans-Pritchard, witch-doctor is synonymous with magician and even sorcerer. He is not alone. Lévi-Strauss makes an equally smooth swerve in "The Sorcerer and His Magic" (1963), in which a shaman constitutes the most memorable "sorcerer" of the three cases that he analyzes. That shaman, Quesalid, is another anthropological trickster, the half-white, half-Tlingit George Hunt, married to a Kwakiutl (now Kwakwaka'wakw) woman and collaborator and main source on Kwakwaka'wakw practices to Franz Boas, founder of North American anthropology. In this particular account of how he became a shaman (as Taussig 2003 reveals, he wrote others), Hunt/Quesalid is even trickier than Evans-Pritchard, occupying simultaneously the positions of skeptical investigator, sorcerer's apprentice, and successful practitioner. After triumphantly learning that his teacher uses sleight of hand to extract illness from his clients' bodies in the form of bloody down, he discovers that when he uses this trick himself his clients get well; a rival begs to learn his secret after Quesalid's technique proves more efficacious.

Evans-Pritchard's account of Zande witch doctors resonates not only with Quesalid's sleight of hand but also with an earlier expert, Sir James Frazer:

> The acuter minds perceive how easy it is to dupe their weaker brothers and to play on his superstition for their own advantage. Not that the sorcerer is always a knave and imposter; he is often sincerely con-

vinced that he really possesses those wonderful powers which the credulity of his fellows ascribes to him. But the more sagacious he is, the more likely he is to see through the fallacies which impose on duller wits. . . . [I]t must always be remembered that every single profession and claim put forward by the magician as such is false; not one of them can be maintained without deception, conscious or unconscious. (1922: 46)

For Frazer, a magician is a swindler who manipulates the gullible. Or perhaps dupes even himself. In either case, nothing he says or does is true. For Frazer, it is impossible to think about the magician without invoking psychology (delusion) and trickery (arts of illusion). Such disenchanting tropes remain durable features of the anthropology of magic.

Much anthropological ink has been spilled in describing, analyzing, and explaining (away) the myriad experts gathered up as witch doctors, sorcerers, shamans, and magicians. Denunciatory zeal and an emphasis on deception—"conscious or unconscious"—remain common. (Evans-Pritchard's focus on tricks goes beyond the usual assembly: the anthropologist's acuity makes him effectively the witch doctor's competitor—a sorcerer himself.) The activities of such experts remain the most common domain of life where anthropologists and other modern authors enroll terms such as magic.

The fraudulent sorcerer or witch doctor has a longer European history, however. As Styers (2004) notes, anthropologists adapted Reformation critiques of Catholic priests to their analyses of primitives. Such critiques are a product of a contingent and entangled history, emerging from theological disagreements between Protestants and Catholics, the end of the witch trials, and political struggles.

Like illusionists, witch doctors, whether or not their repertoire includes prestidigitation, are presumed to be staging performances in order to dazzle and deceive. Instead of temporarily suspending the "real" in the ontological game stage magicians play (During 2004; Jones 2017), they dupe the all-too-enchanted. Such an emphasis shifts attention to culpability rather than reality.[4]

In her bestseller *Eat, Pray, Love*, Elizabeth Gilbert recounts her experiences in Bali with Ketut Liyer, whom she calls a "medicine man." In her book, Ketut Liyer liberally uses the English word *magic* to describe some of his activities: he refers to his "magic paintings," mentions that he learned "black magic" to help clients afflicted by it, and tells her "I do true magic, not joking" (Gilbert 2006: 233). These usages are telling indications of Ketut Liyer's engagements with tourists, expatriates, and their language. No doubt such self-description encouraged David Stuart-Fox, an anthropologist with a decades-long friendship with Ketut Liyer, to title the book they coauthored *Pray, Magic, Heal*, though in not only echoing Gilbert's title but also highlighting magic, he simultaneously targeted readers likely to come across his book in Bali. In this meticulous account of Ketut Liyer's activities, Stuart-Fox explains that Ketut Liyer is a *balian* (Balinese) or *dukun* (Indonesian), terms he glosses as "traditional healer" (2015). How did Indonesians skilled in alleviating affliction find themselves transformed not only into medicine men and traditional healers, but also magicians, witch doctors, and even shamans? What do such translations connect and what do they sever?

In this chapter I tease apart these translational knots by analyzing a report about a different balian, apprehended by the colonial state in 1921. The official who ordered his arrest called him a *wonderdokter*, a charlatan or witch doctor. What Dutch administrator-scholars said about such practitioners, and their responses to particular individuals, constitute illuminating instances of reality politics.

Such reality politics involves conjuring specific kinds of subjects. Calling the man arrested a fanatic as well as a fake, and presenting his clients as both innocents in need of state protection and exemplars of the difficulties of "improving" colonized subjects, the official who penned it runs through a repertoire of accreted colonial positions concerning dukun and their clients.[1] Dukun form a node that gathers up a trio of imaginary subjects through which the Dutch Euro-formed those they ruled: the fanatic, the fraud, and the fool. A cast of characters inheriting Enlightened critiques that identify, reject, and mock superstition, such stock figures populated colonial texts. They are, however, not only pertinent to colonial responses to dukun: they pop up whenever Indonesian practices are diffracted through magic. Their implicit opposite is even trickier and more fantastic: the disenchanted white man of reason, especially the colonial scholar-administrator.

Frauds proved the most common translation machine for turning dukun into witch doctors, as well as the most germane to their metamorphosis into healers. Administrators portray dukun as deliberately or unwittingly devious, using tricks to dupe an ignorant, credulous, and suggestible populace in dire need of protection and education. If frauds are ineluctably yoked to the fools they con, that folly also exerted pressure on colonial governance, in the form of interventions aiming to disenchant.

Colonial translations wrest dukun out of the networks in which they operate, sorting their activities into those Science might potentially recuperate and those to be rejected as nonsense. Glimpses of what this elides and divides—traces of the realities Balinese practices enact—appear in the interstices of this report, offering challenges to colonial claims about Balinese techniques of persuasion, including the much disdained "power of suggestion." Indeed, white men of reason deployed their own techniques of persuasion, efforts to prove the falsity of Indonesian "beliefs."

Disciplining the Sorcerer (If Not His Magic . . .)

In May 1921, Resident Henri Titus Damsté, a senior career administrator responsible for governing the islands of Bali and Lombok, received a frantic telegram from G. J. Kuys, an inexperienced subordinate stationed in Jembrana, in Bali's northwest.[2] According to Kuys, a fanatic (*geestdrijver*) named Nang Mukanis was disrupting peace and order by representing himself as a healing balian and extorting divine veneration from the population.[3] He requested an armed brigade to arrest and isolate Nang Mukanis. Damsté sent two and headed to Jembrana himself.

On Damsté's arrival, Kuys filled him in. Kuys had first learned of the witch doctor Nang Mukanis from an anonymous letter. Its writer informed him that since Nang Mukanis had set himself up as a balian in a remote village a mere two weeks before, a flood of people from all over Jembrana had been streaming to his home with offerings.[4] Because he had heard nothing of any disturbance of the peace from Balinese authorities where Nang Mukanis lived, Kuys initially paid little attention, though he passed the missive to the Balinese district head for comment. The latter's response, however, aroused his interest. Adamantly rejecting the letter writer's charge that he and other Balinese authorities believed in Nang Mukanis's "miraculous power," the district head assured Kuys that Nang Mukanis was no cause for concern. But he was clearly unhappy that Nang Mukanis had come to Kuys's attention. Kuys decided to look into the situation, and, dismissing the district head's protests that it was an uncomfortable and difficult journey, insisted on being taken to Nang Mukanis's compound.

There he found hundreds of Balinese, among them, to his disgust, the chief of police and the wives not only of the district head but also of a member of the judicial council. Signs of ritual activity abounded: colored cloth draped all the pavilions and incense burned before piles of offerings Kuys calculated as worth hundreds of guilders; there was even a decorated sedan chair. Nang Mukanis himself, clad in the white clothing worn by Balinese who traffic with powerful more-than-human forces (usually translated as gods and spirits), was making a circuit around the yard, singing an invocation, while followers held a parasol over his head to mark the presence of a force. At Kuys's unexpected appearance everything stopped. After staring at the interloper ("with eyes full of hate"), Nang Mukanis snapped the parasol shut and walked off. Sitting down, Kuys asked those assembled why Nang Mukanis had become so wildly popular but found their answers—which referred to successful cures—unhelpful. After looking around, Kuys waited in vain for Nang Mukanis to return. He then consulted the Balinese officials, who professed they could not understand why hundreds visited Nang Mukanis daily and declared they had thought the matter too inconsequential to mention.

To Kuys the situation did not appear critical. Once people "noticed that offerings and homage are brought in vain," the mania would surely pass. In the meantime, he asked to be kept posted. An incident a few days later, however, changed his mind.

By chance in Nang Mukanis's district to inspect new roads, Kuys encountered Nang Mukanis dancing with an upraised keris (dagger) at the head of a large procession. Kuys immediately dismounted and strode toward the balian. Keris raised, Nang Mukanis turned in his direction, and (according to Kuys) made defiant movements with his head. At this several girls fell to the ground shrieking, "affected under his influence." As Nang Mukanis headed straight for him, Kuys, who was unarmed, grew alarmed and looked for the district head, who belatedly rushed up and grabbed the fist holding the keris. Aided by the police chief, a constable, and some of Nang Mukanis's followers, the district head led Nang Mukanis into a nearby compound and dispersed the crowd. Kuys noted with displeasure, however, that they made no effort to disarm Nang Mukanis, and entreated rather than ordered him.

Judging things had gone too far, after finishing his inspection Kuys ordered Nang Mukanis's arrest. But that evening the district head and police chief reported they had not been able to follow his instructions. When they tried to take Nang Mukanis into custody, Damsté wrote, quoting Kuys, "He invoked a demon, and immediately everyone [once again hundreds of people were crowded into his compound] was as if possessed! Many fell to the ground shrieking loudly, and others conducted themselves as if insane. And they themselves and the police agents—whose eyes already rolled and were bulging out of their heads!—had ducked out of the dangers threatening them by 'hastily withdrawing'! And they lacked the nerve to repeat the attempt!"

It was then that Kuys telegraphed the resident. But with armed brigades at his disposal, Kuys wanted to return to his previous policy and wait for the affair to run its course. Damsté disagreed. Nang Mukanis must be arrested. To ensure no further mishaps, he charged the police to take him into custody before dawn, when he likely would be home alone, and to say nothing in advance to local authorities. After instructing the brigades to avoid bloodshed, he added that should they not find Nang Mukanis they were "to impound or destroy all of the concrete signs of his holiness." Despite apprehending Nang Mukanis without mishap, they carried out those orders anyway. Damsté reports: "And what under the circumstances was unnecessary, but all the same perhaps also not bad, the decorations in Nang Mukanis's dwelling, his white garments, and the elegant, now dismantled sedan-chair—that had been a gift of homage from the district head!—were chucked in a heap in the yard and burned, without gods or demons retaliating against the police." Later that same day Damsté assembled the Balinese authorities in the district capital for a dressing down. Berating them for failing to protect people against "stupid tricks," he ridiculed their own credulity and derided their failure to inform Kuys about Nang Mukanis, a "mentally impaired commoner." (Since the Balinese officials all were members of priestly or aristocratic families, this reference to rank aimed to shame them further.)

Damsté found much cause for satisfaction with the outcome of events.[5] The Balinese administrators appeared embarrassed and appropriately "disenchanted." Nonetheless, he opined that the incident spoke to the gullibility of not only ordinary Balinese but even those with education and position. He noted with disgust that a member of the judicial council, scion of a priestly household who had, moreover, attended a Dutch school, had even removed the gold from his teeth on Nang Mukanis's orders, and had had to go to Java to repair the damage.

Fanatics and the Disruption of Peace and Order

So there we have it. Nang Mukanis is the target of multiple accusations: he is a fanatic, a witch doctor who claims "miraculous powers" that actually come down to "stupid tricks," and "mentally impaired" at that. What prompts such statements? What do they mean and do?

To answer these questions, let's begin with Kuys's indictment of Nang Mukanis as a fanatic (*geestdrijver*). Not a common element in the making of magicians, fanatic (like its Dutch cousin *fanaat*) derives from Latin *fanaticus*, "pertaining to a temple," but also "mad, enthusiastic, inspired by a god," someone whose devotion exceeded what custom required.[6] *Fanatic's* more familiar meaning—overly zealous, especially in regard to religion, and even "characterized . . . by excessive and mistaken enthusiasm"—dates from the seventeenth century.[7] Note the adjectives, "excessive and mistaken," that modify (the equally problematic) "enthusiasm." Judgment is baked in: an act or claim appears fanatical when it violates the speaker's common sense. The fanatic does not act instrumentally, weighing the best means to reach an end. Instead, swept away by passion or vision, he embarks on potentially dangerous courses of action with no regard for self-preservation. An association with the more-than-human still lingers: outside forces move him to act. Kuys's specific choice of words, *geestdrijver*, literally "psyche driver," has similar connotations.[8]

Fanatic aligned Nang Mukanis with the most alarming specter haunting colonial states: rebellion.[9] Authorities used the term to refer to charismatic men whose relations with more-than-human forces attracted large followings. Even when not instigators of insurrection, fanatics could catalyze resistance to specific policies, laws, or officials. Many of those Dutch officials labeled fanatics were traditional intellectuals: Haji (Muslims who had made the pilgrimage to Mecca); guru (teachers); kiyai (Islamic teachers and scholars, sometimes Sufi masters); and also dukun.[10] Some belonged to prominent aristocratic families; Dutch administrators kept a close eye on branch lines and bastard offspring of such lineages, seeking to domesticate them into the service of the colonial state. Others, like their followers, were peasants. Those followers, of course, saw them differently than the Dutch did: at their most impressive, as the "just king" Javanese texts prophesied, or the Mahdi of Islam (Sartono 1973).

Beginning with the Java War (1825–30), shortly after the Dutch Crown began to manage the Company's former possessions, the Dutch found themselves embroiled in a steady series of conflicts. Even when colonial armies won, victory could come at a high cost. In late nineteenth-century Aceh, for example, an official peace following three decades of outright war hardly meant the end of resistance, which continued to national independence and beyond. Everywhere in the Indies periodic "disturbances" (*onlusten*) plagued administrators. Anxiety over fanatics was as much personal as political. The touchstone was an 1888 incident in West Java in which "fanatics" killed not only Dutch officials but also their wives and children.

Apart from their potential to mobilize, excess characterized fanatics in other ways. Renowned teachers or dukun often engaged in practices that pulled them beyond ordinary social relations. Judged by the standards of a bourgeois bodily hexis, acts of ascesis through which one might acquire or augment a capacity for effective action—removing oneself from quotidian routines, living in isolation in the forest, renouncing bodily pleasures (not only sex but even rice), meditating all night—struck many Dutch authors as extravagant. For the Dutch, such practices involved either delusion or manipulation. At best, they might alter a person's awareness, but they could not affect other people and certainly not forge relations with other-than-human forces; to act as if they could was mad. At worst, some suggested those performing such acts mainly aimed to establish a reputation in order to enrich themselves (e.g., Hoekendijk 1920), moving into the domain of fraud.

The acts and incitements of fanatics, then, exceeded what European officials deemed reasonable. Colonial uses of the term bring a whiff of its original meaning, suggesting traffic with potent more-than-humans as well as mental imbalance. What made such persons troubling, however, was their charisma: their ability to attract adherents. This capacity posed a risk of contagion, of spreading their unreason to others or of congealing their claims into acts that threatened "peace and order" (*rust en orde*), the chief injunction of Dutch colonial rule.

Hence the very first sentence of Kuys's telegram called for action: "For a few days public peace order Tegalcangkring and surroundings seriously disturbed by fanatic Mukanis." Telegraphic technology meant that not only Damsté but also other official eyes would see those words. Calling someone a fanatic who threatened peace and order triggered high alert and mobilized the state's repressive apparatus. By using such terms in a document visible to others, Kuys compelled Damsté to respond—and to report the incident to Batavia. The telegram that set in motion the state's coercive machinery also procured Nang Mukanis a place in its archives.

But why did Kuys use that potent phrase, especially given that he tried to retract it when Damsté showed up? Clearly, Kuys saw in Nang Mukanis someone whose magnetism might catalyze a movement or who could incite followers to oppose authority, if only to mimic his own lack of deference (even palpable indifference) to Kuys's status. But specific elements of their chance encounter at the crossroads undoubtedly provided an impetus. For one, Nang Mukanis approached Kuys brandishing a bared blade. He also had an extraordinary effect on his followers. In addition, like many dukun (and Haji; sometimes kiyai too), he wore white, to mark detachment from mundane life and his association with more-than-human beings. In colonial Indonesia, however, white could also signal an intention to fight to the death. Based on experiences in Java, Sumatra, and Bali itself, officials found white-clad persons (especially crowds) alarming. Not only had people dressed entirely in white as a sign of their readiness to die, and, armed with keris, charged Dutch soldiers during south Bali's conquest in 1906 and 1908, but more recently, in 1916 and 1917, peasant protests against local authorities had involved similar modes of dress and weaponry (Wiener 1995, 1999a).

Kuys's invocation of fanaticism moved Damsté to action, justifying Nang Mukanis's arrest even though popularity or aiding clients violated no laws. The fanatic, however, is of interest for another reason. His purported irrationality resonates with a persistent trope in accounts of witch doctors or shamans: that they are deluded and may even deceive themselves. Anthropological accounts of such figures often note how odd they are—possibly even insane. Such assessments occur in Damsté's report. He refers to Nang Mukanis, once safely in Dutch custody, as a "mentally impaired bungler," with crazy eyes.

Fanaticism rarely figures in accounts of witch doctors and magicians. It is more often associated with religion, befitting its original association with gods. Thus, few fanatics found themselves also characterized as witch doctors or charlatans (*toverdokter* or *wonderdokter*) or as magicians or sorcerers (*tovenaar*).

Frauds

By the time Damsté arrived in Jembrana, Kuys had changed his tune, and sought to present Nang Mukanis as a charlatan rather than a fanatic. Frauds posed different challenges to colonial regimes, and provoked different responses. For one, liars presented no threat to European lives; at least in theory, only natives would be susceptible to a dukun's allure. Fraud also involved a different imagined subjectivity. Unlike fanatics, swindlers are masters of practical reason, experts in cold calculation. A fraud is a *Homo economicus*, using others in the pursuit of money and fame.

Such assessments inform Kuys's and Damsté's responses to the material goods they discover in Nang Mukanis's compound, which they take as evidence he was up to no good. When consulting balian, Balinese bring offerings, topped with a woven palm leaf receptacle containing cash, which the balian ordinarily keeps. Such donations, entirely voluntary, are usually small. (The rest of the offering, mostly food, returns home with the client.) The two substantial chests filled with money discovered after Nang Mukanis's arrest attested to his popularity; the gift of the sedan chair demonstrated his literal elevation.

To Dutch authorities, however, these objects inherently signaled deception. Taking his ability to help as a priori impossible, any compensation could only be illicit. Damsté even briefly wondered if Nang Mukanis might have conspired with the Balinese district head's family (which included the chief of police, a tax collector, and a member of the judiciary) to extort money from the populace. But he thought it more likely they too had been duped, captivated by Nang Mukanis.

Like the fanatic, the figure of the fraud was not new. By the mid-nineteenth century, Javanese dukun pop up in law journals summarizing appeals to the Supreme Court as part of an undifferentiated group of swindlers, people described as claiming to possess "supernatural powers" who traffic in "superstition." Regional tribunals, headed by Dutch officials, administered justice. Just how common it was to try dukun for fraud is hard to tell; journals only report cases where questions arose about sentencing.

But clearly officials did occasionally bring dukun up on charges. Cases involved specific complaints: distributing potentially toxic concoctions, purporting to identify thieves, blessing a burglar's tools, providing water to sprinkle around a house to recover stolen goods, and selling "spells," sometimes by teaching a client, or deploying on his behalf, a *ngélmu* (knowledge). Tellingly, reports have headings such as "swindle-superstition"; they often declare that the defendant took advantage of people's gullibility. One 1847 summary announces itself as "Contributions to knowledge of native character: superstition, fanaticism, and deceit" (*RNI* 1851: 62). As with Nang Mukanis, fanatics, frauds, and fools form a set.

While case summaries judge dukun to be con artists, and draw from magic's lexicon (e.g., "spells") to characterize their practices, as with fanatics these accusations lack specificity. Dukun are only one kind of trickster exploiting local credulity. By the time Nang Mukanis crossed paths with Kuys, however, the fraudulent dukun had developed sharper contours, through (k)nots tying their practices to medicine.

One of the best examples is an entry in the *Encyclopedia for the Netherlands Indies* (*Encyclopaedie van Nederlandsch-Indië*). Offering authoritative digests of matters the Dutch found pertinent to knowledge of the Indies, active and retired civil servants and military officers made up its editorial staff and wrote the entries, among them Damsté. Unlike official reports or abstracts of cases on appeal, encyclopedia entries are synthetic, eliding traces of specific situations. Their generalizing certainty, however, reveals what became taken as settled and cements facts.

Dukun appear in several entries, but two tie the translational (k)not with biomedicine: "physician (native)" and "medicines." The first announces it will cover only those "who practice the so-called native medical science"; unmarked physicians, including Indonesians trained in biomedicine, required no discussion. While dukun engage in many activities, they become (modified) physicians through their treatment of people suffering from corporeal or mental afflictions legible to biomedicine, with plant-based therapies. This structures what the entry addresses. One paragraph scrutinizes the materials and methods dukun use to prepare remedies. The entry on medicines elaborates further, while addressing what colonial scientists had learned about the plants Javanese used to treat illnesses.[11]

As the qualification "native" indicates, dukun are doctors with a difference. Taking biomedicine as the benchmark, what draws attention are deviations. Thus, dukun do not standardize remedies but prescribe dosages in amounts equal in size to mundane household objects (coins, nuts) or to the patient's thumb, intimately tying treatment to person. Moreover, while they administer some medicines internally, as concoctions to drink, they also prescribe unguents to be rubbed on the body. More alarming, many medications involve partial digestion by the dukun or a client's family member, who masticates the prescribed plants and spews the ensuing mash onto the ailing body part, adding spittle to the mix, a practice that appalled bourgeois Europeans. Furthermore, some plants are chosen because their names resemble a symptom or disease.[12]

Such small departures, however, are embedded in more radical ones. Even as it identifies dukun as physicians, the encyclopedia directs readers elsewhere ("see Heathenism"), noting that dukun do more than attempt to cure illness. They "occupy themselves with several superstitious acts"— supplying amulets, interpreting dreams, divining thieves, and leading rituals—and fame accrues to those with potent heirloom objects or spells. To cap it off, they consider "spirits" the primary cause of illness.[13] A small book (on "heathenism") published a decade earlier asserts that the dukun supplements her pharmacy by driving away "evil spirits." It concludes, "The word dukun has become roughly synonymous with native physician or better quack" (Spat 1906: 38).[14]

Deviation from biomedical practice renders the dukun a fraud for two reasons, one of which has little to do with colonial Indonesia. Since biomedicine's authority rests on its credentials as the bearer of truths about bodily affliction, diagnoses or treatments that diverge from its norms invite denunciation. Stengers (2003) argues that because medicine is itself science with a difference, it churns out charlatans. With the suffering human body as its object, biomedicine cannot secure the results sought by experimental sciences: bodies cannot be enrolled in the same way as electrons or chemicals. Consequently, it generates practitioners who insist their procedures also are tried and tested but are accused of trading in placebos and suggestion—an accusation colonial authors also attached to dukun, as I address below.

But dukun were not mere quacks. The encyclopedia's list of acts that find no place in biomedicine makes this clear, as does its reference to spirits. This returns us to Damsté's label: witch doctor, or rather wonderdokter.

Wonderdokter is not fully equivalent to the English *witch doctor*, even though my Dutch-English dictionary offers that translation (Martin and Tops 1991); *toverdokter* would be closer, as the root, *tover-*, similarly recalls witchcraft and witch trials. Where *toverdokter* emphasizes misfortunes caused by witches, *wonderdokter* sarcastically invokes miracles.[15]

FIGURE 1.1: A village dukun from Kandangan, near Lumayang in East Java, 1925 (photographer unknown). Courtesy of Leiden University Libraries, Shelfmark KITLV 36274.

What makes a dukun a witch doctor or wonderdokter as opposed to a generic charlatan? Do offhand remarks about superstition and spirits, evil or otherwise, suffice? To answer, I turn from the encyclopedia, which does not use the term, to a later article, by another administrator-scholar named J. E. Jasper, that does. More precisely, it speaks of *wonderdokteres*, gendered female, which is fitting as most Javanese (and Balinese) dukun were and are women, though famous dukun (such as Ketut Liyer or Nang Mukanis) tend to be male. Jasper was roughly Damsté's contemporary with an even more illustrious career; administrative concerns similar to Damsté's wind through his account.[16] Hence he concentrates on how Javanese practitioners build reputations that bring them wealth and prestige and attract clients who should know better. He also recommends that the regime regulate their activities.

The wonderdokter precipitates out of distinctions Jasper (1932) draws between two types of dukun and treatment methods. The first corresponds to the encyclopedia's "physician (native)": a rural practitioner, who learns her trade from kin and mainly treats neighbors, and has extensive knowledge of the local flora, growing or gathering the plants used in her prescriptions. While Jasper reiterates familiar critiques, he adds an endorsement: though not trained in science and using techniques of little value and potentially some risk, such dukun engaged in a benign and even useful activity, particularly in remote villages without medical facilities or whose residents distrusted doctors.

By contrast, the wonderdokteres merits condemnation. Jasper differentiates the two in every possible way, from distinguishing innocent rural authenticity and duplicitous urban artifice to foregrounding the disparity between knowledge of nature, however limited, and an all-too-skilled manipulation of psyches. The wonderdokteres plies her trade in towns and cities rather than villages. She treats strangers, often those with some status in colonial society: not only native officials, but also Chinese and even Europeans—more often, their wives.[17] But the root of Jasper's rejection lies in an incompatibility between her treatments and biomedical therapies. She has her clients bathe or sprinkle themselves with holy water that she manufactures, make offerings to spirits, and in general does "hocus-pocus."

To Jasper, the wonderdokteres relies on techniques of persuasion that have no actual effect on disease.[18] She is, however, a proficient performer, adroit in generating a seductive aura of mystery and in convincing clients she possesses mysterious powers, in part by claiming to have spirit helpers and in part by her peculiar manner of living. As stories of miraculous successes circulate, her reputation grows. But rapid ascent is frequently followed by equally fast descent, as people become aware "that all [the] hocus-pocus . . . has cost the patient money but bestowed no benefit" (1932: 35).

Jasper compares such dukun to other experts (especially guru) who traffic in esoteric knowledges (ngélmu) to cure, protect, destroy enemies (or undo malevolence), ensure good harvests, or confer invulnerability. While regarding all as frauds, he acknowledges they need not be motivated by greed. Some are mystics, convinced their prayers, incense, and rites really help. He explains their worldly success, however, as due to "almost unlimited credulity even among the better-off and developed [natives]" (1932: 37).

To flesh out his portrait, Jasper narrates the life of an actual wonderdokteres. Originally a farmer's wife in central Java, out of boredom she began to sell kananga oil and dispense syarat (which Jasper glosses as magical agents, tovermiddelen). Her imposture was revealed after she sold a policeman a bottle of oil that she assured him would help to locate a felon. She fled to a large town in West Java, where she attracted a better class of clients (pawnshop managers, supervisors, religious officials, even a regent's wife), whom she provided with amulets. A native district head lent her a small house, where she began to hold weekly ritual feasts (slametan). When she declared that a spirit named Raja Selong occupied a large stone nearby, people installed a shrine and began to make offerings there. She then moved in with another official's family, who provided a room and daily food offerings for her spirit helpers. Only she was allowed into the room (where, Jasper insinuates, she consumed the offerings herself). As stories spread that she could fly and was over a hundred years old, people began to venerate her and bring her gifts. But as failures accumulated, enthusiasm waned. So she moved again, to a large city. There she presented herself as a pious Muslim (by wearing a headscarf) and "wove new mysteries," building an even more successful practice. Jasper drily proclaims that her greatest marvel was attracting many wealthy clients. He ends by regretting that the colonial state had no laws concerning the practice of medicine—and thus could not prosecute such dukun. Calling their activities "excesses in an ordered society," Jasper advocated regulation (1932: 38). Jasper's frustration echoes a complaint in the Encyclopaedie that because statutes on the practice of medicine excluded local treatments, dukun could do just about anything.[19]

For officials, then, dukun either draw on actual if limited knowledge of bodies and plants or engage in deceit. To the extent their activities may be commensurated with biomedical practices, dukun are described as (modified) physicians. Practices resisting such commensuration, however, are "hocus-pocus." *Witch doctor* speaks to the unwelcome intrusion of techniques and entities that find no place in the world modern Europeans make. But note that this accusation presumes afflictions that involve a body—a body, moreover, that preexists therapeutic practices rather than being brought into being by them. The charge *witch doctor*, in short, indicates a profound conflict over ways of doing reality.

Fools

For scholars and administrators, neither fanatics nor frauds would have merited attention had ordinary Indonesians not been prone to trust them. *Fool* is my shorthand for a subject materialized through countless colonial texts, by no means only in Indonesia. Whether amused or alarmed, European authors commonly described those they ruled as naïve, easily duped, and mired in superstition. Assumptions about gullibility and ignorance undergird virtually all discussions of fanatics and frauds. Superstition belongs to the same family. Around the time of Nang Mukanis's arrest, one noted that superstition (*bijgeloof*) "is rightly always mentioned in one breath with stupidity and ignorance" (Habbema 1919: 313). Indeed, in this period in particular officials frequently treated superstition as an administrative problem.[20]

Deriving from Latin, and initially, like *fanatic*, referring to excess—in this case due to "unreasonable" fear of the gods—the term "superstition" has long involved, also like fanatic, a judgment about the beliefs or practices of others. In particular, it judges particular acts as irrational, unfounded, as well as based in ignorance or fear or "excessive" credulity.[21] Which acts, however, merit such assessments is political, an element of struggles among specific communities in specific circumstances, whether those communities are the pagan and Christian communities of Rome, the Catholic and Protestant communities of the Reformation, or the scientific and religious communities of the moderns.[22] While the Latin etymology is not part of Dutch *bijgeloof* (which embeds belief, *geloof*), colonial uses echo such history.

A text by another colonial official-scholar, Jacob Herman Fredrick Kohlbrugge, is helpful for elucidating what counted for some as Indonesian folly, drawing together as it does superstition, spirits, and suggestibility. Unlike Damsté and Jasper, Kohlbrugge was not a career civil servant who had worked his way up the ranks; after operating a private medical practice on Java around the turn of the twentieth century, he secured a position in the Indies medical service. His book of essays on the spiritual—or mental or psychological; Dutch *geestelijk* implies all of these—life "of the Javanese and their overseers" landed him the new chair in ethnology at Utrecht.[23] His first, eponymous essay combines Dutch complaints about "natives," his own experiences as a biomedical physician, and material from earlier colonial authors (whom he quotes copiously; he also lifts anecdotes and whole arguments from them), with concepts from the developing sciences of ethnology and psychology.

For Kohlbrugge, superstition is omnipresent in everyday Javanese life, evident in acts that range from propitiating "spirits" by muttering "meaningless incantations," making offerings, and holding feasts (1907: 11) to calculating auspicious and inauspicious times and directions before embarking on important ventures (1907: 8) to manufacturing objects to bring good or bad fortune to oneself or others.[24] Most superstitious customs, he asserts, seek to avert harm and achieve well-being by establishing relations with "spirits." Living in a world saturated with spirits, who are both capricious and vindictive, leads to constant anxiety. As for the spirits, they are diagnosed as a product of the "unbridled fantasy" and difficulty in distinguishing dreams from reality that characterizes the Javanese psyche (1907: 29).[25]

An overactive imagination constitutes only one of many cognitive defects: "I will not say that they have innately less understanding than us, but the seed, equally present in both, is not developed, logical thinking not trained, they do not form clear concepts" (1907: 30). Nor are Javanese capable of critical reflection or abstract thought.

Conversely, Kohlbrugge claims that Javanese are practical, handy, remarkably adroit, and manifest an "exquisite keenness of observation" (1907: 27). They learn, he says, by imitation. Indeed, a veritable genius at mimicry explains everything from the culture-bound syndrome *latah* to the claim that after seven years his scribe's handwriting was indistinguishable from his own (1907: 36–37).

Taken together, these characteristics—deficiencies in critical and logical thinking, apprehensions about spirits, even skilled mimicry—make Javanese extraordinarily suggestible. More nervous, impressionable, and emotionally labile than Europeans, they accept virtually any claim without question. Suggestibility, then, is a core feature of their psyche. This leads them to rely on experts such as dukun. And dukun, skilled at suggestion, are adept at exploiting these traits, in part by making good use of their own "keenness of observation."[26] Yet, like Jasper, Kohlbrugge thinks it would be wrong to consider such experts merely deceivers. Many operate under autosuggestion, which he attributes to their performance of ascetic exercises and their overestimation of their own abilities as their fame spreads and people treat them as powerful.

Everything about Kohlbrugge's discussion involves reality politics. Simply put, the realities Javanese make through their practices do not, for Kohlbrugge and his presumed readers, exist. He is unusually explicit in declaring them fantastic, products of overactive imaginations. But his primary focus is psychological—or, given his focus on cognition, epistemological rather than ontological.

The White Man of Reason (and Ethical Colonialism)

Each of these accusations—fanatic, fraud, fool—posits an implicit opposite: the white man of reason, precisely the subject making the accusations: Kohlbrugge, for instance. At least in theory, administrators offered the perfect specimen. As contributors to scholarly journals, they epitomized reason in the pursuit of knowledge; as agents of the state, they governed through an impersonal, bureaucratic organization.[27] In contrast to those they governed, theirs was an exemplary subjectivity: temperate and objective, instrumental but honest, and of course skeptical and fully disenchanted.

It is not by chance that I speak of the *man* of reason. Gender, long baked into accounts of reason in Western philosophy (Lloyd 1993), pokes up casually in both Jasper's article and in Damsté's offhand references to the wives of the very disappointing Balinese civil servants. Women, of whatever race, commonly appear in colonial texts as innately more emotional—and, by dint of that, more susceptible to belief and persuasion.

If reason is male, its whiteness also was fundamental, though, as I address in chapter 4, not necessarily phenotypic. Britain's "white man's burden" captures what formed the colonial crux: the duty of Europeans to improve the dark-skinned people they ruled. Damsté and Jasper began their careers as the Netherlands embarked on its own noble project: the Ethical Policy. Formulated at the turn of the twentieth century, its advocates proposed that the enormous profits the Netherlands had extracted from the Indies established a debt that should be repaid. Thirty years of laissez-faire capitalism had produced poverty and famine. This new policy, by contrast, would promote the welfare of colonial subjects—ironically, initially by increasing their number, as the conquest of remaining indigenous polities formerly of little interest to European powers expanded the territorial reach of the Netherlands Indies.[28] Ethicists were committed to extending the reforming and improving projects of late nineteenth-century liberal states to non-European populations. Good governance, they argued, would develop Indonesians, both culturally and economically. They zeroed in on three programs in particular: irrigation, transmigration (the movement of people from densely populated islands, such as Java, to purportedly more sparsely populated "outer" islands), and Western education.

If fanatics had long challenged the colonial state's prime directive, to maintain "peace and order," the state's new concern with development brought attention to fools and frauds. Native naïveté cried out for intervention. The law, an official opined, should "protect the credulous, ignorant population against fraud committed by . . . individuals whose only goal is to part the economically still far from financially sound population from its money" (S. 1921: 33). Jasper's position about the need for a law covering problematic dukun echoes such views. Another complained about the deleterious effects of superstition, which interfered with economic development, wasting time and money: "He may not work then and there, may not begin work before that time, and not end after that time. This must happen thus and that must happen so, otherwise you come into conflict with Déwi Sri, Gendruwo, Puntianak, and other specters and spirits with which his animism populates the entire world" (Habbema 1919: 313).

For ethicists, education offered the ideal path to Euro-form colonized populations, to turn them into men of reason who could (eventually) manage their own affairs. Even if education did not eradicate superstition entirely—as Habbema (1919: 313) acknowledges, superstition persists "even among the most civilized and developed people," including Dutchmen—it constituted a powerful tool for disenchantment. In practice, however, and in contrast to other colonial states, the Netherlands Indies restricted access to schools to indigenous ruling classes—specifically, to the sons of aristocrats who were groomed to replace their fathers in the Native Civil Service (Inlandsch Binnenlandsch Bestuur). This ensured a steady supply of functionaries to fill positions such as district head, judge, tax collector, supervisor, scribe, clerk, and police chief. Such persons would ideally serve as unproblematic intermediaries, flawlessly transmitting orders from above and extracting obedience from below. Ethicists subscribed to trickle-down improvement. Ordinary people would feel immense respect for such persons, who not only would be due deference for their ancestry but would form the face of colonial authority. Out of admiration and a desire to better their own situation, they would imitate their leaders. Moreover, educated natives could gently teach everyone else which traditions merited continuation and which to toss. This would develop the population as a whole, as advanced (i.e., European) ideas percolated to the masses. In turn, such native officials would be reliably inoculated against outbreaks of fanaticism or the allure of common frauds.

No wonder, then, that Damsté was appalled to discover that not only their wives (who, as women, would have no chance at schooling and were presumed more suggestible) but even Balinese civil servants figured among Nang Mukanis's clientele. It was one thing for peasants to consult a wonderdokter. But government employees should be properly disenchanted, robust skeptics about rogues such as Nang Mukanis. Instead, they had proved themselves as gullible as ordinary natives. Nor was this unique to Jembrana. Recall Jasper's complaint that even "better-off and developed [natives]" exhibit "almost unlimited credulity" (1932: 37).

But schools were only one channel through which disenchantment might flow from the rational state. A different pedagogic project took shape alongside trickle-down transformation. Consider Damsté's order to impound or destroy "all concrete signs of [Nang Mukanis's] holiness"; the subsequent burning of his white clothing, "decorations," and sedan chair; and Damsté's sarcastic remark about the absence of divine or demonic retaliation. The order, the acts, and the comments are all iconoclastic. Smashing people's idols—here by burning objects that mediate access to other-than-human forces and by taking Nang Mukanis into custody—aims to make them see the truth, to prove the validity and reality of the world made by white men of reason and the falsity of Nang Mukanis's.

Damsté was hardly the only official to present iconoclastic acts as instructive. Jasper promoted such practices as a salutary supplement to legal proceedings: "The police magistrate could not take better action in the interest of peace in the country . . . than to cause all the reported tumbal, jimat, sacred pieces of iron, sacred stones which they supposed would do evil, to be burned or destroyed in the presence of plaintiffs and defendants, to demonstrate that such hoo-ha is . . . of no value" (1904: 132).[29] As we will see in chapters 2 and 3, journalists articulated similar sentiments in the aftermath of state violence.

Damsté's command draws on a suite of violent acts and statements that are at once pedagogic, spectacular, and ontological. They are pedagogic insofar as officials and pundits make statements about what such acts will teach Indonesian subjects. Presumably, Balinese present at such events would bear witness to the truths they revealed. As dramatic gestures aimed at specific audiences, such acts also may be staged, deliberate performances. And, of course, they are ontological: the lesson to be taught, the message they should send, concerns what is and is not real. Such iconoclastic acts crafted a colonial laboratory for testing worlds through violence. They are what Latour (1988) called trials of strength (or weakness).[30]

For Latour, strength measures the length and breadth of the allies one may marshal. Destroying objects associated with Nang Mukanis's work, and arresting him in the middle of the night, Damsté could extract Nang Mukanis more easily from the networks of allies on which the efficacy of his practices depended. Of course, that in turn depended on the extensive network of allies that Damsté could bring to bear: armed troops, roads, telegraphs, reports, subordinates, and statements that connected this single act to many others across time and space. At that early morning hour, Nang Mukanis was vulnerable, a vulnerability that in part might have been of his own making (see next section). Damsté certainly recognized the advantages of catching him without a yard filled with clients and followers. At the same time, Damsté's iconoclastic acts draw strength from a familiar modern "naïve belief in naïve belief" (Latour 1999, 2010). As he describes matters, the police destroyed "signs" of Nang Mukanis's status (what I have called mediators that opened channels to other-than-human forces), but he suggests that for Balinese they were more: the *source* of Nang Mukanis's power to invoke "demons," or powerful in some way themselves.

Thus, Damsté treats Nang Mukanis not only as a miscreant, but as an opponent in a battle over worlds and the ways they are made and known. For Damsté, when police immolated objects in Nang Mukanis's yard, Dutch reason triumphed over Balinese belief. Reason forms a component of a modern world in which gods and demons don't intervene in daily life—and certainly cannot be brought to earth by a mere mortal.

As we will see, other colonial authors cast even much more violent acts as lessons in metaphysics. Such statements render force as not only inherently demystifying but as an educational opportunity and salutary intervention. As we will also see, Indonesians did not respond to these demonstrations as Dutch authors regularly anticipated. Indeed, there are grounds to argue that Indonesian realities demonstrated the weakness of Dutch realities. Such resilience should come as no surprise given Ketut Liyer's more recent thriving practice, facilitated in part by Euro-American books.

Some Balinese Perspectives

So far, my focus has been on Dutch critiques of Balinese subjectivities—as, of course, they imagined these—and on sporadic responses to the problems these created for colonial rule. But what did and do Balinese make of practitioners such as Nang Mukanis? How do such practitioners' activities weave worlds, worlds that partly cross modern divides?

Nothing reveals the limits of legibility more than comparing how officials construe Nang Mukanis in particular and dukun in general with what Balinese do and say. Balinese positions infiltrate Damsté's report: in the form of the satisfied clients to whom Kuys talked, the local constabulary who failed to arrest him, and the Balinese officials who gave him gifts. What Damsté and Kuys dismissed with sneers and epithets (fanatic, wonderdokter, "mentally impaired bungler"), such persons, and in general the Balinese flocking to request Nang Mukanis's aid, saw otherwise. But I begin with a Balinese critic, the anonymous author of the missive that prompted Kuys's inquiries and led to Nang Mukanis's arrest.

Damsté appended the letter—written in a dense Malay, the language of colonial administration, mixed with smatterings of Balinese—to his official report. In contrast to the Balinese officials who disappointed him so acutely, Damsté's comments on its author conjure an ideal colonial subject: dutiful, vigilant, and suspicious, altogether more suited for high office than Balinese occupying such positions in Jembrana. A glance at the letter shows why: it offers the evidentiary scaffolding for some of Damsté's otherwise cryptic statements. It accuses Nang Mukanis of being both crazy and a clever liar, claims Damsté repeats. The writer complains that Nang Mukanis has managed to convince lots of people to trust in him, including almost all local members of the native civil service; he accuses them of being blind and deaf, given their willingness to be tricked. Moreover, the anonymous writer offers calculations, both economic and political. At least a hundred people seek Nang Mukanis's aid every day, bringing rice and Chinese coins (used in offerings); over twenty days, he must have raked in the equivalent of 350 guilders worth of rice and coins.[31] All of the attention is making him increasingly arrogant. And the kicker: the longer things go unchecked, the more likely he is to become dangerous.

Clearly, the author took pains to craft a letter loaded with triggers. But surely something other than a desire to serve the state motivated him. More crucially, despite his evident awareness of colonial priorities, his concerns about Nang Mukanis do not map straightforwardly onto Damsté's, even when they are most damning. And damning they are, as when he calls Nang Mukanis a "pretend dukun [*dukun palsu*]." But examining his words complicates such readings. The evidence he adduces only partly correlates with the interests of colonial officials. The author is at least as occupied (if not more so) with Balinese debates. What most alarms its author, in short, is not what troubles Kuys or Damsté.

These divergences pivot on uncontrolled equivocations: the author's assertion that Nang Mukanis is crazy (which Damsté simply repeats); that Nang Mukanis claims to be possessed by, and to speak as, a "spirit" (modern Europeans would reject this out of hand); that he boasts he can do all kinds of things (each impossible from the perspective of Dutch officials); and that Nang Mukanis is a pretend dukun (likely to be interpreted as merely a grifter). I read these claims as related.

At least three controversies hinge on that "spirit." First, Nang Mukanis attributes his abilities to entry (*kemasukan*) by a *badan halus*—literally, a "refined body." In English, we swiftly render such statements as spirit possession, though it is worth slowing down for a brief translation detour. Note, for example, that *badan halus* implies that Nang Mukanis was two-bodied, rather than two-spirited. Not only does the conceit of spirits bear the weight of a complicated metaphysics (an issue to which I return below), but possession is equally fraught, entangled with the history of property (Johnson 2011, 2014a, 2014b)—and deriving from a different metaphoric register than either the Malay *kemasukan*, from *masuk*, enter, or the Balinese for such a relation, *karauhan*, from *rauh*, arrive.[32] The author's objection, however, lies elsewhere. Some Balinese are wary of balian whose expertise derives primarily from sources of this sort, *balian tatakson*, rather than from consulting texts, *balian usada*. In my field experience, such circumspection derives in part from questions about precisely what kind of entity-force might have "arrived."

Which leads to what leaves the author aghast. Nang Mukanis identifies the force that he welcomes (the acts the report describes form common ways to invite potent forces to particular places at particular times) as a *Betara*, an exalted term for gods or deified ancestors, not the kind of "spirit" usually associating itself with balian tatakson. Even more scandalous: he blithely names that Betara as Betara Widhi, or, as the writer explains, Allah. Moreover, Nang Mukanis refers to himself (whoever "himself" might be, given periodic dual occupancy) as Betara Widhi. Beginning in 1953, Balinese intellectuals have identified that appellation—now more commonly called Sang Hyang Widhi Wasa—with the supreme deity, equivalent to the Tuhan (Lord) of foundational national documents, and, as the letter indicates, the Allah of Indonesia's majority Muslim population. Prior to that, this Power was mainly relevant and known to Brahmana priests, who asked it to "arrive" during specific rites, though a reform movement in north Bali in the 1920s had popularized it (Picard 2024: 179–80). The letter writer found Nang Mukanis's assertion unthinkable. Betara Widhi would be unlikely to occupy the body of an unconsecrated human, and a commoner to boot, even briefly.

No doubt, though, this assertion underwrote another controversial claim: that Nang Mukanis could basically take care of just about any problem anyone had. The author notes incredulously that Nang Mukanis had declared that he could heal any illness (including blindness and deafness), cure infertility, restore stolen goods, and in general eliminate all kinds of harm (*kejahatan*). Balinese friends of mine would be as perturbed by such boasts, as this unknown author was. A well-known proverb admonishes, "Don't say you can do things; let others say it for you." People who brag raise eyebrows. Those who really "know things" are humble. They recognize that they are not the autonomous source of their own capacities, and they take care not to alienate more-than-human patrons and helpers—especially Sang Hyang Widhi. Arrogating to oneself the amplified powers that depend on relations painstakingly made and maintained is a good way to cut those relations, rendering oneself vulnerable to all kinds of danger.

No wonder the letter writer calls Nang Mukanis crazy! More specifically, he says Nang Mukanis and his brother, Nang Mianis, act like crazy people (*gila-gilaan*), and repeatedly refers to Nang Mukanis as the Crazy One (Si Gila). He even goes further, and dubs Nang Mukanis Si Gelap Pikiran, Mr. Deranged—literally, Mr. Dark Thoughts. With that name he not only decisively rejects Nang Mukanis's identification of the force that aids him but implies that his imprudent words and acts have driven away all benevolent powers—and intimates something about the body sharing his own. Calling a balian "crazy" need not reject the claim to a special relation with a force undetectable by human senses. It may instead suggest that the entity mixed up with/in Nang Mukanis was not only not a deity but something far less benign. That's what being crazy often involves (Connor 1982).

It was not only Nang Mukanis's relations with other-than-human forces, however, that perturbed the author. He notes that he writes anonymously out of fear of retaliation by local officials. While several (including two who are ethnically Javanese) share his view of Nang Mukanis, most, including those with the highest ranks, appear dazzled. But unlike Damsté, what dismays him is not only that these persons are civil servants; they also are aristocrats and Brahmanas. The Brahmanas I know tend to be more skeptical about balian tatakson (though they still consult them), placing more stock in texts. In any event, Brahmanas should know that Sang Hyang

Widhi would not speak through a balian. More important, the Brahmanas in question did more than merely consult Nang Mukanis: they sat below him on the ground, raised their hands in the gesture of homage owed to a superior (the author emphasizes that he considers this highly improper), followed humiliating orders, and made extravagant gifts, completely upending evolving hierarchies.[33]

Which brings us to the claim that Nang Mukanis is a pretend dukun (*dukun palsu*). Is a pretend dukun the same as a wonderdokter? Emphatically no. Unlike officials, the letter writer in no way implies that all dukun pretend. Nor does he class one group of dukun, those who traffic with spirits, as inherently fraudulent or deluded. Instead, he targets this *particular* dukun. What makes Nang Mukanis problematic are specific assertions and acts, many of which fit under the judgment *arrogant*. In their skepticism about individual practitioners, Indonesians are much like people everywhere (a point made in 1937 by Evans-Pritchard with regard to Azande reactions to "witch-doctors"). At the same time, analysis of the letter also refutes Damsté's naïve belief in the schooled native's simple acceptance of the world he takes for granted.

The author, as he himself acknowledges, proffered a minority view, however. Nang Mukanis's extraordinary popularity demonstrates that others did not find his statements and acts beyond the pale, or respect for him unmerited. At the same time, it is hardly unusual for a suddenly popular balian or dukun, especially if his claims or techniques are novel, to arouse controversy. And some traces of how people in Jembrana responded linger.

In 1999, I visited the village where Nang Mukanis lived, on a quixotic quest to locate his descendants or memories other than those in the colonial archive. No one alive in 1999 would have known him by name, as the Father of Mukanis, a teknonym; only his peers would have called him that. Since he died shortly after his arrest, descendants wouldn't have called him by name at all; naming the dead not only is dangerous, but, if his descendants carried out the proper rituals, he would have become a generic ancestor. I asked, therefore, whether anyone had heard about a balian arrested by the Dutch.

Two elderly people seemed to know whom I was talking about—and both described him as powerful (*sakti*). One recalled that not many people lived there then; it was mainly forest and brush. But even at night that balian's compound was busy with carts and horses. Some, she said, thought he could turn himself into a horse, implying he might be a *léak* (shapeshifter), someone who used power of the left (*pangiwa*) to do harm. The other initially appeared to echo the anonymous letter: the balian was like a crazy man (*cara anak buduh*). He didn't know why the Dutch had arrested him, but noted he used to go around on a palanquin waving a keris. Maybe that was it. The Dutch didn't like to see people carried on palanquins. Was he really crazy? I asked. The Dutch thought he was, said the old man, laughing. Maybe because he was always singing invocations (*makidung*). But folks thereabouts found him normal enough (*seger*). People liked him; he cured people. As a boy he once went to the balian's compound to see what was up. Someone had cut himself badly; the balian sprinkled some holy water on it and—just like that!—it healed. After he died, he noted, some said a *jin* had shared his body.

These casual anecdotes testify to Nang Mukanis's power, even as they point to the complex judgments that such persons motivate. One saw him heal, but speculation was rife about what else he might have been up to. And the source of his abilities may have been a jin, a Muslim entity especially relevant in coastal Jembrana, just across from Muslim Java. In a sense Damsté recognized Nang Mukanis's power; otherwise, there would have been no point in arresting him.

Re-Threading the Balian/Dukun through Practices and Relations

Kuys's anonymous correspondent clarifies just what kind of balian Nang Mukanis was: a balian tatakson, usually rendered as "spirit medium." Indeed, on the occasions Kuys encountered him, Nang Mukanis literally may not have been himself. The umbrella held over his head as he sang at the head of a procession and the dance with his keris suggest he was at those times either already two-bodied or in the process of asking "someone" to arrive. So, at least, Balinese might read such acts. But his engagement with "spirits" also elucidates why Damsté called him a witch doctor. In the matter of balian, Dutch officials and Balinese interlocutors highlight different differences. Colonial assessments parse Indonesian practitioners into native physicians and witch doctors through analogies laminated into metaphysical divides such as body and mind, matter and spirit. These operate as well in more positive recent translations, such as traditional healer. How well do they fit what balian make and do?

Native physician clearly constitutes a vast improvement over *witch doctor*. Likening balian or dukun to biomedical doctors accords a measure of respect to Indonesian practitioners for their knowledge and skill. That respect, though, extends only insofar as what dukun do coincides with biomedical practices—which is not very far at all. Where it ends, other assessments (witch doctor, charlatan) come into play.

For colonial experts, what prompted that analogy was pharmacological treatment of physical ailments. But balian (or other dukun) who prescribe plant remedies do not limit their practice to this or consider it their only skill. Nor do those who consult them presume herbal preparations will suffice. Issuing medicines forms only one element in a repertoire of practices. For example, balian also distribute other substances, such as oils, holy water (water transformed by words and offerings), and other material (see chapter 2), but these too are only elements in a broad range of actions that aim to deflect harm, to protect, and/or to realign forces.

Prescribing medicine, though, constitutes an equally small element in biomedicine. Biomedicine rests on fundamental assumptions, and the most fundamental of these is that its proper object is the body, an individual and material reality preexisting the practices that diagnose and treat it. The body ends at the skin but extends to the organs contained within a bounded skin-sack. That body-object is the property of a subject, identified, medically, with the brain, but metaphysically with the mind or soul, which cannot exist without the corporeal substrate it animates. Wherever biomedicine is hegemonic, such views appear commonsensical. Like Dutch officials, most moderns still understand not only the body but this particular body as medicine's object.

A rich literature on both the body and medical practice (as opposed to theory) queers such common sense.[34] Kuriyama (2002), for example, observes that while ancient Greek and Chinese medicine shared an interest in pulses, over time they diverged to focus on different bodies. Greeks and their heirs emphasized anatomical dissection and the muscular body of classical statuary. Chinese doctors, by contrast, grew more attentive to the feel of pulses and the color and texture of tongues. Attending less to structures than to dynamic flows and blockages, they built a cumulative corpus of empirical description that mapped an intricate web of acupuncture points onto the plump body depicted in Chinese medical texts. Excellent ethnographies of Chinese medicine develop a fuller picture of how these bodies have come to interact (Farquhar 1994; Karchmer 2022). Yet even biomedical practices do not yield only one body, argues Mol (2002). She explores the diverse bodies enacted through the various procedures used to diagnose and treat atherosclerosis in a Dutch hospital, from consulting rooms to imaging machines to pathology labs. Sameness is an effect of coordination. That apparently stable object, the body, multiplies.

To this multiplicity I could add Balinese or other Indonesian bodies. (In Indonesia, with its long history of oceanic encounters, multiplicity expands exponentially.) For example, balian usada, balian who rely on texts, refer to the body as a "small world" (*buana alit*) made up of the same elements and relations as the "big world" (*buana agung*), an observation that might sound perfectly acceptable from a biomedical perspective. But those ingredients involve forces that texts represent as a compass rose (a better metaphor in Bali might be a compass lotus), associating these forces with directions, deities, "demons," proclivities, letters, and complex calendrical calculations.[35] This suggests that for balian the body may not be the relevant object on which (as opposed to through which) they work. The practices of balian do more than produce bodies differing from the ones the practices of physicians make. More crucially, they generate new relations.

On the whole, the fields in which biomedical practitioners and balian operate differ considerably. There is little room in biomedicine's diagnostic procedures and treatments for relations between one human body and others, or relations to nonhuman bodies, though this is changing with increasing interest in the microbiome and with growing insistence on the impact of environmental toxins. There is no room in biomedicine for relations to gods (especially plural ones), ancestors, or, even worse, what we call spirits.

By contrast, the dukun or balian does not limit her diagnosis to individual ailing bodies or to dis-eases that manifest corporeally. The suffering that clients aim to alleviate might involve persistent conflicts among residents of a compound, a run of catastrophes, even concerns about a parasitic growth on a flowering tree. Balian may trace such troubles to human malevolence, to ancestors, to more-than-human forces disturbed by activities impinging on their territory, to a person's four invisible siblings, or to additional more-than-humans associated with calendrical conjunctions pertinent to someone's birthday. Apart from misfortune due to humans, most of the other instigators cause trouble because they have been neglected, even if those affected had no prior knowledge of them.

Balian, then, often diagnose inattention to relations as the cause of an affliction. Their prescriptions may entail connecting or extending relations, by insisting that a person or group "remember" (*éling*) a force by building a shrine in a particular place, by attending rites regularly at a particular distant temple, by undergoing a rite or rites, and always by making offerings.

Balian also do not treat individuals, at least not in the way biomedical doctors do. Humans exist in—or even are—a field of relations, that always involves relations to myriad more-than-humans. These include those that are the ultimate owners of the territories humans co-occupy, or those that manifest their interest in specific humans (and their descendants) by sending afflictions or gifts to attract their attention. Well-being, in short, does not end at the skin, but is woven together with kin, territories, and shrines. This is the field the balian works, what they make and are made by.

I've noted that Balinese differentiate between balian who consult palm-leaf manuscripts about the causes and treatment of disorders (balian usada) from those who mediate forces usually translated as spirits (balian tatakson). But observations of and conversations with a Balinese friend who relies on texts made clear to me that all balian solicit aid from more-than-human forces. Sometimes those forces become directly accessible to clients after being invited to double the healer's body. But balian usada also rely on such relations, since texts embody ancestral insight in need of interpretation, and texts themselves are seats for the Power called Saraswati. The aid and care of ancestors also matters to a balian's practice. My friend particularly, however, emphasized the significance to his practice of his four invisible siblings.[36] All humans have such siblings, but not all "remember" them throughout their lives. Balian, he advised me, must: they rely on them for protection as they deal with the sometimes dangerous forces that afflict their clients, and ask for their help. He opined that it is actually his or her spirit siblings who speak through a balian tatakson. Hence, it is hardly surprising that clients bring offerings when consulting a balian, for the balian's more-than-human allies.

Rather than the body, then, could it be said that balian focus on spirits/spirit—or the spiritual? I balk at that for several reasons. First, it purifies in the opposite direction, dematerializing practices. Balian do, after all, prescribe substances, botanical and otherwise, to be ingested, applied to (or under) the skin, or inscribed (in the form of letters) on specific parts of the body. Second, *spirit* universalizes a particular metaphysics. A division between matter and spirit (or mind, if the term for spirit and mind differs; it does not in Dutch) is fundamental to European theologies and ontologies.[37] While historical relations have thoroughly entangled Indonesians with worlds (including Islam) in which that metaphysics is taken for granted, when it comes to Bali at least I prefer to speak of forces and Powers. These terms not only defamiliarize, but they capture something of concrete experience. The translational legibility of bodies and spirits makes it easier to miss what people are up to and forecloses inquiry into what it means to alleviate suffering, if that is indeed what balian always do.

Finally, such translations reinforce the hegemony of biomedicine as well. While divergent treatments no longer are always branded inherently fraudulent or ineffective (as Ketut Liyer's successes show; indeed, nowadays Euro-Americans may embrace and seek them), they are commonly lumped together, as, for instance, not only "spiritual," but "alternative" or "traditional." Such terms reinforce the dominance of particular worlds, even as they establish sometimes robust, sometimes tenuous, and always partial connections to less familiar ones.

Consider the current prevalent rendering of balian as *traditional healer*. While it subtracts the restricted geography of "native," it adds a problematic temporality through "traditional."[38] Even more problematic, like *native physician, traditional healer* draws attention away from the full range of a balian's capacities. For balian and dukun do not only heal; some harm as well. They may use their amplified capacities (whether on behalf of clients or not) to blast well-being, leaving death, illness, blight, or conflict in their wake. When Ketut Liyer noted he had to learn "black magic" (Balinese *pangiwa*, knowledge "of the left") to help clients whose troubles stemmed from such sources, he simultaneously acknowledged he had studied such matters and established their reality. Or recall speculations in Jembrana that Nang Mukanis might have been a *léak*. Even if a dukun never uses such knowledge, people regard it as a tool of his or her trade, challenging translations such as *healer*.

Colonial administrators, at least in their capacity as agents of the state and certainly at the time of Nang Mukanis's arrest, paid little attention to such matters. The malevolent powers of dukun did, however, count in other domains of colonizer experience, such as the intersecting spheres of domestic life, rumor, and popular culture I tackle in chapter 4, and over time. By the 1930s, a young jurist had no qualms referring to dukun as "evil sorcerers," insisting officials had underestimated their ability to affect the "suggestive psyches" of Indonesians at their peril (Lesquillier 1934: 135–36).[39] This dimension of dukun practice also attracted the attention of missionaries and of those who drew on their accounts (e.g., Kohlbrugge). Their focus was neither criminality nor peace and order: it was immorality. Moreover, their own activities generated a reality that, depending on their theology, could offer ample room for both "wonders" and sorcery. For missionaries, dukun might deceive but they also potentially might traffic in black magic. Thus, unlike administrators, missionaries had no problem calling dukun *tovenaars*, magicians or sorcerers.

One missionary even authored a novel, *The Sorcerer* [*Tovenaar*] *of Sunda*, which narrates the rise and fall of a dukun in West Java (Hoekendijk 1920). While his fictional dukun succumbs to the allure of wealth and fame, Hoekendijk also portrays him as effective, especially in his initial treatments of mentally ill clients using knowledge gifted to him (in a nighttime annunciation) by Allah. He eventually, however, agrees to help with requests that go well beyond that gift. Coyly declaring he does not know for sure if this dukun performed any of them, the narrator then describes a panoply of sorcerous acts (*toverijen*) that result in serious harm.

Technologies of Influence

What made Nang Mukanis troublesome wasn't only a potential incitement to rebellion or exploitation of credulity. Even more alarming was his influence. He literally moved large numbers of people: to flock to his compound, to follow him in processions, to offer him homage and gifts. His influence, however, also manifested in less ordinary ways. Kuys witnessed girls fall to the ground shrieking, "affected under his influence," and reported that when Nang Mukanis invoked a demon "everyone was as if possessed," with even more falling and shrieking, and others acting as if they were crazy; even non-followers, such as the police who failed to arrest him, found themselves affected, eyes bulging and rolling in their sockets. Officials appear remarkably incurious about these incidents. How did he do that?

In the broadest sense, texts that manufacture witch doctors often accuse them of staging dazzling performances. For Jasper, for instance, claims about (nonexistent) spirits form part of the wonderdokter's skill at "weaving mysteries." Such accounts grant witch doctors a kind of power: the power of suggestion. The recourse to suggestion is hardly unique to colonial Indonesia; it runs through anthropologies of magic and healing. Mostly such phrases work as offhand explications, vague gestures toward concepts originally developed by psychologists that came to circulate widely in Euro-American mass culture.[40] The power of suggestion not only returns to our familiar cast of characters—suggestible fools or fanatics and duplicitous frauds—but, given its psychological focus, retains a mind–body dualism. Perhaps, though, there are alternative ways to understand influence and skill.

One alternative returns to bodies, but in a different modality—as semiotic actors. Consider what Vinciane Despret (2004) has to say about "talented bodies" and mutual becoming in her analysis of Clever Hans. The

German horse originally achieved great fame for his apparent ability to solve math problems, spell, and perform other cognitive tasks, tapping out answers with his right hoof—and gave his name to a purported methodological minefield in the field of psychology. Scientists invoke Clever Hans with words familiar from descriptions of witch doctors and their clients, such as credulity, fraud, and trickery—as well as from the field of paranormal investigation, a topic of interest to the lead investigator of Clever Hans. According to the scientists who solved the problem that Clever Hans himself posed, Hans was responding to nonverbal communication: Hans found answers by attending to minuscule muscular movements of human bodies, outside of the humans' intentional awareness.

Despret, however, argues that Clever Hans has far more to teach us. Not everyone who interacted with Hans succeeded in getting correct answers. He worked best with those who had both what she terms "talented bodies" and an ability to elicit his interest and trust. At the same time, Despret highlights Hans's own extraordinary talents. Not only could he translate the haptic communication equestrians and horses develop into the sense of vision, but "he could make human bodies be moved and be affected and move and affect other bodies and perform things without their owners' knowledge" (2004: 113). For Despret, influence is a two-way street, grounded in mutual attunement. Such insights—that bodies communicate and can affect one another, that interest and trust matter, and that influence requires multiple actors in attunement—lead Nang Mukanis's achievements into different conceptual channels.

That some bodies are particularly talented at somatic semiotics may be relevant to the practices of balian and dukun. Leaving aside his derogatory distinctions between (European) intellectual acuity and (Indonesian) corporeal capacities, recall Kohlbrugge's admiration of Javanese dexterity, including, he claimed, an extraordinary facility for mimicry. Recall too the role that ascesis plays in dukun apprenticeship.

Turning from colonial texts to my own field experiences in Bali, these mattered a good deal to my friend, teacher, and father Ida Bagus Kakiyang, a small-scale balian usada and ritual specialist. Understanding what predecessors had written required, in his view, an embodied intellect, obtained through investigations of the impact of restrictions in diet, sleep, and sexual pleasure (among other technologies) on oneself. Through such experiments a balian could learn about the forces at work in both bodies and the larger world—and thus affect not only his or her own body but also those of others. Someone who knows such things, he indicated, may read another's intentions in that person's stance and prevent them from acting if those intentions are hostile. He often spoke of what you could see in people's eyes, and of the power of some eyes.[41] Despret's account of "talented bodies," of bodies that teach and learn from each other, points to a potential direction for understanding how dukun and their clients affect one another that aligns with such assertions.

There are further ways the notion of talented bodies intersects with Balinese concerns. Bodily skills matter in both practice and theory. Balinese dance is an exacting discipline learned through the body; it involves extraordinary control not only of arms and legs but of the small muscles controlling eyes and fingers (the hands and fingers figure also in the mudras of Brahmana priests). But another dimension of performance is directly relevant to balian such as Nang Mukanis. The term *tatakson* (in *balian tatakson*) derives from the root *taksu*, a focus of Balinese aesthetics. A more-than-human force, taksu imbues performers with a charismatic energy that draws and moves audiences. In short, influence is cultivated, fostered by acts, rites, and objects that aim to enhance attraction.

A second issue Despret raises is trust. Trust figures significantly in analyses of tricks and dupes, and of dukun and their clients, but only negatively: the dukun takes advantage of misplaced conviction. There is plenty of misplaced faith in descriptions of dukun and balian; some may be merited. But trust involves more than gullibility. As Despret notes, it may entail availability—an availability that leads to change. Openness to care and attachments alters lives and shapes worlds. Such trust is transformative, of both people and situations; sometimes it results in miracles and wonders. Trust, in short, may be generative, yielding new possibilities for living and even new entities. Taken together, talented bodies and trust lead to attunement—not only in relations between dukun and their clients, but in the relations of either to other beings or forces.

Because interest moves bodies and produces attunement, Despret refuses to choose between truth and interest. Following Despret ultimately involves rethinking subjectivity along Whiteheadian lines. Those who speak of suggestion and influence bifurcate the world, dividing it into a stable external world that preexists all accounts, on the one hand, and subjectivity (including the collective subject called culture), with all of the ideas, passions, and interests associated with it, on the other.[42] Such bifurcation is evident in discussions of dukun (and other practices filtered through magic), which distinguish the really real from what people believe. Stress on deception implies reality is given, ignoring the way influence, grounded in interests and affects, may be world-making praxis.

The matter of trust also provokes a rethinking of belief. Like Latour, Despret seeks to replace naïve belief in naïve belief with robust attention to actual situations. Usually interpreted in relation to a fixed reality, belief is invariably associated with delusion or error. But what if instead of appraising the content of beliefs, we shift focus to ask what beliefs "make"? For Despret, relations involving influence and trust may add to reality, bringing more entities into the world as actors affect one another. Hence, she redefines belief as "what makes entities 'available' to events" (2004: 122). This too is promising for thinking about balian. Rather than the familiar figures of the master illusionist tricking hopeful fools, such a definition makes visible a host of entities—including other-than-human forces and Powers, shrines, offerings, and kin—associating in ways they did not previously. The activities of balian and dukun and their clients bring more entities into the world.

While predictable in their assessments, Dutch accounts nonetheless hint at something more. The skilled bodies arousing Kohlbrugge's fascinated admiration, the rigorous efforts dukun make to transform themselves by working on their own bodies, the meticulous cultivation of "mystery" in relations between dukun and clients, the careful elicitation of more-than-human aid all point beyond the impoverished concepts such as credulity and duplicity brought to bear on such activities. That the questions asked of dukun and balian and their clients yield numbingly dull and repetitive answers indicate they are poorly posed. Such questions don't give their interlocutors any "chance to be activated as a subject" (Despret 2004: 128). By avoiding familiar presumptions—that those who consult dukun are docile and gullible, that dukun performances are about deception rather than transformation—richer, more interesting possibilities emerge, not to mention people with many more dimensions.

Like all power, Nang Mukanis's emerged within a nexus of practices, dispositions, things, and talk, many involving alliances with nonhumans and more-than-humans. Removed from its relevant networks, power does not exist—as Nang Mukanis discovered when caught alone and arrested. By isolating people, things, and activities—in effect cutting the networks—the colonial state could weaken and then reassemble them, including by the use of locutions such as "witch doctor" or "the power of suggestion," into a new form that fit and could help to consolidate one reality at the expense of others.

From Witch Doctor to Healer

This chapter has followed some threads in the transformation of dukun into witch doctors and magicians. When administrators drew dukun into partial alignment with biomedicine, the residue of difference made magic. The process rests on divisions: between doctors and charlatans, truth and fraud, rational and irrational, science and superstition, body or matter and mind or spirit, and European and Indonesian. Compared with other practices of concern to Dutch authorities, however, witch doctors formed a weak, tentative knot for attaching Indonesian practices and practitioners to magic. Dukun and balian constitute sparsely inhabited nodes for magic's colonial translation. Despite occasional calls for regulation, they never gelled into a persistent worry, and official responses remained ad hoc. During Dutch rule, dukun did not muster the interest they currently attract.

That attraction takes many forms. In 1996, two years before Suharto was forced to resign as president of Indonesia, I met some Indonesian scholars at a party at Cornell. When I mentioned I was examining materials about magic in Indonesia, one immediately associated the term magic with dukun, and proclaimed to general laughter: "Suharto has all the most powerful dukun working for him—why, he has a dukun in every province! Now that's unity in diversity [Indonesia's national motto]!"

And, of course, as Ketut Liyer's career demonstrates, nowadays dukun and balian no longer elicit the scorn of proudly disenchanted moderns. Non-modern practices are being re-sorted; through new (partial) connections, such practitioners are gaining a variety of allies. This offers possibilities, among them financial. It also knots them more firmly into translational nodes of magic and medicine.

In his 1822 lectures on the philosophy of history, Hegel claims that Africans project power onto "the first thing that comes their way.... [I]t may be an animal, a tree, a stone, or a wooden figure. This is their Fetich—a word to which the Portuguese first gave currency, and which is derived from fei-tizo, magic" (1991: 94). His reference to the Portuguese marks him as an heir to centuries of elaboration of the concept of the fetish, which, at the time he wrote, still constituted the primary trope in European representations of Africa. He writes midway between two developments. Some eighty years earlier than Hegel, the fetish had taken pride of place in the first speculative account of the origins of religions, in what Charles de Brosses labeled fetishism. Eighty years later than Hegel such speculations had become a cornerstone of the new field of anthropology, though key figures assigned only a minor role to fetishes and fetishism, proposing other candidates in their place: souls and spirits in Tylor's animism (with fetishism as a later development), totems in Durkheim's totemism. This is not to say that the fetish disappeared from consideration by European intellectuals. Quite the contrary: it was picked up by Marx and Freud to address capitalism and bourgeois sexuality. It was, however, on its way out in discussions of Africa, to be replaced around the First World War by witchcraft (Pels 1998)—a return, in fact, to its origins.

I want to revisit those origins: the formation of the fetish as an intranaturalcultural product of forgotten but nonetheless inherited pasts. It began on the west coast of Africa in the fifteenth century, in encounters between Africans and Portuguese explorers and traders. William Pietz's exemplary work in tracing the concept of the fetish provides an object lesson in this early moment of magic's translation. Naming unfamiliar artifacts and practices by what they thought they resembled, Portuguese explorers and traders deployed words for the "objects, persons, and practices proper to witchcraft" (Pietz 2022: 14).[1] The one that stuck most firmly, *feitiço*, referred to objects. To explain what they might have had in mind, Pietz tracks the development of Catholic theology (and jurisprudence) regarding material objects, noting that basic tenets (a transcendent divinity who created the material world and incarnated in a human body, the Church as the sole path to salvation) presented two problems involving materiality: relations between bodies and spirits or souls, taken to be radically different substances, and distinguishing objects sacralized by the Church from other potent objects. For the Church, illegitimate potency derived from the devil or his demons (including the "false gods" of pagans). Portuguese voyagers might have differentiated idols (in the form of statues embodying a false god and worshipped) from feitiço (as objects worn on the body for a particular end), but these terms often occur together in their accounts (Pietz 2022: 46). But closer observation of their insistent immanence led to a preference for words for witchcraft. In time, *feitiço* morphed into the pidgin *fetisso*, especially among the (mixed-race) groups that came to mediate trade and communication.

During the seventeenth century, Protestant merchants from northern Europe broke the Catholic Portuguese monopoly. That religious difference was consequential for the way things became caught up in Christian concerns over the difference between spirit and matter. Saints' relics and the Eucharist blended people and things: in the former, as a person who inhered in his or her bodily remains, and in the latter as the Person, invited through rites into a substance to ingest. Protestant reforms rejected these acts and things as "magic," turning not only the Eucharist but the now emptied cross into symbols, evacuating objects of power and attributing the latter solely to subjects—possessed of an interior mind and faith—rather than treating power as potentially a property of material beings.

Books by two Dutch merchants, published a century apart, were particularly consequential for the fetish, revealing how changing European values shaped interpretations of African practices. Pieter de Marees's 1602 book offered the first description of *fetisso*, transporting the term into northern European linguistic repertoires: not only Dutch (*fetis*), but also

German and English. In his account, which presents both continuities with and rejections of Catholic positions, *fetisso* covers a wide range of entities and actions. "They call their Idols (*afgoden*) Fetisso," he writes (1987 [1602]: 67), but he also states they regard their fetisso as their god and speaks of the relation of certain fetisso to evil spirits and the devil. Some trees and fish are fetisso, but fetisso also are worn. Theological debates, old and new, show up not only in the word "idol" but in comments that liken some fetisso to Catholic relics and rosaries. Experts conducting acts involving fetisso are *fetisseros* (another pidgin), which he renders as sorcerers (*tovenaars*).[2]

Over the course of the seventeenth century, the meaning of *fetisso* shifted away from the problematic of witchcraft. Two tropes making up the concept of the fetish (and evident in Hegel's dismissive remarks) coalesced. The first rested on assessments of the economic value of the things Africans were willing to accept in trade for gold—the substance Europeans treated as self-evidently precious. Europeans described these items with words such as *trifles*, *trinkets*, or even *trash*, words that later recur in interactions with non-Europeans well beyond Africa. A second concerned the range of items and practices middlemen termed *fetisso*. Their multiplicity baffled Europeans, who decided that anything at all might become a fetish, according to an individual's "fancy" or caprice. That objects Europeans associated with distinct kinds of being and different domains of practice could all be called *fetisso* came to be taken as evidence of an African mental muddle as well.

The book Willem Bosman published in 1703 displaced De Marees as the go-to source on the fetish and Africa. Unlike De Marees, Bosman, chief merchant for the Dutch West India Company in Guinea, lived there for many years. His detailed descriptions, based on long-term, firsthand experience, quickly made his book authoritative. Not only was it translated into English, French, and German (and widely plagiarized), but among those who read it were Newton, Locke, Adam Smith—and of course Charles de Brosses (Pietz 2022: 84–85). Bosman's work, in short, moved the fetish into the conceptual armature of European intellectuals. His narrative style also garnered interest: mocking and skeptical, in taking particular forms of value and the concept of self-interest for granted, and in its irritation at the impediments fetish practices formed to mercantile relations, it reveals magic's translations through the preoccupations of an emergent modern naturecul-ture. Capitalist rather than Christian iconoclasm dominated his book.

Bosman framed the fetish as marking a fundamental misapprehension of the properties and value of things. That fetishes could affect well-being or possess intention and agency indicated a failure to understand the workings of natural causation and chance. Such arguments became deeply embedded in later European discussions of magic. Writing after Bekker's challenge to dominant theories of witchcraft, Bosman no longer had to consider ideas about the devil or his demonic minions and could instead attribute African practices to delusion and manipulation (Pietz 2022: 86). As the fetish mutated into an index of epistemological hierarchies, differences between European commercial practices and those of African traders were reworked as reasonable or unreasonable understandings of matter, nature, and value. Such views were baked into Enlightenment philosophies that discredited a host of agents, practices, and experiences as not only unreasonable but archaic.

In addition to the fetish's role in the production of magic as a category of commensuration, however, it highlights something more particular: the fabrication of a modern ideology regarding objects and matter. For moderns, the material world no longer is enchanted (at least, purportedly). Agency is a property of human subjects, not the things they make or features of nature. Which returns us to Hegel, whose philosophical corpus focuses on the dialectical relation between subjects and objects, and whose rejection of Africans as historical agents presents them as projecting their own power as subjects onto a jumble of made and found things.

In a discussion of the devastated landscape resulting from the eruption of the world's largest mud volcano in East Java, Nils Bubandt describes a practice through which some Javanese make something hopeful of the bleak terrain: collecting stones of an unusual shape or structure from the mudflats. Good ones, Bubandt informs readers, may become "part of one's arsenal of heirlooms and amulets. Such objects are kept hidden or are fitted and worn in rings for protection. In particular, they are seen to have a magical capacity (*khasiat*) to confer upon the finder of good fortune (*rezeki*)" (2017: G130).

What drew me to this snippet was more than the phrase "magical capacity." Certainly, as I argue throughout this book, the modifier *magical* matters: by using it (it is not part of standard dictionary definitions of the Indonesian word *khasiat*), Bubandt unmakes the world that Indonesian collectors make, while strengthening a world in which such acts and objects may captivate but appear strange. What interests me more, though, are the oddities themselves, which Bubandt characterizes with a much more specific term: amulets. These form an overlooked translational knot in making magic.

Indonesians commonly call objects such as those Bubandt describes *jimat*, a term Euro-Americans, including the authors of dictionaries, invariably gloss not only as amulets, but also as talismans, charms, and sometimes mascots. Certainly, in many ways jimat resemble the items to which these terms refer. Small things that people wear or carry on their bodies, jimat often are hidden from view, whether because they are worn inside of a person's clothing, are wrapped in cloth, or, if in plain view, because not all people recognize their purpose. As I elaborate later, myriad materials may make up a jimat. While some jimat protect their bearer, many confer or extend specific capacities.

That anthropologists have had little to say about amulets may explain why jimat rarely receive mention in postindependence ethnographies of Indonesia despite their ubiquity in everyday life.[1] They turn up, for instance, on only one page of Geertz's *The Religion of Java*, in his chapter on dukun (tellingly entitled "Curing, Sorcery, and Magic") (1960: 103). As this suggests, jimat have some associations with dukun. Finding a small curiosity of nature such as those Bubandt mentions constitutes one way to come by a jimat, but unless the finder is proficient in relevant knowledges he is likely to bring his discovery to a specialist, such as a dukun, for advice on their care and use, or instructions on how to test them to see what they might do. Some dukun, along with the other experts Dutch officials considered potential fanatics, also make and supply jimat to clients and followers, though these commonly look different from the curious stones to which Bubandt refers.

In contrast to current anthropological apathy, jimat excited intense colonial attention. Indeed, the state's response to jimat formed a polar opposite to its dealings with dukun. If some officials bemoaned the regime's indifference to dukun, with whom administrators only dealt on an ad hoc basis, from 1872 on the regime sought to police jimat. Regulations aimed to control their circulation and in 1918 criminalized one specific use. As I discuss in this chapter, authorities attributed three matters of political and jural concern to jimat: theft, perjury, and, most concerning of all, rebellion. At the same time, jimat constituted one of several types of Indonesian objects that Dutch ethnologists labeled fetishes, a topic of scholarly interest.[2]

Insertion into colonial law catapulted jimat into a role in the Indies akin to that played by witchcraft in British colonial Africa. Jimat operated much like practices involving "witchcraft" did, by precipitating laws that proved more complicated and difficult to enforce in practice than in theory (e.g., Fields 1982). And again like African witchcraft, the jimat's inscription in penal codes redounded, at least to some extent, on colonial ethnology's conceptual commitments, though reversing those of British anthropology. Thus, even as the latter turned from the problem of the fetish to the problematic of the witch, Dutch scholars continued to probe archipelago practices in relation to materiality through the conceptual trio of fetishism, animism, and spiritism.[3]

For the Dutch, then, objects provoked more explicit concern than subjects, both politically and intellectually. But responses to jimat were rife with paradoxes. Authorities mocked them as worthless junk onto which Indonesians projected absurd powers. Yet by stressing their significance, singling out their distribution for surveillance, and prosecuting their possession, criminal codes made jimat formidable, even undefeatable, foes. More broadly, their tangibility made them ripe for forensic attention. Unlike other acts, they could be discovered: in markets and homes, in headscarves and hair knots, in pockets or belts, even on corpses. Yet authorities largely ignored their physical properties, instead using them to diagnose what could only be inferred: intentions, frames of mind, attitudes, and beliefs. At the same time they were constantly folded into broader categories: amulet, fetish, and, ultimately, magic. That Dutch commentators discounted their substance to attend to purported animating ideas contrasts with the attention to material qualities Indonesians bring to their production and use. This analytic slide from matter to mentality marks a perduring feature of the category of magic. It also meant that these humble actors, even while caught in the glare of juridical and political investigation and ensnared in theoretical speculation, became and remain barely visible.

Why did small, portable items treated as overvalued trifles and trash accrete such importance for Dutch authorities? More than other practices and things refracted through magic, jimat became embroiled in the edifice of colonial rule; how and why did they provoke such responses? Answering such questions takes us from colonial counterinsurgency to evolving juridical efforts to stem the movement of things that permeate everyday life, and the conundrums to which such endeavors gave rise. Foremost among these was the matter of their materiality. Given the concerns jimat provoked, officials paid surprisingly little attention to the specificity of their composition. Colonial ethnology, which knotted jimat to the concepts of fetish, amulet, and magic, may explain that indifference. But jimat proved too slippery to solidify divides between European and native; their transmutations into amulets and fetishes sent comparisons ricocheting back and forth. Other (partial) connections open a path to think jimat differently: as nonhuman actors as well as outcomes of intra-actions (specifically, what Souriau calls instauration) through which they become real.

Invulnerable Insurgents

On July 3, 1919, Assistant Resident Kal in Garut, in West Java, received word that Haji Hasan (the title Haji signifying he had been to Mecca) in the village of Cimareme had refused to comply with a government order.[4] Anticipating a rice shortage, the regime had mandated all farmers to sell a portion of their yield to the government. Based on his land holdings, Haji Hasan owed forty-two pikol.[5] He requested this be reduced to ten pikol so that he could feed his many dependents. Efforts by the Sundanese subdistrict head (*wedana*) to induce him to pay the original assessment, including threats to seize his crops by force, made no impact. More concerning was a report from the village head, who traced the Haji's recalcitrance to his son-in-law Haji Gajali, a member of Sarekat Islam. Founded in 1911 as an Islamic trade association, by 1919 the group had morphed into a mass organization advocating self-governance. On receipt of Kal's report, Resident De Stuers ordered Haji Hasan's arrest.

Kal, the Sundanese regent, and twenty-seven policemen headed to Haji Hasan's home, where they found forty people wearing white and bearing keris, which Kal interpreted as signs of a willingness to fight to the death. After talking to the Haji, Kal judged matters too volatile to carry out an arrest, but on his return to Garut he received more bad news: people in two more villages were now refusing to sell their rice.

Four days later, Kal, the regent, and the resident, this time with soldiers as well as police, returned to Cimareme. Thousands lined the road to Haji Hasan's house, where he was leading prayers on the verandah. Once again, his entourage wore white and carried keris. De Stuers parleyed with the Haji for an hour while police stationed themselves around the house. When he demanded that Haji Hassan surrender his weapon and come to Garut, the Haji stopped talking and went inside, closing doors and windows. Soon after, those crammed within (later tallied at 116 people) began to chant *zikir*, Sufi incantations to achieve oneness with God.[6]

After repeated calls received no response, De Stuers ordered the troops to fire a warning round through the roof. When after a second round voices inside shouted that bullets couldn't touch them, he commanded a volley through the house. Silence, followed by moans. With that the police forced their way in. Haji Hasan and four others lay dead; the nineteen wounded (one later died) included four women and a child.

Both the Malay-language press and Indonesian members of the recently instituted—solely advisory and thus largely symbolic—"People's Council" (*Volksraad*) demanded an investigation. In its course, the government claimed to have uncovered a previously unknown "Division B" of Sarekat Islam that they pronounced a shadowy revolutionary group. Some declared Haji Hasan's defiance part of an anti-colonial conspiracy, asserting that he had jumped the gun on a Sarekat plot to murder Europeans and install an Indonesian ruling council. Sarekat Islam leaders rejected these claims and denied any knowledge of Haji Hasan.

Unlike the arrest of Nang Mukanis, this incident is famous in the annals of Indonesian history. Dutch alarms about Sarekat Islam, now generally treated as a key organization in the nascent formation of a nationalist anti-colonial movement, have meant historians often comment on this event.[7] Jimat, however, appear nowhere in their accounts.[8] Yet following the bloody confrontation jimat galvanized police, investigators, colonial officials, and journalists at least as much as Sarekat Islam did. Journalists reported that police found a jimat meant to confer invulnerability on Haji Hasan's body. Pundits blamed jimat for people's willingness to follow the Haji's lead. Analysts attributed people's defiance to their conviction that jimat rendered them impervious to bullets. Investigators concluded bloodshed had been inevitable since the Haji and his followers not only were armed (with daggers) and prepared to resist but "believed themselves invulnerable."[9] After the massacre, police combed the region for jimat and jimat sellers. Some claimed that Division B had been making and selling invulnerability jimat, both to generate revenue and to enlist followers to carry out its nefarious plans. The attention paid to jimat bespeaks a remarkable preoccupation with a device supposedly irrelevant to making history.

Dutch officials and journalists had learned to associate jimat with rural insurrections long before shots were fired in Garut. In a series of studies, eminent Indonesian historian Sartono Kartodirdjo, a subaltern studies thinker *avant la lettre*, resurrected from colonial archives an impressive succession of forceful peasant responses across the island of Java to the changing conditions of their lives in the nineteenth and early twentieth centuries. Those conditions included the growing demands colonial policies made on their labor and land, through compulsory production of cash crops for the world market, corvée labor, taxes, capitalization of land, and, as in Garut, the forced sale of staples. The circumstances leading Indonesian peasants to make history, Sartono insists, were by no means solely economic: colonial rule disrupted relations between peasants and traditional elites (many of whom joined the state apparatus), prompting desires for a just order. Such desires drew on prophetic Javanese texts as well as new interpretations of

Islam encountered during the Haj. Colonial administrators characterized these responses as riots, unrest, uprisings, disturbances, upheavals, rebellions, and, of course, fanaticism. In the course of suppressing them, they discovered that prior to such events, leaders—those the Dutch termed fanatics—might dispense or sell jimat to their followers.[10] As Sartono notes, "In studying the development of any particular social movement in Java, one almost invariably comes across practices of an essentially fetishist type [sic]. The most common and significant of these is the distribution of *djimat* (charms) offering protection from danger, illness, and death, or the ability to become invisible or invulnerable" (1972: 79). (I will return to Sartono's decision to characterize these practices as "fetishist.")

A succession of uprisings in the 1860s and early 1870s added momentum to efforts to formalize growing state concerns over jimat, especially as several, including a fatal attack on an assistant resident, occurred in the Ommelanden, the outskirts of the colonial capital Batavia.[11] As a region of large private landed estates Van Till compares to Latin American haciendas, conditions there were especially harsh (2011: 25). By this time Dutch authorities had had enough encounters with jimat to resolve to place obstacles in the path of their all too fluid movement. Police ordinances in 1872 sought to impede their flow by criminalizing the "selling or spreading of so-called jimat, amulets, or other objects under the pretense that they possess supernatural power" (Der Kinderen 1873: 33).[12] In 1918, only a year before events in Garut, a new penal code expanded considerably on this article by subjecting to arrest anyone who "sells, offers for sale, supplies, distributes, or has in stock for sale or distribution" such items (Hekmeijer 1918: 180).

With the link between jimat and insurgency established as colonial common sense and inscribed in law, it is hardly surprising that jimat began to mobilize concern as soon as police inspected the Haji's corpse, and that such concern quickly spread.[13] The jimat found on his body led to others, uncovered during searches in the villages resistant to selling their rice. Authorities aimed to discover caches of jimat, along with their circuits of production and distribution. Discovery of jimat in the house of a former village head from a neighboring subdistrict aroused suspicion. Officials tried to trace all of these jimat back to the Haji or his followers. Even before anyone was shot, authorities found it relevant, for instance, that Haji Hasan's son-in-law Haji Gajali, the Sarekat Islam member, sold jimat.

That the congeries of concerns assembling around jimat following the bloodbath have received little notice from historians shows that the reality politics already evident in colonial law ("the pretense that they possess supernatural power") is ongoing. Items glossed as amulets are unthinkable actors in the one-world world of nation-states and have no place in the modern drama of national becoming. Even Sartono ignores the fuss about jimat when it comes to Garut (1972), presenting the event as a transitional moment, when "modern" structures of authority, motivations, and goals began to displace "traditional" and "magico-religious" ones (1973: 17).[14]

In contrast to the sharp line Sartono draws between tradition and modernity, and the place magic—via jimat—occupies in it, discussions of jimat in the media following the massacre reveal a much messier situation. Not only do these illuminate the extent to which jimat had become a colonial obsession, but different parties enact different relations between jimat and new formations of Indonesian life. These formations include Sarekat, less as a harbinger of nation-building than as a vehicle for emergent strains of Islam, and the new class of Indonesians educated in Dutch schools, the (soon to prove bitter) fruit of the Ethical Policy. Notably, for both Dutch and Indonesian commentators, jimat are actors, capable of making things happen.

Consider a Dutch editorial that appeared sixteen days after the Haji's death under the headline "The Native Press and Native Superstition." Like other journalists who castigated the Malay-language press for denouncing government violence (including massive arrests and legally questionable search-and-seizure operations) but ignoring jimat, De Vries, editor-in-chief of the *Soerabaiasch Nieuwsblad*, enjoined his Indonesian counterparts to recognize jimat as "the most important point of the entire affair" and "the root cause" of Haji Hassan's defiance.[15] To counter outrage at government actions, De Vries strikes back with a novel interpretation of the immorality of jimat. Arguing that the Haji and his followers did not expect to die since they thought their jimat made them invulnerable, De Vries concludes they believed themselves more powerful than their opponents—and to fight under such circumstances is unethical. De Vries's hypocrisy is breathtaking: he clearly "believed" firearms to be more powerful than jimat or keris but does not condemn their use against peasants as morally offensive.

But to reach his main argument, he soon moves to more familiar—and more ambiguous—territory. The Haji proved vulnerable despite his jimat. Adding journalistic force to the state's performance of a considerably more violent trial of strength than the one involving Nang Mukanis, De Vries trumpeted Haji Hasan's death as proof that in a confrontation between bullets and jimat, bullets win. Or do they? De Vries waffles. Only survivors, he noted, would be in a position to benefit from the demonstration. And those with something to gain from convincing people to "believe in the nonsense of invulnerability-making jimat" no doubt already were encouraging those survivors to credit jimat for their continued existence. (If, for the Haji, bullets prevailed, for survivors jimat did.) But others will not profit from this brutal pedagogy, for how would they learn to draw the proper disenchanting conclusions from the Haji's death? Only the Dutch-language press was discussing jimat; even if natives could read such texts, they likely would not find them credible.

Happily, he writes, "We know that among the more developed natives enough are found who do not believe in those things." It is such persons who must seize the pedagogic moment, for "[was] there ever a better opportunity than this to cure those of unsound mind of their delusions?" That the native press featured no articles about jimat raised the disturbing possibility, he opined, that native leaders wanted ordinary people to "remain deluded in their superstitions, so that the best (if not the only) means to move them to revolt will not disappear." Not only does De Vries charge "developed" Indonesians to broadcast the fact that jimat offer no protection, but he gives them an additional brief: to publicize the law. Few natives knew about the new penal code, with its provisions about jimat, and "It is the task of the Native Press to draw its readers' attention to it." He adds: "Doesn't the developed Native feel shame that such a penal provision is necessary for his people?" This is a telling statement; while the code applied to all residents of the Indies, everyone knew that certain articles were aimed at "natives."

Tensions ripple through De Vries's editorial: most pertinent, jimat are both potent (dangerously inciting defiance) and impotent (failing to prevent fatalities). As far as I know, no one replied directly. But several "developed natives" did respond to Dutch acts and words, with critiques of the moral panic to which jimat gave rise. In the process they highlighted not only the limits of colonial comprehension but also the practical and conceptual difficulties of enforcing jimat laws.

Several noted that jimat constituted a ubiquitous element of daily life. Moreover, not all jimat, they pointedly and patiently noted, confer invulnerability; thus, the mere fact of finding jimat in someone's home had little political significance. Hence one argued:

It appears to us that the European papers, a few excepted, deliberately give a false representation of the facts. Among other things, it is asserted that jimat are found almost everywhere in the houses in Garut's vicinity. We would want to ask the European gentlemen if in the entire

Netherlands Indies there is to be found one Native house that is to-tally jimat free. Even in the homes of developed native Officials you still find jimat. Although the men no longer attach value to them, they cannot ensure that their wives, mothers, or grandmothers do not hide jimat in some secret corner. And B.B. [civil service] officials know that very well but bring finding jimat in houses into connec-tion with all kinds of resistance designs. (*Het Vrij Weekblad*, quoted in *SN*, July 21, 1919)

Ignoring the patent gender politics, this commentator highlights the fact that jimat form part of everyday life. Finding jimat in someone's house, therefore, hardly constitutes evidence of intent to take up arms against the colonial state—something the author claims that officials know, making their actions in Garut particularly troublesome.

Several figures now well known to scholars also weighed in. Raden Mas Soetatmo Soeriokoesoemo (hereafter Soetatmo), leader of a short-lived Ja-vanese nationalist movement, elaborates on the omnipresence of jimat in Javanese life: "A Javanese who is *mata gelap* [not thinking clearly; amok] has a jimat in his pocket; a Javanese who undertakes a journey, trades, cultivates his sawah [rice field], or whatever other business he does, always possesses a jimat; even if he goes to solicit a job he first consults his jimat. The Javanese lives with his jimat, and also has himself buried with it. If the jimat is dan-gerous then nowhere on Java is safe" (1919: 161).

Soetatmo emphasizes what colonial alarm obscures: the ubiquity and multiplicity of jimat. Dutch laws and commentaries lump all jimat together rather than recognizing their diversity. At the same time Soetatmo enlists distinctly modern and Protestant rhetoric (Keane 2007), likely derived from his familiarity with theosophy (Sears 1996), when he wryly observes that jimat mean something different to Javanese and Europeans. For Java-nese a jimat is "simply a symbol of his belief" (in what, he does not say), but the European "immediately thinks of death and destruction" (1919: 161).

To be sure, Soetatmo concedes, some jimat could lead a person to think himself invulnerable. But he challenges the next step colonial logic takes: "You are going to argue, aren't you: the jimat leads to belief in invulnerabil-ity and with this belief one easily gets around to organizing a rebellion. It's simple. That conclusion goes without saying, right?" Answering with a re-sounding "no," he poses instead a question: Why do people rebel? Because they feel invulnerable or because they are dissatisfied? Rebellions aim to alter unbearable situations. After all, "If it were true that the jimat procures its owner a rebellious spirit, then a general revolt already would have broken out all over Java." Rather than focusing on the invulnerability jimat purportedly confer, officials should attend to the conditions under which people live. Neatly turning the tables, Soetatmo adds that European authorities rather than Javanese are the ones "infected" with the "jimat-bacillus" (1919).[16]

Raden Mas Noto Soeroto, a Javanese aristocrat famed for his poetry, also comments on the government's "forceful conduct" to uncover "the commerce in jimat" following the Garut massacre, noting that to assess such a response requires "an accurate conception of a 'jimat.' A jimat is nothing but a talisman [sic] or amulet [sic] and consists in most cases of a little piece of paper on which is written a saying from the Korân [sic], which a person always carries with him in a sewn pouch while keeping the maxim continuously in his thoughts. Sometimes a jimat consists of a seahorse carcass or a pouch with soil or dried herbs ... [depending on its aim]. In short: there exist as many kinds of jimat as the various purposes one can pursue in life."[17] But where Soetatmo responds by reversing the arrow of accusation, Noto Soeroto, like a number of Dutch commentators I address later, insists on similarities between Javanese and Dutch practices, which he saw for himself while studying law in Leiden. Calling jimat talismans and amulets (in Dutch, for Dutch readers), prepares the way for further commensuration:

> Naturally there are also jimat to which the ignorant ascribe the power to make themselves invulnerable. But having a jimat does not yet stamp someone as a sinister person, any more than carrying an image of the Virgin Mary in his wallet makes the Catholic a dangerous person. For anyone who believes in the power of prayer, such as the Christian Scientist, or the power of thought, such as the theosophist, and who considers the animation of "dead" objects possible under certain circumstances, belief in a jimat is not absurd in itself. Even in Holland jimat exist, for a wild chestnut that someone carries as remedy for rheumatism and other such things are in fact also jimat.

Tjipto Mangoenkoesomo, a member of the Volksraad, also critiqued those who equated jimat with revolution, asking what native doesn't carry jimat? As he continues, he reveals that some authorities presented the bloodbath as an ontological performance aimed at undermining native claims about invulnerability, to which Tjipto indignantly asked, Why then shoot at chest rather than knee height? (IPO 37 [1919]).

My final (unnamed) example critiques government actions from a different angle, scoffing at the idea that Sarekat, an organization associated with reformist strains of Islam that listed in its bylaws the goal of combating misunderstandings of Islam, might endorse the sale of jimat.[18] Jimat, for reformists, could count among Javanese practices not compatible with proper Islamic practice.

Both the massacre and its repressive aftermath, in short, did mobilize Javanese intellectuals to comment in public about jimat, but by no means as De Vries demanded. They do not declare whether they "believe in" (or possess) jimat in assessing colonial acts and statements. Noto Soeroto uses familiar glosses (amulets and talismans) to undermine the difference implicit in the regime's investigations (and to reverse the direction of translation), while Soetatmo finds the state's equation of jimat with danger ludicrous.

These astute critiques, however, made no dent in the way authorities responded to jimat. Two years later a piece in the *Netherlands Indies Police Guide* reiterated that jimat "deserve the utmost interest and vigilance on the side of the Police" while noting, ominously, that every native on Java and Madura had at least one (S. 1921: 33), perhaps having learned the wrong lessons from Javanese critics.[19] Particularly problematic, the author notes, were jimat that led people to think themselves invulnerable, which emboldened those who ordinarily would fear armed confrontation. Indeed, "In case of *insurrection* against the Netherlands Authority, e.g., we can be assured *that the participants in the revolt without exception are provided with* jimat, while from the subsequent inquiry it continually appears *that education in the practice of élmu* [see below] *preceded the breaking out of the disturbances*" (S. 1921: 33, italics in original).[20] Worse yet, and akin to De Vries, "However often the effect of Netherlands bullets brought disenchantment in a bloody way and proved the invalidity of such hocus pocus notions with facts, the unshakable belief in a possible way to obtain invulnerability continually reemerged" (S. 1921: 34)—requiring, of course, more bullets. Six years later, a brief comment in a standard reference on the Indies pointed to Garut to underscore the political peril jimat posed: "An unusual increase in the sale of jimat . . . indicates the preparation of dark plans; the still recent Garut affair and the history of the notorious Division B. once again furnished evidence of that."[21]

Given these perduring concerns, one might expect detailed descriptions of the jimat inciting insurrections, especially given the heated reactions to the searches following Garut.[22] These do not exist. That Haji Hasan was wearing a jimat when he died is unsurprising. It is even possible that this jimat aimed to confer invulnerability: to make the Haji's body impenetrable to bullets, to deflect their trajectory, to make him undetectable, or otherwise to armor and defend him. Indonesians did wear such jimat in confrontations with the Dutch, to support and protect themselves. It is impossible to do more than speculate, however, about what this particular jimat aimed to do. The thing itself receives no attention, other than the triumphant observation that it had been pierced by a bullet that had then penetrated his skull. Despite the decision that followed to comb the area for jimat, no one describes what jimat that confer such protection look like. Surely it would have behooved authorities to know exactly what they should be looking for when searching people's homes. But commentators focus not on substance but solely on the jimat's semiotic significance, which they appear confident they understand (despite emphatic assertions by Javanese commentators they did not).

This was not, moreover, a new problem. While he no longer lived in Indonesia when events in Garut unfolded, letters that famous Orientalist Christiaan Snouck Hurgronje had penned years earlier demonstrate uncertainty had long plagued colonial officials. Author of numerous scholarly monographs and a former (and future) Leiden professor, who had converted to Islam and made the Haj, Snouck served as adviser for native affairs from 1890 to 1905.[23] In that capacity, administrators from residents to the general secretary asked him to identify suspicious items they had confiscated (mainly texts, bundles of texts, or objects with textual elements, likely sent to him because of his areas of expertise) to clarify the threat they might pose. Were they harbingers of revolt? Clearly, officials didn't have a clue. In response after response, Snouck explains the item sent to him and states it posed no danger whatsoever to peace and order, while patiently outlining the myriad uses of jimat in Indonesian life. For Snouck, moreover, the role jimat played in "political or fanatical agitation" was at best subsidiary (Gobée and Adriaanse 1957: 1229–30).[24] He repeatedly advises his correspondents that the state had chosen the wrong target for monitoring threats of insurrection: instead of jimat, officials should be alert to rumors about the imminent arrival of the Just King (Ratu Adil).

Some intriguing ambiguities filter through government treatment of jimat. Despite regarding them as symptoms of political unrest, officials apparently had no idea what jimat relevant to such events looked like. And while insisting jimat were incapable a priori of doing anything, in practice they treat them as potent, if only psychologically. Some, for example, contended that jimat instilled confidence (e.g., Kohlbrugge 1907: 33–35). Snouck himself wrote that "It is naturally possible that the use of such means—even though their effect is entirely imaginary—results in undesirable frames of mind and dispositions" (Gobée and Adriaanse 1957: 1235). While the reality politics of such statements is palpable ("their effect is entirely imaginary"), they acknowledge jimat "modify a state of affairs by making a difference"—according to Latour, the minimal definition of an actor (2005b: 71).

Crimes and Punishment

While the threat of insurrection particularly perturbed the colonial regime, it was not the only reason to block traffic in jimat. Almost as crucial was their association with criminality. To understand the extent and expansion of colonial concerns with jimat requires fuller examination of how and why jimat incited jurists to inscribe them into law and why they attracted more attention than other criminalized practices. At the same time, unlike jimat taken from purported rebels, texts reveal what some jimat confiscated from thieves (and trial witnesses) looked like. But such enhanced visibility had no practical entailments for governance. It did, however, augment the work of translation, offering fodder for equating jimat with fetishes.

As indicated, peasant insurgency was only one problem that made administrators aware of jimat and triggered a legal response. Officials also had discovered a relation between jimat and criminal gangs. Such gangs, run by thugs sometimes known as *jago* (cocks), had become rampant across Java (Schulte-Nordholt 1991; Van Till 2011).[25] Gangs stole cash, water buffaloes, and portable goods from Chinese shopkeepers and landowners, the occasional European, and Javanese and Sundanese peasants, some of whom had acquired cash by growing crops for export. Gangs also extorted protection money, and some colluded with village chiefs, district heads, and police. Many thugs were renowned for their personal powers, mixing martial arts with esoteric knowledges (*élmu*) and jimat. If the jimat relevant to rebels might render bodies impermeable to bullets, those thieves had other purposes: to break into homes and businesses undetected. Administrators learned, to their horror, of this nexus of criminality in 1872, the same year the first jimat laws appeared. A series of reports, the most damning by a white tobacco planter in Kediri (East Java), highlighted the ubiquity of gangs in rural Java, and the web of fences and native administrators with whom they were in cahoots (Bloembergen 2009; Schulte-Nordholt 1991).

The 1872 regulation is impossibly broad. In theory, distributing or selling *any* jimat—even any *object*—constituted grounds for arrest, since for Dutch officials the stipulation "under pretense that these possess supernatural power" could cover virtually everything: a jimat for moving goods quickly in the market would be as pernicious as one rendering its bearer invisible. Although similar regulations appear in the version aimed at Europeans (and those equated with them), an explanatory memo by Timon Henricus der Kinderen, then director of justice, says nothing either to clarify the concepts or to provide guidance for implementation. What he does say, however, involves not only this provision but the one immediately preceding it, which proscribed professional fortunetelling, dream interpretation, and prognostication. Such acts, he claims, should only "be made punishable when a Native makes himself guilty of them" (1873: 40), adding the same practices do not threaten public order equally in different communities (1873: 45).[26] Later he elaborates, with a comment that surely would have brought insurgency and criminal gangs to mind, as well as the fools, frauds, and fanatics of chapter 1: "Anyone who knows how often the Native especially is the victim of his superstition and how that superstition often is exploited to stir him to embark on undertakings dangerous for public peace and order, will appreciate the benefit of these regulations" (1873: 90).[27] Thus, while similar provisions existed for "natives" and "Europeans," they differed in the eyes of colonial law. This difference is also evident from the penalties for violation, which are significantly higher for natives: more money for fines, though they were less likely to be able to pay them; more time expended in forced labor for those who could not pay.

The 1918 penal code retained both articles, while ramping up penalties and further specifying forbidden modes of jimat circulation, tacking more verbs to the list of prohibitions. It also directed two new laws at "native superstition": an addendum to the jimat law on the topic of élmu, and a second, separate, jimat offense. In theory, the code aimed to reverse prior policies promulgating separate rules for Europeans and natives. Its proponents also prevailed over advocates of *adat* law, culturally relevant laws for specific indigenous populations. Indeed, jurists took as its template the Netherlands' penal code (based on the presumptively universal Code Napoléon, instituted during Napoleon's occupation of the lowlands). But these articles, immediately nicknamed the "occult offenses" (*occulte delicten*), not only deviated from Dutch law, but also once again targeted Indonesians, undermining claims about universal application (Fasseur 1995: 179–80). Thus the "occult offenses" enacted a disjunction between metropole and colony. That deviation from a one-world penal code gelled around language such as "supernatural [*bovennatuurlijk*] power" (and the "pretense" of possessing it) highlights their enactment of reality politics. Featuring in two of the three articles, jimat both materialized and indexed such politics.

The new occult offenses show how jurists resolved long-standing efforts to expand the existing provision on jimat. In 1890, for example, the government secretary asked Snouck to weigh in on outlawing dressing in white or possessing collections of texts, which could include instructions for making jimat. (Both clothing and texts, note, were material objects; they also asked him about whether they might prosecute "spirit possession" under existing laws.) Snouck advised against those extensions, but suggested the government might want to address the use of "magic spells" (*toverformules*), including *jampi* (incantations) and *rajah*, drawings that often formed part of the jimat he was asked about, which were even more prevalent than jimat, as dukun frequently supplied them to clients.[28] That advice may have helped to shape the first of the new offenses. An explanatory memorandum, however, attributed the concern with élmu to a 1904–5 investigation into the welfare of inhabitants of the Indies; respondents purportedly blamed élmu along with jimat for rebellion and criminality (Hirsch 1919: 581; Lemaire 1934: 170).

A subsection of the jimat law, this article (546.2) sanctioned "instruction in élmu or arts which have the intent of generating belief in the possibility of committing punishable offenses without any danger to the perpetrators" (Hekmeijer 1918: 180). A footnote to the explanatory memo explains what élmu refers to: "Élmu (Jav. *Ngélmu* or *ilmu*) means knowledge, skill [*kunst*];[29] in particular it is the knowledge of certain spells (*rapal*) [*toverspreuken*] that—sometimes after a long fast or after long night watches—they rattle off and through which they then come into the possession of some supernatural power or other, e.g., the power to kill someone, to gain victory in a fight, to become rich, to recover stolen goods, to become invulnerable or invisible, etc." (Hirsch 1919: 581).[30] Here the slide from knowledge or skill to the disqualifying notion of belief is the tell in the game of reality politics rather than "pretense" to "supernatural power." However, while this explanation embraces a broad range of abilities, the law only penalized those that led perpetrators to think they could safely commit crimes—in contrast to the article on jimat.

Why, however, yoke élmu to jimat? Some suggested they might complement one another or bestow similar capacities (Poensen 1878), particularly when it came to theft or insurrection. Moreover, activating a jimat could require specific rites or words (Poensen 1879). In short, acts, words, and things formed part of the same false coin. Others argued that jimat offered an easier route to what élmu promised: "One of the most desired things that one hopes to obtain with knowledge of ngélmu or by possession of a jimat is invulnerability, and it is simpler to get this by buying such a charm than through the study of the science of invulnerability or the science of iron" (S[pat] 1927: 266). No need to master the theory of electricity to turn on a light.

The second new occult offense appeared as a discrete article targeting one specific use of jimat. Addressing a practice that irked jurists in Java and Madura, it criminalized wearing or carrying "so-called jimat or amulets" in court by witnesses testifying under oath (Hekmeijer 1918: 180; Hirsch 1919: 582). Dutch officials whose duties included chairing tribunals consisting of a bench of magistrates—members of the local native civil service—had discovered that some defendants requested those testifying against them be searched for jimat.[31] Purportedly, witnesses could negate oaths by strategically placing jimat in their hair knots or the folds of their headscarves and thus below the text of the Qu'ran that religious officials (*penghulu*) held above their heads as they swore to tell the truth. Without fear of divine sanctions, a witness could lie with impunity. This made determining a defendant's guilt or innocence difficult, and frequently led to mistrials (judgments of "unclear," *kurang turang*).

Note that jimat formed an irritant around which two "occult offenses" took shape, and a third was formally attached to them.[32] In practice, jimat excited more attention than fortunetelling or élmu. Élmu, conveyed in words and fleeting performances, leave no residue after a disturbance or crime, and cannot be used to predict one. By contrast, jimat open forensic possibilities, as physical evidence of otherwise undetectable intent. That tangibility likely had much to do with administrative obsessions. Jimat could be treated as sensible traces, indices of motives even of the dead (e.g., Haji Hasan), as well as of specific "beliefs" (invulnerability) and generic credulity. To read goals and beliefs into a jimat, however, requires knowledge of more than the circumstances of their discovery. And what authorities took them to signify, Indonesians do not. At the same time, despite their materiality, jimat often evaded simple observation; while some were worn around necks, wrists, or on fingers, many were carried inside clothing. Though those wearing jimat need not have aimed at concealment, for a regime intent on legibility and signs of hidden plans, such conduct could amplify an impression of menace. It may also explain why the first jimat law outlawed dissemination, in theory easier to track, rather than possession.

To actually implement that law, however, would have required constant monitoring of markets and itinerant peddlers, as well as all the "fanatics" and "frauds" who might provide them. As Garut revealed, it also could lead to invasive searches. The law's generality exacerbated the problem. Limiting it, as the article on élmu did, to jimat relevant to the acts provoking these ordinances, and identifying what these jimat looked like, would seem helpful, especially as by 1918 considerably more was known about some jimat than in 1872.

At first glance authorities grant more attention to jimat linked to criminality or courts than to those associated with uprisings. Indeed, Hirsch's explanatory memo actually describes jimat enabling perjury: "as a rule these consist of bits of paper inscribed with Arabic maxims or words, whether intelligible or not" (1919: 582). A jimat uncovered during an 1890 trial in Madura may have contributed to Hirsch's confident conclusion: court officers discovered "four jimat—namely strips of paper inscribed with unreadable signs—that witness first claimed to have made himself and to have stuffed in his headdress as remedy against headache but finally confessed to have received [from] Kiyai Bringia" (*IWvhR* 1890: 188). We seem, therefore, to have a clear guideline for officials to follow.

Notably, Hirsch does not specify *particular* Arabic maxims or words, which would seem helpful in identifying relevant jimat. Perhaps such maxims or words did not exist. Hirsh's qualification—"whether intelligible or not"—and the "unreadable signs" on the jimat in Madura imply writing that only imitated Arabic calligraphy.[33]

But accounts of other cases undermine confidence in Hirsch's assertion. Consider the packet officers discovered in a headscarf at an 1893 tribunal in Lumayang (Java): a small fold of cloth, containing a piece of coconut shell, six ribs from a coconut palm frond, a clipping of sweet flag plant, and a moth. After confiscating it, officials swore in the witness and asked where he got this item and what it was for. He said his brother had given it to him to nullify the oath. Examining his brother, they found an identical package. He admitted to making both but insisted they forced their bearer to tell the truth. What did authorities make of the fact that, under oath and without their jimat, their stories diverged? The author notes drily: "Evidently, the second brother is cleverer but the simpler first brother speaks the truth" (P. 1894: 209; *IWvhR*). That removing jimat did not guarantee reliable testimony receives no comment.

An incident in Kediri involved yet another item: incense, in a small linen pouch. The witness declared it a prophylactic against fever and illness; the defendant swore it allowed the witness to lie (*RNI* 1909: 509). Could more than one kind of jimat negate an oath? Or perhaps these jimat had nothing to do with that goal and jurists banned all jimat in these circumstances because they didn't know which might aim to subvert their procedures. What counted for them was not the stuff used but where it was worn, in a hair knot or headscarf, though the stated purposes—preventing fevers, alleviating headaches—could also explain that location. In short, the physical properties of jimat that enabled perjury remain unsettled. For authorities, a witness wearing a jimat on his head signaled an unmistakable intent.[34]

No explanatory memo addresses jimat associated with theft, but accounts of these are markedly abundant. The very first publication on jimat describes two taken from a recently apprehended thief (Poensen 1879; see below). Two later articles (Knebel 1898a; Kreemer 1888)—that list a variety of Javanese jimat, and relate what Javanese call them, what they do, and what they are made of—include jimat a burglar might crave. Kreemer notes five (out of twenty) of potential use to thieves, ranging from one (requiring the burial of small bones from a monkey) producing disturbing hallucinations in order to induce people to vacate a targeted site (1888: 353) to the *tosan kuning*, "a yellowish piece of iron as large as a pinkie" that enables its bearer "to break open all possible locks" (1888: 354).

Moreover, jimat taken from thieves could be collected—and even photographed.[35] Meijer, author of a late colonial article on superstition and criminality, had a police photographer named Melis snap mug shots of jimat Meijer selected from the Surabaya Police Museum (1935: 111; see figs. 2.1, 2.2, and 2.3 on pages 89–91).

His article also includes a photo of a group of jimat recently taken from a notorious thief (see fig. 2.4 on page 92), explaining in a footnote where he got it: "Through the friendly mediation of Mr. C. G. M. van Arcken, formerly assistant resident of Magetan, now controleur B. B. at Malang, I ended up in the possession of a photo—made by Catoire, the detachment commander of the Field police—in which appear the amulets from Kuslan alias Abdullah, one of the most feared gang leaders of the rampokkers in Magetan" (Meijer 1935: 121). Arresting officers found them in a pocket in Kuslan's jacket, which was hanging on a post in his bedroom when their surprise raid roused him from sleep. Kuslan tried to reach it, but a revolver pressed to his temple dissuaded him.

What does this wealth of information reveal about the ambitious burglar's tool kit? Some consensus gathers around one jimat: dirt from a grave. While Poensen (1879) merely describes a thief's jimat with such content, others suggest how such unsettling stuff operated. Kreemer (1888: 354) identifies grave dirt as a *jimat penyirepan* (sleep jimat), a "godsend for quick thieves." Knebel concurs, explaining that strewing grave dirt around a site targeted

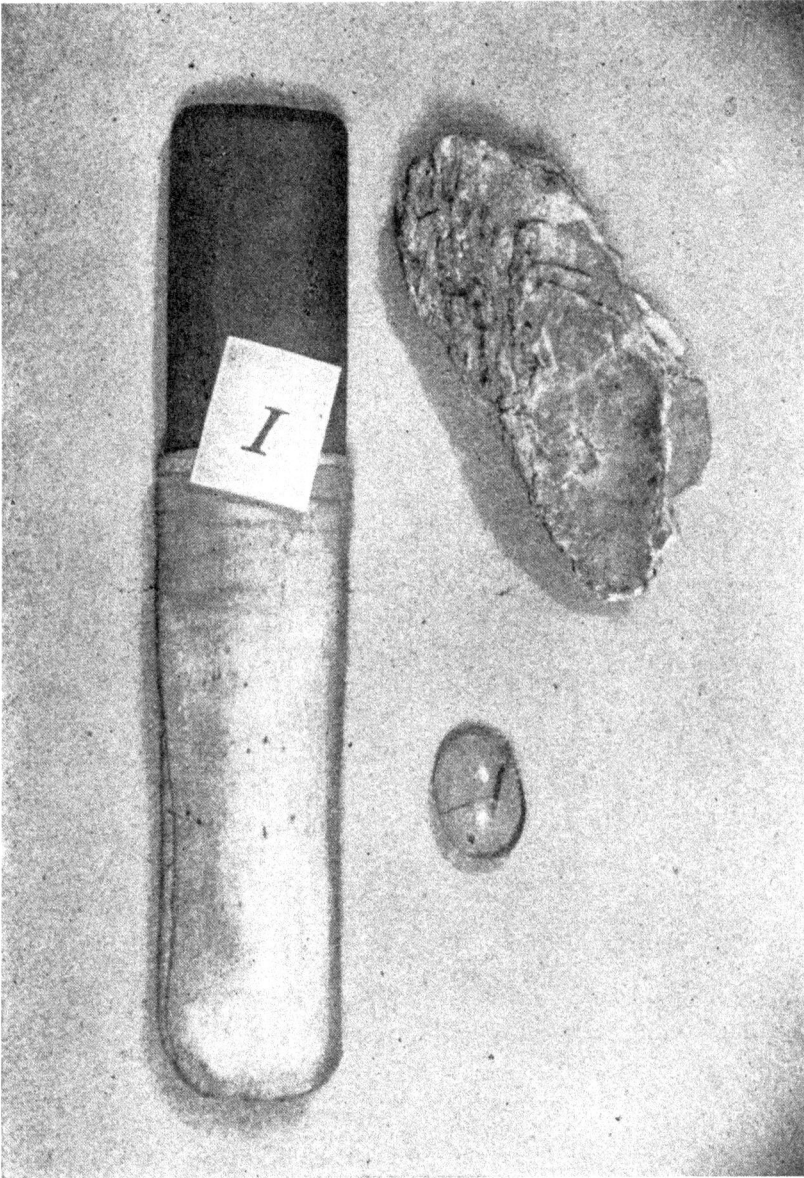

FIGURE 2.1: Mug shot of jimat made of "mineral" materials (stones) at the Surabaya Police Museum, selected by Meijer for Melis to photograph.

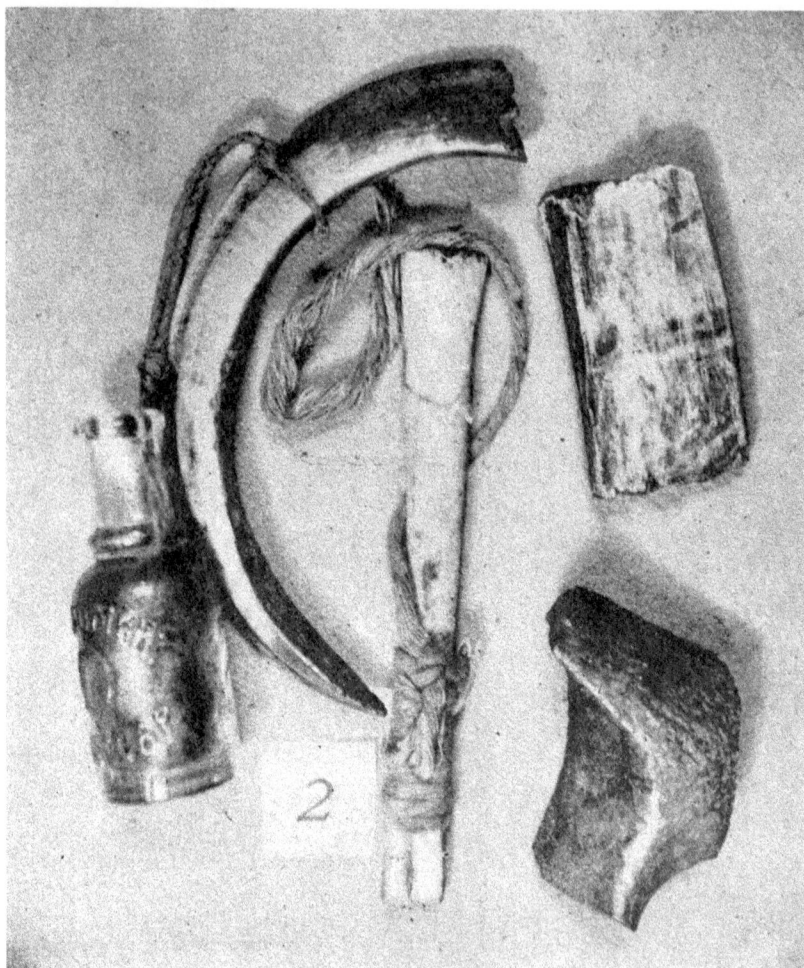

FIGURE 2.2: Mug shot of jimat made of "animal" materials (bone) at the Surabaya Police Museum, selected by Meijer for Melis to photograph.

for burglary plunges those within "into a profound sleep"—and adding a piece of exhumed death shroud guarantees sufficient time to ransack the place (1898a: 506). Following Knebel, who published in a journal widely read by officials and scholars, this association became common sense. Writing in the *Police Guide*, and thus for the most relevant readers, "S" (1921) asserts that jimat made from the dirt and a piece of shroud from particular graves allowed thieves to break into houses while inhabitants slept, while

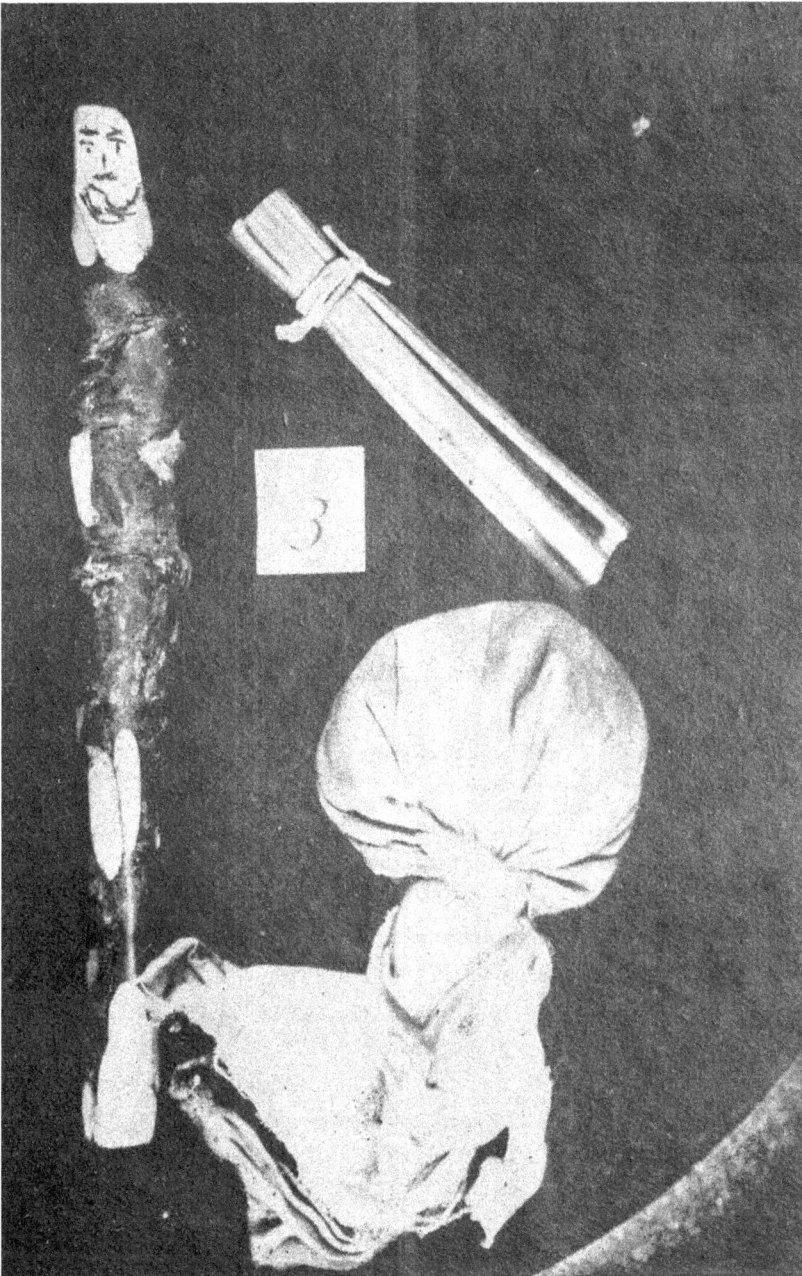

FIGURE 2.3: Mug shot of jimat made of "vegetal" materials at the Surabaya Police Museum, selected by Meijer for Melis to photograph.

Djimatnja Koeslan kepala Rampok

FIGURE 2.4: The Indonesian reads "Head Brigand Kuslan's jimat." Meijer identifies this as "Amulets from Kuslan, brigand from Magetan."

Meijer (1935) casually tosses off the connection without even bothering with a citation in an article otherwise rife with them.[36]

But if officials learned to view possession of pouches of dirt as evidence of criminal intent, it has left no traces. Perhaps the link proved weaker than repetition suggests. Poensen, likely based on a conversation with its owner, said about one such jimat: "In general, it can be kept as a means of defense, and thus also if one goes out to steal; but is also good in all kinds of other circumstances!" (1879: 232). He was, however, writing before anyone mentioned sleep—and the thief might have deliberately misled him. Poensen reports he wanted it back, undoubtedly motive for making it sound as innocuous as possible: a jimat that could induce deep sleep in guards would be of considerable interest to a prisoner. Other experts, though, raise doubts about whether *any* jimat could be conclusive evidence of criminality. On the basis of the texts he examined, Snouck repeatedly insisted that no jimat existed exclusively for use by thieves (Gobée and Adriaanse 1959: 1226, 1232, 1236). Meijer asserted that jimat criminals favored "do not differ from the jimat generally in vogue" (1935: 111).

Yet clearly specific jimat *do* have specific uses, as not only other colonial sources but Javanese intellectuals writing in protest after Garut indicate. It is hard to avoid the conclusion that authorities did not make a concerted inductive effort to draw on accumulated accounts, collections, and photos to discover if those who threatened their "peace and order" favored particular jimat. Meijer, for instance, recaps Knebel's list of Javanese jimat but doesn't try to match any to items in the Surabaya museum. Nor does he say much about the jimat he ordered photographed, highlighting the stuff from which they are made but saying nothing about function. Perhaps such information didn't exist, in itself indicative of administrative indifference in pinpointing the uses of particular jimat. Kuslan's arrest offered a chance to remedy such ignorance, but Meijer's interest in his jimat appears purely anecdotal.

In short, the material form of jimat that could annul an oath or enable breaking and entering (or even make rifles misfire) receives some attention, but not enough to allow officials to predict impending trouble (e.g., on discovering them for sale) or prove illicit intent. If forensic utility focused juridical attention on jimat, officials had no way to reliably relate particular items to the troublesome acts that inspired their laws. The meaning of jimat lay not in their specificity but in what they broadly "said" about Indonesians.

In the next section I turn from government and law to broader translations and explanations, focusing on the developing field of anthropology. These not only echo but clarify the administrative emphasis on the abstract qualities all jimat purportedly shared. But before leaving the law, I want to note that some Dutch jurists found the occult offenses deeply problematic. When the Department of Justice released a draft of the new code for commentary in 1912, a jurist signing himself A. T. wrote a scathing front-page response in a prominent law journal. Tackling each occult offense in turn, he showed how applying it to Europeans would lead to absurdities—and violate established legal principles. In relation to the "queer quasi-fighting of the amulet danger," he observed colonial laws would interdict not only jimat but also items Europeans wore or carried, from lucky horseshoes to Catholic crucifixes (A. T. 1912–13).[37]

Now You See Things . . . Now You Don't

In colonial counterinsurgency and law, jimat generated friction. As objects, they held up the tantalizing promise of serving to prognosticate or prove transgression, but failure to connect particular properties to their operations made it impossible to fulfill such promise. But colonial indifference to correlating form to function was not primarily due to the difficulties this could involve. It was embedded in translation and representation. If their uses and physicality made jimat targets of attention, uncontrolled equivocation with amulets, along with work that turned them into fetishes, had much to do with how authorities dealt with them. Such commensurations performed a kind of sleight of hand, displacing brief glimpses of concrete things with abstractions eliding their materiality, specificity, and diversity. These eased the way to corralling jimat into the capacious hall of magic.

These translational knots appear right from the start, in the very first publication about jimat, by missionary Carel Poensen. The Dutch Missionary Society (Nederlandsche Zendelinggenootschap, or NZG) dispatched Poensen to Java in 1860, and after two years of apprenticeship and work on the language, stationed him in Kediri, where he remained for nearly thirty years. In addition to his missionary work, he produced semi-thick descriptions of Javanese practices for NZG's journal. Given Kediri's role in bringing gangs to the regime's attention, he was well situated to report on theft: first in 1878, in an article on Javanese thieves that included a long discussion of ngélmu (including one inducing sleep); then, in 1879, on jimat, based on two confiscated from a thief. Nothing could be more casual than his gloss on the Malay word: "A couple of years ago a notorious thief was arrested and convicted here. He possessed a, for him, great treasure in the form of some jimat, e.g., amulets, talismans" (1879: 229). The speed of this translation flags it as worthy of attention, all the more as amulets and talismans themselves remain ciphers.

The European formation of these concepts molds their use as translations. Both words derive from antiquity: *amulet* from Latin *amulētum*; *talisman* from Greek *telesm* (τέλεσμα), though neither originally referred to items worn on the body.[38] The words now in use, identical in Dutch and English, emerged during the Renaissance. Talismans, used in natural magic, consisted of jewelry, stones, and small pieces of metal inscribed or engraved with astrological signs (Skemer 2006: 7–8); amulets referred to protective objects, including Catholic reliquaries and medals. The distinction blurred over time, though some translating jimat as talisman appear cognizant of it. Veth, for instance, first to hold a chair in ethnology in the Netherlands (at Leiden University), claims that Hajis "sell jimat (corruption of the Arabic *'azîmah*), mostly consisting of little letters inscribed with Koranic maxims and worn as talismans against misfortunes" (1875: vol. 1,

406).[39] Popular author H. A. van Hien uses *talisman* too, for what he claims is the correct referent for jimat: thin little lead plates, mostly from Arabia, onto which "hieroglyphic-kabbalistic signs are engraved" (1934: vol. 3, 37). For Poensen's readers, however, *amulet* would have invoked more commonplace stuff. Recall references earlier to several Dutch amulets, including horseshoes, horses' teeth, wild chestnuts, and crucifixes. On the whole, amulet conjures portability and vague desires for protection or luck.

The Kediri thief owned two jimat. Poensen found one of them, a bundle of manuscripts with the word *jimat* and the owner's name on the cover, the more interesting, and he devotes most of his article to their content. Replete with examples of élmu (in the form of drawings, prayers, and "incantations"), these largely address the consequences of being born on specific days and the significance of earthquakes, comets, and eclipses. The thief, however, attached more value to the other jimat, for which he had paid considerably more money. Hence before delving into the manuscripts, Poensen takes a couple of paragraphs to describe it and to address jimat in general—and both anticipates and channels his readers' reactions:

> How did that jimat look? Oh, very inconsequential. We even fear that after making its acquaintance you will say: "Is that it? It's not worth it!" But that would show you hadn't considered that the jimat's significance—and this applies generally, to every jimat—doesn't depend on its form or material worth—though that can be very costly— but only on its source and the powers ascribed to it. And so naturally the most wretched object can be elevated to the lofty status of a jimat. It shouldn't be surprising, then, to run into someone in possession of a jimat consisting of skin from a fetus; or a mustika (expensive stone); a little soil from some grave or other; a claw or something else from a tiger, caiman, or crocodile; a gold or silver object even of great value; a ring of precious or nonprecious metal containing a piece of tooth or molar, and what have you. (1879: 229–30)

Poensen assumes a rhetorical position recognizable from travel literature as well as ethnography, moving between the aesthetic and economic valuations of his European readers and elucidation of the "native point of view," even as modifiers (the sarcastic "lofty" and unequivocal "wretched") unmistakably situate him. Unusually, Poensen emphasizes stuff rather than use or meaning, though his remarks about the powers (note the plural) attributed to jimat still perform the crucial reduction. While some items he mentions are familiar (claws and other animal body parts), the indiscriminate jumble of titillating oddments (including disturbing elements such as fetal skin) and his emphasis on value veer into the domain of the fetish. That affinity grows as he literally opens the thief's jimat to inspection:

> See here a package wrapped up in a dark blue, grubby cloth rag. It doesn't look very appealing. That results from the fact that the man used to keep it in his hair knot, the authorized, as well as the safest, place.[40] You can now figure out how large that little bundle must be. We open it very cautiously. A dirty red cloth rag! We undo this too. There you have the actual jimat! A little dirt, containing a stick of metal about a centimeter long and a couple of millimeters thick. The owner says it is wesi-kuning, which others doubt.[41] People say—and who will dispute it? There's no way to know the truth—that it all has to be taken from a specially consecrated grave. There, in the deeply profound stillness of the forest, where perhaps the highly venerated material remains of some kiyai rests, the first owner was given that object in a mysterious way by some inhabitant of the spirit world, after he had spent some time there fasting, absorbed in deep attention and whispering prayers.[42] After that, the man turned homeward again; and everyone was astonished by what they heard of him. And, maybe because the man needed money, or wanted to do his friend a favor, he sold this jimat to our thief, for, he says, f60, after he learned the doa [prayer] or rapal [incantation] going with that jimat and perhaps some ceremonies on a certain day—e.g., Jumungah-Legi—to which he had to pay strict attention. (1879: 231)[43]

In this extraordinary paragraph, Poensen uncovers the emptiness in which the thief places his trust. Removed from its owner, taken from its hidden place tucked into his (implicitly unwashed) hair, a small greasy rag gives way to yet another grimy scrap containing literal dirt, with a fragment of metal. Having broken down the thing itself, Poensen proceeds to unravel the collective that made it, plunging us first into a domain of contested claims and then into fairyland (the dark forest, mystery, spirits), before concluding with incantations and (speculative) rites.

Poensen models for readers the attitude appropriate toward jimat. In iconoclastic prose, he accentuates the absurdity of attaching monetary or cultural value to so much junk: grubby rags, actual soil, a sliver of metal. Like his inventory of indiscriminate and bizarre items and his repeated reference to costs, his emphasis on uncleanliness, sure to appall bourgeois supporters of the NZG, invokes fetish discourse without ever using the term itself: according to Pietz, "the utter worthlessness of fetishes was often expressed through descriptions of their filthiness" (2022: 71).

While unique in its detail, Poensen's default translation of jimat and echoes of the fetish also color later contributions to Javanese ethnography, even as these supply welcome specifics. Unlike Poensen, Kreemer (1888), another NZG missionary (whom Poensen mentored), includes Javanese names and mentions specific functions. At the same time he presents jimat as a hodgepodge of curious and sometimes disagreeable stuff to which Javanese grant what he clearly considers implausible powers. While Kreemer ventures a tentative explanation of the wide range of items used ("[a]nything a bit strange or rare can serve as one"), he also enhances the impression of fanciful formation by noting some originate in a coincidence between name and a goal (1888: 349). Drawing on recent work on animism, he claims Javanese "think the jimat animated, and therefore attribute to them irresistible influence or outcome," before appending his assessment: "[i]t is a childish idea" (1888: 351).

Considerably less editorializing, but the usual gloss, characterizes Jan Knebel's article on "Javanese Amulets," which presents jimat, sympathetically, as forms of care for self and family (1898). Writing in the journal of the Batavian Society for Arts and Sciences, Knebel came to jimat from a professional concern with recording Java's material culture, as an employee (later director) of a new archaeological service. He offers his list (each with Javanese name, description, and purpose) with no commentary, but also with no organization, reiterating the sense of muddle.[44] Meijer, in the scholarly journal *Djawa* (Java), later rearranges Knebel's list taxonomically, into the Linnaean kingdoms, sorting his own jimat mug shots (see figures 2.1, 2.2, and 2.3) the same way: "stones" (mineral); bones and teeth from a wild boar (animal); a carved rhizome, a small pouch with unnamed seeds, and a piece of lemongrass (vegetable) (1935: 109–11).[45]

If all of these authors take the equivalence of jimat and amulet for granted, and spend no time explaining what an amulet entails, they are hardly alone. Amulets have inspired little conceptual elaboration, rarely generating the peripatetic insights called theory. They frequently pop up in this casual manner in accounts of practices temporally, experientially, or geographically distant from their authors. Knebel exemplifies another vein of scholarly work associated with them: the catalog of material culture.

What may be the most extensive body of work on amulets was authored by Walter Leo Hildburgh, a wealthy private collector and prominent folklorist; while covering much literal territory (not, however, the Indies), his publications remain purely descriptive.

But a different body of Indies scholarship does engage amulets conceptually, as a subtype of the fetish, even as it makes jimat themselves vanish. The founding text was a scholarly tome entitled *Animism among the Peoples of the Indies Archipelago*, by G. A. Wilken, Leiden's second professor in the history, literature, antiquities, institutions, manners, and customs of the Indies archipelago and the physical geography of the Indies archipelago. Born in Indonesia (his father was another NZG missionary, stationed in Minahasa, and his mother came from an old creole Ambonese family), he served as a colonial official in Ambon, Buru, various divisions of Sulawesi, and the west coast of Sumatra before taking up the Leiden appointment. Wilken belonged to the international community of newly professional ethnologists developing anthropology as a comparative, evolutionary science of the primitive; he aimed to locate the Indies in this discourse. Arguing that Tylor's concept of animism fit Indies practices, he divides it into two "dogmas": fetishism, based on the notion everything is alive, and spiritism, the idea that spirits or souls wander.

If Poensen never uses the word *fetish*, Wilken never mentions jimat. But Wilken's analysis of fetishism helps to clarify why the substance and multiplicity of jimat could be so easy to ignore. Particularly relevant are his treatment of the material world in his theory of the fetish, his explicit definition of amulets (with a brief introduction of magic), and the all-too-familiar temporality of such evolutionary ethnology.

Wilken picks up more of the historical concept of the fetish than Poensen evokes. In the fetish, he states, the spirit or soul is so seamlessly identified with the object that houses it that the object itself is "worshipped" as a living and powerful being (1885: 113–14). At the same time, his discussion presumes a remarkably broad understanding of fetishism:

> Indeed, the idea everything is alive makes every object a potential fetish, if one only in some way or another came to the conviction that the spirit that lives in that object is a powerful being or for whatever reason must be treated with respect. All the same, the nature of the object, its strangeness or rarity and, in connection with that, its value, are no indifferent matters. Schultze rightly also points out the valuing of objects in primitive society in his famous work about fetishism. Where

one moves in such a narrow world as the savage, where one knows so few objects and has so few representations, it is natural that one must assess the one—and here that is precisely the lower, the sensual—too high, the other—and here that is the higher, the spiritual—too low. As a child attaches great value to what an adult disparages, so the savage burns from fervent desire for what a civilized European views as not worthy of his attention and so the former commits an offense, a murder, to secure possession of things the latter carelessly throws away or the loss of which he hardly notices. The white arouses the savage's admiration. Why? For his high mental aptitude? No. For his hat or his shoes. For shabby attire with which he, the weary traveler, would be ashamed to appear in the streets of London or Paris or any civilized city. To be sure, this peculiarity of the savage offers sufficient explanation how various things of little importance could be objects of such veneration. . . . Both in nonliving as in living nature they find in that way a number of objects that are taken up as fetishes. (Wilken 1885: 114–15)

Wilken speaks of "objects," but the examples that follow indicate he means this in the broadest sense. Beginning with two groups of things he terms "products of art," the second of which are amulets, he moves to "natural objects" (rocks, mountains, bodies of water, plants, animals), embracing by the end the entire material world. Wilken's category of fetishism, in short, encompasses all matter. At the same time, matter (overvalued by "savages") is sensual: what prompts human desires and passions as well as objects of sensory perception. Wilken expresses an attitude both Protestant and Hegelian, rating matter lower than spirit, a position advanced in schemata of human history that placed "primitives" at the bottom of a hierarchy of understanding.[46] It also embeds a dualistic metaphysics in which not only are matter and spirit ontologically fundamental but matter is inert. Inherently, the scholar can identify animism, and presume belief in spirits and souls, by locating any deviance from modern ontology.

But amulets complicate this diagnosis:

As one of the most important expressions of fetishism among the people of the Indies Archipelago . . . we now have to pay attention to the generally occurring use of amulets. It is clear that as soon as belief is established that some object is animated by a powerful spirit gifted with supernatural power, that object will be used by him in whose hands it is found as a luck bringing and misfortune averting tool—in other words, as an amulet. Thus in the nature of things every amu-let, every safeguard, is a fetish [*fetis*]. This does not, however, appear equally clearly everywhere. In many cases the idea that the amulet contains a powerful spirit has entirely disappeared, and the object becomes nothing more than a simple magic charm [*tovermiddel*]. (Wilken 1885: 121)

As he treats spirits as fundamental to the fetish, and the amulet as a type of fetish, Wilken must claim that if "spirits" commonly appear unimport-ant to the workings of amulets, this must be a later development (the idea has "disappeared"). Because the fetish subsumes the amulet, materiality be-comes simultaneously crucial (the fetish must be an object) and irrelevant (since what ultimately matters is a spirit, at least in a presumed historical past). This is not, of course, to say he doesn't address the stuff from which some amulets are made. Most of his examples, though, which mainly come from places Wilken himself had lived, better fit his claim about spirits, consisting as they do of stuff such as human skulls, than jimat do. His ac-count of amulets does end with bezoars (Malay *mustika*), commonly used as jimat, and valued across the archipelago—and beyond.[47]

But at the same time, Wilken's account explains why glossing jimat as amulets draws attention away from specifics by reducing the function of such objects to either bringing good or averting bad fortune. While in keeping with European usages, such functions do not cover the range of concerns, and forms of action, that jimat address. He also introduces magic, through the word *tovermiddel*, *tover-* constituting a venerable Dutch morpheme for sorcery. Note the equation with which he ends: (potent) matter − spirit = magic charm. Wilken, in short, lays out the conceptual ma-chinery through which jimat have been processed into amulet, fetish, and magic. He brings into one frame the abstractions through which colonial encounters made jimat.

Subsequent to Wilken, as both professional and amateur ethnologists drew Indies phenomena further into discourse on primitives, jimat are at best relegated to footnotes, as merely another instance of Indies fetishism; more commonly, they receive no mention. This is even the case in Kruyt's rethinking of Indies animism, which pays much more attention to why In-donesians use some material objects (especially those that are hard, such as iron and stone, or odd, such as strangely shaped twigs) as "fetishes" rather than others (1906).[48] Most lift Wilken's examples of fetishes as well, focus-ing on items from the "outer possessions" rather than stuff familiar from

Java. Thus in the *Encyclopedia of the Netherlands Indies* (*Encyclopaedie van Netherlandsch-Indië*), jimat receive no mention under fetishism, which includes a discussion of amulets.[49]

Jimat reemerge, however, in the 1927 supplement to the *Encyclopaedie*, in the entry for magic (*magie*). A new category in Dutch ethnology, *magie* served as a generic slot for many practices (as animism and heathendism had previously). Its author, C. S., almost certainly was Claas Spat, one of the supplement's editors; the entry—and its brief remarks about jimat—bear signs of Spat's cluster of interests in Islam and Malay literature as well as in cosmopolitan (especially French) ethnology.[50] While referring readers to the discussion of amulets under fetishism, Spat revives jimat in relation to Islam, asserting the term refers especially to amulets inscribed with letters, words, or drawings used in Islamic mysticism (1927: 265). But he takes jimat beyond Java; his examples come from Aceh, where he notes that faith in jimat appears to decline as new strains of Islam rise in popularity—before adding a reminder about the dangers of jimat by referring to Garut.

Jimat's translations move relentlessly from material to immaterial, from concrete particulars to abstract classes. Translating jimat through amulet and fetish not only rendered them more similar to one another than they actually were, but enlisted them in building concepts whose specific and provincial origins became increasingly obscured—as jimat themselves came to be through such translations. Nietzsche noted that concepts are "formed by arbitrarily discarding . . . individual differences and by forgetting the distinguishing aspects" (1979 [1873]: 83). To this, I add Marx's astute observation that "general abstractions arise only in the midst of the richest possible concrete development, where one thing appears as common to many, to all. Then it ceases to be thinkable in a particular form alone" (Marx 1973: 104–5). Marx, of course, was concerned mainly with how under capitalism forms of work and hard-won skills, and the myriad ways individuals may use a commodity, become abstract labor and abstract value. Abstraction, though, is clearly relevant to jimat, objects of striking diversity.

The legal statutes already sum up the common denominator the Dutch extracted from encounters with jimat. The state captured a purported unity in the locution "pretense to supernatural power." Congealed in all jimat, this abstraction renders differences in their material properties, use values, and formation irrelevant. "Pretense" (a disposition) and "supernatural" (a metaphysical claim) replace them.

"Pretense," of course, belongs to one of the imaginary subjects addressed in chapter 1. As for "supernatural," a leitmotif in multiple diffractions of Indonesian practices through magic, no one bothers to explain it, as A. T. (1912–13) points out in his critique of the occult offenses ("Of course, the question arises: what exactly does the legislator understand by the concept 'supernatural'"?). Clearly, *super* implies excess, going beyond the bounds of what Europeans had come to call nature.[51] However obvious such concepts appear to be, "supernatural" was the outcome of historical processes of real-ing that produced that nature. To call something supernatural was to insist it diverged both from what authors took to be common sense and from what Science claimed to discover (rather than produce through experimental apparatuses). In short, this abstraction (k)notted jimat to the making of a particular reality, with a particular political imperative.

That imperative informs an article on fetishism in a popular periodical in the Netherlands, likely written in response to news about Garut. After deftly summarizing ethnological claims about primitive animism, its author underlines the temporality this concept embeds by casually noting that fetishism "is doomed to die out." With more solemnity, he adds, "We must believe [that] if we are serious about the social, intellectual, and moral elevation of the more than forty million Indonesians under our care" (Wiskerke 1919: 862), presenting a particular metaphysics as part of colonialism's civilizing mission.

Yet the same article also demonstrates how commensuration undermines such confidence. Like others—Noto Soeroto, the jurist A. T., even S. in the *Police Guide*—Wiskerke concedes that amulets also exist in Europe:

> Although we will not encounter many Animists in our West European society, we nonetheless still have not so outgrown our own state of nature; here too we still find many amulet carriers, although with many it may be more a freak of fashion than a positive belief in protective properties. Think, for example, of the amulets of many motorists, pilots, and such. But there are nonetheless among us those who still really believe that a horse's tooth in the pocket is a prophylactic against toothache, a sweet chestnut against rheumatism, and also among the "tommies" and the "poilus" in the trenches there were [those] who wore an amulet to protect themselves against the deadly lead of the "Feldgrauen." (1919: 856–57)

Yet even as he points to attitudes ("still believe") and objects (a horse's tooth as mass-produced automobiles began to appear on public roads) that recall Tylor's "survivals" of practices properly past, many of his examples speak to new spheres of action. Carried by motorists, pilots, as well as soldiers in the terrifying combat of the Great War, amulets make innovative attachments at frontiers of risk.

A short story set in the Malay Archipelago offers further insight into amulets in European life, while imbricating them into relations of friendship rather than dominance. In "Karain: A Memory," Joseph Conrad, who knew the region well, centers on ties between British gunrunners (who greatly annoyed Dutch authorities) and a Bugis leader (Karain is a distortion of the aristocratic Buginese title *Karaeng*) in Mindanao, a region not yet under colonial control, at the turn of the twentieth century. After the death of an elderly retainer, Karain comes out to their ship under cover of night to beg his British friends for help. Like so many Conradian characters, he is haunted, in this case literally, by a friend he once betrayed. Or rather he *had* been haunted until he met the old man, a Haji just back from Mecca, who had warded off the ghost. Now again tormented, he finds respite only in the company of his English comrades, whose "unbelief" keeps the ghost at bay. He asks them to take him to England—or, barring that, to give him a charm.

That is precisely, after some thought, what one of the Englishmen provides. He steps inside for a small box containing a girl's portrait, a glove, a packet of letters, and dried flowers. Conrad comments: "Amulets of white men! Charms and talismans! Charms that keep them straight, that drive them crooked, that have the power to make a young man sigh, an old man smile. Potent things that procure dreams of joy, thoughts of regret; that soften hard hearts, and can temper a soft one to the hardness of steel. Gifts of heaven—things of earth" (1977 [1898]: 50).

The first thing he removes from the box, however, is a gilded Jubilee sixpence, perforated near one edge. He tells the other Englishmen: "The thing itself is of great power—money you know," and then Karain: "'This is the image of the Great Queen, and the most powerful thing the white men know.'" Turning again to his countrymen, he elaborates: "'She commands a spirit, too—the spirit of her nation'" (1977 [1898]: 51). Since some of Karain's (Muslim) followers might take amiss a human image, he amplifies his gift's value with something he holds dear. Taking the glove from his box, he cuts a piece from the palm, wraps the coin in it, sews it up, and adds a ribbon so Karain can drape it around his neck. With that, Karain is restored, once again clothed "in the illusion of unavoidable success" (1977 [1898]: 53).

In the mnemonics of white men's amulets (the Jubilee sixpence and personal keepsake), Conrad not only takes commensuration further but flashes on precisely those bourgeois structures of feeling that sent Marx and Freud scurrying to the concept of the fetish. The materials for Karain's amulet derive from the entwined domains of market and state (money and the queen) as well as sexual attachment (the glove, metonym of the beloved).[52] While Marx and Freud take no less critical a position on the fetish than those who invented it—both occupying analytically "the impossible home of a man without fetishes" (Pietz 2022: 16)—they do shake up the purification machine that divides the West from the Rest (Latour 1993).

These reversed commensurations recall Wilken's strange claim that "savages" overvalue material objects because they have so few. What, then, to make of the loving regard for the ever-accumulating objects of bourgeois life—vases, bowls, weapons, fruit, the drape of cloth—in the paintings of Dutch masters? What should we make of the commodities extracted from the labor of colonial subjects for the insatiable world market, not to mention guns and money—or, to point to the next chapter, a growing regard for certain Indonesian artifacts? To echo Soetatmo (and Edward Albee), who's afraid of white clothing, keris, and jimat?

Instauring Jimat

Colonial translations and the reality they support have become common sense even for Indonesian intellectuals, shaping, as already seen, their comments about jimat: recall Soetatmo's description of jimat as "symbols" or Sartono's characterization of Javanese peasant movements as "fetishist"; Sartono, moreover, refers to their "magical elements (belief in charms, amulets, and so forth)" (1972: 79). That colonial understandings of jimat were partly *shaped* by Indonesian reports and acts is less obvious. But consider: European officials would never have recognized jimat on their own.[53] Nor did they occupy the front line when it came to rebels, thieves, or witnesses; search houses for stashes of jimat; or frequent places jimat might be sold or dispensed. Without Javanese and Sundanese soldiers, police, court officers, and civil servants to point them out and explain their possible relevance, jimat would have remained invisible. Moreover, some acted in ways that Europeans could interpret as congruent with their views. Recall Kuslan, the thief whose arrest Meijer learned about from the former assistant resident of Magetan. The latter told him that a Javanese official had convinced Kuslan to plead guilty by neutralizing "the magical force of his gold leaf kris hilt by urinating on it in front of Kuslan" (1935: 122), an iconoclastic act.

Yet these interlocutors also constitute a source of uncertainty. In identifying jimat, they went only so far. Perhaps they did not know enough to match particular things to aimed-for effects. They also may have possessed their own. If jimat could be found in every Javanese household, they might also have been carried, unseen or unnoticed, on the bodies of men employed by the colonial state.

My own sense of jimat has been mediated by Balinese interlocutors. During fieldwork many years ago, jimat came up conversationally, though people generally mentioned them anecdotally, mainly naming types. Given that we were talking about colonial wars, they spoke of kinds that would have worried Dutch officials: *sasikepan*, armor or armament, that could confer invulnerability or make skin impenetrable.[54] I learned a bit about other jimat experientially. I initially didn't recognize the cabochons set in rings—some people I knew wore rings on virtually every finger—as jimat. This changed after my Balinese father had me purchase one for myself from a peddler who stopped by occasionally to show off his wares. He insisted I bring it to a Brahmana priest we particularly respected to see if he was right about what it could do. (According to the priest, he wasn't; but, after telling us what it actually was he informed me it would help me achieve a difficult goal.) Before I had it set, my father instructed me about which hand and finger I should plan to wear it on. As I started to ask about gems and stones, it slowly dawned on me that much (all?) Indonesian jewelry in museum collections—not only rings, but neckpieces, earrings, and arm- and legbands—were not merely decorative but actually jimat.

What I learned from this is that jimat may be hidden to those who lack relevant knowledge, acquired in a number of ways. A genre of Balinese texts called Carcan address particular types of things or creatures that can impart particular abilities or qualities. Carcan Mirah, for example, concern gems and stones, listing names, describing appearances, and briefly explaining what each does.[55] But to describe multicolored semiprecious gems in a way that would permit identification is no easy matter. Hence my father's deferral to the expertise of the older and more experienced priest. And texts also diverge.

I absorbed enough to find myself dissatisfied by the way *amulet*, for all that it usefully highlights size and portability, flattens what jimat do to securing protection or luck. As I discovered before purchasing a second cabochon, many offer the power to attract. To draw others to one's person or words forms a key social capacity, as relevant to writing, teaching, politics, practicing law, selling goods, performing, and making art as to erotic love.[56] That objects bestow an ability to entice others is hardly foreign to the world capitalists make.

These small lessons begin to move beyond habitual translations and the reality they craft. For the jimat is a curious thing: on the one hand, it belongs ineluctably to everyday relations and desires, to the mundane aspirations of ordinary life. On the other, it is a product of practices involving expertise. In this, it resembles a host of common technologies. And that is my first proposal: jimat are tiny technologies that extend capacities in particular domains of experience and practice. More specifically, they are prosthetic devices. Like familiar protheses such as eyeglasses and smartphones, they produce cyborgs with augmented abilities.[57]

Calling jimat technologies (and comparing them to prostheses and commodities) yields different diffraction patterns than amulets or fetishes do. It aligns them to different literatures, counters their dematerialization, and makes them less exotic. Among the useful concepts emerging from science and technology studies' attention to technologies—and *practices*—Latour's attention to what he calls nonhumans as part of a symmetrical anthropology is particularly instructive.[58] Latour argues persuasively that humans always are accompanied by nonhumans; enlisting nonhumans has allowed human societies to become larger and more durable than those of other animals (1993, 2005b). More controversial is his famous insistence that nonhumans act. For moderns, purpose and intention differentiate agents from mechanical causes and are properly solely the property of human subjects, acting in and on a world of passive objects that serve as both resources for appropriation and blank canvasses for projected meanings. Latour's assertion not only challenges this, but, by interrogating such concepts of humanity and nature, threatens the divide elaborated by ethnologists such as Wilken between white men of reason and those they ruled. The outrage and accusations—including fetishist—that Latour's claim has aroused underline the inheritance of such distinctions. For Latour, though, acting has nothing to do with intention; to act is to "modify a state of affairs" (2005b: 71). Thus technologies, documents, deities, skyscrapers, animals, trees, rocks, and microorganisms act, participating in a world's eventful emergence. Any of them may "authorize, allow, afford, encourage, permit, suggest, influence, block, render possible, forbid, and so on" (2005b: 72)— verbs that certainly apply to jimat.

Latour's insistence on nonhuman actors, however, does not yet address the matter of matter, sidelined in colonial texts that highlight what jimat mean. Jimat raise questions about the hegemonic concepts of nature and matter that moderns have inherited, concepts originating in experimental, "experiential, epistemological, and political operations" that bifurcated nature (Debaise 2017: 3). But if the materiality of jimat is crucial to Indonesians, it does not exist in itself, any more than abstracted meanings do. To focus on matter rather than meaning might invert colonial (and dominant social science) practice, but would retain as given the dichotomy embedded in nature's bifurcation. Attending to practices and processes opens other paths. Highlighting doings rather than beings also brings into focus what habit obscures. Not only do the concepts through which jurists and scholars diffracted jimat render their substance largely of anecdotal interest; they also elide the specificity of engagements, the range of procedures, even the acts of experimentation through which jimat come to exist and operate.

Barad's felicitous concept of intra-action challenges all presumption of "individually determinate entities with inherent properties" (2007: 138), including human and nonhuman: "[I]n contrast to the usual 'interaction,' which assumes that there are separate individual agencies that precede their interaction, the notion of intra-action recognizes that distinct agencies do not precede, but rather emerge through, their intra-action" (Barad 2007: 33). Entanglements are everything, even when it comes to materiality. Matter itself is a product of intra-action, "substance in its intra-active becoming—not a thing but a doing, a congealing of agency" (2007: 151), "the sedimenting historiality of practices/agencies" (2007: 180). For Barad, a contrast between materiality and meaning should not, in short, be taken for granted.

Intra-action intervenes, however, at a singularly abstract level. I find more ethnographic purchase in what I take from Souriau's concept of instauration (2015), which offers a way to think about the intra-actions through which jimat come to exist, at least as presented through his apparently simple example of a sculptor or potter facing a lump of clay.[59] For Stengers and Latour (2015), instauration reworks both the concept of creation (the artist or divinity who produces something out of nothing) and the concept of construction (a metaphor long deployed in anthropology—and in accounts, such as Latour's, of the making of facts). Making a pot or statue not only involves two actors, but transforms both sculptor and clay. The statue or pot does not begin as a fully formed intention in a human mind before her hands or chisel or wheel touch the clay. It slowly comes into being through a series of small intra-actions between potter and clay.

Colonial accounts that see jimat as junk made by fanatics and frauds who activate absurd beliefs through the blind faith they inspire pay little heed to such processes.[60] To bring a jimat into existence goes well beyond the contingent encounter highlighted in theories of the fetish, or the observation that jimat may be made of anything strange or rare. The stuff of which jimat are made certainly reveals an alertness to singularities, a form of attention reminiscent of those once informing European cabinets of curiosity or at work in scientific practices such as Barbara McClintock's "feeling for the organism" (Keller 1983). Consider Bubandt's collector of stones thrown by East Java's mud volcano, small things once secreted in the earth. Quite a number of jimat are made of formerly hidden stuff, not only from the earth (precious or semiprecious gems; metals) or sea (corals), but also from living bodies, in the form of enteroliths. These include mustika (bezoars), stone-like formations of undigested material in animal stomachs or intestines; formed through different processes, enteroliths also are found in plants. Certainly instauring jimat entails attention to matter; borrowing from Haraway, it requires response-ability, an ability to respond. But the practices that bring jimat into lively existence do not assume an inert material world or one already composed. Nor do all jimat start from what Euro-Americans take such a world to be. Some jimat involve inscriptions of words, syllables, and/or drawings, but what is inscribed is itself a constituent element of the world rather than a representation of it.[61]

Instauration hardly ends with the selection of a bit of matter. Every additional small act involves a gradual alignment, whether the potential jimat begins as an enterolith, a tree, or an inscription. To discover—or better, recognize, as my Balinese father did in a tray of stones—something that could become a jimat requires knowledge, which involves both intellectual (reading and interpreting) and bodily (meditation, fasting, going without sleep) practices. Jimat that contain inscriptions (of syllables, words, drawings) demand specialized skills.[62] Nor does instauration end when a jimat is worn or carried; it continues through effects on its possessors. Reflecting on my own experience, whenever I happened to notice the stones in my rings, they triggered a manner of feeling, rejiggering perception and affecting my acts. In short, practices make jimat, and with jimat make people, relations, and a world. Jimat galvanize new subjects and things into existence and alter situations, contributing to doings that build a world.

The Case of the Vanishing Jimat

Writing about objects and empire, W. J. T. Mitchell asked, "What kinds of objects do empires produce, depend on, and desire? What kinds of objects do they abhor and attempt to destroy or neutralize?. . . What are the objectives of these objects, their role in constituting forms of objectivity and object lessons?" (2005: 146). This chapter has addressed one kind of object Dutch colonial officials abhorred and tried to neutralize. Arguably, in some ways they also produced and desired jimat, to fix concerns over violations of their peace and order. To address these, I have tracked their emergence as an object of colonial concern, the "object lessons" they prompted Dutch pundits to teach, and the "forms of objectivity" they elicited in Dutch scholarship. This meant following how abstractions and commensurations rendered the things themselves, and the processes that produced them, virtually invisible. In the end, the very notion of "object" is inadequate to the transactions with jimat, whether Indonesian or Dutch, that enact worlds.

For as much as Dutch accounts of jimat dismiss their efficacy, their position in colonial law, including their capacity to remake "universal" legal codes, reveals the opposite—that they helped to build colonizer realities. Not only Indonesians, but Dutch authorities make things with jimat: insurgents, burglars, and perjurers; fetishes and amulets; nature and supernature; matter and spirit; Europe and the Indies; European and "native"— and magic.

For if jimat continue to be glossed as *amulets* with little attention to what that entails, their association with magic also has become stronger over time. Academics use such language freely: recall Sartono as well as the comments by Bubandt with which I started. That translation also may be found at another site that has popped up throughout this chapter: museums.[63] In the fall of 2006, a kind curator at the Tropen Museum took me to the storage area to show me their vast collection of keris. My eye suddenly was caught by a chest-high cabinet labeled *magie*. "What's in there?" I asked. My colleague graciously obliged me by pulling open the narrow drawers. Inside we found myriad small objects, some wrapped, others not, none of them at all prepossessing in appearance. They were, of course, jimat.

INTERLUDE 3 ⌄⌄ COORDINATING DEVICES

Practices of "drawing things together" form a foundational focus of science studies. Such acts make it possible to sort, generalize, and compare an infinite number of discrete observations. At their most potent, they yield artifacts such as the charts, figures, and maps that Latour famously termed "immutable mobiles" (1990) and the standards experts deploy to "sort things out" (Bowker and Star 1999). What Mol (2002) calls coordination is a quotidian version, in which the judgment "same" herds messy multiples into one corral for specific purposes. Coordination brings together locally generated inscriptions, each already interpreted in relation to potentially unstated criteria.[1]

No stabilized standards exist for the category "magic." It commonly moves in the domain of unarticulated assessments and tacit judgments. Every conversation and text that attaches magic and related terms to a particular event, statement, or artifact brings it into being. But there were (and are) coordinating devices that pull these together. Such devices made (and make) magic appear to transcend time and space. Among the relevant spaces for coordination in nineteenth-century Britain I touch on three interwoven ones: the *Encyclopaedia Britannica*, the guidebook *Notes and Queries on Anthropology*, and the Pitt Rivers Museum at Oxford.

Encyclopedias are quintessential Enlightenment projects. Presenting themselves as summarizing compendia of knowledge, encyclopedia entries turned a host of people, places, practices, things, and ideas into mundane markers that could be taken up without controversy. Following entries for magic in the *Encyclopaedia Britannica* over time reveals how magic was transformed from a provincial concept to one that purportedly traversed time and space. What made that metamorphosis possible was the birth of professional ethnology and the expansion of colonial relations. The key figure was a man central to the networks through which ethnology coalesced in Victorian Britain: Edward Burnett Tylor.

Until the ninth edition of the *Britannica*—known as the scholars' edition because of those its editors tapped to write entries—magic did not travel very far. In earlier editions it belongs within the boundaries of what the encyclopedia's authors, editors, and readers considered heritage. Magic not only is geographically local, but its history is lineal, traced to those whom educated Europeans treated as civilizational antecedents and ancestors. All take Greek, Roman, and biblical texts as essential sources, mention the magi, and recall the prosecution of witches. Vague gestures situate magic in fuzzy elsewheres: initially, in European peripheries.

The terse first edition devotes a mere paragraph to magic, noting that while originally it referred to "sublime" knowledge, it came to index an "unlawful" science involving the aid of the devil and the dead (1768–71: vol. 3, 3). The second edition promotes magic to two pages (1780: vol. 6, 4369–70), claiming "ignorant and barbarous" people are suspected of it, including "foreigners": to wit, Laplanders and Icelanders. With the third edition, in six double-columned pages repeated verbatim in the fourth through sixth editions (as well as transatlantically, in the United States), magic begins to move (1788–97: vol. 10, 413–19). While still focused on people, places, and incidents known from the Bible and Greek and Roman sources, it travels beyond such familiar territory, even setting up a continental divide: "magic at all times prevailed among Asians and Africans more than among the Europeans," "an undoubted fact" the entry attributes to the frequency of human sacrifices and the presence of venomous snakes and poisons in such locations (1797: vol. 10, 418). Travelers aid its journeys, attesting that "Indians and Africans . . . perform feats they can't explain." But European witches and their travails still appear, as do Lapland and Iceland. So matters stand until the seventh edition, when magic contracts again to two pages; in the eighth it vanishes altogether.

A radical break occurs in 1883, when Tylor was tapped.[2] Tylor's entry makes magic a universal for the first time, stamping "same" across reports of diverse acts and actors spread over geographic space, while yoking them to confident assertions about human types and history.[3] While he includes considerable material on the ancient world known from the Bible and Greek and Roman sources, magic does not start with Persian magi but forms a feature of human antiquity more broadly. Drawing on accounts of the people coming to be known as primitive, he begins with those considered closest to humanity's origins: Australia's "wild savages [sic]." He follows with "low races" in the Pacific, the Americas, and Africa. Only then does he turn to "the cultured nations of Antiquity," with Egypt and Babylon as the birthplaces of "the higher branches of occult sciences," and on to European ancestors and Europe's familiar others: Greece, Rome, the European Middle Ages, as well as Jews and Muslims. From monotheists he segues to Asia (India, Tibet, China), before addressing the witch trials, the fall of magic (caused, he asserts, by the rise of science), and the demise of "occult sciences" among the educated and civilized.

But Tylor does not only situate magic in a radically expanded history and geography; he also defines and assesses it. That definition differentiates magic from religion, a distinction difficult to make in the "lower stages" since practitioners everywhere call upon spiritual beings ("ghosts, demons or gods"). Insofar as magic involves such beings, it is animistic—hence religious. The residue, though, is purely magical: acts and thoughts based on bad reasoning, an association of ideas that takes ideal for real relations, mere analogy for actual causality (1883: vol. 15, 205).

Tylor proposed a similar demarcation nearly a decade earlier, in the first edition of *Notes and Queries on Anthropology* (subtitled *For the Use of Travelers and Residents in Uncivilized Lands*), a compilation of questions that British anthropologists hoped men on the spot might answer. Among his contributions are two pages on "Magic and Witchcraft," which start by explaining that magic involves two principles. Here the residual (not religious) remainder is described as "sympathetic and symbolic," "a misdevelopment of natural philosophy" (1874: 60).

Distinguishing magic from religion is classic (k)notting. But in the *Britannica* Tylor goes further right from the start, in the second paragraph: "The word magic is still used, as in the ancient world, to indicate a confused mass of beliefs and practices, hardly agreeing except in being beyond those ordinary actions of cause and effect which men accustomed to their regularity have come to regard as merely natural." Thus, all that connects this "confused mass of beliefs and practices" is that they exceed nature, in the form of causal relations. More remarkably, he adds: "The great characteristic of magic is its unreality" (1883: vol. 15, 199). Magic, then, is a tangle of (k)nots: not religious, not natural, and finally not real. No wonder he finds little use for it: "Looked at as a series of delusions, magic is distasteful to the modern mind, which, once satisfied of its practical futility is apt to discard it as fully unworthy of further notice" (1883: vol. 15, 204).[4] Even as he universalized, Tylor could only characterize magic by what it was not, leaving identification a situational practice marked by relations of power.

Both the *Britannica* and *Notes and Queries* drew practices together, the former in a narrative of human development and the latter through questions to be posed in "uncivilized" lands (questions presupposing not only fluency but a language ideology that treats speech as purely referential rather than dialogic and situational). Magic did not, however, play the same role in the third institution in which Tylor played a part. Tylor secured a position at Oxford through his friend Augustus Henry Lane Fox Pitt-Rivers, whose ethnological interests focused on material culture rather than, as Tylor's did, on thought. Pitt-Rivers amassed a large private collection of ethnographic and archaeological objects that he donated to Oxford on the stipulation that they build a museum to house his gift and hire someone (i.e., Tylor) to teach anthropology.

Pitt-Rivers, however, showed little interest in coordinating material culture through the concept of magic. His predilections for collection and display, as in the portions of *Notes and Queries* to which he contributed, centered on technologies—especially weaponry—which could reveal development over time. His vision of ethnology museums resembled Otis T. Mason's in the United States, where debate centered on whether (Native American) objects should be sorted by formal similarity and presumed function or by the groups that made and used them.[5] While Pitt-Rivers's collection included objects identified as "fetishes" and "amulets," these took too many forms to demonstrate progress or even easily identify as to function. Indeed, the range of items that could count as "fetishes" is evident in one of Tylor's queries, which includes as possibilities "images, pictures, odd stones, or bits of wood, claws, seeds and other things" (1874: 60). Today, however, a search for "magic" in the online database of Pitt-Rivers's collections yields 192 artifacts.[6]

The contingency of coordination also is evident from the fact that Tylor's entry for magic was not used in later editions of the *Britannica*. Northcote W. Thomas, a quirky and much less famous former government anthropologist in colonial Nigeria, who authored the entry in the eleventh edition, treats Tylor as one of (by then) many proposing theories of magic.[7]

Announcing "[t]here is no general agreement as to the proper definition of 'magic,'" he adds that it all "depends on the view taken of 'religion'" (1911: vol. 17, 304). More striking to me is that he proposes attending to distinctions societies themselves draw, warns against relying on a concept "made for a very different age and culture," and observes that "our terminology is influenced by the prepossession of alien observers whose accounts cannot be assumed to correspond to the native view" (1911: vol. 17, 306).

A visitor to the Indonesia Room of Leiden's National Museum of Ethnology in 2006 would have found herself almost immediately confronted by the words "Magical Powers" emblazoned in large letters in a sleek, contemporary font across the glass fronts of several display cases. The cases contained keris, several with the undulating serpentine blades for which such weapons are famous. Artfully staged against neutral gray cloth, they were spaced and lit to highlight their gold- and gem-encrusted hilts and sheaths and the gold figurine reliefs running up the spines or at the bases of several blades. A caption introduced the display: "The world of the kris, a two-sided dagger, is full of magic. Krisses can summon the forces responsible for love and sorrow. A good kris is made of various metals. The meteorite iron contained in it established the [*sic*] relation with the cosmos. . . ." [1]

As if not sufficiently enticing, another caption revealed "powers" to be a double entendre: these keris had once belonged to rulers on the islands of Java, Bali, and Sulawesi: "All of his sacred heirlooms, pusaka, are outward signs of a prince's power. Weapons are usually part of the pusaka, with the kris as most important of these. They are mystical objects." While not explaining how these "signs of power" ended up in a Dutch museum, the label for one keris indicated one of the more innocuous paths they might take: "By its nature, a kris belongs to the most important gifts that a king can give. The Dutch royal house possessed various kris, presented by Indonesian kings." Magical powers! Sacred, mystical objects! Kings! Heirlooms! Cosmic meteorites! How could anyone not be enthralled?

Visitors no longer can see this display. The cooler heads of curators prevailed over its designers in the Communication Department.[2] The latter, though, had deployed associations already firmly embedded in the imaginations not only of many Dutch museumgoers but also others—aficionados of edged weapons or Southeast Asia—familiar with keris. At the same time, it surely piqued the interest of novices previously exposed to magical weapons through film or fantasy fiction.

I lead with this defunct exhibit for two reasons: because it featured keris linked to Indonesian rulers and because it used "Magical Powers" to cast its own seductive spell. That phrase does more than weave another Indonesian practice into magic's expanding web. It was in relation to keris crucial to a precolonial dynasty that I first heard Balinese interlocutors speak of *sakti*, the term routinely translated as *magical power* that launched me on this book. (It was also because of these objects that I found myself riveted at my first exposure to the work of Bruno Latour, in a lecture on the factish.) But it is not only because of its role in my own project that discovering this phrase plastered across a display of keris caught my eye. It also marked a remarkable change in the use and effects of these words, a change traceable to practices of empire.

When such keris first became attached to "magical powers," the phrase bore a different valence than it does now, one directly relevant to explaining how some of Indonesia's most famous keris ended up in museums. For while Indonesian rulers bestowed the occasional keris on Dutch monarchs, others found their way to museums as spoils of colonial wars. Then too commentators yoked keris to "magical powers." But at that time the words did not evoke pleasurable wonder—or rather they produced a different pleasurable wonder, turning what Indonesians said of these objects into ludicrous beliefs. If magical powers now fascinate, the phrase once belonged to the arsenal of conquest. I have been arguing that "magical" sorted subjects into rational/modern or irrational/premodern based on acceptance of divisions between body and soul, matter and spirit—or subjects and objects themselves. But it matters that the noun to which that modifier was attached is *powers*. For the situations eliciting the phrase included the brute force of war and the victor's subsequent disposal of people and things.

Less magnificent keris already have appeared in passing: as perceived threats in the hands of Nang Mukanis and Haji Hasan's followers, as the shape of a small rock, and among a thief's treasured jimat. Although this chapter will address keris in general, it highlights those forming vital members of precolonial polities. While not all of the objects making up those collectives were keris—or even weapons—they contributed to many.

"Collective" indicates one of many ways keris differ from jimat, though for Dutch authorities both were fetishes, material objects to which Indonesians attributed outlandish capacities. Yet both discursively and practically their treatment diverged. One reason for those divergences is the different role keris play in Indonesian lives. Jimat are individual concerns; keris, commonly inherited, carry a collective with them. In the case of keris inherited in dynastic lines, these differences become even more pronounced, not only on both sides of the colonial encounter but in its aftereffects. This erstwhile exhibit manifests one marked contrast. Unlike the lowly and visually unappealing jimat, Dutch museums are replete with keris, both on display and in storage, as are private collections. While jimat rarely receive scholarly or public attention, the opposite has been true of keris, about which "thousands upon thousands of pages" have been written since the mid-nineteenth century alone, and they attracted the (anecdotal) attention of travelers and collectors well before they became objects of study (Van Duuren 2002: 7–8).[3] Colonial authors also, through the phrase that caught my eye, attached keris to magic much earlier. A further difference involves semiotic translation: if jimat disappear into the category of amulet, the word *kris* enters European languages, and efforts to commensurate remain unsettled. In short, keris and jimat followed significantly different political, cultural, and ontological trajectories.

I mark one of those differences by calling keris *things*. Like jimat, in the one-world world keris are objects—and European practices treat keris as (or aimed to make them) such. But also, as jimat did, they operated not only for Balinese but for the Dutch as well as actors. Unlike jimat, though, they constituted what Latour, drawing on that word's etymology, calls "things": gatherings that "bring together mortals and gods, humans and nonhumans" (2005a: 23). In that capacity, they contribute to shaping collectives in ways jimat do not. The ones of particular interest to me do so as singular individuals.

This chapter constitutes what I call a resography, from *res*, Latin for thing: an analytic narrative following the trail of a particular thing—in this case, particular keris. It tackles the policies and politics through which keris in general became fastened to magic through an account of the expropriation of specific famed and named heirloom keris following the conquest of Klungkung, Bali's oldest (and arguably paramount) polity. Contemporary comments in newspapers and official correspondence begin the process of affixing these keris to magical powers. Tracking things of this kind into scholarly literatures, museums, and markets, however, shows how associations with magic rebounded in unanticipated ways, producing novel fusions instead of sharp binaries. If modifying *powers* with *magical* may bracket their reality, in relation to keris disenchanting projects amplified enchantment. Rather than defanging their powers, such projects generated new collectives (and actual collectors), adding to the value keris accrued across worlds. Indeed, keris provide a potent introduction to ways magic journeyed back from the Indies to the Netherlands (further pursued in chapters 4 and 5)—even as new practices and modes of circulation reconfigured their capacities in the nation-state of Indonesia.

Latour once presented moderns as tricksters: with one hand they purify by creating sharp boundaries; with the other they proliferate connections. Skilled prestidigitators, they direct all attention to their critical, analytic prowess, diverting it from the suturing accompanying such acts (1993: 10–12). Purification shaped what happened as Klungkung's keris found themselves translated through familiar assessments of native credulity. But these translations worked in part by suppressing commonalities between Indonesian and European practices, even as the movement of these and similar objects amplified connections.

Keris in the Work of Empire

On April 18, 1908, the Déwa Agung, ruler of Klungkung, died in a hail of Dutch bullets at the main crossroads just outside of the Puri Agung, where he lived with his wives, children, and a small town of retainers. In his hands he carried only a keris, though it is impossible to say for certain which. Perhaps it was I Durga Dingkul. Gajah Mada, prime minister of the Majapahit Empire in the fourteenth century, gave that keris to the Déwa Agung's ancestor Sri Kresna Kapakisan when he sent him to rule the newly conquered island. According to stories, when unsheathed I Durga Dingkul paralyzed those in its path. But perhaps it was one of his other potent keris. The Déwa Agung and those who followed him to the crossroads had resolved on a *puputan*, a fight to the death against the combined human and nonhuman forces of the colonial army (hereafter KNIL, short for Koninklijk Nederlands-Indisch Leger, the Royal Netherlands Indies Army). They had prepared themselves and their keris and lance tips by making offerings and using holy water to clear a conduit to ancestors and other more-than-human forces at the Puri's shrines, and by dressing in white.[4] Over one hundred members of Klungkung's ruling class were killed alongside the Déwa Agung. Another sixty were wounded, including his ten-year-old nephew, whose knee was shattered.[5]

This was the not the first time the KNIL had faced a puputan by Balinese ruling classes. In September 1906 two rulers in Badung, to the south, had made the same choice. The news had aroused so much controversy in the Netherlands that the bellicose governor-general reluctantly was forced to make peace with Klungkung at that time rather than complete Bali's "pacification."[6]

While the KNIL, formed in 1814 (and dissolved in 1950, after the Netherlands finally recognized Indonesia's independence), had long engaged in combat against archipelago polities, a stream of wars followed adoption of the Ethical Policy. According to the policy's proponents, repaying the Netherlands' debt to the people of the Indies required spreading the benefits of enlightened European governance to those suffering under the despotism of indigenous rulers. Conflicts once settled diplomatically now led to ultimatums: either sign a short declaration acknowledging Dutch sovereignty or be conquered. This policy had an additional virtue: by cementing control across the archipelago, it forestalled potential competition from the British—or from upstart empires such as Japan, whose success in the Russo-Japanese war had impressed some Indonesians as evidence Asians could prevail over Europeans. By the close of the First World War, the Netherlands Indies stretched from Sumatra to western New Guinea, the territorial boundaries of what is now Indonesia.

Bali's incorporation began in 1849. It took three military expeditions—including an attack on Klungkung during which the Dutch commander, General Michiels (we will meet him again in chapter 5), was killed—to subdue two realms in the north. In the lead-up to the Ethical Policy, complaints to the Dutch by the Sasak subjects of the Balinese rulers of Lombok, the island to Bali's east, led to war. Following Lombok's conquest, the Balinese rulers of Karangasem and Gianyar voluntarily ceded their realms in exchange for retaining some power as regents (*stedehouder*). Tabanan's ruler surrendered after Badung's fall and killed himself while awaiting exile. With the conquest of Klungkung and the capitulation of Bangli, all of Bali came under colonial rule.

Battle over, the commander gave orders to secure weapons and valuables. Survivors surrendered their keris and lances while others were taken from the bodies of the dead and the Puri was ransacked for additional goods. A month later, Bali's resident, George Francis de Bruyn Kops, shipped some five hundred artifacts to the governor-general. Described as "preciosa," they consisted of items made of gold, silver, and gems, and included twelve keris of particular importance. When the shipment arrived in Batavia, De Bruyn Kops was asked to settle two questions: Did all of the objects sent qualify as legal booty? Should any be returned to the deceased ruler's family?[7]

According to a recent decree, only certain items could be taken as spoils of war (*krijgsbuit*): objects belonging to rulers in their capacity as such, matériel (excluding ornamental weapons), and items abandoned on the field of battle.[8] The decree addressed the still unsettled issue of the fate of objects seized during war by insisting on the (European) principle of the inviolability of private property. De Bruyn Kops replied that everything fit these new stipulations. For example, while the gold-handled keris certainly were ornamental, they qualified as weapons because they had been carried into battle. A shield and many of the lances were royal insignia as they always were borne before the Déwa Agung when he processed outside his Puri. As for the valuables found inside Puri walls, it depended on whether or not they belonged to the Déwa Agung as ruler or person.

His assessment was blunt: "it is a matter of common knowledge" that in native states no distinction existed between a ruler's personal possessions and state coffers. The ruler had a right to all the income his realm produced, to dispose of it as he wished. While an enlightened ruler would prioritize his subjects' well-being, Balinese monarchs considered solely their own pleasure. (Here De Bruyn Kops reiterates the justification for the spate of "pacifications" the Ethical Policy set into motion.) They used their wealth to build palaces and temples, to commission gold and silver objects, and to buy textiles. This explained why so many objects made of precious metals and gems could be found in their residences. Yet the ruler was not, for all that, a private individual. His possessions belonged to his office; on his death they passed entirely to his successor.

Although two of the Déwa Agung's half-brothers still lived, according to "Balinese custom" they were entitled to nothing. In war, a familiar principle prevailed: to the victor belong the spoils. Hence the Netherlands Indies government constituted the sole rightful claimant to the estate. Moreover, as the government had exiled all of the Déwa Agung's surviving high-ranking kin to Lombok, they would have no use for such items and inevitably would have to sell them for far less than they were worth.[9] It would be far better for the government to sell all objects with "no special ethnographic, antiquarian, or artistic value," and use the proceeds to indemnify state coffers for the expense of pacification and, should anything remain, cover the costs of maintaining the exiles.

Thus satisfied, the governor-general proceeded to divide the booty into three groups. He ordered 123 "less valuable" articles (mainly made of silver) to be put up for sale in Batavia. Some 135 items, including sixteen keris (several described as "very expensive"), were donated to the Batavian Society of Arts and Sciences. Four boxes containing 225 artifacts were shipped to the Ministry of Colonies in The Hague for dispersal to the Rijks Ethnografisch Museum in Leiden, the Koloniaal Museum in Haarlem, and the Prins Hendrik Museum in Rotterdam. The Batavian Society's directors had declined to make specific recommendations as they did not know what Dutch curators might want or need for their collections. Leiden ended up the main beneficiary, receiving ninety-seven items, including ten of the thirteen ceremonial keris (*staatsiekris*) in the shipment.[10]

Both the Batavian Society and Leiden's Museum formed major Dutch contributions to Enlightened knowledge projects. Founded in 1778, the former was the first learned society in Asia.[11] From the start, it served as a repository for material objects that aroused its members' curiosity, a colonial cabinet of wonders. During the British interregnum in 1811–16, Sir Thomas Stamford Raffles, lieutenant-governor of the Indies, made himself the society's president, in which capacity he pursued his interests in Hindu and Buddhist remains in Islamic Java—as well as in keris. When the Dutch government took control over the Indies, the Batavian Society's president came to be selected from members of the Council of the Indies, the governor-general's advisory board. The society sent collectors to accompany military expeditions, including the first Bali Expedition in 1846, when a Sanskritist working as an assistant librarian went along to gather manuscripts, inscriptions, and images. In 1862, the regime funded the building of a museum, completed in 1868, to house the society's growing collection of artifacts. As for Leiden, founded in 1837, it was the world's first museum (an institutional innovation that replaced cabinets of curiosity) dedicated to ethnographic objects (Avé 1980: 11).

Klungkung's booty, then, was inserted in knowledge projects and assessed in monetary terms. But not all loot had the same political significance, or invoked magic. Both were uniquely true of certain keris, whose "magical powers" figured in both news and official correspondence. The former reiterated in words the trial of strength just concluded through force of arms, by making familiar (though earlier by a decade) assertions about reality. The latter articulated these keris to the immediate political task of establishing control over a newly conquered region. Both knotted heirloom royal keris to the making of magic.

The magical powers of specific keris debuted three weeks after conquest in the colonial newspaper *De Locomotief*, the Ethical Policy's most fervent promoter:

> Among the keris of the Déwa Agung are also some that in the eyes of the Balinese possessed magical powers. To one is ascribed the power to cause earthquakes when the point is thrust into the ground; a second has the power to cause a person to immediately fall down to the earth dead if its tip was pointed at him. It is said that the Déwa Agung had this keris in his hand when he went to meet us, one knows with what result; the belief of the Balinese in magical force will be shaken in no slight measure. A third keris would make someone remain immobile in the position he had at the moment if spiral figures were described with it in the air.[12]

While the reporter casually states that "the eyes of the Balinese" see these keris as possessing magical powers, clearly it is his own that do. No attempt is made to justify that characterization: a description of what they can do suffices. Presumably his readers take it for granted that daggers cannot cause earthquakes, render people immobile, or kill if merely pointed. As in the editorial about Garut analyzed in chapter 2, a journalist underlines the fatal cost of such delusions, since the Déwa Agung, not the KNIL soldiers at whom he pointed his keris, was dead, an outcome that will shake Balinese "belief . . . in magical force." Such comments both exemplify and instruct readers in the attitudes proper to Europeans. And as in similar statements about dukun and jimat, he treats the reputed powers of the keris as something they should manifest in all circumstances. Like kindred articulations, such proclamations suited the Ethical Policy's modernizing mission, even as their iteration shows how such logic was worked out in specific situations. And as with similar predictions this too missed the mark.

The Déwa Agung's death by no means undermined Balinese convictions. Stories I heard in Klungkung attributed the keris's failure to colonial guile, abetted by treacherous (already colonized) Balinese.[13] As participants were preparing for battle, holy water arrived, purportedly from Bali's most important temple. But it was not, in fact, holy water: it was urine. Contact with it short-circuited the keris and cut people off from more-than-human allies. I once found such tales analytically interesting rationalizations; after reading about Kuslan and the training Dutch officials and officers received in ethnology, I find it plausible that colonial authorities and their local allies cooked up such a scheme.

De Locomotief's correspondent clearly had heard tales about Klungkung keris. Certainly the topic was in the air. His article appeared a week before De Bruyn Kops sent a letter about the booty he was shipping. That letter refers to the "magical powers" of twelve particular keris. An appendix lists their proper names and places of origin, with a brief gloss on their powers.[14] He includes the Malay original of the list, compiled with the help of survivors. While the Dutch text enumerates "magical powers," the Malay lists their *guna wasiyatnya*, their inherited uses. De Bruyn Kops substitutes an ontological judgment for what these keris did and their transmission over time.[15] He does not elaborate on the powers he labels *magical*; like the reporter, he likely assumed the list spoke for itself.[16] His language, however, ties the pertinent knot.

In his response to inquiries from Batavia, however, De Bruyn Kops complicates his assessment by linking the keris to the immediate situation. Highlighting the wobbliness of colonial authority in the just conquered territory to clarify why none should be returned to the late ruler's kin, he shifts adjectives: "Among them are several 'sacred' to which the people attribute the possession of supernatural powers. To bring these again into the possession of Balinese lords therefore would not be defensible."[17] *Magical* morphs into *supernatural* and *sacred*, at least for "the people." However defined, their powers made disposition of these keris politically consequential: in the right hands, they could rally opposition to Dutch rule. Political danger here centers not on generic jimat and unknown and unpredictable fanatics or frauds, but on specific objects, mobilized by rival authorities.

Although entangled, De Bruyn Kops and *De Locomotief* do Klungkung's keris differently. The reporter, who aims not only to inform but also entertain, sticks to *magical*; De Bruyn Kops hedges. Though all of his modifiers indicate these keris are not ordinary objects, some uncertainty appears judicious for an administrator about to exert control over new subjects. De Bruyn Kops neither shares the journalist's assurance that KNIL's victory will crush Balinese convictions, nor does he consider the keris potent in and of themselves. On the contrary: he embeds their threat in relations. Hence he advises amputation, severing them from the body politic by shipping them to Batavia, paralleling the exile of hazardous humans.

But there is more to the political significance of these keris than De Bruyn Kops states. His arguments appear contingent on a particular time and place. And they are, insofar as he is responding to a query from Batavia. Yet confiscation of things like these keris was not new, devised for this situation. It had become standard operating procedure. Orientalist L. W. C. van den Berg made this clear in a 1901 publication on Muslim rulers in the Indies.[18]

Van den Berg addressed what he considered a peculiar custom with no corollary elsewhere in the Islamic world: "To be regarded as the rightful King, one must be in the possession of certain objects, usually called in the Indies administrative language Rijkssieraden" (1901: 72), a kind of Excalibur principle. Rijkssieraden, literally realm ornaments, also functioned differently than the regalia of European monarchies: "These objects are not insignia, like, for example, the crown or scepter with us, which in some countries have a certain moral significance as historical objects, but which nonetheless any newly acting Prince could have made if need be" (1901: 72). Instead, they "are fetishes, which control the possession of the throne and the lot of the Realm" (1901: 73). As he rehearses at length, officials had discovered these objects constituted part of the formation and functioning of authority across the archipelago. Indeed, or so Van den Berg claimed, the objects, not the king, embodied that authority. Even if a ruler abdicated or was deposed, if he retained key rijkssieraden people would regard him as the legitimate sovereign. The colonial state had learned on multiple occasions (which he briefly recounts) that failure to secure these articles could obstruct its own exercise of power. Prudence, therefore, required all rijkssieraden be surrendered when archipelago rulers were subjugated militarily or voluntarily relinquished their autonomy (Van den Berg 1901: 76–77). Even in long-rebellious Aceh that policy had had a salutary effect: "The great power of the resistance of the population was, as a rule, broken with the Government's expropriation of the Rijkssieraden" (Van den Berg 1901: 77).

It is difficult to assess the accuracy of Van den Berg's analysis of how rijkssieraden functioned across the archipelago.[19] Since his focus is Islamic realms, it is striking that he ends by expressing uncertainty about whether Bali's "Hindu" rulers possessed such objects; on the basis of the Lombok treasure, he thought they might not (1901: 80). While Balinese royal keris did not work precisely in the way Van den Berg postulated, since taking office in 1906 De Bruyn Kops had learned enough to argue for their removal, though he does not refer to them as rijkssieraden.[20]

Collective Fetishes in the Work of Science

Keris incited little conceptual innovation in Dutch scholarship. The *Encyclopaedie*'s entry for "keris" directs readers to "weapons of the indigenous population," which offers a lengthy comparative discussion of their appearance across the archipelago in a subsection on pointed weapons.[21] Such descriptive accounts are by no means irrelevant to the subsequent fate of Klungkung's heirlooms, and I will return to them below. But they offer little insight into their growing association with concepts such as fetish and magic. Keris also make brief appearances, however, in entries for "rijkssieraden" as well as "pusaka" (heirlooms), both presented as types of fetish. And while not affiliated specifically with keris, the "magical power" of iron, the most important element of any keris, does receive ethnological attention.

Although Van den Berg's discussion covers much more of the archipelago, his claim that rijkssieraden are fetishes builds on Wilken. Wilken actually begins his account of fetishes that are "products of art" with them:

> Among the objects venerated as fetishes in this way, things they have gotten from their fathers as heirlooms, pusaka, assume a prominent place. Especially the royal pusaka—weapons, articles of clothing, etc., coming from ancient kings—summarized by the name rijkssieraden, to which a supernatural power is ascribed and that are considered and worshipped with sacred esteem. Undeniably this is connected with, is only to consider as an expression of, the service of the dead, mainly of renowned ancestors. . . . This reverence for the rijkssieraden plays a large role among the main groups of the Archipelago. (1885: 115)

This finishes Wilken's analysis. He proceeds to offer examples drawn from published sources.[22] Wilken highlights the vernacular terms for such collections (noting that several derive from words meaning "large or great," he suggests they are "signs of greatness"); what they consist of (all involve multiple objects, often including weapons, in many cases keris); and how they are treated (kept out of sight in special spaces, but brought out periodically to be washed and given offerings and incense, frequently by special functionaries).

His two analytic points suggest how rijkssieraden both resemble and differ from amulets. That Wilken, along with several of his sources, speaks of "supernatural power" recalls the jimat ordinances, as does the fact that he notes the weapons frequently confer invulnerability. Some of his sources deploy familiar derogatory tropes: hence Palembang's pusaka "consist of an old rusty keris, a broken gun barrel, or any ancient trumpery to which chance or caprice has annexed an idea of extraordinary virtue" (Wilken 1885: 117, quoting Marsden). These resonances only reiterate their shared classification, however. One difference, though, may explain why Wilken discusses pusaka and rijkssieraden before amulets. Indies practices suggested Indonesians deemed them to be alive, which better fit his definition of the fetish. Hence in Java royal pusaka have a "personal life," with names and titles. Wilken does not explore another difference: their role in human collectives, both kin groups and polities.

Wilken remained the key authority for Dutch scholars and administrators (including the anonymous author of a short manual on "heathenism" published by the Royal Military Academy in Breda during the Dutch pacification campaigns, who lifts passages from Wilken's book). But in 1906 a new study of Indies animism appeared, by Albert Christiaan Kruyt. Like Wilken, Kruyt was born in the Indies to a missionary family (though in East Java) and educated in the Netherlands. Unlike Wilken, he became a missionary himself, sent by the NZG to the Toraja in central Sulawesi in 1892. While periodically nodding to Wilken, his analysis builds on his daily interactions with Toraja; travels across the archipelago in pursuit of comparative data (subsidized by the state and based on conversations with Dutch officials in each region); and anthropologies of Melanesia and Polynesia (Kruyt 1906: vi–ix).[23]

What makes Kruyt of interest is that he retheorizes animism, along with fetishism and spiritism, on the grounds of translation. Europeans, he argued, had rendered two distinct Indonesian ideas as *soul*, neither corresponding to what Europeans meant by the concept: an immaterial personal essence continuing after death. By contrast, Indonesians distinguished one entity that only emerged after death from another relevant only during life. The latter, moreover, was not uniquely human but possessed by all living beings, as well as "lifeless objects." To characterize this "etheric substance," he coined a word: *zielenstoff*, soulmatter or soulstuff.[24] He links it to the Malay *semangat* (discussed by British civil servant and ethnographer Skeat in his book *Malay Magic*), as well as a host of other vernaculars.[25] Animism constitutes all practices involving soulstuff, especially its maintenance, reinforcement, amplification, and transfer from one entity to another.[26]

Kruyt elaborates how soulstuff operates in relation to humans, plants, animals, and objects, differentiating impersonal soulstuff, which is pervasive, from the personal soulstuff some entities acquire through their importance to human concerns. He also differentiates practices in which humans use

other entities to enhance or replenish either their own soulstuff (as in healing, but also through mundane acts such as eating) or that of other beings
important to their welfare (e.g., crops or tools) from those when other entities serve as "mediums" for the dead. Particularly important to his analysis of fetishism is his assertion that some entities have more soulstuff than
others, and are thus more powerful. Kruyt compares this to the Melanesian
concept of *mana* (1906: 201).

For Kruyt, fetishism involves objects with personal soulstuff, which
"animates the object"; indeed, a fetish is "the object itself become person"
(1906: 199–200). Fetishes are "fed" (not worshipped) to make their soulstuff
stronger and more durable. While in theory anything may become a fetish,
in practice only objects with unusually potent soulstuff, which may be used
for their possessor's benefit, do. This leads Kruyt to zero in on material
markers of potential potency, highlighting two features in particular: hardness and oddness. Thus stones draw attention because, unlike plants and
animals, they are not evanescent: they do not rot and cannot be destroyed,
as is also true of bones (he states that some archipelago people regard stones
as the bones of the earth). But rarity and weirdness also count. When people
find something odd, they may not know what it might do, but recognize it
might do *something* (recall Bubandt's stone collector). This part of Kruyt's
analysis recalls instauration.

Kruyt also addresses fetish types, following a logic different from Wilken's
by moving from individual to collective. Hence he begins with amulets, retaining the category without explicit discussion of what it entails other than
having use; he does, however, note that amulets commonly consist of "little
stones, oddly grown twigs and roots, animal or human teeth, all objects that
by their hardness or peculiarity in connection with exceptional situations
justify the conjecture that special soulstuff, and through that special power,
shelters in them," before launching into examples (that once again do not
include jimat).[27] Following amulets, he proceeds to pusaka, which derive
their power from transmitting ancestral soulstuff over time (1906: 221).
He does not mention "family fetishes," which appear in the *Encyclopaedie*'s
entry on pusaka, but the notion is implied as he introduces rijkssieraden:
"If their privately owned heirlooms are for the single family already of such
great significance in advancing their welfare, how much more, then, the
heirlooms that belong to the entire land" (1906: 224).

That Kruyt's analysis made an impression may be inferred from his authorship of the *Encyclopaedie*'s entry on fetishism.[28] There he claims that rijkssieraden "usually are weapons used by former famous kings and valuable gifts

from other lands," calling rulers their keepers. A book aimed at the general public by a former missionary-turned-docent is more explicit: "[T]he so-called pusaka or heirlooms owe their power to their protracted use by former generations, so that a part of the latter's soulstuff still, as it were, clings to those objects. If the heirlooms are [those] of rulers or chiefs, then their value is naturally so much the greater" (Bezemer 1908: 17). But soulstuff appears nowhere in the *Encyclopaedie*'s entries for "pusaka" and "rijkssieraden." Instead, a pusaka is glossed as a sacred or welfare-conferring heirloom, a family fetish to which the soul or spirit of someone who lived in the past is bound (Kruyt would emphatically disagree). The entry on rijkssieraden retains a hint of Kruyt in declaring them the most important pusaka, and objects once in close contact with prior kings.

In juxtaposing two entities that in Christian theology and secular European ontologies constituted a fundamental (and thorny) binary, soul-stuff raises a startling possibility: perhaps Europeans lacked the conceptual tools to grasp Indonesian practices, which at best seemed to bring together what they carefully kept apart. As a commensuration device, soulstuff offered a potentially disruptive opening. But that disruption never was realized. Soulstuff didn't last, even for Kruyt himself. In the leading Dutch anthropology journal, Kruyt lamented that soulstuff had not been taken up. He had been critiqued for using a contradictory term, and for sowing confusion. Snouck even had predicted that some would dismiss his entire argument because they found soulstuff absurd. Both honest and modest, Kruyt admitted that he himself no longer found it adequate. He had come to realize it prevented him from "penetrating more deeply into the thinking of Indonesians," and thus from understanding some Toraja practices (1918). The missionary Kruyt confessed himself converted—to the concept of magical power.[29]

What performed this miracle was a 1916 book-length article by jurist Frederik Daniel Eduard van Ossenbruggen on practices pertaining to smallpox in Java and elsewhere, a contribution (as his subtitle declares) to theories of "pre-animism."[30] A cadre of British and German ethnologists had argued that animism was not after all the most primitive form of thought; it had been preceded by an earlier stage: magic. Or rather by magical thinking, which rested on the association of ideas, an idea taken from Frazer.

Van Ossenbruggen (who cites not only the pre-animists and Frazer but also Durkheim and Mauss) had a long and distinguished career. Born on Java, he studied law in the Netherlands and worked in the Indies as a barrister. He taught in training colleges for native civil servants on Java for several years before being appointed to the bench, where he eventually held the colony's most prestigious judicial post: president of the Supreme Court. In his spare time, he not only helped found the (professionally relevant) study of Indonesian "customary law" (*adatrecht*), a major field of Dutch scholarly endeavor, but also made significant contributions to Dutch ethnology, particularly in his "pox essay."[31] An admirer of Wilken's, he prepared an edition of the latter's collected works, including his book on animism.[32] Nowhere does he cite Kruyt. Yet despite the difference in the concepts they used, they shared an interest in detail. In particular, both sought to explain the use of specific material substances in Indies practices, even if for Van Ossenbruggen matter always ultimately vanishes into mentality.

I will return to Van Ossenbruggen in chapter 4. What interests me here is his use of the concept "magical power"(*magische kracht*), and discussions clarifying its associations with keris. Rather cavalierly, he defines a fetish as "some object to which magical power is linked" (1916: 191) as a result of the association of ideas. Hence amulets, which (following Wilken) he treats as a means of defense, tend to be made of substances that are hard, sharp, and/ or corrosive (1916: 225). Such qualities also explain the magical power of tools and weapons, as "only with hard, sharp weapons and tools is it possible for humans to wound and kill animals and people, to fell large trees, to forge iron and other metals, to manufacture all kinds of things." But "the primitive" mistakenly attributes these capacities to the objects rather than his own aptitude or skill; faced with another's success, primitives credit the magical power of that person's tools or weapons (1916: 239). Most important in regard to keris, however, is the power attributed to iron. Although their hardness and sharpness render shells and stones significant, iron is "the magical material par excellence." Not only is it difficult to obtain— "hidden in stone," it requires fire to extract—but it is the hardest and most malleable of substances (1916: 240).[33] Above all, iron weapons are invested with magical power (1916: 241).

THIS FORAY INTO ETHNOLOGY and kindred disciplines (Orientalism, history of religions) shows some ways that things such as royal keris differed from jimat. But keris also provoked a different stream of publications, not ensconced in the growing Dutch professoriate but entangled with museums and focused on material culture rather than mental processes. The *Encyclopaedie*'s entry on weapons (which appeared in 1921) is one outcome.

Studies of keris—particularly of their manufacture and many styles—began in the early nineteenth century but accelerated after consolidation of the colonial state. Much of it centered on Javanese keris, beginning with Sir Thomas Stamford Raffles's *History of Java*, which offered a detailed discussion of the pamor patterns—produced by hammering together layers of nickel and iron—Javanese smiths had developed.[34] A considerable amount of this scholarship focused on the court centers of Surakarta and Yogyakarta, as did accounts of Javanese rijkssieraden.[35] For example, Isaäc Groneman, a crucial figure, served as personal physician to Yogyakarta's sultan. He became singularly invested in the fate of Java's smiths in the face of rising costs and declining demand. Groneman published detailed accounts of Javanese keris and their manufacture (covering not only forging but even the ceremonial cleansing of court keris) in a Dutch anthropological journal in 1910–13. (His corpus was translated into English in 2009 with an introductory essay by David van Duuren and magnificent color photos of keris in Dutch collections.) Partly inspired by Groneman's anxieties about the disappearance of Indonesian craftsmen, broadcast in colonial newspapers, and partly inspired by colonial exhibitions, the new governor-general at the time commissioned J. E. Jasper (author of texts on dukun in chapter 1) to study the materials and techniques used to produce them. He and Javanese artist Mas Pirngadie coauthored five volumes, beginning with wickerwork in 1912 and addressing metallurgy in the final volume, on the working of base (i.e., not silver or gold) metals, in 1930 (Jasper and Pirngadie 1912–30). As Groneman had feared, keris were vanishing from daily life, though not for the reasons he stated. He was convinced that excellent pamor patterns required the use of nickel-rich meteoric iron—and the meteorite that had supplied this was becoming depleted. But reliance on that meteorite was only true for a limited period of time and in a specific place (the central Javanese courts [Van Duuren 2009: 27–30]), though constant repetition of his claim continues to link meteorites to the magical aura of keris. Instead, Van Duuren (2009: 30–32) argues, forgers lost their market as men sold their keris, partly as a consequence of colonial policies (the Pax Neerlandica ended local wars, and in some regions the colonial state banned carrying weapons in public), and partly due to the arrival of cheap, manufactured European goods and the impoverishment of the population.

Taken together, these modes of knowledge perform a distinction (familiar from chapter 2) between the mental and material, subjects and objects, while doing it differently. Ethnologists sought to map a mental landscape; what Indonesians do with certain objects serves as fodder. Even those—such as

Kruyt and Van Ossenbruggen—who put their analytic skills to work on things and practices, seek something behind these, a procedure common to much later anthropologies too, and crucial to the construction of magic. At the same time, the robust body of scholarship on material culture did not cover jimat. Some of that literature focused on substances (iron, nickel), but much more addressed the techniques of working these into artifacts their authors found captivating.

There was one outlier in studies of keris: an article by Knebel (then assistant resident of a regency in east Java). He reports, without commentary, what a Javanese aristocrat told him about objects—mainly keris, but also lances and other weapons—that Javanese addressed with a name and title, and considered powerful, *ampuh*, or to possess efficacy, *kasiat* (1898b). Describing the varieties of such weapons, as well as what specific named Javanese keris can do, he supplements what he learned from his conversations with tales of the same objects in the *Babad Tanah Jawi*, a chronicle long studied by Dutch philologists. Notably, he never talks of Javanese *beliefs*; nor does he modify the word (with, e.g., *magically*) when he describes these weapons as powerful.

Conundrums of Commensuration

Scholarly categories contributed to the work of purification. Parsing Indonesian practices to yield classificatory schema, they enact a gulf between bounded cultures: Indonesian fools on one side, white men of reason on the other. But if we look at what authorities did with things such as Klungkung's keris rather than at what they say, we find obscured similarities and unexpected consequences. Different differences emerge, narrowing the gap considerably.

I turn, therefore, to the work of translation, in its multiple guises. But before addressing the complex outcomes of the transport of keris over space and time, I want to pause to consider what is and is not made equivalent, and what this reveals about commensuration's politics. Two commensurations especially are eschewed: with European monarchies and with European practices involving edged weapons.

I have already noted one hiccup in my brief discussion of soulstuff. Here I want to highlight that, unlike dukun and jimat, easy translations proved elusive. The word *kris* entered European languages rather than being replaced by purported equivalents; even *dagger* is disputed (some argue for *short sword*). *Pusaka* also gained some purchase, both during the colonial era and later. The pusaka that played a role in archipelago polities, however, posed problems. As noted, contents differed. Keris, while common, need not be among them, or even the most important; some polities included not only other weapons (swords, lances, even cannons), but pieces of clothing, plates and pots, images or containers made of gold, a horse, and/or objects that might have counted as jimat had they not been of collective value. Vernaculars also differed. Dutch authorities, though, sought a general term for a widespread phenomenon. They came up with two: *ornamenten* (ornaments) and the more frequently used *rijkssieraden*.

So far, I have left *rijkssieraden* in Dutch. It appears in no dictionaries. Nor is it used for objects associated with the (young by European standards) Dutch monarchy: symbols of office (crown, scepter, orb) that monarchs never wear but are laid on a bench or carried by officials during the investiture of a new ruler, and crown jewels with no political significance. *Rijkssieraden* is a neologism, one that in-commensurates. Like soulstuff it suggests a limit to making equivalent that could be productive. But it simultaneously performs (k)not-work that renders Indonesians fascinating fools. Recall Van den Berg's insistence that rijkssieraden are *not* like European scepters or crowns: actors rather than symbols, they must be fetishes.[36]

English speakers writing about such things (especially in the Malay states, which were British colonies), however, had no problem calling them *regalia*. British coronations do differ from Dutch investitures: the initiate not only wears the regalia but is anointed with holy oil (as in Netflix's *The Crown*). British regalia alter reality, so perhaps are more like archipelago things, though *regalia* doesn't fully capture how things such as Klungkung's keris operated. We might call them regalia, "but not only," to borrow Marisol de la Cadena's concept (2015).

In addition to matters monarchical, commentators also systematically ignored European practices involving edged weapons—even though some authors had their own experience of these. The dress uniforms of both army officers and high-ranking colonial officials included special swords. Queen Wilhelmina bestowed even more elegant swords on those who performed acts of valor. Such swords received careful, even reverential treatment. They also became valued heirlooms. In short, in a number of ways they resembled pusaka keris.[37]

Such refusals to commensurate make Indonesian practices and things appear stranger than they might. (They also avoid making European practices less familiar.[38]) But the more fundamental in-commensuration lies in the inability to recognize the associations between humans and nonhumans that Latour terms collectives (1999: 304), associations crucial to making—and expanding—polities.[39] Chapter 2 explored some ways objects do more than serve as passive resources or repositories of meaning. Like jimat, regalia coproduce events and worlds, but they also act in ways jimat do not, by enhancing more than individual abilities. They extend collectives over time and space, adding durability and size. While such observations originated in empirical studies of the making of scientific facts, science and technology studies scholars writing about technology have long explored their political ramifications. Latour (1993) addresses such issues in relation to mundane technologies such as Archimedes's lever, infrastructure, and guns. They are equally relevant to regalia keris.

Readers may object that the capacities attributed to keris such as I Durga Dingkul or I Bangawan Canggu, the one that could cause earthquakes if thrust into the ground, are impossible. Apart from noting that what counts as possible also is embedded in collectives, and that in an era of climate emergency it appears far less strange to think that artifacts can have geological effects, it is worth asking what it might do to analytic habits to take such attributions seriously. But for those not willing to concede that keris can do everything credited to them, consider that colonial authorities clearly acknowledged their power, and treated it as more than merely a matter of belief. Regardless of their specific aptitudes, such things could pull people together, strengthen resolve, gather "the great power of resistance." Colonial authors also grasped that such capacities depended on certain conditions, glimpses of which appear in descriptions of archipelago polities. Apart from relations with particular people, these involve forms of care: regular acts of "cleansing" and offering/feeding. In Bali, such acts occur every 210 days on a calendrical conjunction called Tumpek Landep, as well as on special occasions—for example, just before battle. In short, many affiliated actors and practices are necessary for keris to perform. But this is equally true of KNIL's guns. Without skilled operators, proper maintenance, and ammunition, they are impotent.[40] Such similarities recall Latour's factish, a concept he developed to make the point that talk of both fetishes and facts tends to obscure networks, concealing the actors and practices on which they rely.[41] In contrast to the civilizational chasm that *fetish* and *magical power* create, such comparisons yield slighter differences.

What colonial officials termed a native state consisted of a large repertoire of human and nonhuman actors. The humans included descendants of the dynasty's founder and their affines, followers, and supporters, as well as those obligated to them by circumstance or history. In Bali, it also included humans who underwent a series of procedures following their deaths to become ancestors. But not all of the actors making up such collectives were human. They also included more-than-human forces, shrines and temples, palm-leaf texts, architectural forms, rice paddies, and specific keris. Texts chronicling significant events and relationships in a prominent family's past always attend (commonly in the early sections) to how specific men came together with certain keris; in Balinese historiography such encounters mark a dynasty's beginning. Keris were embroiled in history, forming the very stuff of power.

But colonialism enrolled keris in new collectives. And it is to that process and its consequences that I now turn.

From Fetish to Fact via Museums and Markets

If some commensurations were denied, others proceeded apace as extraction propelled things such as Klungkung's keris into the entwined domains of markets and museums.[42] They found themselves translated into commodities in markets, artifacts in museums—and tokens of culture in these and other venues. For only following conquest could scholars offer comprehensive descriptions of the material culture of many Indies collectives, as in the *Encyclopaedie*'s comparative entry on native weapons. A key form of commensuration all of these sites deployed was numeric: historic individuals were rendered in a language uniquely universal by axiom.

For Klungkung's heirlooms, markets remained largely hypothetical. Their political and historical associations, not to mention the materials out of which they were made, destined them for museums—in particular, the Batavian Society's and Leiden's museums. While the policy was to split collections between these institutions, the best pieces—certainly crucial regalia—always remained in Batavia (Ter Keurs 2009). Plenty of other remarkable keris, though, likely heirlooms belonging to other ruling-class men, ended up in the Netherlands.[43] Still, regalia keris were at least partly inserted into the purportedly rational sphere of market economics, if only to be valued by the institutions to which they were donated and insured on their travels. Immediately after Klungkung's conquest, for instance, newspapers reported that certain keris were worth 10,000 guilders, roughly US$130,000 today.

Markets commensurate by translating value into money. By assessing them according to a standard presenting itself as universal, monetary estimates of their worth posited regalia as exchangeable for an infinite variety of other commodities. When the fetish originally emerged as a problematic in market transactions on Africa's west coast, European merchants sought to sever the purportedly inherent value of gold from values they deemed merely superstitious. Klungkung's keris at least had a high monetary value, unlike many other keris and most jimat.

Yet in practice a market for keris, regalia or not, extends only as far as there are potential buyers. An economic calculus based on the law of supply and demand cannot account for the prices keris could command, for on what basis could it operate? What, in short, generated demand? If keris only had value for superstitious Indonesians, why not melt them down for the precious metal and gems of which parts were made?[44] Iconoclasm had its limits. Keris never were treated as an amalgam of substances; they always were worth more than the sum of their parts.

Markets for keris were hardly a colonial invention, or a product of museum collecting. Apart from obtaining keris as heirlooms or as gifts (from human and more-than-human superiors), Indonesian men purchased them, often from the smiths who made them. Europeans, too, had been acquiring keris—as gifts and by purchase—since VOC days, often depositing them in cabinets of curiosity; European monarchs even regifted them to one another (Van Duuren 2002). Rembrandt, a collector of intriguing objects, had picked one up that appears in two of his paintings. But colonial scholarly, collecting, and exhibiting practices accelerated production of the desiring subjects who form their expanding market. And here we begin to sense some of the unanticipated effects of recruiting keris to mock native credulity. For their significance to Indonesians, including their "magical powers," compounds their value—as does documented passage into museum inventories.

When Klungkung booty arrived at the Museum of the Batavian Society, it joined myriad similar objects confiscated during military expeditions, dating back to the VOC era. The museum served as the main depository for regalia seized at the conquest of archipelago polities or surrendered on their submission. Even before the rash of Ethical Policy wars, it contained rijkssieraden from Banten, Banjarmasin, Bangkalan, Gorontalo, and Aceh (Van den Berg 1901: 77). These had been joined by the famous rijkssieraden of Bone and Gowa (South Sulawesi), things from Gayo and Alas (Sumatra), and the celebrated Lombok Treasure before the arrival of booty from conquests in Bali.[45]

Upon arriving at the museum, heirloom keris began to undergo a metamorphosis from named historical actors into artifacts. After being unpacked, each piece received an accession number, a unique identifier written on a registration card and painted onto the item's surface. At least hypothetically, through that number it could be tracked to storerooms or display cases, and its exhibit history reconstructed.[46] Registration cards formed crucial actors in the process of transformation. For in addition to the accession number, they recorded the outcome of a series of examinations. Words fixed items in both space (the geographic region from which they came) and time (the date of their acquisition, establishing a temporal limit to their manufacture). Numbers also calibrated keris in a two-dimensional language through disassembly into and measurement of constituent parts: hilt, blade, and sheath. Each was further disaggregated into the substances from which it was made: blades into nickel and iron; hilts and sheaths into gold, silver, particular varieties of wood, and precious stones.

Such inscription assimilated named heirloom keris to knowledges aspiring to universality as much as assessing their economic value did. But these were not the only knowledges such associations strengthened. Keris became examples not simply of skillfully crafted artifacts but of culture, contributing to emerging ethnographic distinctions. For this, not universalizing but particularizing expertise was needed, requiring collaboration with Indonesians, however much their participation might be rendered opaque. Drawing on the growing corpus of texts on keris manufacture and local classifications, this collaboration surfaces through the vernacular names for the woods favored for hilts and sheaths; for design motifs such as pamor patterns, blade shapes and embellishments; and for hilt forms. Thus when Hendrik Juynboll, as director of Leiden's Ethnographic Museum, produced a catalogue of all Balinese artifacts in the museum's collection, he described a group he called "ceremonial keris," organized by hilt types, subdivided by material (gold or wood) and type: *raksasa*, *garuda*, or nonrepresentational (1912). Through such descriptions specific keris became comparable to keris from elsewhere on the island—or across the archipelago. Such comparisons interested not only curators but also European connoisseurs, and the dealers, auctioneers, and pawnshop employees through whose hands keris could pass.[47] This process rendered both ordinary and regalia keris into signs of ethnic cultures.

The arsenal of techniques operating to transmute a legendary keris into an artifact involved more, however, than registration followed by filing its cards and storage of the thing itself. Keris with historical and political significance, especially those whose appurtenances consisted of precious metals and gems, found themselves destined for permanent display in special spaces called *Schatkamer*, "Treasure Rooms."[48] There interesting blades might be removed from their sheaths, in accord with European conventions for the display of edged weapons. Thus entities formerly secreted away to protect both themselves and viewers faced full exposure. Only after such processing could potent actors appear to become chunks of passive, lifeless matter upon which people might project meanings.

Despite this apparent reduction, however, keris proved adept at entering new collectives, where they again authorized, impeded, inspired, and in other respects acted. Indeed, in setting them apart as treasure and placing them on display, curators enabled keris to drift beyond colonialism's politico-scientific projects. Instead of becoming fully known and mastered—indices of native superstition, culture, or craftsmanship—they not only retained connections to the collectives to which they once had contributed, but acquired new capacities, some quite disconcerting.

Fusions in the Batavian Society

Heirloom keris from Klungkung not only remained in Batavia but were displayed in the Batavian Society's Treasure Room. There they contributed to shaping impressions of the colonial state through the impact that space exerted on visitors, both European and Indonesian. They also once again were caught up with invocations of magical power. On the whole, the Treasure Room brought collectives into existence through novel fusions.

A growing tourist industry supplied many of the museum's European visitors, who were greeted by an array of complex experiences and propositions in material form in the Treasure Room's assemblage of precious and semiprecious metals and gems. Guidebooks directed attention to what might elude a quick gaze. One published well before the conquests that multiplied the room's contents boasted that "[t]he total value of the things appearing here is appraised at more than a half million guilders" (Buys 1891: 18). Such an equation trumpets the affluence of the colonial state, which could afford to keep such costly objects off the market. Following consolidation of the Netherlands Indies, guidebooks identified items by region, underscoring the totality that the state now comprised—even identifying regalia by name (*Gids* 1917, 1928).[49] That so many objects were weapons—trophies of war indexing the power both of defeated enemies and of the regime that had conquered them—proclaimed the empire's might.

The Treasure Room's assortment of gleaming artifacts, however, also produced an unexpected response in a different public the museum called into existence. According to F. D. K. Bosch, former head of the Archaeo-logical Service (and later a professor at Utrecht), "The native inhabitants of Batavia have always been, and are to this day, particularly interested in this collection. It is irresistibly attractive to them, with the result that on Sundays and holidays the number of visitors that throng in quiet enjoyment before the show cases often exceeds 5,000" (1937/38: 122–23). Indonesian visi-tors, sophisticated residents of the capital, may have been impressed by this material demonstration of the extraordinary powers of the colonial state, which had managed to gather in one place so many potent entities.[50] At the same time, the museum allowed these things to extend their reach. Previ-ously, only the functionaries who cared for them and heirs to a dynastic line and their male kin could see such pusaka. But as the eager crowds indicate, now everyone could. The museum reassembled regalia into something akin to their prior collectives, but in a greatly expanded and democratized form.

The way Indonesian visitors engaged more accessible items—antiquities that were not behind glass, as the pusaka in the Treasure Room were—makes this even more evident, while inciting Bosch to use a familiar phrase: "Some of the objects in the archaeological gallery are of special interest to the people, too. There are several stone images, for instance, that seem to them to be filled with magical powers, and sometimes, stealthily, money or flow-ers are offered to these in order to propitiate them with a view to the curing of some malady, the obtaining of revenge, or the like" (1937/38: 123).

Cornelis Christiaan Berg, professor of Javanese language and literature at Leiden, notes further acts such proximity elicited: "In Batavia stands a museum full of Hindu-Javanese idols. On days of free entrance many Indo-nesians come to file past the images there. Art lovers? Nothing of the kind! They try, if the attendants are out, to stroke a statue with the finger to take its sekti [*sic*; he glosses this as 'magical power'] into themselves. This is illicit contact according to the museum's board of directors but falls under per-missible contact according to the native way of thinking" (1936: 75). The museum, in short, constituted a site of promiscuous mixture.

The indulgent tone in 1930s talk of "magical powers" marks a shift in colo-nial attitudes. While still differentiating (level-headed, art-loving) Europeans from Indonesians, it trains attention on acts that transgress bourgeois pro-priety but neither justify nor threaten the colonial project. This is indicative of broader changes in policy, even more evident in invocations of magic in relation to specific Balinese keris exhibited in the Treasure Room.

As Indonesian nationalist ambitions increasingly put pressure on the colonial state, alterity offered new charms. Abandoning the always limited goal of "developing" its subjects, the regime turned to revivifying (and inventing) tradition. This included instituting indirect rule in conquered regions, installing members of old dynastic lines as *zelfbestuurders*, self-governing rulers (at least in name), a policy that launched royal heirlooms into a potential new role as mediators. In 1931 key regalia were returned to the restored ruler of Bone on the grounds that he could not reign without them (Budiarti 2007: 137).[51] Not surprisingly, other rulers requested theirs as well, including Gowa, where items not only from Batavia but even from faraway Leiden were returned (Budiarti 2007: 134–36).

H. J. E. Moll, Bali's new resident, thought this would be an excellent gesture, especially as plans were underway to invest eight Balinese self-governing rulers ceremonially at Bali's most important temple in 1938. Those affected found the prospect even more compelling, dispatching envoys to Batavia to see what was there.[52] Moll's draft to the governor-general notes, "From the nature of the affair it was left to the parties involved which sacred objects they preferably would receive back. Which things [had] the greatest magical-symbolic value for them." All selected named keris and, in some cases, also named lances. Klungkung's new ruler requested I Durga Dingkul, decked out with the hilt and sheath of the otherwise insignificant I Ardawalika, along with two named lance tips.[53] Moll asked Controleur Christiaan Grader to investigate the desired items and Language Officer Roelof Goris to address grounds for restoring them.

"Magical powers" forms part of Goris's analysis. He argues that the most obvious reason to return spoils of war would be that particular items are necessary for the exercise of sovereignty: that they functioned, in short, as rijkssieraden. Basically returning to Van den Berg's question about Bali, he answered it in the negative. Taking Bone and Gowa as his standard, he concludes that the keris and lances Balinese rulers sought were not essential as they played no role in the life of the wider community. Nor were they "ceremonial objects" (*staatsie-voorwerpen*), which he regarded as weaker forms of rijkssieraden, that commonly accompanied the king, as in Surakarta and Yogyakarta, as well as gods in Balinese temples. Instead, he asserts they are merely pusaka, family or dynastic possessions (*famile bezit*), and family fetishes. At the same time, he had to acknowledge they differed from most pusaka in accruing stories about miracles and wonders. In the end, he calls them potent objects that are magically powerful (*magische krachtig*).

Having demolished the strongest argument for their return, he ends by noting there might be other grounds to do so. Moll's letter (to which Goris's report was appended) takes up this charge. Never engaging Goris's conclusions, he offers a corrective while stating his own case for restoration. He insists they are not, in fact, merely pusaka, but *pajenengan*, "objects belonging to the ruling King, in his quality as Ruler," passing not from father to son but from ruler to successor.[54] He also, however, maintained that returning them not only would be a mark of friendship, given how eager the rulers involved were to have them, but that they could serve as an "external sign, a sort of symbol," appropriate to an "Eastern thinking world," diffracting them through both Protestantism and Orientalism. Not only could they serve as useful tokens of tamed authority, but, given solely on loan, they would be "comparable to the old historical institution of feudal lord and vassal," drawing on European history but also in some respects on Balinese legends as most of the items sought originated as gifts from human or more-than-human superiors, and thus created obligations.[55] In the end, none were returned.[56] But the process led to great interest in the museum's collection on the part of the Balinese concerned. Much like the offerings Indonesian museumgoers made to ancient statues, this event produced partially joined collectives.

The very notion of a Treasure Room was another hybrid offspring of partly connected collectives, with its own magical elements. Provoking wonder through its display of items both precious and unique, the Treasure Room hardly conformed to models of the modern museum. According to Bennett (1995), the museum was developed as a site to instruct the public in forms of thought and behavior proper to the modern bourgeois subject. In the Treasure Room, however, science is dominated by art, pedagogy by curiosity. Then too, consider treasure's (magical) associations with lore about dragons and goblins.

Fusions in the Metropole

Over the years, thousands of keris have made their way to the Netherlands. While some arrived as a consequence of the division of war booty, most did not. In addition to the colonial state's donations to Dutch museums, private bequests from former colonial officials, and gifts from archipelago rulers, keris followed many other routes. They accompanied pensioned civil servants, officers, and soldiers; migrated with Eurasians who chose Dutch over Indonesian citizenship at independence; continue to be picked up as souvenirs by tourists; and are hunted and gathered by dealers and private collectors. Older keris often became Dutch family heirlooms. For example, in the nineteenth century, the Dutch king donated a building in Arnhem as a home for former members of the KNIL, many of whom possessed keris or other Indonesian weapons. Over time, a museum became attached to the old soldiers' home. While few (if any) soldiers still reside there, for some years the museum held a "Kris Day," inviting those with keris to come and have them valued and to learn more about keris in general. In 2020 a zoo near Overijssel also held a Kris Day.

Formation of this lively interest in keris deserves extended study, as does what people do with them. But even brief attention reveals some surprising trajectories and indicates that they have become more tightly tied to magic. While some people limit themselves to a single prized possession, perhaps as a decorative sign of cosmopolitanism, others become connoisseurs, exchanging and selling them, and reading and producing materials on keris styles, manufacturing processes, origin and development, and meanings, including their magical powers. As I learned after discovering keris buffs were recommending my first book in an online forum on edged weapons, lore about specific keris or keris in general adds to their appeal.[57] Enthusiasts are drawn to what Indonesians say keris can do. The subjectivities and groups keris assemble are yet another fused offspring of multiple collectives.

Even without stories, however, aficionados value keris—among other things—for their aesthetic qualities. For keris also have been transformed into art, with all of the seductive, moving, and transformative powers this can entail. As in the 2006 exhibit in Leiden, displays contribute to this association. By presenting keris as instances of beautiful craftsmanship, they enable them to participate in enlisting humans in class projects, as subjects whose sensibilities mark socioeconomic and cultural positions.

Yet more surprising fusions may be found in the Netherlands. I opened this chapter by noting that Dutch museumgoers associated keris with magic. Indeed, if many in the Netherlands imagine Indonesia as a place of magic, keris form its preeminent materialization. When I presented a version of this chapter to an audience that included curators working in Dutch museums with extensive keris collections, I discovered that all had been solicited by Dutch owners of keris who had become concerned about their possible magical powers. Often, they suspected their keris might be wreaking havoc on their lives and sought advice on how to neutralize such effects. Some hoped to get rid of them, through donation.

David van Duuren, the Netherlands' foremost expert on keris and former curator at the Tropen, relates several such incidents in a book aimed at the general public. Like most curators—and anthropologists—he finds these experiences disconcerting. But his effort to address them is telling. Even a scholar as sophisticated as Van Duuren cannot help but fall back on familiar purifying responses. Consider what he writes in a section on "superstition":

> In Holland, there are many owners of krisses who feel certain that a soul or spirit lodges in their weapon. People who would never consider rubbing the African ancestor sculpture on their cupboard with the blood of a ritually slaughtered chicken, or even lighting a candle for the image of an ancient Roman-Catholic saint, will place bowls of aromatic flowers in front of their kris. . . . If they do not do these things, some vaguely defined harmony in their homes might become disrupted. While in fact they do nothing more meaningful than keeping artificially alive a set of ideas that has become detached from its cultural context and therefore has become devoid of meaning. (1998: 94)[58]

Note Van Duuren's insight: it is only in relation to keris, things associated with the Netherlands' former colony, that such statements and practices occur. And the practices draw on those of Indonesians, even if they do not fully replicate them.

After commenting on those who seek to dispose of their keris following an unfortunate experience that they have become convinced may be traced to the object, and astutely observing that in the Netherlands keris never seem to confer benefits, Van Duuren dryly notes that none of the thousands of keris in Dutch museums ever has shown any sign of the extraordinary powers they seem to manifest in private homes.[59] His conclusion is adamant: "People who believe that an inherent, autonomous power is present in their kris are superstitious. Its real power is that of a set of ideas, projected into it over the centuries. That of a cultural concept pure and simple, neither more nor less. . . . The kris is part of a now practically extinct phase in Indonesian cultural history" (1998: 95).

Although Van Duuren's position vis-à-vis Indonesians stands in marked contrast to colonial authorities—Indonesians live in a different cultural milieu—his characterization of Europeans who adopt related views shows the limits of the culture concept. By calling Europeans afraid of their keris "superstitious," he reiterates the Enlightened view that treats such claims as properly past, incompatible with modern reason. At the same time, he demonstrates Latour's point about the limits of cultural relativism: as Latour notes, ultimately, all cultures are assuredly not equal, since only the culture of the (modern) analyst possesses a correct understanding of nature (1993: 91–129). Cultural relativism promotes tolerance, at the cost of reality. But as Stengers tirelessly asks: Who wants to be tolerated?

Ironically, given Van Duuren's skepticism, a TV mini-series entitled *Kris Pusaka* that aired in 1977–78 (reissued on DVD in 2007) centered on a researcher at the Tropen who purchased a keris with strange powers at an auction. When an antique dealer with an Indonesian name repeatedly tries to get him to sell it to him, the researcher becomes intrigued. The keris ultimately leads him to Indonesia—and its rightful owners.[60] Several people I met in the Netherlands spoke of the series with great pleasure. Such popular culture forms one of many contemporary arenas reinforcing relations between keris and magic in partly connected collectives.

Things Multiple in Contemporary Indonesia

I began this chapter by pointing out some differences between jimat and keris, especially those that formed crucial members of precolonial polities, highlighting the work keris do as things around which collectives coalesce. Tracking them as they moved across collectives reveals how they became attached to the category of magic. In ending, I want to follow both keris and their association with "magical powers" into the tangle of connections and divergences they have been accruing in the nation-state of Indonesia.

Following independence, Klungkung's royal keris entered a new collective, as artifacts in the Batavian Society Museum found themselves transformed into Indonesian cultural heritage (*warisan budaya*). Renamed the National Museum of Indonesia in 1979, the museum's collections now contribute to a national project by presenting archipelago history and territory as a unified whole. The museum still possesses a Treasure Room in which regalia feature prominently. In and around that space, however, worlds are less fused than uncommoned, with the multiplication of the practices that create them. The Indonesian staff are adept in global museology; however, they also encounter such keris as potent actors needing other forms of attention and care. Periodically (or so I've been told), curators may invite dukun to present offerings so such things will perform as they should in a museum: to be merely an artifact is an achievement.

Such practices point to the place keris in particular occupy in contemporary Indonesia. As in the Netherlands, private collectors abound. Some may simply consider keris good investments. But ambitious men, including politicians, crave keris to help them achieve their goals. Indonesia's first two presidents, Sukarno and Suharto, were known collectors. Joko Widodo, Indonesia's seventh president, also has a vast collection; one of his own pusaka keris went on display in Museum Keris Nusantara, opened in 2017 in the city of Surakarta, one of Java's two historic court centers. The museum showcases several hundred keris, mostly but not solely Javanese. The name Nusantara, from Sanskrit words for *island* and *between*, refers to the archipelago, and is also the name for the new capital this president initiated to replace Jakarta. Nor do only Indonesian politicians possess keris. An article in the *Jakarta Post* at the museum's opening noted that both Vladimir Putin and Recep Tayyip Erdoğan collected keris.[61]

Political and more-than-political ambitions also have animated Balinese efforts to draw on the powers of pusaka keris. Across the archipelago, heirs to former ruling houses have been seeking new forms of influence, often by promoting themselves as leaders in matters of tradition (*adat*), even receiving support from the government, which has sponsored gatherings of such figures as tourist attractions (Van Klinken 2007). In Bali, these efforts dovetailed with commemorations of the centenary of colonial conquests, as the heads of former ruling families in Badung and Klungkung sought to enlist pusaka held by the National Museum in shaping the future. Revisiting the failed colonial proposal to return cherished keris, as members of planning committees they requested temporary loans of the same things desired then. Consulting museum archives, curators sought to match names to artifacts, while conducting negotiations with the parties involved. These spoke to the many tendrils tying these things to the historical processes this chapter has addressed. Hence, they had to be insured, entailing estimates of market value, and they had to be accompanied by museum staff to ensure museologically correct handling. An additional stipulation was that whatever was done to them in Bali had to be undone before their return to Jakarta.

All went smoothly in Badung in 2006 (Brinkgreve and Stuart-Fox 2007). But Klungkung's committee encountered two glitches. First, identifying I Durga Dingkul, the obvious first choice, proved impossible.[62] Instead, they had to settle for I Ardawalika—a keris hitherto notable only for its spectacular hilt and sheath, rather than the powers of its blade—along with one lance tip, I Baru Gnit.

They also had trouble with the matter of insurance. No one explained the problem to me, but I suspect it might have involved cost. Brinkgreve and Stuart-Fox noted that insurers expressed concerns in relation to Badung's

FIGURE 3.1: I Ardawalika. Pusaka keris taken as booty during the conquest of Klung-kung in 1908 and exhibited in the Treasure Room of the Batavian Society for Arts and Sciences (now the Treasure Room of the National Museum of Indonesia). MNI 14905/ E796.

heirlooms. These centered on anxieties about the object's possession of an *ilmu gaib*—literally, mysterious or hidden knowledge, though Brinkgreve and Stuart-Fox translate the phrase with the words perpetually attached to potent keris: "magic power." Insurers worried they might vanish in a mysterious (*gaib*) way (2007: 167). Very likely similar concerns were raised in 2008, but the district had fewer funds. An appeal to the (Balinese) minister of culture seemed to solve the problem.

Both things found themselves boxed up, carried onto a plane, flown to Bali, met at the airport by Klungkung's elected regional head, driven to Klungkung's border to be greeted by marching gamelans and excited people, and walked to the regional capital, Semarapura. Crowds waiting outside the current Puri Agung jockeyed for position to snap photos as Déwa Agung Alit, head of the family, introduced them by name while displaying them in the box in which they arrived. They were then carried along a white cloth path into the Puri to the family shrines where, along with many other keris belonging to members of the clan, they were recharged with offerings they had last received in 1908. Déwa Agung Alit then conveyed I Ardawalika (a half-brother in charge of planning held I Baru Gnit) back to the road, to process with other potent things through the town until they mounted the steep steps to the district office where, after receiving more homage, the visitors spent the night. The following day they were brought down to witness a massive rite to cleanse the earth of the blood of those who died in 1908, listen to speeches, and enjoy some performances before, following a brief rite to divest them of potency, they departed with their entourage of museum staffers for Jakarta.

Although the committee complied with the museum's request to deactivate the borrowed pusaka, no rite actually exists for that purpose. In the normal course of events no one would deliberately drain a keris of power. As is often the case, presumably those responsible modified a rite used to send away more-than-human forces that had been invited into an object at a temple. Sometime later, descendants of the former rulers adapted another practice by building a dedicated shrine to transmit offerings to these pusaka from afar. Such acts transformed I Ardawalika into more than a decorative accessory, and made both into more than museum objects or cultural heritage. Instead, they turned into things—into *pajenengan*—that could gather a new collective.

This relationship between national pusaka and heirlooms associated with rule involves more than partial connection. In both the National Museum and in Klungkung, I Ardawalika and I Baru Gnit may serve as things collective. But unlike keris in the former Batavian Society Museum, diverse sites in the Netherlands, and private collections in both Indonesia and elsewhere—and the institutions threaded into these—specific individuals are at issue. I Ardawalika is no longer only a numbered artifact, but, name restored, it is the target of multiple, diverging practices. In Jakarta, it dutifully performs its role in the Treasure Room, responding to the care of experts adept at preserving and exhibiting material objects, who are attentive to iron's reaction to the oils of human bodies and to air circulating through ducts. It also may periodically receive attention from local dukun. Yet in operating as a pajenengan, it has become a "thing multiple," a member of a diverging collective.[63]

This chapter has highlighted some paths by which magic—through the phrase "magical power"—became associated with keris, especially those belonging to precolonial rulers. Claims about native beliefs in the power of such things not only affected decisions by civil servants about what to do with and about them but motivated analysis. Cycling through such mutually enforcing genres, the magical powers of keris contributed to making colonial difference through the category of magic.

As with jimat, colonial accounts of keris fail to pay adequate attention to the making of worlds, perpetually deferring to inferred inner states—individual beliefs or shared values—rather than attending to nonhuman actors and the practices and associations they mediate. But in many regards, keris, especially heirloom keris, are unlike jimat. Not only do some have venerable lineages, singular identities, and personalities, but as a class they demonstrate a remarkable ability to move beyond their places of origin. In addition, the stuff of which they were made, and the act of making itself, garnered attention. Produced by skilled craftsmen (many with royal patrons), they could be admired as aesthetic objects and develop entourages, especially when the materials used for accoutrements were of a kind that on their own generated high market prices. As a result, they could be incorporated into numerous European collectives—not only those involving colonial administrators seeking to control unruly subjects or colonial scholars aiming to make a mark through their analytical adeptness. By contrast, the knowledge needed to instaure a jimat occasioned little respect among European scholars or collectors. Instead of specialized craftsmen patronized by aristocrats, frauds and fanatics such as dukun and Hajis, purveyors of preposterous ngélmu, manufactured jimat or certified their capacities. While the circulation of keris entailed more or less orderly succession (particularly in ruling-class families), the movement of jimat speaking to the common concerns of ordinary people was unpredictable. Royal heirloom keris travel the world in special exhibits, attracting ever more admirers. Jimat remain invisible; when they do make their way into museums and collections, it is often in unrecognizable forms.

In the case of keris, moreover, the very operations that produced a yawning difference between colonizer and colonized simultaneously created connections. If the role some keris occupied in Balinese polities enmeshed them in Dutch efforts to establish a one-world world, their talent for gathering interrupted that very world. Colonial binaries elide not only myriad connections and commonalities, but also the fresh competencies keris acquired in moving between worlds, from affecting European sensibilities to recomposing former dynasties. Numerous bridges exist between the collectives keris gather, with brisk traffic across them.

Keris in European collectives need not have capacities identical to those they possess in past or present Indonesian collectives. But if "magical powers" once implied fantasy, it should be evident that many keris have considerable powers, including building new, partially fused, collectives. Even setting aside keris owners who suspect their sinister impact or who light incense to maintain peace, no one can deny they produce pleasure, wonder, and lust for possession. They gather admirers, who exchange information about them—even circulating stories about their magical powers on social media.

And keris are fastened ever more tightly to magic. A recent book on Balinese keris, for example, is subtitled *Metal, Masculinity, Magic* (Kam 2019). Even more significant is UNESCO's 2008 decision to include keris as one of its Masterpieces of the Oral and Intangible Cultural Heritage of Humanity. UNESCO's website presents them in an all-too-familiar way: "Both weapon and spiritual object, the kris is considered to possess magical powers."[64] Strands of old scholarship converge, merging admiration of objects demonstrating skilled craft with their European associations with magic. The abstraction *keris*—rather than a particular object with a name, storied past, lethal blade, and gleaming accessories—now forms a pusaka of the endangered collective *Homo sapiens sapiens*. Ironically, modern efforts to banish magic have made it an increasingly solid feature of increasingly connected worlds.

INTERLUDE 4 ⋮ GETTING CAUGHT

I have only once seen witchcraft on its path. I had been sitting late in my hut writing notes. About midnight, before retiring, I took a spear and went for my usual nocturnal stroll. I was walking in the garden at the back of my hut, amongst banana trees, when I noticed a bright light passing at the back of my servants' huts towards the homestead of a man called Tupoi. As this seemed worth investigation I followed its passage until a grass screen obscured the view. I ran quickly through my hut to the other side in order to see where the light was going to, but did not regain sight of it. I knew that only one man, a member of my household, had a lamp that might have given off so bright a light, but next morning he told me that he had neither been out late at night nor had he used his lamp. There did not lack ready informants to tell me that what I had seen was witchcraft. Shortly afterwards, on the same morning, an old relative of Tupoi and an inmate of his homestead died. This event fully explained the light I had seen. I never discovered its real origin, which was possibly a handful of grass lit by some one on his way to defecate, but the coincidence of the direction along which the light moved and the subsequent death accorded well with Zande ideas. (Evans-Pritchard 1937: 34)

In this extraordinary paragraph, Evans-Pritchard invites readers to share a field experience of witchcraft as an element of everyday life by drawing on narrative conventions of spooky tales of the supernatural. Yet after presenting what he translates as witchcraft (Zande *mangu*) as real, he abruptly shifts gears, brusquely swerving from what he saw and heard to reductive speculation. It wasn't witchcraft but a fluke; with that, he dismisses the incident. After conjuring a world in which witchcraft exists, he exorcises it with words such as "real" and "coincidence."

This is one of several passages where Evans-Pritchard engages reality politics, transforming Zande entities, statements, and practices into mistaken ideas, and explaining away things he saw or Azande said. Repeated use of "we" distinguishes Zande "idioms" from the knowledge of what's *really* real that Evans-Pritchard shares with his presumed readers. For all that his work troubles assumptions about irrational Africans, it buttresses the one-world world. Azande believe in witches. White men, especially educated white men, know better. Evans-Pritchard is blunt: "Witches, as Azande conceive them, cannot exist" (1937: 63).[1]

Elsewhere, though, Evans-Pritchard anticipates and works to counteract Euro-American reactions, for instance, by noting his own adoption of Zande forms of life. Exhibit A: he casually comments that he consulted oracles and found that practice "as satisfactory a way of running my home and affairs as any other I know of" (1937: 270).

These swerves can give a reader—okay, *this* reader—whiplash. It's hard not to read the bit about what he *really* saw one night or his blunt statement about witches as reassurance to readers who may wonder if he's gone too far—even "gone native."

In his analysis of how colonialism shaped anthropology, Asad perspicaciously remarks that those supporting research expected what it yielded to "confirm them in their world"—which is to say the one-world world. Moreover, he comments that no anthropologist has "been won over personally to the subordinated culture" studied, though the opposite is commonplace and even presumed (Asad 1973: 17). Asad was not referring to anything as fraught as activities translated as magic or witchcraft, but these observations are especially relevant to such doings, which have a singularly subversive potential. To be sure, Evans-Pritchard would have had a hard time keeping himself stocked in young chickens and *benge* in his rooms at Oxford, let alone trying to operate an oracle without help, but the very idea seems ludicrous. Not because consulting oracles is inherently ridiculous (he insisted it is not), but because, like any practice, it is embedded in a socionatural ecology. Evans-Pritchard's swerves not only assure readers that he has not "gone native," but make clear who he expected those readers to be: educated English speakers, fellow anthropologists, and political authorities for whom that possibility is anathema—as well as making evident who he aimed to be.

By contrast, an ethnography published a year after *Witchcraft* by Gikuyu author (and future president of Kenya) Jomo Kenyatta offers a different mode of disciplining magic in its preface, supplied by Bronislaw Malinowski, with whom Kenyatta studied anthropology. While Malinowski gently chides Kenyatta for making too many comparisons with Europe and using too many European terms ("Church, State, 'legal systems,' 'economics,' etc." (1956 [1938]: xi), he says nothing about the term *magic*, to which Kenyatta devotes an entire chapter. He also remains silent about Kenyatta's defiance of anthropological conventions by declaring, after a discussion of "love magic," "The writer is happy to say that he had the privilege of trying one of the spells, and it undoubtedly proved successful" (1956 [1938]: 289). Maybe the silence marks respect for his student; maybe he regards it as evidence that Kenyatta is still, after all, a "native." He does, however, single out Kenyatta's explanation for magic's efficacy (telepathic communication) as something "some anthropologists may question" (1956 [1938]: xii), and refers to "Mr. Kenyatta's somewhat ingenuous remarks" (1956 [1938]: xiii).

Anthropological concerns about "going native" in relation to practices translated through magic hardly vanished with the end of formal colonial rule (though not colonial worlding); as structures of feeling, they continue to inhabit (and inhibit) ethnography. Consider Harry West's (2007) reflections on Paul Stoller's account of becoming a sorcerer's apprentice in *In Sorcery's Shadow*.[2] West notes (and treats as "going native") Stoller's insistence on full acceptance of the "beliefs" of those studied even when they clash with "ours": Stoller's claims that he had developed the power to harm others, and his assertions that more potent sorcerers had caused his temporary paralysis and illness. West—whose Muedan friend suspected West had suffered a sorcery attack after he became dangerously ill during prior fieldwork—seeks to avoid that path, though, like Stoller (and many of us), he makes use at home of something (a packet of "medicine") he was given in Africa (2007: 74).[3] He implies Africanists received Stoller's book critically—puzzling, since most reviewers thought it opened possibilities for ethnography at a time of great interest in experimentation.

Throughout, West is alert to how various interlocutors—undergraduates who ask if he believes in Muedan sorcery lions, anthropologists who avoid doing the same, Africanists who might dismiss his work, Muedans who insist sorcery lions are not, contrary to his first stab at analyzing them, symbolic but real—do and might receive his work. Such attentiveness resembles the French peasants Favret-Saada (1980) describes—who know all too well how talk of witchcraft will sound, having grown up with schools, media, biomedicine, and the Church.

Most of those peasants accept the official discourses of French institutions. Only those "caught" or "taken" by witchcraft know it as real, and they are careful about whom they talk witchcraft with. Only because she herself was "caught" could Favret-Saada learn how it alters one's reality. Drawing on her experiences to critique the distance underlying much anthropological practice, she argues the importance of "being affected," a phrase that—like being caught or taken—emphasizes something that happens, rather than willful action (2012).

As someone who lives in a world in which matters translated through witchcraft or magic are not supposed to exist, I like the phrase "getting caught" better than "going native." Going native is active, something someone does; getting caught implies reluctance. To become a "native" suggests abandoning a prior identity (as if that were ever fully possible); to be "caught" or "taken" is to find oneself not only vulnerable but living across plural realities.

Stoller acknowledges that he was caught—not by his willingness to learn from Songhay experts but by his alarmed discovery that what he had learned was deadly serious. He did not recognize the dangers when, a naïve young anthropologist, he embarked on the adventure of apprenticeship: what an opportunity! By contrast, Evans-Pritchard was never at risk: he makes it clear that his status (as a white man) meant he could neither be accused of mangu nor apprentice himself to "witch-doctors"—though the latter were unlikely to extend such an offer. Which of these shapes current structures of feeling?

In a 2010 memoir, a German telecommunications engineer named Geerken, who lived and worked in Indonesia from 1963 to 1981, declares that "incomprehensible and bewildering things happen in Indonesia. Things which I would previously have considered impossible" (2010: 113). Prime among these is *guna-guna*. While he tends to use the term for anything vaguely strange, a chapter on "Guna Guna and Magic" is more specific: "the double word guna-guna is like a black hole: witchcraft, black magic, love magic. All at once" (2010: 296).[1]

I had heard of guna-guna in Bali, in reference to practices that induced an inexplicable attraction. People brought it up to speak of couples who struck them as badly matched: for instance, when one party seemed oblivious to deficits of character, status, or beauty obvious to everyone else. But this guna-guna bears only a partial relation to Geerken's, whose expansive gloss conveys what it came to mean to Europeans in the Indies and whose chapter offers a slew of what I call guna-guna tales. Such tales focus on a white man, confident that sorcery is a benighted native belief, who becomes a target of "witchcraft, black magic, love magic." The author of his misfortune is a Javanese or Eurasian woman seeking a commitment or retaliating after being jilted. Products of conflicting desires, such tales are offspring of relationships that not only cross colonial racial divides but destabilize ontic certainties.

I first came across such stories by chance, in a 1936 book by Geoffrey Gorer about a "pleasure trip" to Southeast Asia.[2] Smack in the middle, he reports a shipboard encounter with another German, badly shaken by such an experience. I soon discovered that tales of this sort had circulated in the Indies for some time. In fact, once you look for them, anecdotes about Europeans affected by "incomprehensible and bewildering things" pop up not only in the Indies but in and about other colonized places, especially in memoirs and travel books.[3] Some recount firsthand experiences; others, tales heard at clubs, on colonizer verandahs, or in casual meetings of the kind Gorer relates, in transit or at hotels.

Such stories are a staple of fiction, whether with colonial settings—what Brantlinger (1988) calls "imperial gothic"—or not—as in Jacques Tourneur's 1957 film *Night of the Demon*, based on M. R. James's 1911 short story "Casting the Runes." The main character is a skeptical white man, often well educated, who becomes a victim of what he insists cannot exist. Guna-guna abounds in Indies fiction; undoubtedly, literary plot lines, figures, and storytelling techniques helped shape nonfiction narratives.

But there is more to guna-guna than insight into European imaginaries. By highlighting transactions that have no place in judicial, administrative, and ethnological concerns with objects, activities, and talk identified as "native," guna-guna opens different zones of magic's formation to inspection. Following keris to the Netherlands registered a change in concepts of magic as what (and whom) keris could gather expanded. Guna-guna also moved beyond the Indies; however—at least initially—it aroused considerably more ambivalence. Unlike the human and nonhuman actors that incited attempts at colonial control, guna-guna evaded official notice, involving as it did the intimate, affective lives of Europeans—the white man of reason at home. Initially a topic of gossip, guna-guna burst into public view when changing colonial policies and technological developments led to an intensification of guna-guna as a practice while propelling rumor into print. It is no accident that the genres through which accounts reached those unfamiliar with guna-guna speak to personal experience, where epistemic murk, to borrow Taussig's (1987) felicitous phrase, need not be dispelled by an impulse to explain. Although some ethnologists mention guna-guna in passing, it contravened their remit: to decode how natives think. Indonesian beliefs were, precisely, Indonesian (and merely beliefs), ending at the boundaries of Indonesian communities. But, as chapter 3 showed, borders may be breached. Guna-guna smashed right through them.

This is not to say that no ethnologist addressed it. As I will show, a handful did. How colonial science handled guna-guna both reiterates and makes explicit familiar procedures: dividing nature from culture and European from native, while eliding the myriad nonhumans guna-guna required. But stories participated more in magic's formation than glancing attention from authorities did.

Guna-guna tales recognize an ontic risk, insinuating that reality is less stable than learned discourse and colonial—and modern—politics could acknowledge. Bewitched Europeans could have no place in scholarly articles or official correspondence because they challenged the structures these worked to assemble. Such materials trouble political and epistemological hierarchies, not least because of their capacity to invade psyches supposedly resistant to them.

These tales offer a different angle on the white man of reason, as well as the dukun. Guna-guna reveals that the former was made, not born: to become or remain such a person required work.[4] As for dukun, they figure less as frauds than as practitioners of knowledges beyond the ken of Science, indeed provincializing the latter as European.

A Shipboard Encounter

It was a balmy night in 1935, on a steamer from Batavia to Singapore. Geoffrey Gorer had come on deck to enjoy the sea breeze. Suddenly he realized that he was not alone. Only yards away stood a fellow passenger, a mysterious German named Muller. Muller had refused the usual shipboard conviviality to a marked degree. He had emerged from his quarters only at meals, which he ate with his eyes locked on his newspaper. Such behavior had aroused Gorer's curiosity. Crew members had told him Muller would be traveling all the way to Europe, the steamer's sole passenger to Amsterdam.

Muller obviously was in great distress; tears rolled down his cheeks. When Gorer asked what was wrong, he replied, brokenly, that he was terribly lonely. But when Gorer invited him inside for a drink, Muller let loose a stream of invective against the crew. He was returning to Europe to get away from Asians. For five years, he had been forced to spend his time surrounded by their "brown faces." It was enough to drive one mad. He even dreamed of them.

And with that, Muller began his tale. In happier days, he had helped his uncle run a hotel in Berlin, until financial woes led to his uncle's suicide.

Muller then parlayed his local knowledge into a precarious living, leading tours of Berlin's nightlife. In this way he met Jan, a wealthy Indies rubber planter who took a fatherly interest in him and offered him a job. Muller had no desire to leave Berlin, but Jan left passage with a shipping agent in case he changed his mind. When the economy continued to slide downward, Muller headed to Java. But by then the Depression had affected Jan as well and he had no work to offer. Stuck in Java, Muller eventually found a post supervising the native staff in a hotel near Batavia, the colonial capital.

There life proved unbearably lonely. He could not fraternize with guests, and he would not with staff. Eventually, he became involved with a Eurasian woman named Anna. Anna considered herself European, but as her Dutch father had never acknowledged her, she was legally a native; Muller certainly regarded her as such. She lived with her Javanese mother and uncle, whom Muller described as "'a thoroughly disreputable old fellow, who made a living by doctoring the sillier natives and giving them amulets and love philters.... I thought he was an old rogue and let him see it'" (Gorer 1936: 121).

Muller soon found himself supporting not only Anna but also her family. Still, he was content with the arrangement until Anna announced that she was pregnant and insisted that he marry her. He refused but did offer to acknowledge paternity and continue supporting her. Anna, however, was determined her child be legitimate. So incessantly did they quarrel that Muller refused to see her. But she made embarrassing scenes at his hotel until he called the police.

With that, Anna stopped contacting him, but her uncle began dogging his steps. One day, when Muller was at the barber, the uncle dashed in and grabbed a lock of his hair. Not long after, on a rainy day, he materialized to scrape up a patch of mud where Muller had stepped. This alarmed a Javanese waiter at the hotel, who urged Muller to leave town before the man could make a spell, or at least to seek protection from a dukun. But, Muller told Gorer, "'Of course I couldn't do a thing like that; everybody would know about it, and my position would become impossible. And, anyhow, I didn't believe he could do anything except perhaps poison me; and I took good care not to eat anything which I hadn't seen others already eat'" (Gorer 1936: 123).

Time passed. Then Muller received a letter from Anna. She admitted she had been unreasonable, but as the baby was nearly due, would he come see her? At first Muller tossed it aside. But she was, after all, the only person with whom he had any intimacy, and, he confided to Gorer, not bad for a Malay. On his next evening off he dropped by.

Anna and her mother fussed over him and prepared a feast. (Muller, still cautious, only ate what they ate first.) Everything was fine until, dinner ended, Anna again raised the question of marriage. At first cajoling, she then began to threaten him, and he headed for the door. Throwing herself before him, Anna grabbed his legs, demanding that he explain his refusal. After all, he had liked her enough to spend two years with her, and she swore she would take good care of him. Muller, thoroughly annoyed, said that if she had to know he would tell her—she was a Malay, and he didn't want to spend his life with someone of her color. She became furious and swore that he wouldn't marry anybody of a different color, adding, "You won't see anybody who looks a different colour!" She then bit his hand. Muller wrenched free and left.

The next morning, he was minding the front desk at the hotel when Anna walked up. Furious, Muller shouted at her to leave, or he would call the police, but she responded with astonishment and in English, a language Anna did not know. Then up walked Anna's uncle, who berated Muller, also in English, for frightening his wife. Baffled, Muller recognized the voices of a British couple staying at the hotel and apologized. At noon he went to the hotel dining room and was stunned by what he saw: "'Every table was occupied by Annas and her uncles. Every white woman I saw looked like Anna, every white man like her uncle. It was horrible, and what was worse, I couldn't do my work properly any more; when all the clients looked the same I never knew which were speaking to me'" (Gorer 1936: 126).

The local (Dutch) doctor thought at first he was joking, and when he realized he was not, recommended that he wear dark glasses. The staff guessed something was up, however, and the Javanese waiter again urged him to see a dukun. Muller, who by now hated Javanese, and could not accept that he had been bewitched, refused. But finally he could take no more and agreed to a consultation.

After hearing his symptoms, the dukun confirmed that Muller had been ensorcelled. He suggested that he marry Anna, since that would end the spell, but Muller refused. In that case, if Muller could bring him a lock of Anna's hair, some nail parings, and a drop of her blood, the dukun would work a counter-spell. Muller told Gorer: "'But we're in the twentieth century; I can't go about picking up other people's nail-clippings, even if she'd give me the chance, which wasn't likely; and apparently it wasn't any good if anyone else did it. So the magician said he couldn't help me.' But as I was going away he added: 'It won't travel over water'" (Gorer 1936: 127).

Muller held out as long as he could but finally decided to return home. If distance didn't work, a psychoanalyst might. In the meantime, he avoided looking at anyone. When Gorer protested that he had been looking at him, Muller responded that Gorer's back was against the light, which obscured his features. Gorer concludes: "I didn't reply but lit a match so that the flare lit up both our faces. After that I went back to my cabin, for the expression on his face showed clearly enough how mine had appeared to him" (Gorer 1936: 127).

Sexual and Racial Politics in Colonial Java

Muller's vexed relations with Anna involved more than personal biases and desires. What made them simultaneously available and unavailable to one another were intersectional dynamics of sex, race, and class—shaped by historical and changing colonial policies, technological innovations, and semiotic-material forms of life.

As Taylor (1983) shows, from the start the VOC preferred to hire bachelors, opposed immigration by European women, and forbade marriages to non-Christians. Hence its merchants and officers formed households with *nyai*, Indonesian (mainly Javanese) or Eurasian women who ran their homes and shared their beds. Some legitimized these ties: ambitious men wedded the mestizo daughters of their superiors. Licit or not, such liaisons produced a hybrid colonizer culture: while VOC employees dressed Dutch and remained nominally Christian, their domestic lives were primarily Indonesian.

Such mores long outlasted the VOC. Well into the 1920s, old colonial hands counseled new arrivals to find themselves a nyai. But such arrangements produced offspring whose status required clarification. Those whose fathers acknowledged them counted as European themselves. Admitting paternity had other consequences: men had to support such children, while Indonesian mothers lost parental rights.

Policy changes began to bring this blended Indies culture under scrutiny. In 1870, advocates of free trade came to power in the Netherlands, prompting a boom in capitalist investment in the Indies. Partly in response to the problematic consequences for Indonesians, an alliance of business and religious groups instituted the Ethical Policy addressed in chapters 1 and 3. More and more Europeans—including bourgeois women—headed to the Indies seeking opportunities. The European population doubled from 1860 to 1900 and increased fourfold again from 1900 to 1930 (Van der

FIGURE 4.1: A Javanese nyai (name unknown), circa 1870. Part of a series of visiting cards of nyai by the famous photographic studio Woodbury and Page. Courtesy of Leiden University Libraries, Shelfmark KITLV 30794.

Veur 1955: 87). But numbers alone don't explain their impact. New transportation and communication technologies—the steamship, the telegraph, and the Suez Canal—facilitated contact with the metropole, making it easier to regard the Indies as a merely temporary home.

These developments set in motion a process Locher-Scholten (1994) calls "totokization." A new vernacular identity, a *totok* was someone born in Europe who planned to return there, and thus remained oriented to metropolitan norms and practices. Totoks set new standards for colonizer culture, drawing attention to departures from European norms. Increasingly, colonizers distinguished those judged culturally European from those colonial law classified as European because European men had acknowledged paternity.[5] Europeans born and raised in the Indies—recognizable by their distinct habitus—became known as "Indies people." Indies people often came from families who, having lived in the Indies for generations, had Indonesian ancestresses. Others, whose mixed background was evident from not only their behavior but also their appearance, were referred to as "Indos," from "Indo-European."

But totokization proceeded slowly and was never complete. For one, the longer totoks remained in the Indies, the more likely they were to adopt elements of Indies culture. Moreover, their children, raised by Indonesian nursemaids (*babu*), could become Indies people. Such hybridity marked domestic life into the start of the twentieth century. The semi-Indonesian drag even totoks wore at home scandalized and bemused visitors, as did their midday consumption of semi-Indonesian fare (the famous *rijsttafel*), invariably followed by a nap (De Wit 1984 [1912]; Scidmore 1984 [1899]).

Adoption of the Ethical Policy brought pressures to solidify distinctions. Since the superiority of European civilization justified colonial expansion, the policy presumed a clear gulf—in manners, morals, and mentality—between Europeans and Indonesians. Everyday Indies life confounded such presumptions. Much boundary work ensued, especially in regard to routines most in conflict with metropolitan norms. Sexual mores, and practices judged superstitious, provoked particular concern.

As religious groups played a crucial role in supporting legislators promoting the Ethical Policy, it is hardly surprising that cohabitation came under attack. Vice alone did not serve as grounds to condemn carnal relations with natives, however. For some reformers sexual license damaged European prestige, especially when practiced by administrators (Adelante 1898; Kohlbrugge 1907; see also Van de Doel 1994). Not only did extramarital sex raise questions about European morals for some subject populations, but, said reformers, white lechery aroused local ire, threatening peace and order. Such relationships could also encourage unseemly familiarities by the woman's male kin, potentially leading to corruption and nepotism. As the heads of local European communities, critics asserted, administrators should model propriety for both Indonesians and other Europeans. In short, by bringing European superiority into question, interracial sex undermined colonial rule. Such arguments convinced policymakers, who banned cohabitation by Dutch civil servants early in the twentieth century (Van Marle 1951–52:

486). As anticipated, the prohibition had a broader impact. At least in Java's urban centers, such attachments no longer were conducted openly or sanctioned socially.

But as Muller's story shows, they nonetheless persisted.[6] Demography offers one reason why: although their numbers continually increased, white women remained in short supply. The 1930 census (about when Muller arrived in Java) counted only 884 European women to every thousand European men. Men like Muller—who did not work in the civil service, as plantation managers, or in business—largely lacked the cultural and economic capital to wed a white woman. It took time even for better situated men to accumulate the resources needed to establish a European household, and many saw nothing wrong with dalliances in the interim. Then too, for many men the tropics embodied a zone of indulgence, beyond the constraints of bourgeois respectability. Thus totoks continued to regard Indonesian and Eurasian women as fair game for erotic adventures, despite changing mores and, increasingly, objections by Indonesian nationalists. Some still kept a nyai until they could afford to marry, while others engaged in casual fornication; prostitution rose as cohabitation declined (Van Marle 1951–52).

By the time Muller arrived, racialized boundary formations were at their peak. Activism by Indonesian labor unions, communists, and nationalists had brought the Ethical Policy into disfavor; Dutch opponents insisted it had produced an underemployed and overeducated native class with radical ideas. Alarm over disorder, and skepticism about progress in the wake of the Great War, precipitated policies promoting indirect rule and revivals of tradition (see chapter 3). A new separation marked interwar life. Returning to the Indies after a twenty-five-year absence, Couperus (1924) noted that colonizers had abandoned most remnants of previous forms of life. Totoks became more insular and judgmental of Indies people, even forming a political party that reflected the racism growing worldwide. For some totoks, little differentiated Indies people from Indonesians.

Given the time and place, Anna and Muller made a likely pair. Both found themselves on the peripheries of colonial society, Anna by virtue of race and Muller by virtue of class. Since his position as hotel manager barred him from socializing with European guests and put him in constant contact with Javanese, Muller may have found it vital to emphasize his whiteness. Although legally a native, Anna's paternity may have made her a more acceptable mistress. In turn, Anna's position—on the fringes of both European and Javanese society—no doubt rendered her susceptible to Muller. According to Van der Veur (1955, 1969), some Eurasian women in this period were obsessed with the desire to marry totoks. Like others in her situation, Anna tried to parlay her ambiguous identity into a relationship that might lead to commitment, and opportunities for her child. Anna had reason to have high hopes of Muller: in the Indies, Germans had a reputation for being less racist than Dutchmen and Englishmen, and more likely to marry their mistresses (Van der Veur 1969: 75). Such circumstances afforded ample opportunities for friction.

Desire and Danger

Totokization stimulated guna-guna, both as a practice and as an object of discourse.[7] As a practice because Indonesians had more cause to resort to guna-guna as more Europeans came to the Indies, for shorter sojourns, and European endogamy became more plausible. As an object of discourse because new arrivals found stories about bewitched men intriguing. Indies life appeared full of novelties—especially regarding sex and superstition. Guna-guna offered both. Before, few media existed to disseminate anecdotes (Nieuwenhuys 1978); Europeans lived in a primarily oral culture, in which the art of conversation thrived on gossip: an ideal medium for sharing, embellishing, and evaluating guna-guna tales. Passage from word of mouth to less ephemeral published texts, however, allowed guna-guna stories to proliferate promiscuously.

The most detailed description of guna-guna appears in a quirky work by H. A. van Hien, a totok renowned for his numerous books documenting Javanese practices.[8] An unconventional figure, Van Hien was born on the coast of Guinea in Africa (then a Dutch colony), but, after his father's death, his grandfather raised him in the Netherlands. He came to the Indies to serve in the KNIL infantry. Following his discharge, he obtained a civil service job as a low-level supervisor in the forestry division until a dispute cut his colonial career short. Such positions put him in contact with Javanese. He stayed in the Indies, supporting himself by writing. Van Hien devotes a section to guna-guna in his magnum opus, *The Javanese Spirit World (De Javaansche geestenwereld)*, a compendium of entities we call spirits, powerful places and objects, rites and invocations, divination techniques and creation tales, framed by concepts drawn from ethnology and theosophy.[9] It went through six editions after its initial 1896 publication; the last (consisting of three volumes) appeared in 1934, during Muller's residence on Java:

Guna-guna means to unite or bring together; also, a means administered in secret to make someone absent-minded, *"bruwet,"* a condition allowing one to get what one wants from him or her. . . .

Someone is in love with a girl, but she wants to have nothing to do
with him. The man goes to a *dukun guna-guna* . . . [who] then tries to
come into contact with the girl and administer to her by secret channels, usually via female servants or family members, a powder made
of *Jaka tua*, a small beetle, that is fed *kecubung* leaves before being
killed, dried, and pulverized.[10] If this succeeds, the *dukun* places a
guna-guna before the door of the girl's house the next Monday or
Thursday evening. This guna-guna consists of two cut-out dolls,
representing the girl and the man who desires her, which are buried
in the ground. On that day she has managed through a servant or
housemate to obtain a few of the girl's hairs, that—combined with the
lovesick man's hair, incensed with *stanggi*, and wound with *kenanga*
flowers—are hidden in the girl's pillow.

The administration of the *Jaka tua* befuddles the girl (*"bruwet"*) . . . and she then is inclined to do whatever one wishes. The
dukun now has to do nothing more than try to speak to her, at which
opportunity she imperceptibly touches an uncovered portion of the
[girl's] body with *minyak duyung*, i.e. mermaid's tears, and asks her to
come to the lovesick man. . . . Usually this succeeds, and the *dukun*
conveys the girl into the arms of the enamored man. (Van Hien 1934:
vol. 3, 46–47)[11]

Van Hien draws together actors that appear only in part in other accounts of guna-guna: human intermediaries, dukun, kecubung leaves, pulverized beetles, buried images, hidden body debris, incense, flowers, and
"mermaid tears" (dugong oil). He also provides a suggestive gloss for the
term *guna-guna* itself: its double inflection as a means both to make someone succumb to another's desires and to unite what otherwise would remain apart.[12] The latter is striking, for ultimately colonial guna-guna is all
about mixing. Among other things, it marks a form of engagement that
works against purificatory technologies of race and rationality.

So far, Van Hien's description appears purely ethnographic, a description of curious customs among the Javanese, although not framed, as that
genre often is, with phrases such as "Javanese believe." But shortly after, he
continues:

Although rare, you also find victims of *guna-guna* among Europeans. During our journeys collecting data for this work, we had the chance to get to know a few such miserable beings. They declared they did not know how they hit on the idea of taking that woman or girl as spouse.

Those who formerly had a housekeeper and cast her off for a legal union with another woman lay themselves most open to *guna-guna*. But the goal then is mostly revenge; seldom is affection still at stake. If the revenge is directed against the man and the *guna-guna* doesn't have the desired effect—to carry him back to his former housekeeper's arms—they resort to malignant *tumbal* or to secret poisons that usually cause a stomach illness through which he is sacrificed. If the revenge is directed against the woman, then it ends, if she doesn't quickly leave the house, with her death.

How many young women did we see during our investigations sink into the grave after having been married only a few months; and how many a promising young man, who after much labor obtained a position that allowed him to marry, did we see lie in a coffin, face contorted by the pain preceding his death. . . .

Sometimes you see European youths hanging out with Native women who are neither amiable nor pretty, are even past their youth, to whom they are as subservient as a slave, literally doing or having done everything desired of them. Do not be surprised by that, reader. It is the result of *Guna-guna*, that, continually employed, makes the man vacant, gray before his time, and after only a few years totally unfit for marriage. (Van Hien 1934: vol. 3, 48).

Here Van Hien links the mystery of attraction with fear of subjection and painful death: as discrete ends and acts or in the unfolding of a relationship over time. The impressionable Javanese damsel in distress, duped by unscrupulous men and their venal accomplices, vanishes, to be replaced by a manipulative, devious, spiteful femme fatale. White men materialize as victims, kept in place by induced docility, or, for those who managed to escape, subjected to fearsome retribution.

Van Hien distinguishes guna-guna from acts that may follow from it, aimed at causing illness or death. These involve poison or *tumbal*—assemblages of materials, often from the victim's body, as well as items such as needles and eggs, buried where the target regularly walks. Most authors are less fastidious; indeed, such blurring became constitutive as Dutch uses of the term guna-guna increasingly deviated from Malay meanings.[13]

But at its publication debut, guna-guna's meaning remained close to vernacular uses. In 1889, totok journalist P. A. Daum published a novel entitled *Goena-Goena*, after serializing it two years earlier in the *Bataviaasch Nieuwsblad*, the newspaper he founded and edited and one of the most widely read in Java (Beekman 1996: 332). Contemporaries considered Daum's novels romans à clef. Thus, although technically a work of fiction, he likely based it on rumors about people he knew, changing names and circumstances to avoid charges of slander or libel (Beekman 1996: 333).[14]

In the novel, a Javanese *babu* or nursemaid and her dukun son help an Indies woman named Betsy dispose of one totok husband and nearly capture another. Daum highlights the transformations then occurring in the Indies, starting with a description of a town in the throes of the new era of investment—with rice fields and coconut palms displaced by sugar cane, factories, and a rail station—before moving to a social world beginning to feel the impact of totokization. Bronkhorst, the man Betsy desires, is happily married to a blonde, blue-eyed totok he met on a visit to the Netherlands. Daum portrays in detail the various acts and objects involved in preparing and administering guna-guna; indeed, the novel has a quasi-ethnographic character, as in a chapter describing the dukun's trip to Java's south coast to purchase *minyak duyung* (dugong oil). Repeated exposure to guna-guna draws Bronkhorst under Betsy's spell; he loses interest not only in his family but in his greatest passion, his work as a notary. (That Bronkhorst is professionally in the verification business is suggestive.) His wife, however, who shocks the European community by her constant cooking and cleaning, proves "too strong" to succumb to the materials (a tumbal; substances slipped into her coffee) meant to drive her from her home. A scandal ensues, leading to Betsy's forced departure. Forty days later Bronkhorst returns at last to his senses. In the novel's final words, "the guna-guna was spent" (Daum 1964 [1889]: 223).

Daum's guna-guna tale differs from most in that the woman at its center is technically European. As Van Hien indicates, guna-guna became increasingly relevant as a way to explain involvements with Javanese or Indo women. In portraying such women as seductresses, guna-guna tales mark a growing disapproval of mixed-race alliances while exonerating white men. Consider this characterization of Javanese women by an opponent of interracial liaisons: "Whatever the abominable means employed—whether they mingle their spittle or blood or some other filth in his food; or whether they know how to invoke and use secret powers unknown to us to make him a supine tool in their hands—they dominate him completely, more fatally than the hypnotist dominates his subjects" (Koot 1905: 13, quoted by Ming 1983: 82).

This comment pinpoints why guna-guna could appear sinister. In rendering its victim tractable and sapping his will (recall Van Hien's *bruwet*), it eerily targets colonizer masculinities. The sense of superiority proper to male colonizers rested on an authoritative and self-assured agency, based in reason. What could be more insidious than an unknown force that could exact compliance, rendering white men subject to those (natives, and women to boot!) they should command? In effect, guna-guna emasculated European men. Or emasculated them further. Seduced, rather than seducers, they already were feminized.

Daum's Bronkhorst serves as a good example. As he succumbs to guna-guna, he becomes dominated by desire rather than duty. A model paterfamilias and responsible public figure, respected for his sound judgment and successful investments, he turns into a moony adolescent, consumed by longing and indifferent to social mores.

So inflected, guna-guna tales constitute a male genre. European women narrate them differently, affording more nuanced insight into the motivations that might inspire such acts, and even sympathizing with native women as victims of their fickle lovers (or of rivals [Rush 1990; Taylor 1983]). One totok, for example, claimed that Javanese women mainly resorted to guna-guna to stay in the relative comfort of a European household and ensure continued contact with their children; some managed through guna-guna to become legal wives (De K. v. W. 1907: 192). An American traveler, less likely to share intimacies with Javanese, offers a keen observation on the impact of guna-guna stories on white men: "the chilling tales of slow, mysterious deaths overtaking those who desert Malay wives or return to Europe without these jealous women, act as restraining forces" (Scidmore 1984 [1899]: 120–21).[15]

This reference to "chilling tales" marks a metamorphosis from guna-guna's vernacular meaning. As cohabitation with Javanese or Indo women became a temporary stage in the lives of white men rather than the norm, guna-guna tales focused less on seduction and more on revenge. Stories highlight the excruciating deaths not only of men who abandoned their mistresses for white women but also (as in Van Hien's account) of their innocent white wives or fiancées.

In these late nineteenth- and early twentieth-century accounts, only occasional traces of the language of magic appear. Van Hien (1934: vol 3, 47) mentions "bewitching" (*betoveren*) in noting that guna-guna often is used against married men. For Daum, a Javanese servant recruited against his will to help thinks of the dukun as a sorcerer (*tovenaar*) and the dukun's mother as a witch (*toverheks*) after noticing in the dukun's room jars containing beetles and kecubung. As I show below, this changed in the 1920s and (dramatically) in the 1930s, when guna-guna commonly is translated as magic, often as black magic.

Discipline, Denial, and Disdain

Having originated in gossip, guna-guna tales flowed easily into conversational and experiential print genres. Apart from novels and travelogues, guna-guna found its way into essays, commentaries, and memoirs. Casual uses of the term in newspapers and magazines mark such stories' ubiquity. Guna-guna, in short, inserted itself even into the experience of white skeptics, if only in the form of piquant rumors and anecdotes.

Under the circumstances, scholar-administrators certainly would have heard guna-guna tales. But given that these stories concerned the private lives of white men, it is perhaps unsurprising that most had nothing to say about them. Even guna-guna as a purely Indonesian phenomenon attracted scant attention: it offered little of theoretical interest to those focused on animism and fetishism, and was not of obvious political concern as a threat to peace and order. Yet tracking even brief accounts of guna-guna into the work of such authorities over time proves illuminating, both in terms of the types of experts who weighed in on it and for following its growing translation through magic.

Guna-guna entered colonial science by piquing the curiosity of two totok physicians who encountered it through their work. Each draws on agents familiar to medical science to account for guna-guna's effects. Starting from different mechanisms (indeed, their explanations are mirror opposites), each reduces the panoply of practices and actors Van Hien described, selecting certain elements and ignoring the rest. More specifically, they distribute guna-guna as physiology or psychology.

In 1893, Adolphe Guillaume Vorderman, superintendent of the Civil Medical Service for Java from 1890 to 1902 and a pioneering researcher of Javanese plant remedies and poisons, offers what may be the first scholarly account of the phenomenon. Vorderman came to the Indies as a naval medical officer, joining the Civil Medical Service in 1871 and moving to Batavia in 1881. He addresses guna-guna in a short piece on two native poisons that had come to his attention. Defining guna-guna as a means to make someone ill, he then effects a purification, precipitating out what belongs to the sphere of nature from the domain of culture. Specifically, he divides guna-guna into "charms" and "superstitious acts" (e.g., burying bones in someone's yard) and "the administering of foreign supplements in the food or drink of the person to be manipulated" (Vorderman 1893: 81–82). Leaving the first to ethnologists, he claims the second as the domain of scientists such as himself. Implicitly, he considers "superstitious acts" harmless. But substances added to comestibles are another matter since these might affect organic function. More than merely a division of scientific labor, Vorderman's distinction is ontological, extricating acts belonging to the realm of nature, by having observable consequences for the bodies of biomedicine, from customs with no material effect.

The substance that interests him comes from trapping small black beetles (species unidentified) and feeding them the leaves of a kecubung plant; the ensuing fecal matter is used in guna-guna. While Vorderman notes that it works "toxically on the human organism" to produce a "chronic poisoning," he does not specify the effects. He does, however, identify kecubung as the plant botanists then knew as *Datura alba* (now *Datura metel L.*), allowing knowledgeable readers to infer possible symptoms, such as hallucinations, disorientation, memory loss, and anxiety. Vorderman does not address how passage through a beetle's digestive tract might modify its action. Nor does he indicate that datura is not just any toxin; it traverses the literature on magic, popping up in accounts of European witchcraft and Amazonian shamanism.

By contrast, J. H. F. Kohlbrugge, introduced in chapter 1, has no use for poisons or ingested substances in his much lengthier discussion of guna-guna: instead, he zeroes in on the "charms" Vorderman ignores. For Kohlbrugge, guna-guna works by subconscious projection and suggestion. He offers a detailed analysis of how these operate in Javanese subjects, centered on signs that allow a victim to infer that she (as with Van Hien, the victim in this imaginary scenario is female) is the target of a spurned suitor; convinced that guna-guna works, she succumbs. Here guna-guna safely remains a (false) native belief.

But what happens when guna-guna is directed at white men, who by definition do not believe, "occasionally with excellent results" (Kohlbrugge 1907: 18)? Kohlbrugge recognizes his readers may have learned about this, as well as about the fearful consequences of spurning former nyai, from novels and travel books. Moreover, he acknowledges that he personally had treated men who insisted their mistresses had poisoned them. This he rejects: in no such case is there evidence of poisoning. Here suggestion works on belief as well, albeit a different belief: "It is a fact," Kohlbrugge maintains, "that many Europeans believe in guna-guna's influence, that most young people are afraid of the deserted housekeeper's poisons." This triggers a psychological mechanism: "The feeling of not having acted in harmony with their own moral concepts, thus the sense of guilt, suppresses cool thinking and suggests belief in guna-guna and poison" (Kohlbrugge 1907: 18–19). Moral scruples lead men suffering from mundane maladies to find gossip about guna-guna newly credible. As for those who blame guna-guna for their attraction to unsuitable women, Kohlbrugge prefers psychopathology: men with sadistic tendencies unconsciously feel the pull of passive, masochistic Javanese women.

But Kohlbrugge does not limit diagnosis to his patients. He also takes aim at the popular Van Hien. Commenting on the passages I quoted earlier, he asserts: "See, a European can only write so who is already strongly Indicized, who has experienced the suggestive influence of animism" (1907: 19). To take reports of white victims seriously indicates pathology, serving as evidence one is no longer fully European.

Kohlbrugge contributes here to discussions of the mutability of European psyches in the tropics, a matter of considerable concern to colonial states.[16] Later, some argued that Europeans became more volatile in the Indies, showing an increased tendency to react to stimuli (Hermans 1925; Kerremans 1923). In extreme cases, this led to nervous disorders (such as tropical neurasthenia) marked by irritability, overexcitement, or excessive anxiety. While some attributed such syndromes to the debilitating effects of nature, others blamed society, noting the stresses generated by isolation from racial and status peers, homesickness, absence of a "normal" family life, even "the entire complex of atmospheric nuances that we call the mystical East" (Van Wulfften Palthe 1936: 358).[17] Such assessments percolated into popular wisdom—recall Muller's complaint that spending so much time surrounded by "brown faces" was enough to drive one mad. Doctors held that these disorders would "not travel over water": returning to Europe would effect a cure. Indeed, doctors diagnosed more than half of those repatriating for medical conditions in 1915–25 with tropical neurasthenia (Van Wulfften Palthe 1936: 356).[18]

Kohlbrugge is not claiming that Van Hien suffered from a mental illness; even those who apparently functioned well could be altered by the Indies. Kohlbrugge's position was radical; he maintained, for instance, that no one raised in the Indies could remain European—even if both parents were totoks. Moreover, "their descendants . . . shall be still less [European]; they metamorphose, if slowly, then nonetheless surely, into Indos, and finally into Javanese" (1907: 112).[19] Van Hien's lapse from cool reason suggested he was heading in that direction. But how did Kohlbrugge account for such transformations? Like others, he highlights not only climate but also social life, including interactions with natives. He agrees, for instance, with those who cautioned that too much contact with Indonesian servants (especially nursemaids) could make children fearful and superstitious.[20] Kohlbrugge insinuates that affairs with Indonesian women could incite similar results. Europeans in such intimate associations risked contagion: belief in magic could be a sexually transmitted disease.

Guna-guna, then, had to be purified to be dealt with scientifically. It also required border work to render colonizers distinct from those they colonized. Neither doctor fully elucidates guna-guna, however. Vorderman shows it involves a psychogenic substance but does not account for its specific effects: how, for instance, it might make a particular person attractive, or produce remarkably precise hallucinations such as Muller's. In noting its "toxic" effects, Vorderman implies these should be universal. But accounts of datura from other parts of the world show they are not: its biological activity is locally mediated. For Kohlbrugge, guna-guna is a mental phenomenon, an effect of the power of suggestion. While acknowledging that guna-guna involves "certain finely mashed beetles that have a stupefying effect," they play no role in his analysis (1907: 17). And that any substances interesting to toxicologists could be relevant to his patients's complaints, he dismisses out of hand. Only minimal material supports appear necessary, although Kohlbrugge does acknowledge that European psyches may be made amenable by exposure to "superstitious" Indonesians in tropical environments. Precisely how suggestion operates remains vague. Suggestibility strangely resembles the mental state that guna-guna aimed to induce.

If initial efforts to grapple with guna-guna parse it into binaries (a universal nature for Vorderman; psychopathology and Javanese culture for Kohlbrugge) and ignore many elements Van Hien mentions, they nonetheless treat guna-guna as a practice with tangible and real effects. But in the 1920s, ethnologists enlist guna-guna to speak to *magie*, a new theoretical object. In the process, both European victims and guna-guna's efficacy vanish.

According to Alkema, a former missionary and Kohlbrugge's colleague at Utrecht, *magie* came into vogue (along with *primitieve*) with "the modern ethnologists," whom he also calls the "men of magic" for their insistence that customs previously analyzed as animist would be better explained by magic (1930: 24–28). *Magie* had different connotations than the older *to-verij* and *hekserij*, which dragged with them the historical memory of the witch trials: it was foreign, theoretical, and altogether sexier.[21] Once subsumed under the category of magic, any sense of its relevance to European lives disappears.

Alkema's main target was Van Ossenbruggen. The latter concurred with British and German ethnologists who maintained that the earliest stage of human thought could not have been animist (as the eminent Wilken had argued), since, as its Latin root implied, this required spirits or souls: a metaphysical partition between a material world perceptible to the senses and incorporeal essences or forces. Van Ossenbruggen disputed animism's relevance in favor of "magical thinking," that is, mistaking associations between ideas for connections in nature. Such associations arose from chance conjunctions in time and space, resemblances, or strong emotions. While the "associative mechanism" formed the basis of all human thought, advanced peoples subjected associations to reason.

Van Ossenbruggen briefly brings up guna-guna in a short article, to demonstrate how magical thinking lingers in practices others call animist:

> [W]hen the animist wishes to get someone to do something, wishes to influence him, he will not try to do this psychologically but purely magically. The native love agents, guna-guna, are, like all magic charms [*tovermiddelen*],[22] magical thought. Generally they consist of administering something of yourself to the person whose love you are trying to win, e.g. saliva, little pieces of skin, etc., or even beans that are swallowed and remain hard, undigested, which are burned, ground, and mixed into coffee, which you then give to the one desired. None of this has anything to do with the soul. Influencing the "treated" person's disposition, will, psychologically is simply lacking; this person is entirely unaware of the magical influencing, happily for him. (1926: 298–99)

Like Vorderman, Van Ossenbruggen highlights the ingestion of noxious substances, but he is remarkably vague about the stuff itself (note the "et cetera"), finding the particulars unimportant. Whether corporeal fragments or something passed through the alimentary canal, what counts is a relation to an amorous body, an anticipatory fleshly encounter. Did he choose his examples (saliva, flakes of skin, a bean recovered from excrement) to invite disgust or to speak to a shared understanding with readers familiar with guna-guna anecdotally? While chapter 3 showed Van Ossenbruggen paying meticulous attention to specific materials, they do not concern him here except as evidence of the associative mechanism. At the same time, he adamantly rejects psychological explanations. Guna-guna is meant to work mechanically rather than by altering consciousness.

Not surprisingly, then, he says nothing about white victims, although he surely heard stories, having been born and living most of his life in the Indies. He does, however, observe that even well-educated Europeans may manifest magical thinking, especially when overcome by emotion. But he props up the white man of reason by insisting that the European "system of thought" is "rooted in rigorous logic, [which] gives us a correct view of cause and effect and makes us find and understand laws of natural necessity" (1926: 296).

Guna-guna also appears under *magie* in the *Encyclopaedie*'s 1927 supplement (S[pat] 1927: 263–71).[23] As prior editions contain no such entry, that *magie* now demanded lengthy treatment (eight pages!) testifies to Van Ossenbruggen's persuasive powers (recall his impact on Kruyt, chapter 3), even as his theories proved less enticing: while guna-guna receives only cursory attention, Spat, a totok, presents guna-guna squarely as a form of magic rather than an expression of magical thinking.[24]

Written as it is for an encyclopedia, Spat's text gathers a wide range of practices under magic's umbrella. Guna-guna appears near the end, in a paragraph on "the bewitching of one person by another," through "charms" intended to "arouse love and sow hate, get power over someone and so on." Most often these involve spells and incantations, though examples from the Malay peninsula involve substances familiar from Muller's story: small wax images, incorporating the victim's hair and nail clippings, which, aided by a magical formula, capture the victim's soul; and earth from the victim's footprint, to put him under one's power.[25] Spat also cites an Indonesian book on *mantra guna-guna*, "formulas said for love magic and the concoctions to use with these" (1927: 270). For Spat, guna-guna is primarily a semiotic technology, consisting of prescribed speech acts or expressive performances. Nowhere, however, is it potentially part of his own or his reader's reality.

For Van Ossenbruggen and Spat, guna-guna remains an ethnological curiosity, an element of Indonesian culture irrelevant to their readers' lives. It serves solely to illustrate how natives think. Their boundary work severs guna-guna from its scandalous promiscuity in popular culture by rendering it purely as a scholarly object, one of many specimens of magic.

A final scholarly treatment not only firmly maintains guna-guna's identification with magic but amplifies it, specifying it as "black magic" and analyzing it as a matter of potential concern to colonial administrators. It appeared in a dissertation in jurisprudence in Leiden, on "customary law (*adatrecht*) offences in the magical worldview (*magische wereldbeschouwing*)." Its author, Nicholaas Willem Lesquillier, was an Indies boy: he proudly notes "born in Sigli (Aceh)" under his name on the title page (Lesquillier 1934). His parents too were Indies born, his father in central Java and mother in west Sumatra. Adat law was a uniquely Dutch field of scholarship and policy recommendations, established at Leiden around the turn of the twentieth century by Cornelius van Vollenhoven. Adat law experts sought to reveal the underlying unwritten laws that informed *adat*, an Arabic loan word for indigenous practices, traditions, and customs. Van Vollenhoven was indefatigable in eliciting materials from "men on the spot" across the archipelago and making colonial legislators take them into account.

Lesquillier organized this project around what he termed a "magical worldview." Building on colonial ethnology (including Van Ossenbruggen's work), he declared that for the Indonesian (*Indonesiër*) a dynamic force operated in all things—humans, gods, ancestors, plants, animals, and objects. These entities existed in a delicate balance: acts that upset equilibrium constituted offenses; sanctions sought to restore it.

Much of what Lesquillier addresses concerns reviewing specific legal cases involving what jurists in different places across the archipelago had translated as beliefs in "witchcraft."[26] As a specialist in adat law, he advocated that colonial law and policy accommodate community concerns in such matters. But he differentiates "witches" from those he termed "black magicians." While witchcraft is an act attributed by others who may or may not have anything to do with deliberate actions on the part of the one accused, "black magic" (*zwarte kunst*) is an intentional act that involves material mediations and may leave material traces as evidence. It is such black magic that he links to dukun and guna-guna.

He is clear that the purview of practitioners such as dukun not only involves doing harm, but encompasses curing the sick and warding off danger. But since Europeans regard magic as based on fantasy or a failure of reason, they cannot recognize when the activities of Indonesian practitioners veer into the domain of criminality, especially when Europeans treat doctors and scientists as arbiters of the factual basis of the activities involved. European physicians, Lesquillier observes, regularly fail to explain sudden deaths, illnesses, or psychological disturbances (even insanity) in the Indies. Since medicine continually evolves and the power of suggestion remains poorly understood, rather than taking the efficacy of the means used as the basis for deciding whether the use of black magic has been unlawful, the perpetrator's intention should serve as guide. Someone Indonesians consider capable of making people ill or killing them is dangerous to community welfare and should be treated as a criminal. Because Dutch law had nothing to say about such matters, the colonial state ignores what Indonesians deem serious crimes. Reviewing several cases of such "black magic" (such as the use of materials to try to seduce a married woman) in *RNI*, Lesquillier argues that the fact that they know they cannot be tried for a crime empowers unscrupulous persons.

His proposed solution is an addendum to the penal code's (admittedly problematic) occult offenses. He even proposed its form: "Anyone who by magical means (*magische middelen*) intentionally tries to cause another harm, whether misfortune, illness, psychological disturbance, death... is punished," with the details to be worked out (1934: 138). He added later that "misfortune" could include exerting undue influence on authorities (1934: 228).

It is not clear what happened to Lesquillier or if he ever returned to the Indies after receiving his degree. In any event, nothing came of his proposal. Perhaps it would have aroused more interest over time. His dissertation appeared only a year before an explosion of British publications on witchcraft, with the special issue of *Africa* to which Evans-Pritchard contributed, which in turn prompted a Leuven conference on witchcraft in mission fields to which C. C. Berg, Professor of Javanese at Leiden, was invited (though his contribution said nothing about witchcraft).

Like the ethnologists, Lesquillier's concern is with Indonesian perspectives. He says nothing about guna-guna tales. Yet his remarks about the limitations of colonial science and law leave open the possibility that guna-guna might in fact affect Europeans. As I address below, arguments resonant with his already had been circulating in Indies communities. Indeed, if Dutch scholars purified or ignored guna-guna tales, elements of what they say turn up in popular culture. As Rush notes, "If one were to believe [the] stories, being poisoned was one of the commonest ways to die in colonial Indonesia" (1990: 155). Suggestion had its advocates too.[27] But it is telling that while Kohlbrugge invoked suggestion to dismiss guna-guna's reality, men convinced they were its victims consulted him. Guna-guna tales did more than reflect colonial anxieties; they shaped Indies experiences, molding colonizer subjectivities.

"Now Don't Sneer"

While guna-guna tales never ceased to be an element of Indies life, they boom in the 1930s. They also undergo several alterations: in the social relations they report and enact, in those who narrate them, and in the technologies through which guna-guna operates. Even more crucial: they cement guna-guna's translation through magic.

Consider this passage from a second novel entitled *Goena Goena*, published at the very start of the decade. In it, Henk Daeman, the totok main character, ponders with surprise an implied proposition regarding a housemate's baffling illness:

> Guna-guna . . . was a word that people used much and much too much and too easily. People who were in the Indies three or four days knew the word, without knowing its full significance.
>
> For guna-guna did not exist. It cannot exist, because magic did not exist and what is the Dutch translation of guna-guna other than pure: magic [*toverij*]?
>
> No . . . when you wanted to classify Native poisons under the heading guna-guna . . . yes, all right . . . then you could speak of guna-guna, because Natives knew many queer poisons and almost every Native is a born toxicologist. (Kijdsmeir 1930: 81)

It would be hard to find a plainer statement of the reality politics at work in rendering an Indonesian vernacular equivalent to the Dutch *toverij*. My own translation of the latter is, of course, itself too simple, since *toverij*'s use here pulls magic in the direction of sorcery and witchcraft. If "guna-guna cannot exist," it is because for a post-Enlightenment white man, magic, especially in that form, cannot exist. Once knotted to magic, guna-guna loses any claim to reality—unless it can encompass poisons, even those only Indonesians know. At the same time, like other contemporary texts, this novel, even this passage, challenges totok certainty.

The reality politics of this era form its most important feature. But this novel also serves as an entrée to several key transformations of guna-guna tales. The quote itself starts by referencing the speed of their transmission to parties new to the Indies, a harbinger of Gorer's transient encounter with Muller. Its plot brings to the fore the racial dynamics informing both relationships and narratives, a matter its authorship oddly underscores: Caesar Kijdsmeir Jr. was the Indo-sounding pseudonym of totok Albert

Zimmerman, editor-in-chief from 1923 to 1937 of *D'Oriënt*, an illustrated weekly with the largest circulation in the Indies.

Blonde, blue-eyed Henk, a businessman, falls in love with and marries a light-skinned, well-educated Indies girl, who speaks nearly perfect Dutch and has blue eyes herself.[28] Her darker, culturally and linguistically more "native" distant cousin, once Henk's secretary, has become infatuated with him, however. Her obsession leads to a deterioration in her mores and morals: she moves from wearing a guna-guna "amulet" with Henk's photo under her blouse to consulting a Haji to kill Henk's wife, and from sleeping with other men and once with Henk, to prostitution. After the death of his wife and child, Henk flees the Indies in terror. The Eurasian ex-wife of Henk's totok housemate is presumed responsible for the latter's illness and death. In the novel, the darker a woman's skin and less European her manners, the more she engages guna-guna.

As this plot suggests, 1930s texts pay more attention to race. As in Kijdsmeir's novel, some mapped attitudes toward guna-guna onto racial categories, with skepticism marking European reason (the totok view) or European ignorance (the position of Indies people and Europeans residing longer in the Indies). Notably, Javanese nyai no longer appear in guna-guna tales at all; Indo and Indies women replace them. Indos and Indies people also sought to establish guna-guna's reality by translating it as magic. As the scholars did, that translation allowed them to knot it to networks beyond the Indies, while reversing the goal.

Eurasians could hardly avoid tackling guna-guna, and not only because some depicted them as its instrument. As racial lines sharpened, Indos and Indies people found themselves on the defensive. Caught between a desire for recognition as European and their intimate local knowledge, they worked hard at mediation, testifying to their own experiences and those of acquaintances while confronting totok derision.

Indos bear witness to both the use and effects of guna-guna. Contrary to Kohlbrugge, they insist that guna-guna was not a product of febrile European psyches. Consider the testimony of an Indo who followed her Dutch husband to the Netherlands after independence:

> Many Dutch boys and men were subjected to *guna-guna*. Now don't sneer! The men were made groggy by the constant use of herbs and sometimes excrement from the women's body mixed with their food or drink. This is no story. It is something very important—even though many sneer about it—in breaking down and confusing will

power. It absolutely, to put it bluntly, forces the person in such a violent way to continue intercourse that, combined with all that guna-
guna, he is spiritually broken for the time being. I saw it used much
by *muntjies*, the wives of regular soldiers. (quoted by Van der Veur
1969: 76)

Note the speaker's anticipation of disdain. Still she persists, presenting herself as a witness to guna-guna's use (while mentioning a particularly transgressive ingredient).

Indo testimony repeatedly registers such sensitivity to Dutch sneers. Anyone seeking to speak to experience on this topic had to present himself, at
least initially, as a skeptic. Schenkhuizen sets the stage this way: "Strangely,
we Indos who grew up with black magic, called *guna-guna* in Indonesia,
were kind of skeptical about it and had the idea or the feeling, 'Well, that
won't happen to me. That can only happen when you're afraid of it, or believe in it'" (1993: 138). Having signaled her reliability, she recounts the
events that changed her mind. Chief among them was a diagnosis of an
otherwise unexplained illness by a "doctor" with "psychic powers," who
discovered in her home a pillow sewn shut with black thread. After her
fiancé opened it, and the doctor disposed of the object within, her symptoms vanished. Schenkhuizen, like the anonymous Indo above, betrays a
constant awareness that interlocutors might be dubious, or dismiss her as a
native. To establish her European credentials she adds that her strong Christian faith no doubt protected her from even worse effects. She also calls on
allies beyond the specific racial problematic of Indies life: "You can read for
yourself that such dark powers, sometimes called voodoo and sometimes
by another name, are found all over the world, no country excepted. In one
country it may be more out in the open than in another, but magic has been
used as long as the road to Rome has been in existence" (1993: 139–40).

Many maintained that biomedical physicians could neither diagnose
nor cure illnesses involving "black magic," whether these afflicted the body
or the mind, including so-called tropical mental disorders. Consider this
passage in an autobiographical novel by the scion of an Indies family:

Every night, at exactly two o'clock, [my father] would wake up fright-
ened, as if he had been called. He thought he would go insane; nothing could interest him. In short, he seemed to be going through an
early stage of the later neurasthenia which baffled all his European
doctors and which they couldn't even diagnose. At the time a village
chief in Tjitjurug sent my mother a *hadji* woman who was famous for

her powers against black magic. She prayed over a bowl of water in which seven kinds of flowers were floating, and she walked through the garden looking for the evil. Under the *bungur* tree she found a little doll buried, rusty pins stuck through its head.... The voodoo doll was used to drive him mad. Perhaps it was the power of counter-suggestion, but the *hadji* woman achieved her goal. After he had seen the little doll unearthed, my father slept quietly again and the neurasthenia disappeared. (Du Perron 1984 [1935]: 81)

The narrator moves between magical causes and religious cures and medical labels and explanations ("counter-suggestion"). Efforts to translate "black magic" into psychiatric language leave out elements featured by those working the translation in the opposite direction. Doctors like Kohlbrugge linked guna-guna to disease through suggestion, mental illness, and going native; Indies narrators through dukun (here a Haji), enmity, and "voodoo dolls."

Indies authors refuse to reduce guna-guna to poisoning or suggestion. They emphasize guna-guna's materiality, but the substances highlighted are not ingested; rather, they are buried or hidden in proximity to their target. And, contrary to Kohlbrugge, only with the discovery of such objects following the appearance of symptoms does the sufferer consider "black magic" their cause.

A particularly detailed and sophisticated defense of guna-guna appears in a series of articles by an author calling himself Hitzka (1930). Translating guna-guna as unmodified magic (*magie*), Hitzka argues that it involved facts of nature, however unfamiliar to science. To make his case, he not only draws on local knowledge, anecdotes about the Indies, and Van Hien, but crosses time and space to establish magic as real. Indeed, the first two installments say little about the Indies. Quoting from sources in Latin, French, and German, and from scholarly and quasi-scholarly materials (including occultist investigations), he argues the global ubiquity of certain practices despite local differences in materials—insisting as ethnologists did on sameness, while rejecting evolutionary explanations. Instead, he presents guna-guna as an Indies variant of a universal matter of fact.[29]

Hitzka also treats guna-guna as more ominous and omnipresent than usually acknowledged. After lauding science and refusing to blame biomedical doctors for their ignorance (how could physicians trained in the Netherlands be expected to recognize and treat illnesses caused by Indonesian experts?), he takes guna-guna beyond the vicissitudes of amorous relationships, intractable illness, and inexplicable death to timely matters such as bankruptcy, loss of employment, and stalled careers. Invisible to the colonial state, with no risk to themselves, practitioners could come under the politically sensitive radar of officials, seeping into the consequential domains of government and law. Since the regime neither prosecuted practitioners nor took their abilities seriously, why not try to influence the outcomes of trials, remove interfering administrators, and commit felonies?[30] Through their ignorance the totoks running the colonial state not only promoted malfeasance but failed to protect its subjects.

Different interests spurred another body of texts: travelers's accounts of guna-guna, which is not always mentioned by name and invariably is rendered as magic. Many of the Europeans and Americans making use of the growing infrastructure of transportation, hotels, guides, and travel agents that private and government enterprises developed between the wars came to the Indies in search of the exotic. Fussell (1980) argues that after the Great War a new restlessness seized hold of metropolitan middle and upper classes; declaring bourgeois conventions stifling, some avidly sought novel experiences. Reason had lost its luster, stimulating interest in its purported opposite. Little wonder that travelers found guna-guna riveting. And unlike Europeans living and working in the Indies, it never put their status or welfare at risk. On the contrary: they engaged it to make their reputations, by publishing books with broad appeal.

Typically, they refer to guna-guna in passing, in brief anecdotes to add local color.[31] Some merely present guna-guna as an ethnographic curiosity, an instance of peculiar native beliefs (Childers 1933). Others use it to amplify exotic mystery; hence, "even Europeans" tell "odd stories" of the power of Javanese dukun (Ponder 1990 [1942]: 109). Mostly, however, they put Indies tales into wider circulation, with several new elements.

For example, De Leeuw arrives at guna-guna ("a sinister side of native and European superstition") via a discussion of (female) Eurasian "half-castes," whom he characterizes as volatile and vindictive. Starting with familiar claims, he then introduces some novel technologies that others mention too:

> Debilitating drugs are concocted for use on the beloved, making him weak, physically and morally, and thus open to mental and imaginative suggestion.
>   These actually do work, and produce of course not love, but simple animal passion. But guna guna goes much further than this. Ground glass, tiger's whiskers, shredded bamboo fibre, and similar devices are

used to cause slow agonizing death, puncturing the internal organs.[32] Such is the skill in the use of these delightful weapons that they can be administered unnoticed, and may be timed to take just so long to produce the desired effect. (1931: 137–38)

Yet then he changes course, introducing two tales of white men whose abandonment of their Eurasian lovers proved fatal with the words: "Superstition? Perhaps, but . . . ." The first concerns a German-American living next door to De Leeuw at Batavia's Hotel des Indes, who told his Eurasian mistress of his plans to bring his fiancée to the Indies and marry her. As the wedding drew near, he became haggard and anxious. Still, he wedded on schedule, and the couple boarded a steamer to Singapore for their honeymoon. Then word came of their tragic double suicide, induced by guna-guna. Acknowledging his readers will find this incredible, De Leeuw shifts to a tale about a doctor who decided to return to Britain. His mistress "warned him that if he left without her he would not live beyond the Suez Canal. We later learned that he died while his ship was passing through the Suez. Possibly a tiger hair or ground glass" (1931: 139). As in Muller's story, the words of a woman scorned become literally true, even as the "possibly" undermines De Leeuw's earlier assurance. And, as with Muller, guna-guna follows its victim beyond the Indies.

Writing for audiences enthralled by tales of magic, especially in exotic settings, travelers produced guna-guna as an object of pleasurable fascination. Associations with the low and forbidden energized it with appealing transgressive possibilities, and genre conventions made such tales legible.

Gorer's is an exemplary instance of those conventions, drawing on familiar narrative strategies such as the meeting with a mysterious stranger and the ambiguous ending. He relates Muller's story without comment, allowing its testimonial structure to buttress credibility. His own narrative persona resembles Conrad's Marlowe: the trustworthy, tolerantly cosmopolitan, no-nonsense Englishman, lending an ear to a younger, unstable Continental enmeshed in a situation he badly misunderstands.[33]

Gorer never uses the term *guna-guna* or even the word *magic*. But a long digression to an account of his visit to Bali preceding this anecdote proposes something he calls "M.E.": mental or magical or mystical energy. While for three hundred years, he comments, Europeans had specialized in mastering the material world, taking it to be identical with reality, people in places such as Bali, West Africa, and Tibet had perfected techniques to use the mind as an energy source. Such energy could be deployed to affect objects at a distance or make mental creations visible to others (Gorer 1936: 87–94). Perhaps this is an implicit explanation of what happened to Muller. Its West versus the Rest dichotomies, however, remain problematically familiar.[34]

Reports by travelers, Indos, and Indies people partly coalesced. All translated guna-guna beyond the Indies and rendered it as magic. Unlike ethnologists or totoks, however, they insisted on its efficacy, including its capacity to afflict skeptical Europeans. By knotting it to metropolitan networks, they also challenged divisions between a European science uncovering a universal nature and native belief bounded by culture (at best) or ignorance (at worst).

Into the Twilight Zone

Tracking guna-guna tales over time makes it clear they did considerable work, from domesticating newcomers to contesting and ramifying knowledge formations to comprising a field for magic's translation. For Indonesians, guna-guna is about coercing infatuation from someone who did not reciprocate a suitor's desire. But guna-guna's meaning morphed as it moved beyond Indonesian speech communities. While Dutch accounts initially use the vernacular for the same kinds of situations that Indonesians do, guna-guna not only expands its referents but is increasingly glossed as *toverij*, magic, especially sorcery or witchcraft. Some parties also knot guna-guna to the task of universalizing magic—though knotters had differing stakes in that project. In guna-guna talk, magic emerges as a complex boundary object (Bowker and Star 1999), simultaneously a site of discipline, danger, derision, and desire.

Gorer's narrative is more than a token of a type, however. The form guna-guna takes in it clarifies the moral, political, and conceptual issues at stake. It foregrounds not only race but also magic's temporality. The destabilized differences that permeate this tale reveal the vulnerability of the moderns who count among those Stengers (2018a) calls "the frightless ones," and the colonial legacy of reason as a structure of thinking and feeling.

Indonesians talk about guna-guna to comment on bizarre relationships, in which a person appears besotted with someone others judge that person's inferior. We might call guna-guna a glamour, in its old sense of enchantment or magic. I learned from my Balinese family that there are those—like Anna's uncle—who can shift the shape of what others perceive, causing people to see things other than as they are or to see what others cannot. Such abilities hardly are limited to Indonesia: they saturate advertising and, increasingly, politics.[35]

But Muller's is not just your average guna-guna tale. Whenever I tell Muller's story (and I have, often) and end with Gorer striking his match, I imagine Rod Serling stepping out of the shadows to intone its moral, accompanied by the eight notes of *The Twilight Zone*. For this particular guna-guna tale definitely yields a moral.

Consider Muller's fate. Unlike other victims, Muller does not contract a ghastly illness or die a lingering death. Instead, what happens to Muller targets his sight. With surgical precision, Anna's dukun uncle obliterates the possibility of making the discriminations racist systems require. Since all Muller could see of Anna was her "color," what could be more apt? Muller no longer can "see white": he can neither see whites—who all look like Anna and her uncle—nor see like a white, prone to differentiate people by appearance. Clearly Muller had to leave the Indies: What place could there be for a colonizer incapable of such distinctions? Though it is by no means clear how a man who no longer sees white will fare in Nazi Germany.

The more I think about Muller, the more useful I find the figure of the "twilight zone." As a time when the gathering dark makes it hard to distinguish colors and shapes, twilight appears a fitting characterization of Muller's condition. But the phrase speaks to more than a transitory interval. Challenging the clear boundaries on which coloniality and racism depend, twilight zones are domains of epistemic murk where familiar divisions— including the real and the imaginary—offer no guidance.

Yet Muller's story offers even further insights. His desperate efforts to restore the world familiar to him highlight the temporality and geography of the reality politics constituting magic for moderns—and of guna-guna as one of magic's translations.

When in desperation Muller finally consults a dukun, he is horrified to learn that relief from his condition would require not only renewed intimacy with Anna, but also enacting the reality such practices produce—the world Europeans sought to eradicate. Balking at collecting nail clippings, he resorts to one of reason's counter-spells as he tries to prevent his reality from unraveling: "we're in the twentieth century!" That phrase hammers home magic's temporality. Not only does it deny the dukun's "coevalness" (Fabian 1983), but it enunciates what Stengers (2018a) identifies as a (modern) commandment: "thou shalt not regress." While she speaks to the power that commandment holds for academics, the latter are only one of many communities bound by that decree. In performing it, Muller bares its colonial ecology, the ground in which (having been planted in the Enlightened rejection of the reality of European witchcraft) it flourished. Both sorcery and the fear of it—and hence the prosecution of its purported practitioners, implicating those who, by prosecuting, took it as real—belong to the white man of reason's past. That white man of reason need not be well educated, a contributor to the making of knowledge. It obliges even a hotel manager. To treat sorcery as real is to "regress," to return to a former state, a conceptual palimpsest through which is visible Freud's annexation of what Tylor termed magic's "revival." In "the twentieth century" it can only exist as a false belief proper to "primitives" or the white children and neurotics who think like them. For the one-world world, reality involves a one-way temporal arrow—embedded in words such as *advanced, developed*, or, regress's opposite, *progress*.

If such "magic" refuses to remain in the past, it also traverses space. The dukun upon whose advice Muller can't act declares it won't travel over water. (What happens in Java stays in Java!) Gorer's match-lit face destroys that hope. Indeed, Gorer himself facilitates guna-guna's transit, as do all the authors who inscribed such tales. Through their texts, guna-guna establishes a foothold wherever there are libraries, books, and readers.

Nor has guna-guna only traveled in books; it also has moved with people. In 2022–23, Amsterdam's Stedelijk (Municipal) Museum—the foremost Dutch museum of modern and current art and design—planned a special exhibit on "Guna-Guna: Design, Contemporary Art, and Diasporic Magic."[36] "Diasporic magic" highlights guna-guna's path to the Netherlands, while reiterating the claims of Indos and Indies people who made it synonymous with magic more broadly. The call for submissions connected guna-guna's arrival in the Netherlands with the "Indonesian diaspora," that is, the Indos and Indies people, who, identifying as European, fled Indonesia following independence. In the Netherlands, the population category "Indo" includes their descendants as well as offspring of recent mixed marriages; the two art historians curating the exhibit were Indo women.[37] The call completes guna-guna's transmutation. It leaves behind not only vernacular practices (to induce infatuation), but also colonial meanings (entailing malign acts): guna-guna may, so the call read, be "productive, protective, deflective or destructive." It is defined as "animism, voodoo, vodou, popular belief, witchcraft or magic, as well as . . . ritual acts, spells and metaphysics," virtually everything (from anywhere) that magic covers.

Guna-guna now allures by a different form of seduction, as something (or some thing) tantalizing, mysterious, inexplicable, and mystical. Artists and designers were enjoined to propose "objects, sculptures, and other projects" that presume and convey the feeling that "objects may possess a soul or supernatural force." If the ethnologists' *magie* made guna-guna notional, a way of thinking, collectible art rematerializes it, without, however, nail clippings, ingested substances, or dukun practitioners.

INTERLUDE 5 ⌄̇ THE MAGIC OF MAGIC

Magic—the very word seems to reveal a world of mysterious and unexpected possibilities! Even for those who do not share that hankering after the occult, after the short-cuts into "esoteric truth," this morbid interest, nowadays so freely ministered to by stale revivals of half-understood ancient creeds and cults, dished up under the names of "theosophy," "spiritism" or "spiritualism," and various pseudo-"sciences," -ologies and -isms—even for the clear scientific mind the subject of magic has a special attraction. . . . [M]agic seems to stir up in everyone some hidden mental forces, some lingering hopes in the miraculous, some dormant beliefs in man's mysterious possibilities. Witness to this the power which the words *magic*, *spell*, *charm*, *to bewitch*, and *to enchant*, possess in poetry. (Malinowski 1948 [1925]: 50–51)

This passage by Malinowski attests to the magic of the word *magic*—its potency and capacity to allure even those presumed insensible to such things, those fortunate enough to possess a "clear scientific mind." He surely is right that responses to magic and associated terms have to do with hope, though he isn't very specific about what is hoped *for*. The American activist Starhawk is more explicit: a good reality. Magic aims to transform situations through an "art of changing consciousness at will" (Starhawk 1993: 152)—not only one's own.[1]

Malinowski's comments about contemporaries drawn to the occult, however, suggest he would not be comfortable with Starhawk's practices and views. While he argues that magic functions to instill optimism and confidence in situations where there are limits to human control, this is properly only necessary for "primitive man." Magic no longer is relevant in a "developed civilization" because science and technology have replaced it. Those he condemns for engaging in "stale revivals" of "ancient creeds" would likely include Starhawk, who calls herself a witch and calmly labels her practices magic and is explicit that she is engaged in a process of reclaiming.

Malinowski's comments are rife with tension, acknowledging magic's appeal while rejecting what he considers cognate enterprises. His denunciation—grounded in a temporal theory—is not unique. Both his language and distaste recall Tylor's *Primitive Culture*. After claiming that magic ("one of the most pernicious delusions that ever vexed mankind"; 1958 [1871]: vol. 1, 112) primarily exists in Europe as a survival, Tylor diagnoses its disturbing *revival* in the form of spiritualism. Bad enough that there are "tens of thousands [of spiritualists] in America and England," but some are even men of "distinguished mental power." Granting this mix of "superstition, delusion, and sheer knavery" (1958 [1871]: vol. 1, 142) might contain grains of fact meriting scientific investigation, its fundamental concepts resurrect "savage" philosophies (1958 [1871]: vol. 1, 155). No wonder he ends his book by declaring anthropology a "reformer's science" that, by exposing traces of primitive thought, may expunge them from modern society (1958 [1871]: vol. 2, 539).

Malinowski expresses a similar urge to purge in his preface to Kenyatta's monograph. He responds at length to Kenyatta's assertion that magic "is a way of transmitting thoughts telepathically" and his claim that science may prove "that there is something in it which can be classified as occultism, and, as such, cannot be dismissed as merely superstition" (1956 [1938]: 290), with an adamant critique of "occultism." He undercuts Kenyatta and recalls Tylor by equating occultism with superstition, even as he tries to defend his student. He asks: "How can *we* [*sic*] criticize Mr. Kenyatta for believing in . . . occultism and telepathy and spiritism?" given its appeal to Europeans, as evidenced not only by these practices but by the rise of Hitler? Calling "[s]uperstition, blind faith, and complete disorientation . . . as dangerous a canker in the heart of our Western civilization as in Africa," he nonetheless adds that "we know better [*sic!*] and have all the means to combat superstition among us" (1956 [1938]: xiii).

Such exorcism is not so easy to accomplish, however. Tylor's analysis of spiritualism had rested on reading the ample literature its practitioners produced. But in November 1872, he went to London for an intense bout of participant-observation: eight séances in two weeks, several with well-known mediums. George Stocking stumbled across his field notes on a dusty shelf in the Pitt-Rivers Museum.[2] Nothing in Tylor's publications hints at what Stocking calls a shift from total skepticism to "perplexed uncertainty" (1971: 101). Stocking offers a sociological explanation: while Tylor could easily dismiss mediums who were his social inferiors, as were the first few whose sittings he attended (he uses epithets such as *stupid, ugly, coarse* to describe them[3]), it was hard to mock those—both mediums and the bourgeois men and women attending, with whom he frequently discussed the sessions—he found respectable, people who did not strike him as "morbid," "hysterical," or credulous.

I find another intriguing thread running through Tylor's notes. At his first séance and two others, spirits inform him that he could be a medium: two saw a light around him and the third (channeled by Kate Fox, one of the movement's American founders) said he could produce physical manifestations. At the last two séances he attended his presence had a dampening effect. At the first, people thought he was interfering with the spirits, and he left for a while. On his return he was informed a lot more had happened in his absence than before his departure. A male medium he had befriended said this also happened to him as well early on and called Tylor a "powerful but undeveloped medium" who had absorbed the energies. At the same séance his friend fell into a profound trance. Tylor felt himself becoming sleepy and others thought he might become entranced. He writes he felt partly under a "drowsy influence" and partly "consciously shamming, a curious state of mind" (Stocking 1971: 100).

These ancestral reactions to "occultism" reflect discomfort with its enthusiastic embrace by peers, an apparent abandonment of the ascetic skepticism and view from nowhere ideologically associated with Science. It matters that these new practices are presented as unintentional resurrections and gathered under the category *magic*. Such strong condemnation also indexes the danger of slipping—as Tylor almost slipped into a trance in London.

But another way to avoid magic's magic is to subvert reader expectations, a kind of anthropological letdown, as in Evans-Pritchard's explanation of the mysterious light he saw one evening. Malinowski takes a related approach in the paragraphs following the one with which I started: "Yet when the sociologist approaches the study of magic, there where it still reigns supreme, where even now it can be found fully developed—that is, among the Stone Age savages of today—he finds to his disappointment an entirely sober, prosaic, even clumsy art, enacted for purely practical reasons, governed by crude and shallow beliefs, carried out in a simple and monotonous technique. . . . Primitive magic—every field anthropologist knows it to his cost—is extremely monotonous and unexciting, strictly limited in its means of action, circumscribed in its belief, stunted in its fundamental assumptions." Prosaic and practical, clumsy and crude, monotonous and unexciting. Malinowski declares magic boring; anthropology classes and texts may make it so. The hapless undergraduates who sign up for classes on magic rarely encounter the ancient wisdom, spells, or ways to transform their reality that they desire. Instead they find analysis of symbolic expressions of social relations, idioms, and systems of thought.

Malinowski links this now dulled magic to a perverse entrepreneurial fantasy: "Follow one rite, study one spell, grasp the principles of magical belief, art and sociology in one case, and you will know not only all the acts of the tribe, but, adding a variant here and there, you will be able to settle as a magical practitioner in any part of the world yet fortunate enough to have faith in that desirable art" (1948 [1925]: 69–70). If anyone could set up shop anywhere people yearn to believe, magic, the same everywhere, would entail no actual knowledge or skill.

Nowadays, interactions with the dead no longer loom as a threat. But I find myself balking when faced with middle-class white folks seeking Oriental wisdom in Bali. And some anthropologists feel dismay faced with peers or students who call *themselves* witches. (On the other hand, nowadays some anthropologists are practitioners.)

If the term magic connects, its analysis historically has purified, distancing practices so identified from the anthropological tribe that by speaking its name also makes it be. Does anthropology remain a ghostbusting praxis?[4] Or is it a queer science (even a Nietzschean gay science) that aims to make the familiar strange?[5]

5   HIDDEN FORCES

In 2015, Ivo van Hove brought to life a classic of Dutch literature in a dramatic staging in Amsterdam. *The Hidden Force* (*De stille kracht*), a novel written in 1900 by Louis Couperus, narrates the unraveling of a white man of reason, in the exemplary form of an ambitious official with a plum post as resident in East Java.[1] The production's website summarizes the plot as a "clash between two cultures": "One is ostensibly open, rational and bureaucratic. The other is concealed, magical [*magisch*] and mysterious. The westerner dominates and controls, but he can't fight the hidden force of the east, which imperceptibly permeates and slowly erodes everything."[2] In its Orientalist bluntness, this précis points to an inheritance—a geographic imaginary attached to the concept of magic. The novel helped to fashion that attachment. Hailed as a literary masterpiece in the Netherlands, in the Indies its appearance comprised an event, coalescing a complex sensibility, prehending or grasping a feeling, through both its title and tone. Almost immediately, Dutch residents of Java adopted *de stille kracht* (the phrase echoes through the book) for what they found curious or perplexing there, whether sinister or alluring. It soon encompassed much of the territory now associated with *magic*, including its use in selling commodities.

It would be impossible to address magic's translation via the Indies and ignore *The Hidden Force*. But while it gives this chapter its title, the novel is not my focus. As I initially learned from the introduction to its English translation, and then found regularly mentioned in biographies and reviews, accounts of an event that occurred some seventy years before inspired the uncanny incidents leading to the main character's unraveling. Couperus remains an active node for that event's transmission into the present. But my primary concern is the event and its impact rather than his imaginative reworking.

Assistant Resident Karel von Kessinger, in whose Sumedang home it occurred, did his best to describe what happened in a report requested by the governor-general:

> On the 4 February 1831, being the first day of the Javanese month Puasa, returning home from a completed inspection, I noticed at some distance from my house that the latter was surrounded by a great number of people. Not being able to understand what that signified, my wife told me, on arrival home, that in the sitting room [*binnengaanderij* [*sic*]] and inner room of the house stones fell without anyone being able to detect where they came from. Hearing this I became somewhat angry, saying that a person with healthy eyes could very well see by whom the stones were thrown, and to that end I placed myself in the center of the room where the greater part of the stones fell, satisfying myself quickly, however, that such a thing could not happen through human hands, because the stones sometimes fell down thickly before my feet perpendicularly without stirring and without anyone being in the vicinity.
>
> I then examined the ceiling boards one by one and found that they [were] all fast and lay next to each other without the slightest intervening space. At this I had all the people living both in and by the house assemble at an open place in front of the house, guarded by a few police servants, [and] then went indoors—after previously having closed properly all shutters and doors, accompanied only by my wife. But then it was much worse and stones came flying from all sides, so that I quickly was obliged to open the doors and shutters again. This kept up steadily for a period of sixteen days. On one day a thousand stones fell, some of which weighed nine pounds. With this I must not forget to say that mine is a plank house, built of dry jati-wood, the windows being provided with wooden lattices removed ± two thumbs from each other and also that the throwing usually began at 5 o'clock in the morning and kept up until about 11 o'clock at night.
>
> The peculiarity that the stones mostly fell in the proximity of an eleven-year-old native girl, yes, even seemed to pursue that child, I

pass over in silence, because that pertains less to the affair, and also would make this report too detailed. (Van Swieten 1872: 495–96)

Note the trouble Von Kessinger had in articulating what he saw: stones apparently materializing from nowhere, landing gently, sometimes targeting (but not hitting) a specific person.

These oddly behaved stones form this chapter's core. The rocks deposit a dense trail of intertextual traces across time and space. Stubbornly refusing to leave them in the past, colonial authors resurrected the stones virtually generationally. I follow their uptake as they are knotted over time into efforts to make and maintain worlds.

That the substance involved is rock plays no small part in the impression the incident made: the primary component of the earth's crust, for European thinkers rock often exemplifies nonliving, passive, inert stuff. These rocks violated not only taken-for-granted expectations but also purported laws of nature: As the literal ground of earthly existence, how could rocks materialize inside a house, their mineral heaviness at odds with the way they move? Adding to the mix, those attesting to what happened included men whose word usually went unquestioned. In discussions of the stones, disrupting as they do the certainties and habits underwriting the world colonialism presumed, reality politics becomes particularly unsettling. In short, the rocks have the potential to slow us down and make us think, as Isabelle Stengers often urges.

But this is not to say they did—or do. On the contrary. Iterations continually revisit one or both of two sets of what (riffing on Pignarre and Stengers 2011) I call pernicious alternatives, one ontic and the other epistemic. The first set, seeking to explain what happened, speculates on the agents or entities responsible—human and not. The second pair demands a choice between belief or skepticism, about either incident or testimony, training attention on the reliability of sources as well as on what counts as a proper attitude toward strange phenomena. What makes these alternatives pernicious is that they channel thought into predictable grooves. And as I've discovered in presenting this incident, they retain their vigor.[3]

Such responses build on repertoires of epistemic practice and associated moral economies. Both pairs have implications for colonial reality politics. As shown in prior chapters, colonial experts found it easy to dismiss Indonesian assertions about forces and entities or knowledges associated with them. These were, for them, products of the inferior, and backward, mentalities of subjects in need of European tutelage and rule, self-interested charlatans, or claims by fanatics who deceived even themselves. Some sought to make what happened in Sumedang about Indonesians, but it was hard to make this stick. The incident does not conform to any Indonesian field of practice or vernacular. Indonesian communities show little interest in recalling such occurrences. Indonesians certainly appear in Dutch texts, not only as possible perpetrators but as witnesses and interlocutors. More crucial: there was no getting around the fact that white men of reason had attested to the event. Such testimony required different forms of engagement, as those making them could not be shoved a priori beyond a shared moral-intellectual community—though insisting on what they saw blatantly transgressed the norms of their own.

Modest Witnesses

Sumedang, 1831. One of several regencies in West Java making up what the Dutch called the Preanger, and the Sundanese who lived there knew as Priangan, Sumedang had long been woven into colonial projects and the political economy of global capitalism. In the seventeenth century, the voc demanded Priangan regents supply them with pepper, indigo, and cotton free of charge (Furnivall 1944: 37).[4] In the eighteenth century, the Company found its hilly uplands eminently suitable for growing the coffee Europe's new bourgeoisie savored.[5] Shortly before it declared bankruptcy and its assets (and extensive debts) were taken over by the Dutch government, the voc introduced the "Preanger System," involving the forced, supervised cultivation of coffee. In 1808, Sumedang became a stop along the Great Post Road, a massive infrastructure project built with corvée labor that connected Batavia's port to centers of production in West Java and, along the northern coast, to the rest of the island.[6] And in 1830, only a year before rocks fell in the Von Kessinger house, Java came under the Cultivation System (*Cultuurstelsel*), a policy that intensified colonial demands even further.

What led to the policy's adoption were the combined effects of inherited voc debts, the Napoleonic wars, Belgium's secession, and the five-year Java War on the Dutch treasury. When Johannes van den Bosch proposed to King Willem I, who controlled Dutch colonial possessions after the Netherlands became a monarchy in 1815, that the Indies could not only eliminate the deficit but even generate a surplus, the king made him governor-general to carry out his plan.

The Cultivation System merged the voc's Preanger System (while extending it over Java and generalizing it over a wide range of agricultural products) with the land rent introduced by Raffles, a follower of Adam Smith, during British control of Java.[7] Each village had to grow and sell specific crops to the state, for fixed prices. (A government monopoly, the Netherlands Trading Company, transported them to Amsterdam.) According to Van den Bosch, peasants would benefit. They could continue to grow rice (for subsistence and as tribute to regents), plus, in a good year, sell surplus cash crops. In practice, only coffee grew on land unsuitable for rice: sugar and indigo diverted land, labor, and water; and indigo depleted the soil. Moreover, since local officials set quotas and received a percentage of the profits, they would demand more than required. When prices fell (or colonial costs rose), the state increased its demands.[8] For the Dutch crown, however, the Cultivation System was a rousing success. As exports nearly tripled between 1830 and 1835 and more than doubled again by 1840, the deficit vanished (Furnivall 1944: 127). The Netherlands came to depend on an annual colonial surplus, and Amsterdam again became a hub of global trade as coffee and sugar brokers made fortunes.

This brief survey explains the presence in that time and place of a group of Europeans who observed the rocks fall in the home of Karel Gotthard Ehregot von Kessinger.[9] Von Kessinger concludes his report with a list of "the most reliable persons who witnessed the aforesaid continuously or periodically, and who, I don't doubt, if it were demanded, would corroborate by oath" what they had seen (Van Swieten 1872: 496). They are identified by the positions they held in 1834, the time of writing, as follows: Michiels, lieutenant colonel aide-de-camp; Ermatinger, ex-inspector of coffee cultivation; Dornseiff, innkeeper at Sumedang; Born, foreman-bricklayer; Adipati Soeria Laga, Sumedang's ex-regent; Tommagong Soeria di Laga, his chief minister (and successor); Soema di Laga, chief prosecutor; and the two head *penghulu* (mosque officials), various district heads, and the heads of the audience hall.[10]

The Europeans listed index past and current colonial projects transforming Sundanese land and labor. The Priangan coffee business is represented not only by Ermatinger but also by Von Kessinger himself, who began his career in its service in 1821, first in Sukapura and then, as Ermatinger's assistant, in Sumedang. In 1831 he was a "supervisor first class" of coffee cultivation, a post that included liaising with Sundanese leaders (and evolved into *controleur*). By 1834 Von Kessinger had been promoted to assistant resident, and signs himself as such. The bricklayers Born was supervising were building a factory not far from Sumedang to process indigo. Finally, its location on the Great Post Road meant Sumedang could support Dornseiff's inn for travelers to or from Batavia to stop and rest. That inn brought to town the most important person listed, Andreas Victor Michiels, then a major in the colonial army.

Von Kessinger's report, with the list that concludes it—what he includes, whom and what he excludes, how he narrates what he did and saw—along with a second account by the innkeeper, Johann Joost Dornseiff (1853), prompt me to recall the now classic figure of the modest witness. Shapin and Schaffer (1985) conjured this figure to examine the invention of experimental science in seventeenth-century England, a time and place far removed from the doings of a handful of European men in 1831, all but one employed directly by the Dutch colonial state and neither men of science nor men of independent means. Of the three interconnected technologies (material, discursive, and social) that, according to Shapin and Schaffer, became crucial to making matters of fact, one is entirely absent, arguably the key one: no nonhumans, in the form of fabricated machinery, produced, testified to, and (potentially) replicated the fall of the rocks. What occurred in Sumedang, of course, was hardly an experiment, but a happenstance event that started and ended abruptly. Nonetheless, Von Kessinger and those he recruited clearly investigated within the technical limits of their abilities and situation. And the social and semiotic techniques relevant to making facts are evident in the actions human witnesses took, including their inscriptions. Certainly elements of experimental science had percolated into European common sense, infiltrating broad conceptions of the world, especially as they overlapped with legal practices of witnessing.[11] The point of all three technologies, after all, was to establish veracity, to convince others to add to the stock of existing entities and forces, in part by multiplying witnesses to secure confidence in the reliability of observations. Everything Von Kessinger did shows a keen appreciation of the importance of numbers.

To demonstrate this requires Dornseiff's testimony. When put side by side, the two accounts differ, though not fatally. Dornseiff dates the incident some six months earlier, claims it lasted only eleven days, and estimates the child's age at seven. (On these points Von Kessinger is likely more reliable, both because more time had elapsed before Dornseiff put pen to paper and because Von Kessinger knew the child.) Of greater interest is what Dornseiff adds to Von Kessinger's terse report.

We learn from Dornseiff that Von Kessinger actively sought others to see the stones and join him in trying to determine their source. Dornseiff was the first and remained involved to the end. While Ermatinger turned up on his own, Von Kessinger dispatched Dornseiff to fetch Born (since, Dornseiff explains, apart from the Von Kessingers and himself, no other Europeans lived nearby). Von Kessinger and Dornseiff then "waited impatiently that a traveler might pass through," landing Major Michiels, who stopped by chance at the inn about a week into the incident. At the same time, Dornseiff notes Sundanese aristocrats not only came by, but on leaving each "took along a few stones as souvenir, perhaps to use as obat (medicine)" (1853: 184).

Dornseiff adds more about their rough attempts at measurement, as well as matters the report leaves out. He calculates the stones were thick as a fist and fell from a height of three to four feet. Those present apparently gathered them, filling half a wine case daily, though on the fourth day twice as many fell. Oddly, they stopped when the Von Kessingers took their midday meal and slept (restarting at five a.m.). Dornseiff also says more about the child: occasionally, a stone landed (as if laid by a hand) on the child's shoulder, and a doll in her lap. Whenever she went out, she felt someone pushing her from behind, though no one was visible.

Unlike experimentalists, the sole aim of these investigatory acts was to make sense of a baffling experience. When Von Kessinger called people to his home he did not yet anticipate having to convince anyone of what had happened. That began with his report, which drew on specific genres and tacit conventions to enact credibility. Writing turned him—and Dornseiff—into modest witnesses. Despite aiming at different kinds of readers (see below), they deploy rhetorical forms mirroring the "discursive technologies" of experimentalists. For one, they are restrained: they describe only what they observed, making no effort to explain it. Stylistically, their language is plain and unadorned, semiotically indexing an author neither prone to exaggeration nor swayed by emotion. Their texts also share a feature not part of scientific prose but central to authenticating practices. Von Kessinger asserts those he listed would, if asked, "corroborate by oath" what they saw. Dornseiff concludes by declaring himself ready to swear "a solemn oath" that what he recounted had happened. Both, in short, invoke a potent speech genre that binds the speaker to a moral community, gesturing to a socio-epistemological world in which specific words, spoken by particular people, may establish truth. An old procedure involving more-than-humans, the oath, a juridical act, is also pertinent to Indonesian forms of life (see chapter 2).

Oaths as sureties of honesty count among colonial "social technologies," practices addressing relations between truth and trust. Shapin (1994), assessing these for seventeenth-century England, notes that not only laboratory manipulations but also reports from afar proposed myriad novel phenomena. Mercantile and settler colonialism, and associated voyages of discovery, transported from distant places a host of astonishing things and tales, contributing to a period of unusual ontological openness. But this did not mean novelties were readily accepted. Ontic additions depend on judgments about those advancing them. Assurances of credibility become more acute when claims defy the taken-for-granted inventory of existents. In short, as Shapin (1994: 302) lays bare, "thing-knowledge" depends on "people-knowledge."

But such technologies bake hierarchy into appraisals of credibility. In Restoration England, those likely to be regarded as reliable were gentlemen of independent means. Dutch colonizers based sincerity on different criteria.[12] Von Kessinger's list doubly ranks witnesses: Europeans before Sundanese; for each, by occupation. His ordering proposes that Europeans, even a foreman supervising manual laborers, have greater credibility than Sundanese aristocrats holding an office underwritten by the colonial state.

Note whom Von Kessinger excludes: his wife and servants, including the "native girl." Though he reports his irritated remark about his wife's visual incompetence—trumpeting his skepticism—what disqualified her was likely gender.[13] Dornseiff not only records testimony from Mrs. Von Kessinger about the night stones began to fall (initially against, not inside, the house), but mentions she ordered eight guards and six stable boys to watch outside. Apparently, the word of women, servants, and children could not warrant truth. In seventeenth-century England, such persons were dependents, a status raising questions about their freedom to speak (Shapin 1994). Perhaps this was relevant in the Indies—though Europeans generally discounted Indonesian discernment. Here only those vetted by the state could ratify a European official's statement. To amplify Haraway (1997): not only gender and class but also race was baked into colonial objectivity.

The man who tops Von Kessinger's list deserves special attention, not only because as first he is "most reliable," but also because of his prominence in later narratives. Given his occupation, Michiels serves as the incident's guarantor. As an officer, he adhered to an old European code of masculine honor that demanded physical violence as a response to challenges to his integrity. Moreover, when he stopped by chance at Dornseiff's inn, he was well embarked on a spectacular career.[14] First tasting action as a teenaged second lieutenant at Waterloo, he came to the Indies in 1817 and a year later was a captain. Service in the Java War led to a knighthood (in the

FIGURE 5.1: General Andreas Victor Michiels, created by C. W. Mieling circa 1850, probably for his obituary. His full dress uniform explains why stories about him in Klungkung refer to him as I Bintang Tujuh, "Mr. Seven Stars." Courtesy of Leiden University Libraries, Shelfmark KITLV 47A20.

Military Order of William) in 1828 and promotion to major in 1829. Not long after his visit to Sumedang he received the appointments appearing beside his name in Von Kessinger's report: in 1832 he was promoted to lieutenant colonel and aide-de-camp and adjutant to the governor-general. Thus Michiels had considerably more social capital than the other European witnesses. The more decorations he received, and the higher he rose in rank, the more expectations about his integrity clung to him.

But Michiels was more than the incident's primary guarantor; he also formed the key vector for its transmission and inscription. As adjutant and aide-de-camp, he was the confidential adviser to the colony's commander in chief. In that role he informed Jan Chrétien Baud about the rocks when the latter became governor-general in 1833, leading Baud to request a report from Von Kessinger, by then Sumedang's assistant resident. In 1840 the king appointed Baud minister of colonies in The Hague, and, after he left that office in 1848, he was elected to the Dutch parliament in 1850. Those offices put Baud in position to spread news of the affair in the upper echelons of the government.[15] Michiels also spoke of it to friends, especially fellow officer Jan van Swieten, who further transmitted the story.[16]

None of the other five European men present could either warrant the truth of what occurred or spread the news as Michiels could. Neither Born nor Ermatinger wrote about what they saw, and they quickly fade from view. Von Kessinger may well have talked about what happened in his house, but he left the civil service—and the Indies—in 1839, never advancing beyond assistant resident. Dornseiff did, of course, write about what occurred, but his profession may have compromised his reliability. While a successful entrepreneur (in addition to an inn, he later owned numerous stores and warehouses in Cirebon, near Priangan), as someone who presided over a site for exchanging and embellishing stories (perhaps entertaining guests with the rocks), he had less credibility. He also published his account in a popular magazine, a textual extension of his inn.[17] Moreover, I suspect, given its date, that Michiels indirectly prompted him to submit his memories for publication. Michiels was trending in 1853, due to the regime's recognition of Michiels's later accomplishments and recent death. The accomplishments included a second knighthood in 1832 (in the Order of the Netherlands Lion), a stint as civil and military governor of Sumatra's west coast after he led the Dutch to victory there in 1837, further exploits in battle leading to his 1843 promotion to the rank of major general, and appointment as KNIL's temporary commander. In that role he led the Third Bali Expedition in 1849, during which he was killed by a bullet in a night attack by Balinese in Klungkung. Such a record—and death as a war hero—could not go unheralded. In 1853 a commission was established to construct a monument in his honor, a task completed in 1855 with two: one in Batavia and the other in Padang (Sumatra).[18] In the years between his death and his iron and marble resurrection, he definitely was a topic of conversation.[19]

As the key figure who could vouchsafe what occurred as a matter of fact, however, impugning his reputation offered a crack for later skeptics. Despite the care Von Kessinger took to certify the event, the rocks violated what European considered self-evident at a time and in a place with a considerably tighter attitude about ontic expansion than in the seventeenth century. Michiels's credibility—or credulity—became a focus. Some found relevant critiques of his governance of Sumatra's west coast by advocates for liberal reforms.[20] The first round of stories, however, took different directions.

Traveling Rumors

Dornseiff's is not only the sole published account by an eyewitness, but also the first publication about the stones. Two anecdotes in travel books, however, provide additional evidence that Michiels's commemoration sparked the circulation of stories. While their books appear in print later, both authors were in West Java in 1852. Neither refers to Michiels by name, but he clearly forms the model for the sole investigator of the peculiar events (and the sole European) in their tales.[21] That rumors had been spreading orally is marked by their disinterest in specifying where and from whom they heard them. Their narratives differ significantly from eyewitness accounts, especially in two respects: they add a second bizarre element, and they offer explanations, one of which introduces a specific version of the category of magic. Before considering these matters, I present them in the order they appeared in print.

Famed Austrian travel writer and amateur ethnographer Ida Pfeiffer visited the Indies on her second round-the-world journey, arriving in the Malay Archipelago in 1851 and leaving the Indies by 1853. She stayed mainly with colonial officials and German residents. Any of her contacts could have been the source of what she reports:

As I was just speaking of peculiar things, I also want to mention a perplexing event that took place on Java several years ago and made such a stir that it even demanded the attention of the Government.

There was a small house in the Cirebon Residency that, people claimed, was badly haunted. As soon as evening broke, stones began to rain and sirih to spew from all sides in the dwelling. The stones, like the spit, came down right next to the people who were inside, but never hit anyone. That spook seemed directed mainly against a small child. So much was spoken of this inexplicable affair that the Government finally delegated a trustworthy staff officer to investigate it. The latter had the house surrounded by handpicked loyal soldiers who prevented anyone from entering or leaving, carefully examined everything, and then sat down in the notorious room, taking the child on his lap. As always, a rain of stones and sirih began in the evening, falling close to the officer and the child but without touching them. Again, they inspected every corner, every hole—but found nothing. The officer could not make sense of it. He ordered the stones to be collected, marked, and concealed at a remote location—

to no avail, the very same stones, with their markings, flew back into the room at the same hour. To put an end to this incomprehensible tale, the Government had the house demolished. (1856: 278–79)[22]

A haunted house, in Cirebon, a place she herself never visited. As Dornseiff moved there in 1831, I read its mention as a trace in the chain of transmission that led her to hear the tale: likely, it included someone who heard it there. Another detail (that the officer put the child on his lap) may point to a different chain, this one leading to Michiels: it recurs in later accounts.

Unlike Pfeiffer, the second traveler, Steven Adriaan Buddingh, was an Indies insider. Affiliated with the Dutch Reformed parish in Batavia, he had served as president of the church council. Duty, not pleasure, motivated his journey: in 1852 he was dispatched to inspect churches and schools across the Indies, an excursion that lasted for several years. One of the places he visited was Sumedang. After a lively description of the approach from Bandung on the Great Post Road, he pauses:

> [A]s an example that the natives have obtained great proficiency in magic [*toveren*] or performing tricks [*goochelen*]—striking also in their *cemin* and *gedebus* performances and other stunts—I will impart a story that is common knowledge on Java concerning a former, private house at Sumedang demolished around 1840. For many years (they say) small gravel stones or lava stones fell down in this house without anyone being able to see where they came from, and at that always in the room a child, a girl of 9 or 10, was in. They fell down from the ceiling from time to time around the child, and no one noticed them until they were almost on the ground. The child was, moreover, time and again besmirched with sirih saliva, and no one saw who did it or where it came from, and no one but this child was made dirty by the sirih spittle! . . . In vain they tried to discover the secret. In due time an aide-de-camp of the late Governor-General van den Bosch would institute a close examination in situ or on the spot. He had (they say) *prajuits* or native residency soldiers surround the house and even placed several on the roof, but in vain. The little stones fell down all the same and the child was besmirched for all that with sirih juice!—So runs the story, and the aide-de-camp's official report must still exist. The house finally had to be demolished and replaced by a new house at the same place, but the phenomenon since is no longer observed. The Sundanese joker has certainly not been able to produce his tricks in the new house. (1859: 104)

Buddingh then returns to the two performances he mentioned, which he saw in 1846. As Wolter Robert van Hoëvell had already described them, he only offers a brief account.[23]

Before examining contrasts between these travelers' tales, they share several differences from eyewitness reports. Both suggest these events went on for some time, stopping only when the house was leveled. Neither indicates the house belonged to a European, or an official. Each mentions only two people: the child and the officer. Pfeiffer calls the latter "a trustworthy staff officer"; Buddingh is closer, referring to him as Van den Bosch's aide-de-camp (Van den Bosch appointed Michiels to that position).

The most dramatic divergence, of course, is the addition of a second peculiar thing: *sirih*. More geographically specific than falling rocks, it indexes a practice once widespread across Asia and Oceania. Technically, *sirih* refers to the leaf of a plant, *Piper betle*, a member of the *Piperaeae* family and kin to both peppercorns and kava. Smeared with a dab of lime from crushed shells, and wrapped around slices of betel nut (*Areca catechu*), until well after Indonesian independence it was widely chewed. Apart from producing a feeling of relaxation and calm, it both stimulates the salivary glands and turns saliva bright red. Not only must the chewer periodically expectorate, but what comes out resembles blood. More crucially, sirih made relations: offering these ingredients constituted *the* basic act of hospitality. Although coffee has replaced it for human visitors, sirih remains essential to welcoming more-than-humans and ancestors in rites across the archipelago.[24]

voc merchants initially adopted the custom, only giving it up in the mid-eighteenth century when Indonesians began to add a wad of tobacco between lips and gums, a practice Europeans found unsightly. Europeans new to the Indies found sirih disgusting, including Java's new rulers during the British interregnum (Reid 1985; Taylor 1983). Their revulsion marks changes in the metropole, where spitting, once considered healthy, was becoming associated with the lower classes (Elias 1978). Since by the end of the nineteenth century health initiatives condemned public spitting in Europe, European rejection of sirih was doubly purifying: expectorate was not only "matter out of place," but racialized, a bodily practice that helped to erect the divide between the (civilized) West and the (barbaric, repellant) Rest.

The sudden appearance of sirih in these tales is as mysterious to me as its sudden appearance in the incident they report. In both cases, it is impossible to discover where it came from. Perhaps sirih spewing occurred in the Von Kessinger home and witnesses chose not to mention it. Von Kessinger indicates he has left things out in the interest of being succinct. But Dorn-seiff published in a popular venue, so why would he feel constrained? Perhaps sirih was added as the story circulated. But if so, why and by whom? Certainly, the addition has effects: injecting sirih into the event cemented it to the Indies.

For my purposes, more striking than the sirih is the way explanations fill the space witnesses carefully left empty. These introduce the first pernicious alternative: attributing what happened either to an uncanny agent or tricky Indonesians.

Ghosts in some ways provide the simpler interpretation. Pfeiffer merely repeats what "people claim," and "people," finding the incident eerie, held invisible agents responsible. For Europeans, this meant ghosts, the disincarnate dead. If Pfeiffer is reporting what she heard, she is not offering an interpretation. But she also may have filtered what "people claim" through the spread of spiritualism and the rising appeal of ghost stories, which increasingly appeared as filler in media aiming at mass circulation.[25]

Buddingh does not ascribe agency to ghosts. His profession (and denomination) made intervention in the world by immaterial beings problematic. Instead, he treats the incident as a prank, drawing on nascent colonial knowledge of Sundanese rites and practitioners and Van Hoëvell's prior interpretation of two performances as tricks. The first, which both Buddingh and Van Hoëvell call *cemin*, involved setting wooden puppets to dance to music. Both authors treat the puppeteer as an illusionist; Van Hoëvell claims the audience not only found the movements inexplicable but "bordering on the supernatural" (1849: 25). *Dabus*, which they describe in greater detail, is a rite associated with a Sufi order, in which men in trance stab themselves with iron spikes to the accompaniment of rhythmic music and under the guidance of the group's leader without incurring any wounds (Vredenbregt 1973). A Haji led the performance Van Hoëvell witnessed; he dabbed the tip of each spike with saliva from his mouth before blessing and handing it to each performer. Not surprisingly, Van Hoëvell insists the spikes only *seemed* to go into the bodies of those wielding them, presenting the rite as an example of how Muslim leaders secure their influence (1849: 26–27).[26] Buddingh also attaches illusionism to what happened at Sumedang: in addition to *toveren*, he adds *goochelen*, magic in the form of tricks and sleight of hand, a word not deployed in relation to other practices I've addressed.

Buddingh opens a controversy by associating stories about Sumedang with performances he had witnessed and Van Hoëvell's explanation of these as legerdemain. What Van Hoëvell termed "priestly deceit" slotted practitioners and spectators of such performances into the familiar categories of frauds, fools, and fanatics. Neither Van Hoëvell nor Buddingh shows any curiosity about what talented bodies (to recall chapter 1) might become, in this case with music, the chanting of legends, prayers, spikes, and other mediators, including saliva—or even about what skill in directing attention might involve.

In this first iteration, explanations are offered in passing. Pfeiffer recaps what others say, and Buddingh offers no evidence to support either Van Hoëvell's assessment of Sundanese performers or their relevance to the incident. Neither mentions earlier interpretations—at least in English—of odd stones, which multiply what appeared to be a singular event.

Consider an early report that gave strangely acting stones a name: *lithobolia*. Such is the title of a 1698 pamphlet about an event in New Hampshire.[27] According to its author, a "spirit" threw stones inside his landlord's house. Local theories blamed the devil, working at the behest of a witch angry at those afflicted for stealing her land. These stones hit their targets (Chamberlayne 1698). For nineteenth-century Europeans, though, witchcraft no longer explained anything, unless one was willing to open oneself to mockery or a charge of regression.[28]

Closer in time, and potentially more attractive, the 1832 *Encyclopaedia Britannica*'s entry for the meteorological category *rain* presents "rain of stones" as one type of "preternatural rain," attributing it to volcanic activity. Had these travelers or their interlocutors heard such speculations? Pfeiffer uses the locution "rain of stones" and Buddingh claims that what fell included "lava stones." Sumedang lies at the foot of Mount Tampomas, though it has not erupted in historic memory.

Apart from their explanatory impulse, colonial relations pop up in both tales. In the story Pfeiffer retells, the government both investigates and puts an end to the situation: the regime is victorious even over the dead. As for Buddingh, like Van Hoëvell he presumes white men of reason can suss out the cause of anything exceeding what they already know.

Pfeiffer's brief account had repercussions Buddingh's did not. Her fame led to the immediate translation of her book into numerous languages, including English, Dutch, French, and even Malay. Those translations brought the stones—and sirih—to the attention of those calling themselves spiritualists (or spiritists), who engaged a new experimental field: practices aimed at communicating with the dead.

Spirits, Sleights, and Cites

In the 1870s, two new accounts displace travelers' tales. Embedding witness reports, they focus more on what happened than how. Ushering in the second pernicious alternative, they introduce materials pertinent to securing historical facts by naming witnesses, providing testimony, and referring to archives and documents. They also begin to build a new archive: from this time on citations abound. This is not to say the urge to explain disappears. Rather, the choices become more elaborate and specific. Pfeiffer's ghost transmogrifies into spirits, in response to both spiritualist activities and the ethnography of Javanese spirit *beliefs*. Allegations of prestidigitation introduce motives. Two other changes also occur: stories are simultaneously emplaced, firmly attached to Sumedang, and pluralized into an event type known by a name—or different names: rains of stones, following Pfeiffer; stone-throwing, implying an agent; and a Sundanese term, one of several glimpses of Indonesian interlocutors that begin in this time.

An account published in 1871 remains grounded in the 1850s, as it claims to be based on materials gathered during an official investigation in 1854. It appears, however, in *Die Gartenlaube*, a German illustrated weekly targeting bourgeois families, under the title "Spooky Stone-Throwing" ("Das gespentige Steinwerfen"). The author, Friedrich Gerstäcker, was another traveler and popular writer who visited Java from November 1851 through January 1852, shortly before Pfeiffer, during an unexpected stop on a three-year voyage around the world. He claims he heard about the stones then, though no mention appears in either his book or a Dutch translation of the Java section (Gerstäcker 1853, 1855). Like Pfeiffer, he did not go to Sumedang; the farthest either ventured into Priangan was Bandung. This piece was not, however, based on what he heard in Java. While his name is attached to it, he wrote only seven paragraphs. These frame text, set off by quotation marks, by someone Gerstäcker identifies only as a "friend" who "lived half of his life on Java," whose "superior education" made him unimpeachable. Such statements (he also remarks that in 1851 "quiet and reasonable men" had assured him that those who relayed the tale—"believable people, educated Europeans"—could "hardly be doubted") reiterate the role of race, gender, and class in securing credibility. They also signal a shift from widely known story to a possible event.

The "friend" mixes material reported by eyewitnesses with the tales circulating in the 1850s and adds some novelties. He mentions the Von Kessinger home; that the stones fell during the day, straight down, only becoming visible about six feet from the ground, and filled a box daily; and Michiels. But a sudden splattering of sirih on the girl's clothing heralds the incident's start and Michiels is sent by the governor-general. Among the new elements: it identifies Mrs. Von Kessinger as "an Indies-born lady" and Michiels as author of the official report. Of greater interest, the incident no longer is unique. Claiming Indonesians take such events for granted, he mentions other cases in Priangan involving Europeans: as witness, near witness, and target.

More remarkably, the "friend" affords glimpses of Sundanese reflections. While opening with colonial clichés (about "simple" Sundanese who let "fantasy run wild" and "believe in a spirit world"), he introduces a vernacular purportedly referring to the "throwing of stones or falling of pebbles or sand": "Gandarúa or Gundarúa."[29] Ethnography would soon reveal that he misconstrued that word's meaning: rather than labeling an event type, it marks a Sundanese effort to posit a possible agent responsible for what happened, equivalent to European speculative explanations. It is, moreover, not the only such hypothesis in the text. The "friend" notes that when he discussed "this puzzling phenomenon" with "bolder" regents, the regent of Ciamis ruminated there must be families whose members had the power to make themselves invisible. The regent of Sukapura, who witnessed a similar incident in the 1830s at the home of the French overseer of an indigo factory, noted the house stood on the edge of the steep bank of the Ciandug River (an observation to which I will return).

Such materials support the "friend's" assertion that he is reporting the results of an 1854 inquiry; indeed, he seems to have conducted it.[30] What prompted that investigation was the discovery that Von Kessinger's report was missing from the government's archives. In its place, a note stated Baud had taken it to the Netherlands. The author speculates that Baud told the king about the incident, which resulted in a personal commission from the government to Sumedang's "Resident [sic]." This statement—Sumedang was a division of the Priangan residency—is the only reason I question what I suspect to be the case: that Gerstäcker's "friend" was Albert Kinder, Sumedang's assistant resident in 1854. I deduce this from the fact that he writes he was located in Sumedang and living in Von Kessinger's house as well as from his unusual interest in language: Kinder began his career as a student in the Institute for Javanese in Surakarta, and *Gandarúa* is a cognate in Sundanese and Javanese.[31]

Having laid out his version of events, Gerstäcker's friend explains its sources. He notes at least twenty witnesses still lived in Sumedang, mostly "natives" but including two Europeans: Misters Dikhuis and Dornseiff. Their statements, taken independently, were key. While Dornseiff was an eyewitness, Nicolaas Dikhuis was, however, not; in fact, he only arrived in Priangan in 1838.[32] As a newcomer himself (he had just been appointed assistant resident), Kinder may not have realized that, given his haziness about dates.

He evidently tried to locate other witnesses. He reports the Von Kessingers had long since left; the regent had died; and the sirih-plagued girl, now a grandmother, worked for a tea planter. He also discussed the matter with others to whom his rank provided access. The regent of Sukapura, who recalled the misfortune that befell the French factory overseer, was under his jurisdiction. Related events came up in conversations with his colleagues. Tjalling Ament, longtime resident of Cirebon, had had a disconcerting experience as a young inspector of coffee cultivation, at the home of a Sundanese woman living near the then assistant resident in Bandung. Both officials saw something grab the woman by her foot and drag her inside, and a handful of coarse sand hit Ament in the chest as he stepped through the door. In 1859, Visscher van Gaasbeek heard of something odd that ended before he could get there.

The reference to Visscher van Gaasbeek offers a clue about how the author knew Gerstäcker. Gerstäcker's Indies connections stem from his visit from November 1851 through January 1852. In Batavia, he befriended (and lodged with) a German merchant also named Kinder, who provided a letter of introduction to his brother-in-law, Alexander G. C. Visscher van Gaasbeek (Gerstäcker 1855: 553). The merchant would have been Gustav Kinder, recently wed to Visscher van Gaasbeek's sister.[33]

Gerstäcker—like Pfeiffer after him—writes of his warm reception by Visscher van Gaasbeek, who, like Kinder, invited him to stay at his home. Born in Hanover, Visscher van Gaasbeek, Bandung's assistant resident from 1850 to 1860, spoke German.[34] His relation to Gerstäcker, moreover, continued beyond the latter's visit: in 1863, Gerstäcker married Visscher's daughter in Bremen. Visscher van Gaasbeek would have known Albert Kinder, as they served together in Priangan.[35] Gerstäcker could have become acquainted with him through Visscher van Gaasbeek. But why hide his identity and use Gerstäcker as a conduit? And why wait to publish? The second, considerably more transparent, account, provides some clues.

At the end of 1872, an article entitled "A Missing Document about the Incident in 1831 in Sumedang" appeared in the "Miscellaneous News" section of the *Tijdschrift voor Nederlands-Indië*, the premier journal for serious students of the Indies. Its author, Jan van Swieten, was well known. Commander of the Netherlands Indies Army from 1858 to 1862, upon his retirement he became politically active, even representing Amsterdam as a liberal member of the Dutch parliament. In 1873 the Ministry of Colonies recalled him to the Indies to head the Second Aceh Expedition. He also was Michiels's close friend and colleague. Their bond dated from the Java War, but they served together often: Van Swieten was on Bali as battalion commander when Michiels was killed.

As its title indicates, Van Swieten confirmed that Von Kessinger's original report had gone missing, while making it publicly available for the first time—indeed, this article served as my source for that document. In addition to disseminating the report, he provides a secondhand account of Michiels's testimony, while shedding light on reactions to it during and after Michiels's lifetime. With these we enter the terrain of the second pernicious alternative: Michiels did not like to talk about the incident, "because he assumed in questioners and listeners the tendency to scoff at his credulity or ascribe his observations to delusions" (Van Swieten 1872: 493). But he confided in trusted friends such as Van Swieten, who also twice heard him repeat the tale to others. Michiels both affirmed and expanded on what Von Kessinger wrote. He told Van Swieten he had locked himself in a room with the child, and, seated on a chair with his feet propped against a wall and the child between his legs, had observed the stones for hours. The more attention he fixed on her, the more stones fell. (Like other eyewitnesses, he said nothing about sirih spit.)

Van Swieten reveals himself to be another vector of transmission. He talked of the incident to a French admiral in the late 1830s and asked Michiels to repeat the story to German Major General Baron von Gagern, sent by now Minister of Colonies Baud to report on the colony's defensive capabilities. Von Gagern had heard the tale in The Hague, where many took it to be a "fairy tale" (*sprookje*); Baud, however, not only corroborated it but promised to show him the report, only to discover it was neither at the ministry nor in Batavia.[36] Informing Von Gagern that he had a transcript, Van Swieten presented a copy for him to forward to Baud.[37] By putting it into print, Van Swieten broadcast it well beyond the intimacy of face-to-face relations. For the first time, narratives by the two witnesses deemed most credible became available for inspection.

Unlike Gerstäcker's friend, Van Swieten explains some of the circumstances prompting him to publish the report. He notes that a recent visit to The Hague by Herne and Williams, two British mediums, had stimulated considerable discussion of spiritualism—and reminded many of the stones.[38] Herne and Williams were among several English practitioners who recently had become physical mediums, producing what were called manifestations or materializations.

But their performance in October 1872 was not the only spur to recollect the stones. Earlier that year, a publication called *Something for Everyone* (*Elk wat wils*) translated Gerstäcker's article into Dutch. The editor remarked that most readers may already have heard something of the haunted house (*spookhuis*) on Java, a sign of the tale's uptake in the Netherlands that carries forward Pfeiffer's interpretation (Koopman van Boekeren 1872: 46). Whether or not Van Swieten read it, others likely did. It may, in fact, have led to some impressions he sought to correct. Such anticipation of readers' familiarity with the broad outlines of the incident derives, however, from its intimate association with the formation of spiritualist organizations and periodicals in the Netherlands.

Spiritualists had homed in on Pfeiffer's brief report. It was excerpted and published in 1859 in a French spiritist periodical (followed by a transcript of an interview with her recently departed spirit). The Hague formed the site of a major spiritualist circle, consisting of men connected to the Indies and each other as former members of the colonial civil service and/ or by lineal and affinal ties. Key figures adduced the stones as evidence of the truth of spiritualist claims, drawing on the story to recruit members (Ackers 2007). The centrality of their Indies experiences even led two experimenters to deploy adolescent Javanese servants as mediums, despite their reluctance. The experiments of Dutch spiritualists differed from better-known ones in Britain or the United States in other ways too. For one, they only took place in intimate gatherings in homes rather than also in public presentations. They also engaged the interest of figures in high government circles (Ackers 2007).[39]

In the Netherlands, Herne and Williams followed their hosts' lead by conducting their séances in private. Ackers (2007, chapter 10) wonders if Van Swieten was the "high-placed old Indies officer" mentioned as attending a sitting in The Hague. But he need not have been there to have heard the talk they inspired.

The new phenomenon of manifestations may have sparked Gerstäcker's publication too. I find it suggestive that, in addition to stones and sirih, the author writes that tables, chairs, and plates moved, and mentions "the imprint of a moistened hand running over a mirror" (1871: 398). Gerstäcker also refers to "stone-throwing" incidents in Germany; in a footnote, the editors recall a much-discussed occurrence in Zittau—enjoining readers to contribute explanations (1871: 399).[40]

But spiritualism was hardly universally accepted. Considerable skepticism—even appalled opposition—met its forays, especially in Dutch newspapers and pulpits. This might explain why Gerstäcker's friend concealed his identity. It certainly informs Van Swieten's insistence that by presenting Von Kessinger's report he by no means wished to "choose for those who seek in the incident at Sumedang assimilation with spiritualism's manifestations," or anything beyond human abilities (1872: 493).

As the (predictable) alternative, Van Swieten selects prestidigitation, even as this complicates his impassioned defense of Michiels. To doubt the event occurred, he avers, would be to impugn Michiels's reputation. But while he insists Michiels was not a man "who let himself be deceived by appearances or robbed of his sound judgment by tricks, however adroitly executed," almost immediately he implies he was. While not arguing with anything like Buddingh's (1859) conviction, he gestures to "examples of the dexterity of the natives in the performance of tricks or conjuring that are equally inexplicable" (1872: 495), mentioning the adroitness of "Hindus" (likely itinerant South Asian performers) and Javanese "Dawoes."[41] Along the same lines, he proposed treating the incident ethnographically, "as a contribution to the knowledge of the Indies natives and their dexterity in displays of tricks" (1872: 494).

Van Swieten not only feels pressure to choose a pernicious alternative, but in the process reveals the other option had been rearticulated: from ghost to "spiritualism's manifestations" (1872: 492). It also entailed endorsing spiritualism more broadly. But his choice involved a conundrum: in seeking to vindicate his friend, he had to accept that, for all his "sound judgment," Michiels had been duped. All Van Swieten could say of those who managed that feat is that such adroitness deserved attention.

It did not take long for this to happen. In 1877, an article entitled "Gandaroewa (Invisible Stone-Throwing) in the Preanger. Observed and Explained by A. G. Vorderman" appeared in a journal dedicated to the natural sciences in the Indies. The title takes the vernacular—and its putative translation—from Gerstäcker, and promises not only to describe but also to explicate it. Its author is the same Vorderman who linked *guna-guna* to *Datura alba*.

In 1874, Vorderman, stationed in West Java, received word from a friend about "strange things" happening at the home of a woman in Cianting: "all kinds of things are thrown after her by an invisible hand." Eager to witness such a phenomenon, he grabbed an engineer colleague and set out for his informant's house, only to learn they were too late. Despite their disappointment, all three men decided to check things out. They found the victim, Ebbot, seated on the verandah with her husband, mother, and several guests. She cordially answered their questions (in Malay), as did the others, and showed them the stone that was the last object to fall. After looking around her one-room home (Vorderman estimates its length, width, and height), they expressed regret at missing such a fascinating occurrence. Just then, a ripe areca nut fell amid those present. Ebbot, dejected, noted it was starting again. At that, the guests left, Ebbot went inside, and a rock the size of a man's fist fell in the doorway.

Suspecting a scam (*bedrog*), Vorderman and his friends searched inside and out; he then had his friends keep watch outside while he joined Ebbot. She told him she suspected her recently deceased first husband's ghost or spirit (*geest*) might be responsible, and became quiet. As the three men conferred in the doorway, a lump of palm sugar brushed past Vorderman's head, followed by a stone and other small objects. Unable to tell where they came from, he writes he only noticed them when they were about a yard from the floor. Then a large quantity of green beans fell.

Noting Ebbot's calm, Vorderman began to suspect she was responsible, and decided to pay close attention to her hands. Alerting his friends, he instructed them (in French, in case Ebbot's husband knew Dutch) to ignore her until he said otherwise. Casually glancing at Ebbot, he noted she seemed to be hiding something under her hand. He then told his friends in Dutch that he thought the objects were coming from a particular place (in the opposite direction from Ebbot), adding in French that the next object thrown would be white and a bit larger than a woman's hand. For some time, nothing happened. And then a piece of coconut, just the right size, flew against his body from her direction. Triumphant, he accused her of being a charlatan: *she* was the source of the "putative persecution." One of his friends chimed in, stating that before the beans fell, she moved a basket; upon examining it, they found beans within. She met these allegations with heated denials, which left them unmoved.[42] Mystery solved, they returned home "cheerfully."

But Vorderman does not end there. He recalls prior incidents, both the famous one in Sumedang and episodes in Gerstäcker's piece. While commenting that the situation he observed was much simpler than nine-pound rocks, and that he does not mean to lump all these events together, he proposes that a clearer understanding would require prying "more deeply into native household life" than Europeans usually do. Take Sumedang. Even slight acquaintance with native "character" and "inclinations" leads one to wonder, he writes, if someone sought to turn the Von Kessingers against the beleaguered child, to remove a girl on the brink of puberty from their supervision. His analysis suggests that lust, greed, and a desire for attention motivate such incidents. Europeans become mere bystanders in indigenous dramas.

Vorderman is the opposite of a modest witness. He coyly keeps the reader suspended: on the one hand, a "mysterious semidarkness" he finds "uncanny" (*unheimisch*) pervades the interior; on the other, from the start he suspects a con. He is the story's hero, leading the investigation and solving the puzzle. He confronts Ebbot, calling her an imposter (*bedriegster*) to her face and dismissing her protests—ignoring that she was the target and that objects continued to fall for a week after his departure. How did she manage to throw things at herself, let alone keep it up for two weeks? Nor does he reflect upon his own use of ruses and misdirection, trickster tools, to out her. No wonder the trio are cheerful, having reestablished the world as, for white men, it should be, their cunning reason victorious over her purported fraud.

Vorderman engages both sets of pernicious alternatives. He confidently chooses prestidigitation and offers possible motives. The second set is tacit. He not only cites prior publications but highlights testimony, drawing on Dornseiff, quoting in full the "authentic official document" (Von Kessinger's report via Van Swieten), and ending with Gerstäcker. But given that he solves the case in a matter of hours, he makes Michiels look both gullible and incompetent, shredding his credibility.

Once again, traces of Indonesian responses come into view. His friend claimed the (Sundanese) district chief sent the regent of Bandung not only a detailed report but also some of the "thrown" objects. He also informed Vorderman that the crowds flocking to Ebbot's house brought rice, chickens, and coins (Vorderman adds "according to adat," or custom). And there is Ebbot's conjecture about her first husband.

Ebbot's comment about what might be responsible for the events in her home forms one of many speculations discernible in the interstices. Earlier I suggested that "Gandarúa" was misunderstood; corrected, it forms another complex Sundanese response to Dutch inquiries. In the same issue of the journal in which Van Swieten's note appears, an article corrects that translation. Jacob Adolf Bruno Wiselius, a scholar-administrator stationed in East Java, published an ethnographic piece on Javanese spirits (*geesten*) that included an extensive list. At its top is *gandroewa*: a malicious spirit who hangs out in the tallest trees in forests or residential areas and throws stones at passersby (1872: 26).[43] Wiselius does not mention Sumedang and is reporting what he heard at the opposite end of Java. But his description raises the possibility that in conversation with an insistent European official someone might have suggested that perhaps a "gandroewa" was involved—especially as the Cultivation System was leading to the felling of their forest dwelling places (Boomgaard 1995).

It took another decade before the connections became explicit, and before the word's meaning—though not yet its spelling—stabilized. Pieter Johannes Veth, founder of academic Dutch anthropology as the first to hold Leiden's chair, mentions *gandaroewa* in the Sumedang section of his magnum opus, a three-volume study of Java's geography, ethnology, and history.[44] Unlike his successor Wilken, he had little interest in broader trends in ethnology and no direct Indies experience. He built academic ethnology (and geography) on detailed knowledge of the Netherlands' prime colony, based on secondary sources. While citing Wiselius, he also adds to what he wrote by calling gandaroewa a *plaaggeest*, a spirit who teases, who delights in not only "throwing stones" but also "spitting sirih." This flows into a recital of events in Sumedang, which draws on (and footnotes) every prior publication: not only eyewitness accounts, but also travel tales—as the mention of sirih already suggests. He notes that while the "authentic documents" say nothing of what happened later, "the tradition at Sumedang" is that the government leveled the house.

But this is not the end of Veth's discussion. He then makes the decisive anthropological turn, the god-trick that establishes gandaroewa as merely the native's point of view, by explaining what occurred as sleight of hand.[45] While in Sumedang the perpetrator was never caught, other cases exist "in which all the dexterity of Javanese magicians [*goochelaars*] who delighted in throwing stones and other objects has not been able to protect them from the sharp gaze of European observers" (1882: 240–41). Not surprisingly, Vorderman exemplifies that sharpness. Like Van Swieten, Veth also praises Javanese skill, noting their tricks (*kunstgrepen*) reveal a "quick-fingeredness [*snelvingerigheid*] that goes far beyond European understanding" (1882: 241). He also refers readers to an earlier section of his work, where he briefly discusses magic tricks (*goocheltoeren*): humorous performances in East Java that included stunts similar to (and as incomprehensible as) those attributed to Indian magicians (*goochelaars*)—all the more impressive as they made no use of the devices crucial to European illusionists.

By 1882, then, the authoritative position treats the stones as evidence of Indonesian skill in magic tricks, while presenting Indonesians as attributing such acts to a spirit. Unlike the spirits of spiritualists, that spirit is not a disembodied person, the dematerialized essence of an individual human, but something even less plausible in the reality Dutch scholars made. *Gendruwo* (to give the word its current spelling) became a social—and ethnographic—fact, the illusory object of a generic subject.

Veth's assertions soon found themselves translated both back to the Indies and into popular culture. Hence a guidebook aims to pique visitors' interest in Sumedang by mentioning gendruwo and memories of the mischief one caused by throwing stones and sirih at a native girl there—noting that rains of stones are not infrequent on Java but due to conjuring tricks (Buys 1891: 139). Van Hien treats Veth as an authority in introductory remarks in the first edition of *The Javanese Spirit World* in 1896, which includes an entry on gendruwo. Both stone-throwing and sirih-spitting appear among the gendruwo's attributes.[46] Perhaps he learned this from Javanese subordinates during his brief career in the forestry service; more likely he got it from Veth.

Gendruwo have both lost and retained the associations Veth made. In postindependence ethnography, gendruwo show up in accounts of Javanese "spirit beliefs": Geertz (1960: 18) calls them "frightening spirits" who toss rocks on roofs at night (no sirih). In Indonesian cinema, they feature in horror films (again, no sirih). My Indonesian-English dictionary defines *gendruwo* this way: "ghost, *esp.* a garden/forest spirit that manifests itself by throwing stones and other objects on the roofs of houses, by spitting at or spattering s.o., an animal or other objects with red sirih-juice, by knocking on doors and windows, or by shaking them" (Stevens and Schmidgall-Tellings 2004).

From this point on, such phenomena never entirely disappear. The press, for instance, periodically reports incidents involving stones or sirih. This persistent low-level buzz contributed to the atmosphere when Louis Couperus and his wife arrived in Batavia in March 1899 to begin a yearlong visit, during which he wrote *The Hidden Force*.

Novel Forces

Couperus's book revivified talk of Sumedang. Along with sporadic recirculation by occultists, it continues to resuscitate the stones to this day. The novel triggered several crucial changes, however. For one, it offered a name both broader than "rain of stones" and less specific (and Indonesian) than *gendruwo*.[47] It also prompted a shift in the producers of texts, away from expertise based on position to personal experience and its genres. Couperus's most critical intervention, however, was to conjoin inexplicable phenomena to colonial politics. "Hidden force" not only challenged the epistemic and ontic domination justifying European superiority but presented Javanese as possessing unthinkable yet real capacities. Even as he tightened the knots binding magic to non-Europeans, he proposed it might not only work but threaten.

The novel itself grew out of experiences in and of the Indies. Couperus and his wife Elisabeth (a cousin) had deep connections to the colony. His family had long served the colonial state and still owned a private estate on Java. He spent part of his youth in Batavia; Elisabeth was raised in Batavia and Sumatra. During their visit, they mostly stayed with his sister's husband, Gerard Valette, the resident of Tegal, who was reassigned to Pasuruan during their visit. Pasuruan provided a model for Couperus's fictional residency, Labuwangi. From Valette, he learned about a resident's concerns, inspiring his main character, Otto van Oudijck.

Couperus portrays Van Oudijck as the quintessential white man of reason: he even describes him (repeatedly) as logical and masculine (*mannelijk*). Self-assured and decisive, Van Oudijck takes pride in his deft management of the regent, Sunario (his Javanese "younger brother," as the regime characterized the relation between a Dutch resident and Javanese regent), drawing on mastery of the pragmatics of Malay (e.g., using flowery, respectful language to impose his will). While cordial, the two despise each other. Van Oudijck considers Sunario—who frequents dukun, organizes activities according to auspicious and inauspicious days, and so on—a superstitious fanatic (*fanatiek*). In turn, Sunario bitterly resents Van Oudijck's obtuse authority. And with that Couperus begins to suggest the limitations of colonizer certitude. Van Oudijck's obliviousness—both to what is going on domestically (his wife is sleeping not only with her stepson but also a handsome Indo) and to the eponymous hidden force building to an explosion beneath the surface of everyday routines—drives the plot.

Initially, only his wife and children encounter manifestations of that hidden force: sightings of a tall, silent Haji in white; small stones whizzing past; moans high in a banyan tree. In the novel's famous climax, Van Oudijck's hedonistic wife flees naked in terror from her bath after blotches of sirih, spat from the room's corners, plaster her alabaster body. Once his family departs, Van Oudijck becomes the target: he hears constant hammering overhead; a large stone smashes a mirror; one whiskey glass breaks and another yellows. Finally, he summons several officers and a company of soldiers; with his secretary and controleur, they all spend a harrowing night in the bath house. After swearing everyone to silence (eventually a lieutenant leaks tales of a rain of stones, sirih spewing, a heaving floor, and something unmentionable in the water), he orders the bath house torn down and hand delivers a signed report to the secret government archives in Batavia. Upon his return, he talks to Sunario, and the eerie episodes cease. But his inability to make sense of these experiences destroys his confidence in the world white men of reason make real. By the end, Van Oudijck has resigned from the civil service and lives with a young nyai in a village near Garut.

Almost immediately, the novel revived talk of Sumedang. In rejoinders to a Dutch reviewer critiquing Couperus's "mystical point of view" as implausible, journalist Samuel Kalff and spiritualist Willem Bosch brought up the 1831 incident, the latter claiming he heard about it from Michiels himself.[48] Kalff (under a pen name) elaborated in a series on "Indies Mysteries" in the *Java Bode*. Citing all prior texts, he called Couperus's novel the most recent recollection and proposed it as Couperus's inspiration.[49] This set the pattern for recurring references to the present. Many later invocations seek to explain how Couperus learned about it: from family members (his father served with Michiels in Sumatra; he and his wife were distant kin of Baud); access to secret archives; or both.[50]

Yet the resemblance between what happened in the novel and in Von Kessinger's home is thin. Stones are few and far between and never violate expectations of how stones behave. What seized Couperus's imagination was the sirih. This, along with other details (officers summoned to investigate; tearing down the affected structure) recall tales circulating since the 1850s.[51] Links to Sumedang appear less a matter of access to unusual sources than of relations early commentators forged to channel hidden force into familiar grooves.

Couperus, however, offered hitherto unconsidered options for the first alternative. If prior texts linked the stones to magic by tossing off claims about tricks, Couperus translated a different form of magic to Java. Consider his deployment of words rooted in *goochel*—magic as arts of illusion— versus *tover*—magic as acts that shape reality. "Magic tricks" (*gegoochel*) is Van Oudijck's predictable public explanation for the creepy events in his home, and the European community follows his lead.[52] But Van Oudijck (and other Europeans) claims that Javanese think Sunario commands magic power (*toverkracht*). So far, this gap between what Javanese supposedly think and European "truth" resembles Veth, except sorcery substitutes for spirits. But Couperus does not leave things there. Van Oudijck acknowledges the regent's responsibility for what occurs: when he threatens him, the strangeness stops. But for Van Oudijck (and Couperus), *tover-* words prove inadequate. What happened exceeds his categories; he is catapulted into what De la Cadena (2021) calls "not knowing," but a not knowing that cannot be productive because colonialism has no place for such a position (hence, he resigns). He calls what he experienced "that," "the thing that happened," and "it" (Couperus 1985 [1900]: 226). For Couperus, "it" is "the hidden force," a substitute for the *tover-* words he uses and then refuses. Nonetheless, the sense of sorcery persists: Couperus links "it" to a Javanese capacity to manipulate unknown forces.

For Couperus, that force is more than human but immanent: in the soil, under the volcanoes, on the wind—even in the rain. A dangerous landscape translates traces of Javanese world-making that pop up in other colonial texts: not only gendruwo (as "tree spirits"), but comments about places to which people bring offerings, or complaints about the annoying Javanese insistence on holding rites before or after new construction, whether in European homes or public works.

An article by J. E. Jasper, then just starting his colonial career, testifies to Couperus's skill at grasping colonizer apprehensions. Jasper treats hidden force as synonymous with his own *tover-* coinage, railing in frustration that "the European population at the expense of everything comes more and more under the influence of the morbid myth concerning magic power [*tovermacht*] in the native" (1904: 132). Some officials, he grumbled, "imagine so much of the hidden force that emanates from the Javanese . . . that [they] also ascribe to him the great power to make [the] perfectly hale and hearty suddenly seriously ill, by administering mysterious, not existing, or having no effect, sometimes indeed entirely innocuous, things."[53] He especially condemns administrators who hesitate to carry out official tasks out of fear of Javanese retaliation, mentioning anxieties about contravening Javanese interdictions on examining ruins or antiquities or felling large trees (1904: 129–30). According to some, the latter preceded two 1890s episodes.[54]

Most who picked up Couperus's phrase skirted recognition of Javanese resentment, and certainly of any capacity to modify material reality. For many, hidden force spoke to experiences (for which Couperus uses a different *tover-* word, *betoverde*, to speak of the night or moon) that enticed rather than threatened. English equivalents—*enchanted, fascinated,* and *magic* itself—make up a parallel semantic history and structure of feeling, which has largely displaced sinister ones.[55] In the Indies, this sensibility rejected *tover-* words in favor of *hidden force.* The phrase not only came to index the Indies but, deployed across a host of cultural products—by 1902, the *Koloniaal Weekblad* ran stories at the bottom of the front page under the banner "Hidden Forces in the Indies"—became entangled with markets, just as *magic* is now routinely invoked to sell commodities. A manufacturer of patent medicines based on Javanese remedies even made *stille kracht* its brand, advertising one product as working with a "salutary and healing hidden force."[56]

Nonetheless, deployment of Couperus's phrase frequently took familiar paths. Headlines reporting possible episodes offered a familiar option: "hidden force or deceit [*bedrog*]," "hidden force or practical joke [*baldadigheid*]."[57] The choice between human and nonhuman (or not-only-human) agents appears immediately after the novel's publication. When a reviewer in the Netherlands insisted that Dutchmen living in the Indies for decades "unanimously" held pranksters responsible for rare cases involving stones or sirih aimed at disturbing Europeans' peace of mind, a spiritualist adamantly disagreed, even as he condemned those who failed to differentiate frauds perpetrated by charlatans from the real thing.[58]

Such acknowledgment of the possibility of scams indexes metropolitan battles between skeptics and adherents—of not only spiritualism but its offspring and competitors. Professional illusionists developed a side gig discrediting manifestations as faked.[59] Other debunkers included members of the Society for Psychical Research, dedicated to investigating what increasingly came to be designated by the prefix *para-* (as in *paranormal* or *parapsychology*) rather than *super-*. Like Bosch, defenders might concede that some phenomena were bogus—but by no means all were.

The most elaborate case for chicanery drew liberally on the techniques such debunkers had developed. If prior claims about deception offered little evidence, in 1916 Creusesol (the pen name of Isaac Pierre Constant Graafland) advanced a rigorous argument for trickery in a pamphlet entitled *Does Hidden Force Exist?* Born in Semarang (Java) in 1851, he worked as a plantation manager and railway official before becoming a journalist and man of letters and moving to The Hague in 1899. Noting that hidden force stories seemed more common in the Netherlands than in the Indies—

he blames returning totoks—he accuses them of vagueness about what occurred, where, and to whom, asserting that all such accounts ultimately derived from either Couperus or Sumedang. These serve as his focus.

Creusesol builds his brief on two fronts: technique and motivation. For the first, he speculates about how Javanese might produce the famed effects.[60] Discussion of the Mango Trick and Rope Trick, for which itinerant South Asian troupes were famed, serves as prelude to explaining how spewed sirih and falling rocks could be rigged. His reconstruction rests on claims about both Javanese and the Europeans at whom such tricks were aimed. According to Creusesol, Javanese techniques of the body involve remarkable agility. Not only can they squat for hours, but they can deftly turn bamboo into an extraordinary range of useful items, ranging from living quarters to containers. Moreover, dark skin and hair make them invisible (especially at night), like black-clothed helpers on metropolitan stages.

Creusesol's Javanese possess a proficiency in misdirection as wondrous as anything occult. The mechanisms he proposes are extraordinarily complicated. For the stones: loading them into bamboo catapults, or placing them on ceiling beams, to be launched by the warming and cooling of the heat of the sun. For the sirih: bamboo cylinders filled with carefully collected spittle from spittoons in the servants' quarter, hung to escape detection and each with a hole just large enough to allow the liquid to fall out at a precisely timed moment.

What prompted such elaborate ruses, however, were routine disputes. Taking his lead from Couperus, he identifies resentment as the motive, while grounding hostility not in regents chafing under Dutch authority but in the mundane relations of everyday life. There are indeed "hidden forces" afoot, in the silent omnipresence of Javanese servants in European households, with the most intimate facets of colonizer life open to their gaze.[61] In short, he materializes the master–slave relation as magical praxis: deception becomes a weapon of the weak. But these maneuvers work better on totoks and officials than on those with Indies backgrounds (such as himself). Totoks, habituated to neither people nor place, are particularly susceptible. As for officials, insulation from the lives of Javanese and frequent transfers make them easy marks. Not once had Creusesol heard of such a thing happening to a planter, whom Javanese know better than to try to fool.[62]

Considering how long stones fell in Sumedang, to maintain such devices would be remarkably time-consuming—and it is hard to understand why stones never hit anyone. Such explanatory strategies contravene one of Boyle's strictures: namely, that different causes may yield the same effect (Shapin and Schaffer 1985: 24, n. 3). That ingenious apparatuses could produce such effects does not prove they did. In treating Javanese as trickster trollers, Creusesol is as speculative as prior advocates for deceit.

Skeptics may have considered Creusesol's explanation definitive. Certainly, more publications argue the other side. However, there is a good deal of trotting down familiar paths despite filling the signifier "hidden force" with several new possibilities. Most favor universalizing explanations, involving scientific discoveries and/or metropolitan occultism. Though Java figures as a site for unusual experience, Javanese entities, agents, and speculations mostly vanish.

A major exception is Van Hien. Later editions of *The Javanese Spirit World* add to gendruwo two other explanations for stone-throwing and sirih-spitting, both involving human control over other-than-human entities. One, *medi*, he calls an elementary, using a theosophical term (*elementaar*), and glossing them as "the soulless astral body of a person who has lived very badly and, as we say figuratively, has lost his soul" as well as the "astral bodies" of those who died bad deaths.[63] Using formulas, Javanese may command them to "pursue revenge" or trouble someone (1934: vol. 1, 250). *Jin* are "Mohammedan" spirits who also may be incited to such acts by the right words (1934: vol. 3, 43).[64] He also published a tiny book of *Formulas for Hidden Force* (1924).

Despite highlighting Javanese entities, however, Van Hien knots stones (and sirih) to theosophy, not only in glosses such as elementaries and astral bodies but in short sections referring to theosophical texts.[65] Theosophical concepts ("astral regions," "etheric doubles") also dot Kalff's (1925) article in a popular Dutch journal. No one, curiously, mentions that Blavatsky (1881) herself addressed "stone showers" in response to a query from a Dutch spiritualist. She rejected the view that malevolent or disembodied human spirits were responsible in favor of physical mediums sensitive to magnetic forces—or, in the absence of people, in favor of the "Forces of Nature" theosophists called Elementals. In the Von Kessinger household, the girl plagued by the stones was a medium. Such mediums attract stones (or other objects) while also repelling them (so they are neither touched nor hurt by them).

If Blavatsky anticipated a shift from spirits of the dead to the bodies of mediums, it took until 1926 for that position to be elaborated, in *The Problem of the Hidden Force* by a A. Baudisch, who calls himself a doctor.[66] A counterpoint to Creusesol, it rejected the latter's argument as too extreme.

While Baudisch concedes that Javanese saboteurs might account for some cases, especially when victims are recent arrivals from Europe, this can hardly be true of what happened in 1831, for which "authenticated documents" exist (his emphasis on textual evidence contributing to the second pernicious alternative). Like Creusesol, he concentrates on Sumedang but also addresses Couperus's novel as public opinion had followed Couperus in attributing such phenomena to Javanese (1926: 14).[67]

Baudisch poses two questions: Can such things happen (the quintessential second pernicious alternative issue)? If so, can they be consciously produced, as in the novel? Responding "yes" to both, he pulls together a plethora of sources: published reports of similar phenomena by parapsychologists from other regions, experiments (mostly British) on physical mediums (mostly women) conducted by natural scientists, theosophically informed Orientalism, and recent findings by physicists about the relation of matter to energy. The first show that falling stones are not unique to Java; the second reveal the agent responsible: physical mediums produce such phenomena spontaneously and psychically. Thus such incidents form a poorly understood element of nature.[68] Unlike Europeans, however, in whom the ability to produce material effects is rarely under conscious control, in Java, heir to "Hindu" traditions, some know corporeal and mental exercises whose mastery produces such abilities—a claim contributing to the Orientalism inherited through Couperus's novel. The theosophists (re)knotted magic to the East (though farther east than the Persia from which the word came) as ancient wisdom. Baudisch also connects falling stones directly to magic. Glossing occult phenomena as inexplicable events contradicting normal experience, he insists they have been reported in all times and places. Medieval Europeans attributed such magic (*toverkunsten*) to saints (*heiligen*), sorcerers (*tovenaars*), witches (*hexen*), and magicians (*magiërs*).

Others endorsing "hidden forces" eschewed explanation. Authors often quote (in English) Hamlet's "there are more things in heaven and earth," harkening back to an era when wonder constituted a mode of serious inquiry.[69] While some cite or quote accounts of 1831 or allege a (tenuous) connection to a witness as evidence,[70] others claim to have been "converted" (an epistemic framing in the language of belief) by experience.[71]

By forging a link between uncanny incidents and colonial politics, Couperus suggests the limits of European mastery. Beneath the smooth surface of Javanese compliance lurked hostility, manifested in ways officials could neither acknowledge nor address.

Before leaving those Couperus inspired, I want to note opposing re-marks by two authors who claim they elicited Javanese views. To establish that Javanese had never heard of such powers, Creusesol spoke to those with whom he (purportedly) had relations of mutual trust: native leaders, old overseers, and servants of his family and friends. As "Natives" are reluc-tant to speak of their "folk beliefs," he approached the topic casually, asking if people existed who could throw stones without touching them, or if one might be at risk from stone-throwing spirits in particular places. Even the most "superstitious" answered no. Van Hien explains such silence differ-ently: "Every Javanese knows how those mysterious teasings were evoked but he will seldom speak about it, afraid of kindling the spirits' displeasure, and he finds it better to pretend innocence toward the European" (Van Hien 1934: vol. 3, 43).

Between Rocks and a Hard Place

Writing about the unthinkability of the Haitian Revolution, Michel-Rolph Trouillot noted, "When reality does not coincide with deeply held beliefs, human beings tend to phrase interpretations that force reality within the scope of these beliefs. They devise formulas to repress the unthinkable and to bring it back within the realm of accepted discourse" (1995: 72). Narra-tives about the stones funnel them into just such realms.

While I've spoken of two sets of pernicious alternatives, the first—efforts to explain—was considerably more relevant to colonial reality politics. Whether highlighting technologies of deception or proposing unknown (but not unknowable) forces, explanations recuperate European superiority in the face of a dual threat to the coloniality of the one-world world. Apart from the affront to natural law, that men whose eyes serve as instruments of domination fail to find the cause or agent responsible yet insist on what they saw makes a mockery of European authority.

Assertions about duplicity and legerdemain are a god-trick of white men of reason—while giving birth, via Veth, to a decisive scholarly position.[72] They restore authority through their command of logic and a penetrating gaze that can see beneath mere appearance. Reasserting the orderliness of nature, they insist the only actors are humans, whose skilled deceptions and motivations can be plumbed. European reason triumphs over duplicitous natives and unruly nature.

The other position treats falling stones as supernatural or paranormal, "super-" and "para-" doing telling work by treating what they modify—the natural and normal—as settled. Those attributing falling stones to spirits subordinate their troubling materiality. Albeit controversial, spirits are familiar as agents or subjects, indeed as the essence of agents or subjects. (Those who favor the unconscious projections of mediums remain in the domain of human causality.) However contentious occultism may be, it remains colonial insofar as it supersedes and ignores "the native point of view." Strange phenomena become another raw material to be processed in the metropole.

By contrast, the second pair of pernicious alternatives—preoccupied with evidence—speaks more powerfully to academic reality politics. These alternatives only became possible in the 1870s since what circulated before that were stories, which some in The Hague called "fairy tales." Von Kessinger's report and Gerstäcker's friend changed the terrain. From then on there is attention to testimony, especially to "authentic" documents that authors not only cite but quote at length. Still, no one seems to doubt what happened—though those arguing for legerdemain invariably speak of thrown rather than falling stones. While skepticism about "hidden forces" in general may have existed, and explanations involving Indonesian trickery implicitly made Michiels a fool, no one argues that nothing happened or tries to take testimony apart. But when I first talked about the stones to an academic audience, some immediately challenged the event or the testimony. One colleague proposed that Van Swieten fabricated the purported report; another asked if it matched the style of Von Kessinger's other reports. The most common response was to ask if I *believed* this incident had happened.

Anthropologists rarely ask such questions. But then usually when we talk about matters that academics deem impossible, we are addressing other anthropologists about the subjects of our research. Cultural difference elides the question of reality through the sleight of hand of relativity, in which the analyst's faith that she comes from a society that knows what is *really* real remains unacknowledged. Here, though, the "informants" are white men—and the academics were not anthropologists.

To respond to demands for adjudication, however, would close the small space the stones open to query what counts as real. To answer "no" to the question of whether I "believe" stones fell would comfortably confirm a shared reality; to answer "yes" would undermine my credibility, shutting down inquiry before it begins. Both leave "reality" in place. Surely, these are not the only possibilities. How else might strangely falling stones—so far from the inert philosopher's stone—be attended to? I offer two paths that have the virtue of unfamiliarity.

The first ponders the trail of citations. Instead of using them to secure a historical fact, what other effects do they produce? Over time, sheer accumulation lends weight to the remembered rocks. The accretion of attribution and argument becomes an actor itself, spurring conversation, speculation, investigation, deduction, and more narration. Its tendrils even stretched to a now vanished Barnes and Noble bookstore, where I casually picked up a book entitled *Supernatural Tales from around the World* to discover "Javanese Poltergeists," excerpted from a report by Northcote W. Thomas for the *Occult Review* (1905), which relied in turn on Gerstäcker (Hardin 1995).

A second possibility moves yet further from preoccupations with explanation and evidence. I am lured by interstices, in two senses. The first are the Indonesian reactions glimpsed in the interstices of European accounts. They include speculations in conversations initiated by Europeans, hints about what leads to such incidents, and responses. The second is Isabelle Stengers's concept of interstices (2011b). Perhaps what appeals to me is the happy coincidence not only of the word but that in presenting this concept she imagines a wall made of—well, stones. The weeds growing between the stones may eventually lead to its collapse. Such walls recall European experiences of what they call nature in the Indies. Stones appear inert, though like everything else they are not. But the volcanic stone used to build walls, shrines, and statuary quickly appears ancient, as humidity encourages the growth of lichen and mosses.

In what I take from Stengers, a "culture of interstices" involves the possibility of originality rather than the habits that constitute societies. Interstices are potential openings to something new. In passing, she also calls trance and divination experiences that open a collectivity to an "intrusion" that "suspends habitual functioning" (though in Indonesian societies such intrusions have established accommodations).

To be sure, certain explanations proffered for the stones are also interstitial: those in which the dead or psychic powers intrude upon—and reorient—some European lives, weeds that could crack the walls of one-world worlds and their forms of knowledge. But, as noted, they also are among the stones making up a Eurocentric, colonial wall in which Indonesians are barely visible. I want to pick up on hints in those fragments of curiosity.

These fall into several different—and differently illuminating—types. As already noted, some involve speculations about forces or entities that might be responsible for falling rocks. Only one appears to have been offered spontaneously; most are elicited by white men in positions of power with limited command of Indonesian languages or worlds. Ebbot suspects her dead first husband might be causing her troubles—though Vorderman, while recording this, did not ask her why. Van Hien associates *medi* with the dead—did Ebbot's husband die a bad death? The regent of Ciamis muses about an inherited ability to become invisible. Was he speaking of humans or more-than-humans? And then there is the unknown interlocutor (or interlocutors) who suggested gendruwo.

Concerns about gendruwo—who dwell in forests or gardens—appear implicated in repeated references to felling trees. Sometimes Javanese try to warn the European victim to leave large trees alone (always noted after the fact). Recall too Jasper's exasperation at officials whose apprehensions led to hesitation about cutting them down. Trees are not the only mark of Indonesian cosmogeographies. The regent of Sukapura mentions that the French victim of an incident lived above a ravine.

Such comments bring Sumedang—and Priangan—back into view. Some places, I learned from Indonesian friends, are more prone to encounters with more-than-humans. Mountainous Priangan (from the root *hyang*, a potent entity or force), including Sumedang, is filled with such sites, remnants of the dynamic geological processes (active volcanoes, waterfalls, hot springs, deep ravines) and relics (of pre-Islamic polities) that produce the geographies more-than-humans favor.[73] The coffee inspectors and indigo factory of 1831 signal further alterations to land long subject to extractivism. Over the course of the nineteenth century, colonial projects led to deforestation across Java.

What led me to connect falling stones with changing landscapes was what I learned from an American acquaintance living in Bali about an incident in the town of Mas at the end of 1999 or start of 2000.[74] Small stones fell on, around, and under a pavilion (rather than inside a closed structure). Her sources included the Brahmana priest of the family of those affected, who requested his help. He told her that a *wong samar* (what we would call a spirit but literally an imperceptible person; hence my question about the regent of Ciamis) was responsible; recent construction had invaded its territory. Mas was in the throes of development, as people built businesses to sell or export handicrafts.

Faced with the intrusion of falling stones, Indonesians take different actions than Europeans did, readily socializing odd occurrences. The priest in Bali conducted a rite, provided protective devices, and suggested the family build a shrine to make offerings on a regular basis. Such incidents offer an opening to connections with a more-than-human, beginning with a welcome. In Bali, responses involve not only establishing but maintaining relations of hospitality, through acts repeated at regular intervals. Intimations of something similar appear in Dutch accounts, when Vorderman records that people brought rice, chickens, and coins to Ebbot's house, "according to 'adat.'" These imply help with ritual costs. Perhaps references to sirih are a distorted glimpse of greeting the force at work in Sumedang.[75] In short, making offerings (and building shrines) answers a query initiated by an other-than-human. Identifying the agent matters less than responding well.

These reflections, like European explanations, deflect attention from the stones themselves, however. The well-trodden alternatives constantly draw our attention to subjects—their credibility, credulity, their knack for deception—at the expense of things. But among casual remarks in Dutch texts appear glimpses of the interest some Indonesians on these occasions showed in the rocks themselves. Dornseiff notes the regent, Patih, and "other native leaders" "each took a few stones as souvenir, perhaps to use them as obat (medicine)." A district official sent several objects that fell at Ebbot's house to the regent of Bandung. And according to the buzz in Bali, a visitor or visitors who came to gawk pocketed a stone—though, or so the story goes, something scary happened to him that night. Their strange behavior suggested the stones might have properties that could enhance human capacities. Rather than a souvenir or medicine, likely what interested people was whether a stone could be instaured as a jimat or pusaka.

Whether or not they were is impossible to say; this is not the kind of topic about which Indonesians write or tell tales. Perhaps stones that fell in Sumedang remain among the heirlooms of descendants of the Sundanese who came to Von Kessinger's house, without anyone recalling their origin. Like a shrine, an heirloom is a material archive, a remnant of events no longer necessarily recalled *as* events.

These glimpses reveal responses that do not narrow focus to the question of whether rocks fell or attempt bifurcated explanations. Nor do they involve what anyone—Indonesians, witnesses, those talking about the incident, including me—believes, as if this were a useful concept. To follow how worlds are jointly made by humans, nonhumans, and more-than-humans is to work in the interstices. It is to move beyond belief—and the analytic of magic with which it is often entangled.

INTERLUDE 6 ⌄⌄ THE MAGIC OF SCIENCE STUDIES

> In short, to him magic is always an art, never a science; the very idea
> of science is lacking in his undeveloped mind. It is for the philosophic
> student to trace the train of thought which underlies the magician's
> practice; to draw out the few simple threads of which the tangled skein
> is composed; to disengage the abstract principles from their concrete
> applications; in short, to discern the spurious science behind the
> bastard art. (Frazer 1922: 11–12)

In this passage from *The Golden Bough*, Frazer offers insight into what
founders of the anthropology of magic meant by Science, a concept that
doubly obsessed them. If as an academic discipline they sought recognition
for anthropology as a science, as an object of study, they conjured magic as
science's opposite—or its dark twin, a rudimentary but empirically false
science replete with faulty reasoning and inadequate theorization. Perhaps
it is fitting—or perversely satisfying—that the magic anthropologists made
later served as a doula at the birth of science studies, through multidisci-
plinary discussions partly inspired by Evans-Pritchard's analysis of Zande
witchcraft.[1] And here I introduce the first of three engagements between
magic and science studies: David Bloor, who along with his colleague
Barry Barnes founded the strong program in the sociology of scientific
knowledge.

Beginning in 1970, several edited volumes debated the universality versus relativism of rationality, especially in relation to the Azande.[2] Both Bloor and Barnes contributed to these discussions. But it was especially Bloor's *Knowledge and Social Imagery*, a book that Steven Shapin, in a blurb on the back of its second edition, calls a "classic in modern science studies—indeed, perhaps the first classic text," that linked the new field to anthropology's magic. To be sure, Bloor (1976) spends fewer than ten pages on what Evans-Pritchard calls a contradiction in Zande claims about the heritability of witchcraft, and thus in their logic. But in defense of the Azande, Bloor poses a parallel Euro-American contradiction, a subtle example of what the strong program called symmetry. Unlike prior sociologies of knowledge, which explained beliefs (in, e.g., magic), ideologies, and superseded knowledges such as alchemy, as products of society, and science by nature and reason, symmetry meant accounting for all knowledge claims—true as well as false—using one explanatory framework.

Bruno Latour explicitly endorsed—and expanded on (despite Bloor's objections)—symmetry as both concept and method. Less obviously, he inherited the debates on rationality and relativism to which Bloor had contributed—and which remained a focus of anthropologists writing about magic into the 1990s. Which is not to say he chanced upon anthropology through Bloor. Latour's introduction to, understanding of, and long-standing regard for the field derived from encounters with French ethnographers, themselves captivated by issues raised by magic's reason. It likely dates from his national service in Côte d'Ivoire in the early 1970s, at a development agency headed by Marc Augé, then involved in analyzing sorcery among inhabitants of the lagoons near the capital.[3] Latour's early works often cite not only Augé on this topic but also Jeanne Favret-Saada on witchcraft in rural France. His references to magic suggest the imprint of such analyses.

Latour deploys the term *magic* to turn the tables on the moderns, mainly in two books. The first is the provocative and remarkable *Irreductions* (1988);[4] the second, the daunting *An Inquiry into Modes of Existence* (2013; hereafter *Inquiry*), in which he delivers—in the personage of an imaginary female ethnographer—on the "anthropology of the moderns" toward which he previously had gestured (Latour 1993).

Irreductions blends the way moderns accuse others of magic to present (and elevate) themselves as rational, logical, and scientific, with magic's ambiguous ambient meanings: trickery that yields the appearance of extraordinary effects but also actual marvelous phenomena. Magic refers as well to "potent words" that dazzle or cast a glamour on those who hear or speak them: words such as *rational, true, universal,* and *objective.* Such language and associated conceptual habits conceal the arduous task of building particular connections and "paying their cost" (a favorite phrase). Arguing for immanence rather than transcendence, for bringing science especially—but also religion and power—back down to earth, Latour insists we need to show our work (as math teachers like to say) rather than eliding the actual processes—and necessary infrastructure—through which ideas and practices spread. Insofar as he uses the word to address how moderns make things mysteriously appear or vanish, magic entails unreality.

Inquiry takes his analysis further. In a grand synthesis of some of his earlier work, Latour reworks the Big Ideas (among them, Nature, Matter, Objects, Subjects, Society, Religion, Morality, Economy) that make up the common currency of both popular and academic discourse. In their place he proposes a series of what he terms "beings," adopting a set of novel abstract descriptors to perform a symmetrical anthropology. This allows him to mutate familiar abstractions to (at least) two ends. First, to demonstrate the gap between these familiar concepts and what moderns actually do. This is a move recognizable from the hidden work of translation Latour (1993) identified as occurring alongside articulations of the work of purification, a deflection reeking of legerdemain—a "look at the right hand, not the left" practice. Second, these strange new categories—for example, beings of reproduction and beings of metamorphosis—that describe the moderns' modes of existence form a reflective anthropology that undoes the moderns' pretense to universalism, opening possibilities for future negotiations with others.

Magic and related words weave in and out of the text, sometimes elaborating earlier themes. *Irreductions* referred to "magicians of reason" who "travel beyond their bodies" (1988: 186). A section of *Inquiry* labeled "and the magic of rationalism vanishes" states, "With one stroke of the magic wand—and it is really a question of magic here, except that magic is the source of the idea of Reason!" (2013: 118). He talks of black and white magic to characterize words that wound or soothe. On the whole, Latour emphasizes that assertions moderns make about themselves—whether these make them smug or sad—rest on contrasts with those they label primitive, traditional, backward, and superstitious.[5]

Latour's thinking was entwined with Isabelle Stengers's, with whom he engaged for decades in generous acts of what Haraway calls cat's cradling.[6] But unlike Latour—or Bloor, whom her early work discusses—Stengers develops magic and sorcery into concepts.

Like Latour, Stengers is conversant with how ethnologists have addressed such topics. "Do you believe in sorcery?" the title of a chapter asks, in a book on capitalism coauthored with Philippe Pignarre (Pignarre and Stengers 2011). To answer, they succinctly dismiss the usual suspects deployed in accounts of sorcery (metaphor, belief, the supernatural, culture), noting that ethnologists presume at best that sorcery is a survival in our own society (2011: 39). But they insist that sorcery—in a society where no one calls themselves sorcerers and where such things are presumed definitively past—renders precisely how capitalism captures people and turns them into its minions.

But it is *magic* that comes up repeatedly in Stengers's work, where it refers neither to the moderns nor to those from whom they distance themselves. Her interlocutor is Starhawk, and the latter's articulation of why and how she and other ecofeminists have *reclaimed* (a position that does not presume a continuous survival of peasant traditions) the words *witch* and *magic*. Of particular interest to Stengers, in keeping with her work's focus on situated practices rather than ideologies or theories (not to mention beliefs), is the specific practice in which that magic is performed: to wit, casting a circle and invoking a "Goddess" associated above all with change.[7] Stengers repeatedly stresses how such events enable participants to learn to think and feel differently. There is much more to say about what this practice—and her encounter with Starhawk—has provoked Stengers herself to think and feel (each mention includes small gems of insight—some of which I discuss in the epilogue). I find especially satisfying, however, the way Stengers reverses the valuation of magic and the understanding of science that marked the work of ethnologists such as Frazer. Inverting what once was a negative, Stengers calls magic a craft, an art, a recipe, a procedure, a technique, sometimes preceding these words with the word *experimental*.[8] Emphasizing its pragmatism, she insists (in contrast to Frazer's critique) that it cannot be theorized (2018b: 148).

I began this book with the promise of an adventure, by accompanying *magic* on some of its journeys across time and space. These followed two paths. The first explored a series of encounters between Dutch authorities or other Europeans living in the Indies with Balinese, Sundanese, and Javanese people engaged in life-enhancing, world-assembling practices. My five chapters opened with practices, practitioners, things, or events now routinely presented as magical, before going back in time to discover the arrival of the judgment *magic* and subsequent mutations in its meaning and entailments. Each of these accounts revolved around stories concerning particular historical incidents, which served as gathering points for discussion. In each I also proposed alternative routes—different translations—by drawing on glimpses of Indonesian responses.

The second path wove through the interludes, related contrapuntally to themes arising in the chapters. These focused on the formation of magic (and related words and concepts) in the anthropology I learned to practice—a magic jolted by what I heard and experienced in Bali. Shaped by the times and places in which such words and concepts developed, they fashioned the discipline not only in the work they did as descriptors and categories, but by molding habits and structures of feeling. The latter in turn fed other magics, in other disciplines as well as "modern" collectives.

This adventure included an experiment: *magic* and related terms were analyzed rather than used as tools for analysis. Or rather, in the chapters,

Dutch terms, such as *toverij* and *magie*, which do not entirely overlap with English relatives. That the persons and language that transported magic to the archipelago were Dutch matters. The Dutch were shaped by different pasts than the British. *Magie*, cognate with *magic*, came into use late, through ethnology. While *toverij*, closer to the English *witchcraft* and to witch trials (with which the Dutch had different experiences than the British), circulated in Dutch colonial texts, it was not taken up in colonial administration and law (and anthropology) as was the case in British Africa.

What interested me in embarking on this journey was how, when, and with what consequences particular practices, practitioners, and things found themselves enrolled in magic's conceptual field. In the Indies, this meant tracking magic's uptake in colonial laws and policies, ethnological theories and exhibits, rumors and popular culture. The trajectories of these particular translations demonstrate that magic does different work in different circumstances. In these diverse zones and times magic operated not only to construct hierarchies but also to challenge them, both fabricating and subverting sociological distinctions (of race, gender, and class), epistemic distinctions (between reason and irrationality, truth and belief), and ontic distinctions (between nature and culture, material and immaterial, matter and spirit—not to mention real and imaginary).

At the same time, having learned from reading Isabelle Stengers to take seriously the matter of inheritance, the latter issue also has run through my inquiry, in the interludes. From whom do we want to inherit? What do we want to carry forward and for what ends? My field of anthropology began by suturing itself to magic, attaching Europe's safely passed past to the ongoing practices of others, distant or not. Such magic has been seminal, fertilizing the productive activities of generations of (mainly male) ancestors. This fateful alliance had many unanticipated consequences. Proclamations by metropolitan theorists had their own magical effects, acting at a distance on other lives. Some wielded their concept of magic to discipline sympathizers at home, treating even members of their own circles who spoke to the dead (or nowadays call themselves witches) as beyond the modern pale—even calling for exorcisms, at least in Tylor's vision of anthropology as a "reformer's science" (1958 [1871]: vol. 2, 539).

Even generous and sympathetic anthropological routines—descriptive, analytical, conceptual, affective—may obscure magic's politics, however: not only the colonial processes that transported it around the globe, but ongoing struggles over the really real. To become cognizant of these politics is to recognize that magic often remains a technology of empire. When such magic is conjured, it sediments colonizing projects of making, unmaking, and remaking worlds. At the same time, if magic's translations have brought the realities of nonmodern collectives into question, those translations also have bounced home, to enchant the purportedly disenchanted.

That the death of magic among the moderns has been greatly exaggerated is something to which I will return. I also want to take up an issue involving anthropology's magic not yet addressed: namely, the trio of magic, science, and religion. Indonesia—or more accurately, Indonesian—will play its part in that consideration.

Here let me note that my dual adventure also could be regarded as an extended experiment in what Marisol de la Cadena (2021) calls *not knowing*, a concept to which I have previously referred. Like not knowing, it runs counter to the "categorical imperative" that slots unfamiliar practices and statements into Euro-historical constructs.[1] Such not knowing strikes me as a richer intellectual and ethical position than those usually informing magic as a scholarly analytic.

Magic, Science, and Religion

As mentioned above, anthropology's founders often treated magic as part of a theoretical trio, with science and religion as its other two members. Peter van der Veer (2014) has offered an intriguing interpretation of their entailments. He argues that as the success of the sciences in accounting for and manipulating material processes threatened Christianity's authority, European intellectuals redefined religion's meaning and purpose. Religion morphed into the province of morality rather than earthly creation; culture, not nature, became its proper purview. But the reworking of religion to avoid clashes with the accumulating corpus of matters of fact enacted a cultural arithmetic that left a remainder. All practices that dared to compete with the sciences, which insisted they could transform reality rather than only human souls, found themselves labeled magic.

Such definitional niceties, and the histories they drag with them, are crucial to the translations that still haunt not only magic but studies of what gets called religion. Other scholars have had much to say about how Protestant Christianity became the implicit model for religion and about how religion came to encompass more than the three monotheisms. Pietz's history of the fetish already complicates Van der Veer's claim that it took until the nineteenth century for Christianity to marginalize myriad techniques, objects, and speech acts through the label magic—as do later developments (e.g., the practices embraced by evangelicals or Mormons that secularists often render as magic). Still, Van der Veer's proposal clarifies later (k)not-work. Not only does it underscore how magic came to be trapped particularly between the Scylla of Religion and the Charybdis of Science, but this referential reshuffling zeroes in on the period when Europeans carried their magic (with its *nots*) furthest.

For North American anthropologists, as well as for scholars in religious studies and history, religion counts more than science now in discussions of magic, at least pedagogically, a crucial domain of continued transmission. Magic occupies an indispensable place in both textbooks and courses on the anthropology of religion rather than those on the anthropology of science. Yet consignment to religion elides the formative role that magic as "not science," and (as Van der Veer clarifies) thus not about reality, performed in making anthropology. Making sense of practices identified as magic, preemptively walled off from the real, incited considerable resourcefulness—no less than a full-on invention of culture and cultural relativity (Wagner 1975). At the same time, the desire to be a Science undermined anthropologists' capacity to learn from and not only about their "others."

In addition, while the trio was an organizing structure for disciplinary pioneers, religion often proved a far less interesting contrast with magic than science was. Frazer and Malinowski were among those who found this trio compelling. Frazer (1922) placed them in an evolutionary sequence: magic starts things off as a false science, but religion, though morally superior (confirmation of Van der Veer), is inferior to true science, the culmination of human thought. Malinowski (1948 [1925]), at least when he sticks to what he learned from Trobriand Islanders rather than generalizing about "primitives," offers more nuance: recognizing that Trobriand Islanders possessed a fount of empirical knowledge, he proposes that "magic" (in this case, specific words) fills the gap between the skilled application of such knowledge and inevitably indeterminate outcomes. But in the end, he contrasts the uncertainty of "primitive" life with the security technology has procured in "civilized" society. His faith in technoscience now seems inconceivable, given what was unleashed in World War I trenches and has accelerated since, leading to nothing less than an imminent planetary catastrophe.

But let me enter into these treacherous waters from a different direction, by backing up onto the terrain of translation in the mundane sense of finding ways of saying in one language something originally expressed in another. How do magic, science, and religion translate into Indonesian?

Across the archipelago much preceded (and proceeded alongside) the arrival of Europeans. Long before the first Portuguese ships sailed through the Strait of Malacca, inhabitants of islands across the archipelago had been exchanging all manner of things with one another and with seafarers from farther away, transmuting them in the process. Language preserves traces of these exchanges. Unknown events and untold stories rumble in the background of quotidian words and their pragmatic uses. English is shot through with mementoes of past engagements, with its mixture of Celtic, Anglo-Saxon, Germanic, and Romance languages, along with Latin and Greek terms and roots—including *magic*, which harkens back to Persian practitioners and the unfamiliar practices they introduced to the Greeks. Indonesian is similarly replete with vestiges of past and recent encounters. These are visible in the words Indonesian-English dictionaries interpret as the trio Van der Veer addresses.

Agama, invariably understood as one of five major world religions (Islam, Catholicism, Christianity [covering all Protestant denominations], Buddhism, and Hinduism), though each has its particular Indonesian inflections and histories, comes from Sanskrit, where it meant something more like doctrines or precepts (Zoetmulder 1982: vol. 1, 23). That Sanskrit term has undergone decided transformations of meaning due to the impact of both Christianity and Islam, along with colonial developments and nation-building.[2]

Science involves more complications. It is translated by not one but two words, with different roots, which may be combined. One is Malay: *pengetahuan*, from the root *tahu*, to know. The other is *ilmu*, from Arabic *'ilm*, which referred initially to religious knowledge. Science is *ilmu pengetahuan*. But as these glosses suggest, Indonesian does not distinguish science from knowledge in general. Indeed, *ilmu* covers such a vast territory that a list of specific kinds (indicated by the word *ilmu* plus a second noun) takes up two columns in the most comprehensive Indonesian-English dictionary.[3] Not only does the list encompass natural sciences, social sciences, and humanities (with many varieties of each), but it does not differentiate theoretical from applied knowledges. Know-how, skilled practice, is, moreover, another form of knowledge (as it should be, since abilities acquired through experiential learning are basic to all knowledge). Ilmu is a copious category, generous and generative, in which science/knowledge is action as much as abstraction.

Not surprisingly, many of the natural sciences are on the list (some also are known by words adapted from English). But so are over forty entries that could be placed in the domain of magic. More than half a dozen are rendered "mysticism" (sometimes paired with "occultism") without further clarification. They include *ilmu kasaktian*, from the root *sakti*, power, which partly prompted this book. I suspect several refer to particular Islamic (and Javanese) practices that by no means would be identical to one another. Others are explicitly identified with magic. Three involve language: spells to make someone invisible, incantations to injure or kill at a distance, and the art of casting spells. Four more directly refer to the practice of magic or sorcery (at least according to the dictionary). One involves putting someone to sleep (recall chapter 2!); four are simply presented as *black magic* (one also offers "occult science" as a secondary meaning), including *ilmu hitam* (literally black knowledge/science), and only one white magic (*ilmu putih*, again literally white knowledge/science).[4] The absence of distinctions among these could mean they are simply synonyms, or perhaps they point to different objects with different ways of engaging them, a multiplication rather than a subtraction of possibilities. In any event, Indonesian presents epistemic equivalence where Euro-American philosophy finds incompatibility, a judgment relevant to magic's history.

Clearly the last clump of ilmu I've discussed appears to correspond with what English terms magic, of a particular kind. But looking up *magic* itself yields three Indonesian words: *sihir*, *sulap*, and *gaib*. The first and third derive from Arabic. *Sihir* involves doing harm, "sorcery, witchcraft, magic," though it raises questions of what this implies should we delve into its Arabic origins and ask what might linger.[5] *Gaib*, however, is by no means self-evidently interpretable as magic. It is glossed as "hidden, concealed" as well as "mysterious, occult"; pursuing these meanings might move into world-makings of an even less familiar kind. The archipelagic *sulap* speaks to another meaning of English *magic*: magic as a performance art. It also connotes deception. Dictionary equivalents include *sleight of hand* and *conjuring tricks*, though some usages, like English, blur meanings: *serperti disulap saja layakn*ya, "as if by magic," or the verb form (*manyulap*) as "to turn/change something into something else." If *ilmu* goes well beyond *science*, no single Indonesian word covers the multiple meanings of the English *magic*. Dutch works a bit better: *toverij* partly overlaps with *sihir*, and *goochelarij* is a good match for *sulap*. But there is no Indonesian for *magie* or Dutch for *gaib*.

What this foray into Indonesian reveals is that its speakers have inherited different encounters and make different distinctions. And importantly: what is deemed equivalent to *magic* is not a *not*.

Is Another Magic Possible?

To translate not only words but acts and objects as magic proposes that categories forged in Europe's past have equivalents elsewhere—even everywhere. The differences among the topics of my chapters partly clarify my focus on magic's *translations*, for it is by no means self-evident what *dukun, jimat, keris, guna-guna*, and the stones in Sumedang might have in common. Nor is it self-evident what they might have in common with any of the other matters across the globe that were lumped together and coordinated as magic in encyclopedias and museums, as well as in legal codes, reports, memoirs, and travelogues. They have been shuffled together by their apparent similarity to acts and words in Europe's benighted past—or benighted present, in the form of "superstition."

Similarity, in short, appears to lie in the eye of the beholder. In anthropology's formative years the association of ideas (a concept British empiricists developed) was held to be a universal feature of human thinking that ran amuck (or, in the original Indonesian, *amok*) in magic, as "primitives" mistook merely mental correspondences for real, material connections. According to Sir James Frazer, magic rested on "two different misapplications of the association of ideas," with the first, sympathetic magic, based on similarity. Its error lies in assuming that things that resemble one another are actually the same. Ironically, Frazer's own opus is organized by similarities, arranged into a fable about the advancement of human mentality. If finding similarities and making something happen through them to transform the world is a feature of magic, then the entire anthropological corpus on magic is itself an extraordinary example of sympathetic magic.

As a basis for comparison, however, the concept of magic has flaws. It appears to be among those categories, originating and handed down in worlds identifying themselves as Euro-American, that have historically been used to intimidate, silence, destroy, even exterminate opponents, beginning with those closest to home. Like myth, groups seeking to establish their own authority have used it polemically, to attack others (Stengers 2011a: 56–58). Historian Owen Davies, focused more narrowly (and not surprisingly) on religion, makes a similar point: "across the centuries, religious groups have accused others of magic as a means of self-identification and to reinforce political and cultural legitimacy" (2012: 5).

Rendering practices, things, and statements as magic pulls them into the orbit of a dense European concept that was enmeshed in conflicts well before a handful of European nations divvied up most of the planet.

It simultaneously casts them as unproblematically similar to one another, without making explicit in what that similarity consists. If Van der Veer is right, what they share is vexing indeed: a fundamental unreality. This is signaled when people presume magic implies supernatural. By entailing what is not natural (more [k]notwork!), it is yoked to the remarkably vague concept of nature.

Given its history, should magic and its kin be banished from scholarly tool kits? What (if any) value do such words/concepts have for characterizing practices and claims or as concepts with which to think? Does magic remain useful as a category, and if so, to what ends?

In a conversation about the Anthropocene, a term that makes anthropologists twitch by suggesting that all humans share responsibility for the cascading catastrophes affecting the web of life, Tsing advocates that rather than subtracting problematic words, we should instead add meanings to them. But unlike Anthropocene, magic already is crowded with meanings. Should we layer even more onto the many it has collected over its long history? While Haraway indicates that she tends to agree with Tsing, she mainly promotes multiplying meanings to "do different work differently situated," a suggestion I find promising (see below).[6]

Another kind of addition might be found in De la Cadena's advocacy for "not only," a different concept than not-knowing. This one she learned directly from Mariano Turpo and uses as a strategy for translation and partial connection (2015). In the Andes, it enables useful partnerships. Although it is "not only" a mountain, when translated that way the earth-being Ausangate invites alliances with environmentalists (2010). If we use the word *magic* modified by *not only*, could alliances be activated?[7]

On the whole, I find it more interesting to treat magic as an ethnographic object rather than a comparative category. My own rule of thumb: the less familiar a practice might be to an author and her readers, the more cautious she should be in characterizing it with words such as magic, witchcraft, or sorcery—or in speaking blithely of belief. These words work like a god-trick, placing the practice at a distance and the reader in an Enlightened nonspace of knowing. Such magic may benevolently tolerate difference, but at the cost of avoiding its challenges. Moreover, the creativity that magic in this vein may prompt will lie with the analyst, not practitioners or their practices. The latter bring nothing new into being but only endlessly reiterate. But rather than banishing such language, I would urge caution, especially in using it to talk about those who do not use it to talk of themselves. Magic is not innocent. It is important to recognize what is inherited with it. In traveling down that road, it helps to take heed of yellow warning lights, slow down, look around carefully, and prepare to stop.

Instead of identifying what others do this way, what might it mean to describe "modern" forms of life with a magical vocabulary? Such concepts, after all, arose and developed among those who considered themselves such. Anthropologists are used to saying other people's practices "really mean" something else, something nonmysterious. What if we reverse this, and consider the mystery of what appear to be familiar mundane practices? This use of magic involves an art of transformation, shifting the real. In skilled hands, it can be amazingly potent.

Most of what attracts me in this vein involves dominant or hegemonic collectives, defamiliarizing what they take for granted about what it means to be modern, secular, developed, advanced (to list some familiar magical words). Consider those who draw on words from the magic family to characterize the workings of modern institutions, especially capitalism and the nation-state. Marx set the precedent in his analysis of commodity fetishism. His heir Raymond Williams (1997) called advertising, not yet part of the capitalism Marx analyzed, a magic system. What makes it magical is its ability to link the purchase of commodities to the promise of love, economic security, success, happiness, and personal value. Such promises are also magical in their deceptive substitution of false for real sources of satisfaction. This is magic in the vein of sleight of hand or deceptionism (see below). Similar to this are those who find the magic of the moderns in their concepts and forms of knowledge, as in Latour's "magic of rationality" (interlude 6) or what Muecke (2021) identifies as the "whitefella magic" in the god-tricks of anthropology, archaeology, and other human sciences.

More conceptually and analytically complex is Pignarre and Stengers's diagnosis of capitalist sorcery, already discussed, in a world where people do not accept sorcery as efficacious and therefore have lost the capacity to defend themselves (recall Muller). The complexity partly lies in their refusal to treat sorcery as a metaphor, while also rejecting insistence that this implies naïve belief in an illusion.[8]

Michael Taussig has developed such reversals with particular brilliance, in dialogue not only with field experiences and colonial and anthropological history but also with thinkers such as Benjamin and Bataille (e.g., 1980, 1987, 1993, 1997, and, more recently, 2020). From the devil at work in Colombian mines to colonists in the Amazon seeking the magical expertise of "wild men" to the magic of the state, Taussig seductively writes of the reenchantment of . . . well, everything. Including the really real.

A different dimension of advertising's (and public relations') aim to confound the real involves performance magic's descent from the stage to the staging of such worldly and consequential theaters as war, spy craft, political campaigns, and political life more broadly. In noting these developments, artist and magician Jonathan Allen (2007) refers to their practitioners as "deceptionists at large." And what about the sleight of hand at work in hiding from view the earth from which we live from the one on which we live (Latour and Weibel 2020)? Perhaps Pignarre and Stengers spoke too soon in claiming capitalism involved no actual sorcerers.

These examples mainly treat magic as a concept and deploy it for the purpose of critique. But the "magic of the moderns" also is of considerable ethnographic interest. Raymond Williams's analysis of advertising was strangely prescient in that magic has become omnipresent as an explicit referent in selling products and experiences. Disney not only calls its theme park the Magic Kingdom but bills it "The Most Magical Place on Earth." Other than the now commonplace Magic Markers, there is Mr. Clean's Magic Erasers as well as a program of the same name for editing photos, and a host of cosmetic companies with magic in their names or that describe products as working magically. The beauty and fashion industries in particular deploy such language (including words whose magical meanings are no longer explicit, such as *fascinate*, *glamour*, and *charm*) to captivate consumers, as Moeran (2017) shows in an analysis of the copy in fashion magazines.

Such cynical, commercial functions by no means exhaust magic's circulation. As Stengers has noted, magic comes up constantly in considerably more positive veins: "the magic of a moment, a book, a gaze, everything that enables us to think and to feel differently" (2005a: 1001–2). Magic does different work than it does elsewhere in the world-building of fictional genres of fantasy, speculative fiction, gaming, and the fan activities these have spawned. The efflorescence of such materials and the inventiveness of their followers in fan fiction and cosplay testifies to its capacity to spark different modes of thinking and feeling, as does the domain that triggered Stengers's interest in the topic. It is remarkable how many (women in particular) now claim the identity *witch* for themselves and their (often creative) practices. Kitchen witches, for instance, are only one of many subcategories on #witchtok. As Stengers continues, "calling themselves witches and defining their art with the word magic are already 'magical' acts, acts that create an unsettling experience for all those who live in a world in which the page is supposed to have been definitively turned" (2005a: 1002).

Stengers here is writing about Starhawk, who practices a craft dedicated (as Starhawk explains it) to bending reality. Reclaiming magic for such practitioners is about speaking defiantly to the power of change, of immanence, of the earthiness of soil, of the capacities of those who had been told they had none, to alter the shape of the world they have inherited in the name of making new possibilities for living.

With this in mind, I wonder about how *this* magic might translate, and what it might inspire. Throughout this inquiry I have referred (anachronistically) to Indonesians. Nation-states have their own version, however, of the coloniality of power, especially when it comes to the hegemonic process of development with its devastating naturalcultural effects. I wonder what some Indonesians might reinvent from forms of life destroyed by older and newer colonialisms. Perhaps the reclaimed witch may yet heal the translated colonial witch doctor and together they might multiply worlds rather than adding meanings or subtracting words.

Afterword

Isabelle Stengers

I am not an anthropologist, not even a science and technology studies (STS) researcher, only a philosopher engaged in the question "what made us 'moderns'?" It is as such that I write this afterword, in a double hope. First, I hope to show the crucial relevance of Margaret Wiener's reality politics to discuss not only the modern relation to other peoples but also what happened to those Bruno Latour called "Moderns" when they referred to themselves as "having Science." But the other singularity of Margaret Wiener's book is that she dares to take seriously what many of her colleagues would no doubt despise, the contemporary attempt by neopagan self-called witches to translate magic in reclaiming terms. Reclaiming is an activist word, and the magic rituals of those witches, as explained by Starhawk, are self-consciously designed to reclaim what reality politics has separated us from. I wish to add to the diagnostic of the disaster which weaponized sciences into Science (which I take as a quasi-synonym of reality politics) the same kind of cautious hope Wiener associates with those witches: sciences, each science in its own way and with its own risks, might possibly reclaim or claim what would be their common but not unifying question: how to make matter what they address, that is also, how to learn from or with, and not about, or how to produce worthy, and not disenchanting, facts. I will translate what I hope for by the term "gravitas," this ancient Roman virtue that will lose in translation its connotation of solemn virile dignity but will rather evoke what Whitehead (1968) called "the solemnity of the world." As the reader will discover, gravitas was used by scientists who, with their own means, learned to take magic seriously, that is, did not explain it in negative terms (cheating manipulations) but recognized its positive and irreducible force.

To put it in a nutshell: it might be possible for sciences to escape the bifurcation of nature. And it is because of this "might be possible" that I gratefully welcomed Margaret Wiener's choice of "reality politics" instead of speaking of the "ontological turn." This turn is undoubtedly important as it marks the will of some contemporary anthropologists to abandon concepts that, whatever their intentions, situate them in the position of "knowing better." They feel a duty to "take seriously" their inability to explain in their own terms the worlding practices of "others." But this turn raises another question: how to avoid following the path taken by Philippe Descola, for instance, when he labeled us "naturalists." How to avoid attributing to "us" some kind of ready-made ontology reliably correlated with Science. The danger lies in associating "our" ontology with the epistemic will that, as Bruno Latour emphasized, sent ethnologists all over the world but not to the places where this ontology supposedly ruled supreme: the science labs. This is why STS research is so interesting for contemporary anthropology, but all the more so if it aims, as Bruno Latour powerfully did, at "taking seriously" the entanglement of matters of concern associated with so-called modern practices.

To me the "ontological turn" is thus an interesting change of perspective, as it dethrones Science as universal. But it is vulnerable to the poison of "debunking," as marked by the temptation of adding "only"—only one way among others to make sense of the world. Far from inspiring gravitas, it recalls the way in which, in its polemical youth, the STS field was poisoned, identifying the successful agreement between scientists that marks the history of some sciences with an "only social" one about a resolutely mute reality. Indeed, STS's first case studies were iconoclastic, addressing claims unanimously recognized as belonging to the great story of "scientific progress." "Dubious" scientific claims such as those associated with psychology, for instance, would be ignored as "too easy."[1]

When Bruno Latour insisted that construction did not mean the possibility of deconstruction, that it rather imposes the problem of what facts are well or badly constructed, associating well-constructed facts with what he then called "factishes,"[2] he took what is to me a decisive step. On the one hand, the problem he points to refers to a concern—and it might be a transversal concern, bearing elsewhere not on "facts" but on what other peoples make matter and how they do it. This is why, in my *Cosmopolitics*, I introduced factishes to comment on the obligations of scientific practi-

tioners, and tentatively associated obligation with the term *practice*, referring to all practices, that is, all activities that cannot be defined by a simple
means–end relation. When a practice is concerned, all means are not of
equal worth, and some ends impose obligations. On the other hand, Science in the singular does not do justice to the multiplicity of scientific
(and technical) constructive practices. On the contrary, it mobilizes them
all under a single war banner heralding objectivity or rationality. And this
war is not only waged against far-away peoples whose "beliefs" must be
defeated. It is also an internal war against what is called opinion, that of
the ordinary people who are unable to understand Science and are liable to
rebel against its authority.

I myself became interested in this war when I began exploring scientific fields outside my first domain of interest, the experimental sciences.
For experimental scientists, the difference between well-constructed facts
and what they call artifacts is vital, but artifacts are not related to opinion,
belief, or subjectivity. What matters for experimenters when making a
crucial difference between facts and artifacts is the possibility of a very particular achievement, which has nothing to do with objectivity as generally opposed to subjectivity. It is rather an event—the coming into existence of something that has the power to produce agreement among them.
That is, among those not only who know how to pay the kind of attention
which the experimental situation concerned demands, but who also share
the same passionate quest, assigning value only to what has obtained the
power to enforce their agreement. They share a collective concern: a fact
has to resist their objections, demonstrate that they are unable to separate
it from the interpretive claim it justifies—that it is really a reliable answer to
the question the experimental device was designed to ask. Only those facts
have value, because the possibility of relying upon them means that they
are potential ingredients in a cumulative process, allowing new questions
to be asked or new instruments conceived. In other words, experimental
scientists do not grant power or authority to facts as such. What they call
"objective" facts are uncommon, the products of their highly selective practice. If something matters for experimental sciences, it is not some "ontological" truth; it is the "advance" of *their* knowledge.

My surprise, when addressing other sciences, was that their so-called
objective facts often appeared related to a methodological duty or to new
instrumental possibilities of measuring, not to a risky and demanding
achievement. What they called "advance" was rather a unilateral conquest.
"Serving Science," I realized, entitled them to address and objectively

define whatever they had the means to address. But I also understood why experimental scientists usually do not object when their work is assimilated to Science. They know very well that their facts are highly specific, indeed theirs, answering their own questions, not unveiling an objective reality hidden behind subjective appearances. But this knowledge is inscribed in their practices, not in the words they use in order to communicate what these practices have obtained.

It might appear that experimental scientists operate a kind of secret society, keeping for themselves what really matters to them and heralding news about Man discovering the secrets of the universe. But there is no clean divide between what they keep for themselves and what they herald. Typically, once they have succeeded in obtaining a reliable answer, experimentalists seem to forget about the passionate, risky, and always more sophisticated sociotechnical assemblages they had to achieve in order to create the questioning relation required by their hypothesis. They seem to forget that there is no answer without such a relation and do as if this assemblage were only a scaffold that, once it has played its role, can be relegated to the status of an incidental accessory, leaving the rational, scientific mind face to face with what preexisted, awaiting its disclosure.[3] The "secret" society does not even know how to initiate new members, the students who learn public versions of "discoveries" before facing, when and if they become researchers, what their practice will demand.

Bruno Latour once contrasted "ready-made science" with "science in the making," portraying them as a two-faced Janus (Latour 1987: 4). He illustrated the latter as a beardless, lively youth, representing the risky production of scientific facts and their sociotechnical assemblages. The other face was that of an old, bearded man explaining the robustness of established science by its truth, its objectivity, its respect for settled matters of fact, and so on. But I would add that the beardless youth dreams bearded dreams.

The question, however, is whether we can relate this Janus-faced situation to an ontology. Can we respect it in the same way ethnographers claim to respect the people they learn to meet? Alfred North Whitehead, who turned from mathematics to philosophy in order to reclaim a meaningful understanding of the reality we experience, would answer "no!" For him, there would be no "secret" but rather an incapacity to articulate the facts that Science represents as self-supporting with the willful, passionate activity they required. This is why Latour spoke about factishes—we break our factishes into irreconcilable fragments. In so doing we perpetuate the bifurcation of nature Whitehead protested against.

For Whitehead, the bifurcation opposing nature as it "is," an objective, causal nature, and nature as we experience it subjectively, gifted with meaning and sensitivity, was an absurdity that, since the seventeenth century, has ruined modern philosophy and destroyed the very possibility of a coherent ontology. Philosophers have "oscillated in a complex manner between three extremes. There are the dualists who accept matter and mind on an equal basis, and the two varieties of monists, those who put mind inside matter and those who put matter inside mind. But juggling with abstractions can never overcome the inherent confusion introduced by the ascription of misplaced concreteness to the scientific scheme of the seventeenth century" (Whitehead 1967: 55). And the consequences of the bifurcation do not concern philosophy only: "This radical inconsistency at the basis of modern thought accounts for much that is half-hearted and wavering in our civilization. It would not be going too far to say that it distracts thought. It enfeebles it, by reason of the inconsistency lurking in the background. After all, the men of the Middle-Ages were in pursuit of an excellency of which we have nearly forgotten the existence. They set before themselves the ideal of the attainment of a harmony of the understanding. We are content with superficial orderings from diverse arbitrary starting points" (1967: 76).

Arbitrary starting points, maybe, but related to a shared imperative. Where the scientific enterprise is concerned, many among the motley variety of "facts" that parade under the name of Science share this imperative under the name of objectivity. To characterize this imperative, I will refer to William James, who may have been Whitehead's most important source of inspiration. In his *Will to Believe*, he characterizes Moderns by a passionate "horror of becoming a dupe" (1979: 24–25). What is a concern for experimenters wondering about the possibility of an artifact has become a homemade generality about humankind: humans are at risk of being duped, and the duty of Science, and of all enlightened persons, is to accept as true only what will not turn them into dupes. While in experimental sciences skepticism refers to the duty of a new experimental claim to resist objections that test its reliability, it has become a hallmark of Science, which must again and again make nature bifurcate between what is "really real" and what is "only" a manifestation of our imagination. This, indeed, far from being an "ontology," is an ontology-destroying machine.

When Margaret Wiener speaks of "reality politics," rather than the "West's" ontology, we must thus keep in mind that this politics is not only part of colonizing operations, or else that such colonization did not only operate in faraway lands but also in the West. The horror William James characterizes is perfectly reflected in Tylor's or Malinowski's strong reactions against the interest in "spiritualism" infecting "Western civilization," including enlightened persons such as scientists.[4] Typically, Malinowski even refers to Hitler; and the danger of fanaticism, already feared by officials in Java, has become a classical argument for the intellectuals' vital mission to disqualify any approach that would open a door or even create a crack in the wall that must protect all of us against dupery.

While sciences would require that what they address be able or enabled to make a difference that matters, while experimenters have, in so doing, gone on freely populating the universe with beings gifted with uncommon properties—very strange and local "ontologies" indeed, opened to sudden revisions—Science systematically closes the door to the possibility that what might trouble public order might matter. It is now replete with so-called scientific methods aimed at dismembering and disenchanting uncommon experiences or performances by humans or living beings (see the case of Clever Hans recalled by Margaret Wiener). These methods do not, like experimental labs, care to provide the relevant ecology required to learn from or with what they study.[5] They impose on it the rarefied and suspicious ecology required by statistical tests. What matters is not to learn but to make the bifurcating difference between "objective" and "illusory."[6]

Recognizing reality politics at work might be what Bruno Latour (2004) called a shibboleth when he finally accepted what I and Vinciane Despret insisted on: that it is possible to discriminate "good"—that is, interesting—sciences from bad ones without referring to a normative epistemology. The discrimination here would concern the bifurcating challenge "is it real?" as it was engaged by colonial agents, but also by the agents of Science. When Muedans insisted that sorcery lions are not symbolic but real, they did not ask Harry West to "become native"; that is, they probably did not take real in the sense of reality politics, meaning "really real" or "truly real," as defined by the horror of becoming a dupe. When "real" is doubled by "really" or "truly," the stakes concern—or should concern—everybody. This is why, during the "science wars" in the nineties, physicists defending Science repetitively used the same argument, trusting that it would work for anybody: if you believe that the laws of nature are just a construction, throw yourself from the window of my flat (the number of floors being optional). In so doing they insulted Galileo's achievement, as if he had demonstrated that heavy bodies fall and the higher the starting point the stronger the crash. What Galileo achieved concerned only physicists—the possibility of defining and measuring the variation at each moment of the continuously changing velocity, what we now call acceleration.

As Wiener writes about reality politics, it bears on "what does and will count as real, what claims and practices may be subject to mockery, what futures are and are not achievable." Reality politics is real as it makes a lot of differences that matter. It is related to what I call *bêtise*, which unhappily is usually translated as stupidity in English. Stupidity, derived from stupor, implies a sleepy quality while bêtise is nasty and active, feeding on the power it actively designs to mock and destroy what counts as real for "credulous" people. It embodies the horror of becoming a dupe William James diagnosed, and gives pride of place to scientific claims that may confirm its leitmotiv, the reductive "only." In biology, for instance, it enthusiastically endorsed the brutal simplification that turned Darwin's interesting proposition into a one-size-fits-all monotonous explanation, valid from bacteria to humans.

But biology does not have as its main task to teach people how wrong they are. It was hijacked, but not absorbed, by reality politics: the concern for "details" that might matter could not be eradicated. The plurality of scientific practices manifests itself each time scientists prioritize adventurous questions and succeed in giving to what they study the occasion to disclose what they are capable of. Nowadays, it is exhibited by experimental biology, evolutionary understanding, and ethology. Words are getting new meanings. Life is now associated with a web, no longer with a common property of living beings, and we belong to this web together with the others who (rather than which) participate in its weaving. World is now plural and becomes a verb rather than a noun: worlds are in the making through ongoing processes generated by interdependent agencies, human and nonhuman. If ecology has become a transversal concept, it is because nature and "natural laws" have gotten a divorce. For contemporary biologists who learn to decipher the subtle intricacy of the relations that involve the most heterogeneous beings, it could be said that "there is nothing natural in nature."

As a result, when activists cry "we are not defending nature, we are nature defending itself," it can no longer be heard as a "romantic" protest against a disenchanting scientific bifurcation. It can be, if not relayed, at least understood by researchers. But the activists' cry is not a scientific claim. It is addressed to those who have systematically unmade worlds and who have also made us "moderns." Activists reject what has "unmade" them to produce so-called free individuals, who are actually dependent on the imperial and industrialist infrastructures[7] without which they would be unable to live, and which today threaten the very livability of the earth. Their cry expresses the need and will to reclaim a nonbifurcated nature.

It was in 1998, when I discovered a bit by chance Starhawk's *Dreaming the Dark* (originally published in 1982 but constantly reedited since), that I understood the double and intricate meaning of "reclaiming": both struggling to recover what we have been separated from, and healing, recovering from that separation. It is what turned me into an apprentice "activist philosopher," deliberately jeopardizing my reputation as a "serious" philosopher, trying to introduce in France, where reality politics has the crushing authority of a republican principle, the real difference "neopagan witches" and their reclaiming practices made in our way of thinking and situating ourselves.[8] Reclaiming, because it speaks of the need to heal, implies what may be at the core of a typical activist cry when contemplating the disaster: "It did not need to be like that!" This cry demands actively refusing any consideration that would "normalize" the disaster, which would link it to some fate "the Anthropos" was unable to escape when he left His cradle and entered the path of progress. What happened has nothing to do with an emancipatory coming to maturity and the tragic discovery that freedom means accepting being alone in a meaningless world. We need to heal because it is violence that created the "modern individual," which destroyed, and is still destroying in each new generation, practical ways of togetherness with others, thanks to others, and at the risk of others (human and nonhuman). Reclaiming activism in this sense is a direct intervention in the domain of anthropology, and if I dare to write this afterword despite not being a specialist in this domain, it is because Margaret Wiener, as an anthropologist, dares to take seriously what Starhawk called "magic," rather than reduce it to some Californian fad.

If, as Wiener writes, Starhawk "calls herself a witch and calmly labels her practices magic," it does not mean she claims to resurrect what was destroyed. What we know about those who were prosecuted as witches comes from the inquisitors as well as from the enlightened thinkers for whom they were just victims, eradicating them a second time. To call oneself a witch is itself an act of magic, defiantly activating the living memory of the "burning times," is becoming aware that the "The smoke of the burned witches still hangs in our nostrils." Certainly, enlightened thinkers could claim it was part of an outdated past since the witches' prosecution was a matter of religious belief. But reality politics has its own inquisitorial power: to claim to be a witch, a practitioner of magic, is to expose oneself not to physical death but to mockery and sniggering.

Furthermore, is it "only" a matter of religious belief? Starhawk (1997) made it clear,[9] as did Silvia Federici later, that the burning times cannot, in England at least, be abstracted from the destruction of rural communities and their customary commoning rights. Those were considered a relic of the past. Owners needed exclusive property rights and the enclosures enforcing those rights were part of a wider operation of dispossession. They coincide with the colonialist "terra nullius" doctrine: lands occupied by "lazy savages"—who enjoyed natural resources without working to make them profitable and who did not even care to define what they occupied as individual properties—were available, free of rights. For the neopagan witches, pagan means rural, and healing or recovering means becoming capable again of practices and customs that presuppose and affirm (more-than-human) interdependency and their common belonging to the earth. Calling themselves witches, they remember the violence from which the modern individual was born. This violence went on without the help of religion since it was committed by the new intertwined powers of capitalism and modern states for whom the customary immanent obligations associated with interdependency were obstacles to the transcendence of both the rule of profit and the rule of law.

From this perspective, a form of colonial violence extended to Europe as well as to faraway lands. This does not enable us to claim that we "also" are victims. The point is rather about "resurgence," when the seeds of what seemed to have been successfully eradicated begin to sprout again but, given the hostile environment, need renewed power. The Goddess who, the witches chant, "returns" is not a matter of belief. It may be a matter of myth, but "the ending of this myth is not yet written. Has the Goddess reawakened only to preside over the destruction of the earth? Or will our awakening come in time? For unlike other deities, the Goddess does not come to save us. It is up to us to save her—if we choose. If we so will" (Starhawk 1987: 311).

What Starhawk calls "will" is not a matter of decision, which belongs to the lexicon of the moderns as a quasi-synonym of arbitrary choice, of freedom escaping causality. It rather means the obstinate "will to life" that resurgence manifests. Resurgent magic is an act of will, as is the will to remember. Or, as Monique Wittig wrote, "Make an effort to remember. Or, failing that, invent" (1969: 126o–27, quoted in Christ 1979). Such an understanding of will could be related to what William James opposed to the definition of truth by the horror of becoming a dupe: "the will to believe" in the kinds of truths that make our lives worth living. For him too, what Margaret Wiener calls reality politics defined a violence against what he defined as "congruous with human nature."[10]

Just as the Goddess is not a transcendent power, magic, as a craft cultivated by the neopagan witches,[11] has nothing supernatural about it. It is, as Margaret Wiener writes, "about speaking defiantly to power" but also, as she adds, about pragmatically, experimentally, enacting what it speaks of: "of change, of immanence, of the earthiness of soil, of the capacities of those who had been told they had none, to alter the shape of the world they have inherited in the name of making new possibilities for living."

Magic is an art of effects, effects that are real but do not need to be explained (that is, disenchanted) by a "true" cause. As David Abram discovered, balians in Bali and dzankris in Nepal were interested in his sleight-of-hand tricks, as they demonstrated that he had "at least some rudimentary skill in altering the common field of perception" (1997: 5). And this alteration, when explored by neurophysiologists who learned not about but from and with masters of illusion (in other words, who did not serve Science), becomes the source of a nonbifurcative experience for them: "After years of living magically, we will never watch a magic trick the same way again. Our appreciation of magic has been deepened, and it has been given gravitas to the nth degree by the knowledge that all magic, every little sleight, is really happening in our mind" (Macknick and Martinez-Conde 2011: 259). "Really happening in the brain" does not mean here explained by the brain. What inspires "gravitas" is rather the brain's reality-shaping force, in close relation with which every little sleight has been crafted. No politics of reality here, no explanation of misperception by the misdirection of attention or "cognitive biases," that is, by weaknesses "illusionists" would exploit. And no opposition between this "weakness" and a "scientific mind" who would pay the right attention and enjoy unbiased access to a preexistent reality. Learning from those we call illusionists to decipher ordinary experience in neurophysiological terms rather intensified the scientists' appreciation of what is required by so-called ordinary experience. The art of misdirecting attention has been enabled to thwart the temptation to consider that we know what we are saying when we demand that someone "pay attention." I can only dream of teachers who would know that it is not "normal" for students, if only they are attentive enough, to understand, and would learn how to induce and then to celebrate the event "now it makes sense!" as something that had to really happen in the classroom. Something that communicates with Whitehead's "full solemnity of the world."

Sciences, when they escape Science, do add to reality, rather than subtract from it. And to do so, they, like experimental sciences but differently for each, have to learn from or with, not about. The experience of "gravitas" might characterize the way each is then transformed by what it learns. Contemporary biologists learning that living beings become themselves through their relations with others, or neurophysiologists learning to appreciate both magic and what the brain is capable of, are witnesses to the nonbifurcative character of this experience: they have given what they address the power to touch them and open them to transformation. But such a transformation is also what reclaiming witches call for through their magic rituals.[12] They chant, "She changes everything She touches, and everything She touches changes" or "we are the weavers, we are the web," and both chants artfully and positively escape the bifurcation between active causes and passive effects. "She" is not causing the change. It could be said that Her touch is empowering or inducing it, but it is the one She touches who "actively" changes. Similarly, the "active" weaver is also woven into the web or, as today activists cry, "we are not defending nature, we are nature defending itself."

We might be tempted to relay such syntactic twists resisting any bifurcating opposition between active and passive as an ontological proposition, but then ontology would not be dealing with a characterization of natural or human beings or as what preexists the way they relate but would address an immanent generative power which may be exemplified by the familiar experience of being touched by a force that one may name but not define, a real happening, the meaning of which is yours to give, at your own risk.

"Have a care, here is something that matters! Yes—that is the best phrase—the primary glimmering of consciousness reveals, something that matters," writes Whitehead (1968: 116) against bifurcating psychological explanations, while reality politics demands that we psychologize such happenings. What such explanations might explain, on the other hand, is our vulnerability to forces that others are able to manipulate without us recognizing what they are doing. "Wild," uncultivated magic runs free in the "West."

Gravitas, becoming able to appreciate or to wonder, may be an interesting word for an anthropology that would learn to escape the grip of reality politics and add to reality. I perceive gravitas when Margaret Wiener writes about answering an inquiry initiated by an other-than-human force: "Identifying the agent matters less than responding well." And when she does not deride neopagan witches remembering the burning times—that is, also the destruction of collective ways of doing, feeling, and knowing; of felt, immanent obligations that make (and do not define) the difference between using and abusing, between power-with and power-over. Paying, as Margaret Wiener did, "close attention to the worldly engagements through which magic was transported across the planet" indeed demands gravitas since it is tracking "the making and unmaking of worlds." Becoming capable of close attention is in itself a transformative engagement, the capacity to resist even well-meaning interpretive abuses. I, as a philosopher, can only read with gravitas the ending sentence of her book: "Perhaps the reclaimed witch may yet heal the translated colonial witch doctor and together they might multiply worlds rather than adding meanings or subtracting words."

Notes

Epigraph: Callon 1986: 19.

1   Images during the witch hunt bore little resemblance to Halloween witches. They often depicted naked women with bare heads and long, flowing hair.
2   The roots of terms translated as *translate* in both Indo-European Dutch (*vertaling* from *taal*) and Austronesian Balinese (*mabasan*, from *basa*) refer to language, not movement.
3   This includes removing a dead body from one place to another. For nineteenth- and twentieth-century European elites, magic arguably was just such a dead body.
4   For a brilliant account of translation as movement, see Montgomery (2002).
5   *Sakti* also has been translated in the OED's first sense, moving to Indonesia from India.
6   Barber's Balinese-English dictionary (1979) defines *sakti* as "strength (esp. spiritual); magic power; supernatural power." Stevens and Schmidgall-Telling's Indonesian-English dictionary (2004) has "1. supernatural power.... 2. To have, possess magic power, magic." The dictionary I had in the field defines it as "1. Supernatural, divine power...; 2. having magic or divine power...; 3. sacred" (Echols and Shadily 1992). Of course, bilingual dictionaries are themselves complicated linguistic phenomena, with an implicit metapragmatic ideology that equates language with reference. At least one dictionary, however, does not use any modifiers in equating sakti with power: Zoetmulder's *Old Javanese-English Dictionary*. Old Javanese (or Kawi) is a textual language in certain literary genres as well a register of Balinese in specific performance genres. Kawi is rich in Sanskrit lexical items. Zoetmulder's

dictionary is actually trilingual since it includes Sanskrit terms too. Glossing San-skrit shakti as "power, ability, strength, might; regal power, energy or active power of a deity personified as his wife," Zoetmulder renders Old Javanese *śakti* as close to this: power, strength; or powerful, mighty (1982). Nothing magical about it.

7 Translation forms an omnipresent feature of contemporary experience in media (subtitles!), international politics, and transnational business (see also Leavitt 2015).

8 Thus Asad (1993) demonstrates how Christian theology informs Ernst Gellner's discussion of Islam among Berbers. In a similar way, David Schneider (1984) in-sisted that anthropological accounts of kinship were smuggled in Euro-American relations of blood (nature) and law (society).

9 De Saussure complicates this by noting that even in languages in one family signi-fieds do not map onto each other. Hence English distinguishes animals from meat (sheep versus mutton, hen versus chicken, cow versus beef, pig versus pork), unlike French, where zoology and cuisine overlap (*mouton, poulet, boeuf, porc*).

10 I previously used Annemarie Mol's (1999) term "ontological politics," even as I bent it to situations different from those for which she coined it. However, anthropologists use "ontology" in myriad ways, not all of them deriving, as my own interest has, from engagement with science studies work that is in dialogue with Whitehead's speculative metaphysics. "Reality politics" clarifies what is at stake: what does and will count as real, what claims and practices may be subject to mockery, what futures are and are not achievable. It also better captures Latour's assertion that the real is gradients of resistance (1988: 158–59, 188).

11 See, for example, Barad (2007); Haraway (1991, 1997); Latour (1987, 1988); Latour and Woolgar (1986 [1979]); Shapin and Schaffer (1985); Stengers (2000).

12 During (2004). Jones (2017) analyzes illusionism's impact on nineteenth-century anthropology in depth.

13 See the epilogue for some enchantments of so-called moderns.

14 Malay was the language of the Sultanate of Malacca. What the Dutch adopted was Bazaar Malay, a pidgin.

15 One might make a case for playing Philias Fillagap or Lucy Lacuna (Cohn 1987: 21–22), though intellectually this is hardly compelling.

16 Bekker mentions Javanese in passing in chapter 7, but says little about them.

17 Dutch domination of maritime trade went beyond the Indies. By the mid-seventeenth century, for instance, the voc imposed a monopoly on trade with Japan. The Dutch also controlled most sea-based trade in Europe. For Moore (2010), this European (and Atlantic) trade marks the Dutch role in making a global political economy.

18 See, for example, Brook (2008) and Buck-Morss (2000).

19 Reliance on De Marees is evident in Bekker's account of fetishes in Guinea (Bekker 1695: 38–39; De Marees 1987 [1602]).

20 The Dutch West India Company, chartered in 1621, received a monopoly on the Atlantic trade, covering the Americas and Africa. Its raison d'être was not only commercial but political: due to the ongoing conflict with Spain, the Dutch sought to undermine Iberian interests. Most of the work already cited on Dutch centrality

in forging a global political economy has focused on the West India Company and not the voc.

21 The fetish maintained a conceptual robustness in Dutch ethnology that it lost in Africa, where a new concern with witches displaced it (Pels 1998).

22 See Pietz (2022).

23 Or so Dutch texts describe these phenomena. Indonesians have their own names for them. A caveat: Europeans translated Indonesian entities, stories, and practices through magic on myriad occasions other than those I address.

24 Magic also can do useful knotwork. Linking practices to a category decreed universal empowers by providing a host of potential allies (see chapter 4).

25 When I began this project, I expected to follow magic into the work of Indonesian intellectuals, but Dutch materials required more thinking than anticipated. One weakness I readily concede is that I do not historicize the Indonesian practices I draw upon to disrupt European categories and claims. But my goal is not to write a history but to track usages.

INTERLUDE 1. WITCH DOCTORS

1 For anti-witchcraft ordinances and the category of the witch, see, for example, Fields (1982), Gray (2005), Luongo (2011), and a special issue of *Africa* (3, no. 4) in 1935 to which Evans-Pritchard contributed; most of the other contributors were colonial officials grappling with the category and legal remedies for a practice they found problematic.

2 Its third meaning is another telling extension: psychiatrist.

3 More interesting is *diviner*, which, like *oracle*, associates Zande practices with the classical world Euro-Americans claim as ancestral.

4 Taussig (2003) is a major exception in noting that a diagnosis of deception may elide a clash in realities. Based on ethnographies of Kwakwaka'wakw shamanism, he suggests the shaman does not act alone but in conjunction with spirits. The shaman's movements compel spirits to mimic him, and thus cure; the bloody down he takes from his mouth indexes the disease the spirits actually remove.

CHAPTER 1. TRICKY SUBJECTS

1 As important figures in Indonesian life, dukun also populate travel literature and novels, and appear as the butt of amused anecdotes in journalism. See chapter 4.

2 Mailrapport 514, in V. 13, April 1922, no. 119, Ministry of Colonies archives, Algemeen Rijksarchief, The Hague. Damsté had been an administrator for twenty-seven years, and, at forty-nine, was three years away from retirement. Kuys had entered the civil service only three years before.

3 Some balian specialize: in childbirth, finding lost objects, or mediating conversations with the dead. For balian, see Connor, Asch, and Asch (1986); Lovric (1987); and Stuart-Fox (2015). For Javanese dukun, see, for example, Ferzacca (2001); Geertz (1960); and Woodward (2011).

4 Damsté sent a copy of the letter to the governor-general, whose office forwarded it to the minister of colonies. See below.

5 He continued to be pleased long after, publishing an account of this incident after his retirement as one of a series of short pieces relevant to Bali's administration and concerned with Balinese culture (Damsté 1924).

6 *Fanaticus* remains a Dutch word for a fanatic.

7 Online Etymological Dictionary, http://www.etymonline.com/, accessed June 1, 2013. Online Oxford-English Dictionary, http://www.oed.com/view/Entry/68008 ?redirectedFrom=fanatic#eid, accessed June 2, 2014, lists as *fanatic*'s second meaning "Of persons, their actions, attributes, etc.: Characterized, influenced, or prompted by excessive and mistaken enthusiasm, esp. in religious matters," as well as "a mad person," "a religious maniac," and "an unreasoning enthusiast."

8 *Drijver* is cognate with English *driver*; *geest* covers psyche, mind, spirit (in both senses), and ghost. I am tempted to think Kuys chose *geestdrijver* because, unlike *fanaat*, it not only suggests Nang Mukanis's state of mind and impact on others, but subtly invokes a relation with spirits (see below).

9 For casual references to such concerns, see Een Ooggetuige (1898), reprinted from *De Locomotief*, which also uses the word *geestdrijver*; and Kohlbrugge (1907), especially chapter 1. See also Sartono Kartodirdjo (1966) and Snouck Hurgronje's advice to the government about fanatics and Islam (Gobée and Adriaansse 1957–65, especially vol. 3).

10 Frequently, they disbursed protective objects or taught esoteric knowledge (*ngélmu*) to followers (see chapter 2). See Sartono (1973) for dukun and guru as leaders of protest movements.

11 Indonesian preparations offered scientists the possibility of discovering new drugs—an interest that still fuels bioprospecting. While such attention appears to accord respect to local materia medica, it ignores the role dukun play in testing and modifying flora.

12 Some Dutch authors recognized that dukun might have skills biomedicine ignored. One observed that while dukun, who did not perform surgery, lacked anatomical knowledge, their lexicon for body parts and diseases testified to extensive knowledge. He also remarked on their highly developed sense of touch (Maijer 1918: 6).

13 *Encyclopaedie van Nederlandsch-Indië*, s.v. "geneeskundigen (inlandsche)."

14 This is from a paragraph about dukun in *Heathenism in the Dutch East Indies*, published by the Military Academy at Breda, where officers trained for service in the Indies, and where its author, C. S. Spat, taught ethnology and Malay (Spat 1906). A contributor to and editor of the *Encyclopaedie*, he also may have authored its entry on native physicians (and/or heathenism).

15 In an account of practitioners in Frisia in the Netherlands, De Blécourt translates *toverdokter* as *witch doctor*, and suggests they were seen as countering witchcraft, and *wonderdokter* as *miracle doctor*, claiming the latter relied on herbal treatments (1991: 157, 166). However, elsewhere he mentions someone who was a *duivelbanner* (exorcist) and wonderdokter (1989: 253). I suspect officials didn't call dukun toverdokters because they had little interest in witchcraft (Wiener 2015).

16 Like Damsté, Jasper rose through the ranks during the Ethical Policy, although achieving much greater heights and fame (see chapter 3). His discussion of dukun, a republication in a pharmaceutical journal of an article written for the colonial newspaper *Java Bode*, purportedly draws on earlier pieces: on medicinal plants (published in 1904) and Javanese village life (originally 1916).

17 Jasper's description indicates how the growth of urban centers offered new opportunities to dukun, including incitements to develop novel techniques. In contemporary Indonesia some urban dukun make excellent use of media, appearing on television and advising prominent political figures (see Ferzacca 2001, for example), just the kind of flamboyance that aroused Jasper's ire.

18 Jasper exaggerates their differences. Not only do urban dukun commonly administer herbal remedies, but, as he himself notes, the rural herbalist seeks to "increase the effect by connecting a little superstition to her pharmacy" (1932: 34).

19 *Encyclopaedie van Nederlandsch-Indië*, s.v. "geneeskundigen (inlandsche)." Others later insisted the state's indifference to dukun encouraged criminality (see chapter 4).

20 Authorities often compared colonial subjects to children, who believe nonsense until they are old enough to reason or are properly educated. At least if they are male and middle class. European women and lower classes might never grow up, a view transported to the Indies. Hence if Indonesians in general were childlike, in need of white guidance, Indonesian peasants and women were doubly so.

21 Here the *OED* is again instructive.

22 For example, Protestant authorities called not only astrology and mesmerism superstitious, but also Catholic masses and pilgrimages. Yet those engaging in such practices would "strenuously object to being lumped with some of the others, which they themselves might be happy to term superstitious" (Davies and De Blécourt 2004: 6).

23 Scholars at Leiden, site of the Netherlands' first chair in ethnology, contemptuously called Utrecht "the petroleum university," funded as it was by entrepreneurs profiting from extracting fossil fuels in the Indies. Snouck Hurgronje, one of the Indies's most famous scholars, wrote a scathing review of Kohlbrugge (1907).

24 Kohlbrugge lifts much of this from Harthoorn and Poensen, the first missionaries sent to Java.

25 For Kohlbrugge, the relations Javanese establish with spirits reveal the latter to be materialistic, vindictive, arbitrary, and easily beguiled—thus unworthy of human attention. He finds native deities equally contemptible. Gods are simply stronger than humans rather than sources or models of ethical precepts (1907: 31).

26 Kohlbrugge writes:

> A certain Javanese A. is furious with his neighbor B. He calls on a famous Dukun, renowned for his powerful tumbal, ngelmu, and such. He promises to give him a calf or horse if his neighbor becomes severely ill. The dukun or guru goes on a journey to a short distance from the desa [village] where the enemies live. He takes a piece of paper, writes B.'s name on it, pricks some figures in it, buries it in the ground, pronounces the necessary

magical formula or curse, and B. actually becomes seriously ill. . . . [B.] fears dying; the guru hears that and to kill two birds with one stone he sends an accomplice, who says to B: 'I know by which spirit you became sick. Pay me and I will cure you.' B. eagerly accepts. He has to swallow the ash of a black dog's burned tail and heals. Now the accomplice returns and says: 'the illness was A.'s fault, do you want to make A. sick?' 'With pleasure,' says B. Naturally he must pay for it. Before long A. threatens to succumb. . . .

From this actual incident . . . is very clearly shown that suggestion alone is this illness's source. In a village, everyone knows everything about everyone; therefore, they know that A. went on a journey to that powerful guru or dukun and heard that that guru went on a journey in the desa's direction. B. needs know no more to become sick from terror. . . . He was cured of that painful illness as soon as he believed that his physician or the latter's ngelmu is more powerful than the spirit of the illness. . . . [O]ne way or another the dukun makes sure that the victim knows what was done to him. (Kohlbrugge 1907: 15–16)

27 Apart from presuming Indonesians to be cognitively irrational, the Ethical Policy justified conquest of independent polities on the grounds of political irrationality as well: "native states" were purportedly run by despots who tyrannized their subjects and enriched themselves (see chapter 3). The Dutch would bring good governance, the rule of law rather than whim. Such governance was exemplified by the state's very structure. In contrast with the arbitrariness, despotism, and nepotism of indigenous polities, the colonial state was a meritocracy with a clearly organized and explicit hierarchy. Lower-ranking officials reported to higher-ranked ones with greater experience and broader powers, all the way up to the governor-general (and minister of colonies in The Hague). In practice, matters were more complex (Wiener 2003).

28 They were also racing against other European powers to control the region.

29 For jimat, one of the items Jasper would smash and burn, see chapter 2.

30 Haraway (1997: 23–39) rightly points out the martial, manly qualities of this early Latourian concept, but they fit such colonial situations. Trials of strength need not entail actual violence; some deploy trickery. Thus French officials brought famous illusionist Robert-Houdin to perform before the Muslim leaders they called *marabout* in colonial Algiers, an event that ambiguously aimed to impress them with the superiority of French power or impress upon them the proper attitude toward apparent miracles (Jones 2010). Frank Hives, a British district officer in Nigeria, made use of his own more modest skills in sleight of hand to impress those he ruled in an effort to ensure their compliance (Hives and Lumley 1930). I have not encountered such examples in the Indies. On the other hand, Indonesians likely carried out their own trials of strength. Consider the theft of curtains from the home of the resident of Madiun (Onghokham 1978). Since Javanese knew that thieves consulted local experts and sought jimat to aid and abet their profession (see chapter 2), this incident likely made quite an impression, especially since many wondered if Europeans could be affected by dukun and other experts (Habbema 1919: 314).

31 He puts this in more locally meaningful terms as well. The atmosphere, he notes, is even livelier than a cremation ceremony (*ngabén*), big rites involving as much labor (neighbors and kin) as those holding them can muster.

32 Dictionaries render both *kemasukan* and *karauhan* as possession. The practice of some Javanese dukun also involved "spirit possession" (Gobée and Adriaanse 1959: 1226).

33 Schulte-Nordholt (1986) argues the Dutch solidified once flexible hierarchical distinctions, a familiar colonial pattern.

34 See Scheper-Hughes and Lock (1987) on the metaphysics of biomedicine's body.

35 For letters, see Wiener (2016).

36 In turn, balian tatakson may or may not consult texts.

37 This made incarnation a thorny problem for Catholic theologians. The question of when and how minds and bodies combine still drives Euro-American debates about life's beginning and end.

38 See, for example, Karchmer (2022) on "traditional Chinese medicine" or Langwick (2011) on Tanzania.

39 He went further by arguing that European medicine and psychology might be incapable of evaluating either their techniques or materia medica. While not uncommon views at the time among some Indies residents (see chapter 4), they were unusual for those in the colonial service.

40 Less vague are Lévi-Strauss's (1963) discussions of "the efficacy of magic," including what Cannon (1942) called "voodoo death," and famously explained by proposing the psychosomatic.

41 For further discussion, see Wiener (2015, 2016).

42 Rejection of the bifurcation of reality is fundamental to Whitehead's speculative metaphysics.

INTERLUDE 2. THE FETISH

1 Three crucial articles appeared in the journal *Res* in 1985, 1987, and 1988. These and other essays were reissued in 2022. I cite that book rather than the articles.

2 I consulted both a 1987 English translation and a 1912 Dutch reprint.

CHAPTER 2. TROUBLING OBJECTS

1 Tambiah (1984) is an important exception to anthropological indifference to objects translated as amulets. W. L. Hildburgh, who wrote a remarkable number of studies of amulets—mostly European but also from Egypt, Japan, Bhutan, and Burma—was a folklorist, having served as president of the Folklore Society in London.

2 See chapter 3 for different objects knotted to the fetish, which galvanized other enactments.

3 Just as witchcraft remains a potent a legacy for Africanists, the fetish continues to magnetize Indonesianists, even when they show no awareness of its colonial importance. Unlike African witchcraft, however, fetishes foment no passions in

postindependence Indonesia. No doubt this has much to do with the different histories of the witch and the fetish, including the place witchcraft continues to hold in some forms of evangelizing Christianity. For more on the entwined histories of the witch and the fetish, see Wiener (2015).

4 West Java is known as Sunda; the vernacular is Sundanese. I stumbled across jimat and Haji Hasan while on the track of a different topic in colonial newspapers. My account draws on newspaper reportage for what it reveals of contemporary concerns. I supplement this with Locher-Scholten (2002), who consulted Ministry of Colonies archives. Sartono (1972) notes that investigations at the time indicate the Haji's refusal had something to do with deteriorating relations between Haji Hasan and the wedana of Leles.

5 A pikol was a unit of measurement that initially referred to one of the two loads Javanese peasants carried on a pole over their shoulders. At this time, it referred to a fixed weight.

6 According to Carl Ernst (personal communication), zikir or *dhikr* is a Sufi practice, involving the meditative chanting of praises to, or specific names of, Allah. The goal could be to lose oneself in the divine or to take on particular divine attributes.

7 For examples of the "Garut affair" in accounts of the growth of Indonesian nationalism, see Shiraishi (1990: 113–14) and Van den Doel (1994: 380–81).

8 The exception is Locher-Scholten (2002), but her focus is a different issue.

9 This comes from news of the commission's report.

10 I was unable to track the development of administrative concerns with, and knowledge of, jimat through colonial archives.

11 Two other "disturbances" occurred in Central and North Java, one in 1865–69 in Klaten (where a certain Mangkuwidjaja claimed to be the Just King or Ratu Adil prophesied by Jayabaya in the twelth century), and a second that began in Pekalongen in 1871 Sartono (1972). I suspect such incidents (and those discussed in the next section) supplied momentum for the regulations.

12 Two sets of regulations passed, one applying to Europeans and the other to "natives," though in 1872 most people legally classified as Europeans in the Indies were either Eurasian or more culturally creole than Dutch (see chapter 4). My quote comes from Article 3, no. 14, in the ordinances for natives; the identical phrase appears as Article 5, no. 14, in the ordinances for Europeans (Der Kinderen 1873: 15). The main difference involved penalties. Convicted Europeans could be fined twenty-six to sixty guilders or imprisoned for five to six days; natives could be sentenced to thirteen to twenty days of forced labor in lieu of a fine. Note that the reference to "other objects" opens the door to virtually anything authorities might connect to "supernatural power."

13 For instance, see Kohlbrugge, who asserted that uprisings usually could be traced to persons trafficking in esoteric knowledges and amulets (1907: 32–35).

14 Such contrasts between "tradition" and "modernity" themselves belong to struggles to establish a one-world world.

15 Second page, July 23, 1919.

16 For Soetatmo, see Sears (1996: 139–43, 157–63).

17 Reprinted from *Het Vaderland* under "De djimat-kwestie," *IG* 42, no. 1 (1920): 161–62.

18 *SN*, August 15, 1919.

19 Perhaps an anxious response to Soetatmo's insistence on ubiquity?

20 For élmu, see below. S. refers here to a provision in the 1918 penal code.

21 My source is the 1929 Supplement to the *Encyclopaedie van Nederlandsch-Indië*, s.v. "magie" (page 266). I discuss its likely author below (note 49).

22 They could have drawn on Kreemer (1888) and Knebel (1898a), discussed below. Kreemer describes one jimat that could make a rifle misfire (1888: 353) and another that renders its bearer invulnerable and his enemy defenseless (1888: 354); Knebel, one that shields its bearer from gunshots (1898a: 503) and two that protect someone away from home from enemies (1898a: 505), all plausibly relevant. Two that Knebel describes are made of quotidian foodstuffs, albeit unusual (coconuts with only one eye and sugarcane with nodes unusually close to one another), which may have rendered them easy to miss.

23 Apart from scholarly expertise, Snouck developed a pragmatic appreciation of Sundanese mores, as he married and had children with the daughter of a local aristocrat. He later wed and had a child with a second Indonesian woman.

24 He does, however, condone intervention when jimat are distributed as part of a movement taking shape around a charismatic figure.

25 Schulte-Nordholt (1991) attributes this to the impact of colonial rule. In her more extensive study, Van Till (2011) argues that while it might be tempting to link the rise of banditry to the political economic forces that motivated some peasant rebellions, her data don't support this.

26 This may have aimed to exempt the growing numbers of Europeans dabbling in recreational séances as spiritualism became popular.

27 Given these intimations of danger, one might expect Der Kinderen to explain how jimat came to arouse official concern. He does not. Presumably, it went without saying.

28 These terms appear in my Indonesian-English dictionary thoroughly modified through magic. Thus *jampi* (listed as deriving from Sanskrit) is defined as "incantation, magic spell, charm, mantra," with *berjampi* as "magical" or "under a spell," and *air jampi*, water over which a magic spell has been intoned; *menjampi*, the verb form, is "to cast a spell/incantation on, treat s.o. with magic spells," and so on. *Rajah* is glossed as "(magic) sign, rune, figures used as a charm/talisman (to ward off sickness, etc.)" (Stevens and Schmidgall-Tellings 2004).

29 *Kunst* can also imply a knack or a trick.

30 *Rapal* is an interesting word choice. Unlike *jampi*, Stevens and Schmidgall-Tellings (2004) list it as Javanese, derived from Arabic *lafal*. Its first meaning is a saying or maxim. The second meaning is shot through with magic: "incanation, spell, charm, magic formula." *Élmu* (modern Indonesian *ilmu*) also derives from Arabic, and refers to multiple kinds or practices of knowledge (see epilogue). Like jimat, the colonial focus on élmu likely derives from experiences in and texts about Java (e.g., Poensen 1878).

31 See, for example, *RNI* 1909, extract from a court session in Kediri, Java, in which a defendant asked that a witness be required to remove his headscarf and submit to examination of his hair.

32 For the occult offenses, see Fasseur (1995); Hekmeijer (1918); Hirsch (1919); Lemaire (1934).

33 Knebel (1898a: 499) lists a jimat with unintelligible Arabic (a Javanese aristocrat told him it resembled "Buddhist writing") that had nothing to do with perjury. For some the term jimat could only refer to items with Arabic inscriptions (see below).

34 No one raises the question of why witnesses might not want to help convict or exonerate defendants. Could it be fear of jago and gangs? In any case, as with uprisings, the law deflects a broader problem of governance onto jimat. At the same time, the familiarity of the rite of testifying—modified to suit a non-European, non-Christian population? adapting existing procedures?—suggests Dutch blindness to objects in their own habitual routines. How it became commonplace to swear on a Bible would be worthy of study, as would its transmutation into holding a Qur'an—more properly, a *mus'haf*, since Qur'an refers to the message rather than the thing that mediates it—above a witness's head. (See Suit 2020 for a fascinating discussion of *mus'haf* in Cairo.) If colonial reports about jimat uncovered in courtrooms find them ridiculous, someone unfamiliar with Euro-American courtrooms might find procedures equally absurd.

35 The 1872 regulations required such objects to be destroyed (Der Kinderen 1873: 33); this was dropped by 1918.

36 While Meijer casually refers to "a Javanese method" for housebreaking—"throwing dirt from a cemetery while murmuring prayers on the house where one wants to go burgle" (1935: 114)—he does not call this a jimat. Both Meijer and S. likely learned about grave dirt from Knebel's article.

37 In addition to crucifixes, he mentions the uses theosophists make of specific colors, shapes, and symbols. He comments too on the ontological implications of the notion of superstition, observing that figuring out what is actual or real and what is merely superstitious is not as simple as it may seem: for example, predictions sometimes come true. For A. T., governments are in no position to adjudicate such matters.

38 Although some uncertainty prevails about these etymologies, I base myself on the OED. Skemer (2006: 6) claims that *amulētum* comes from Arabic *hamalet*; those who cite this origin define a hamalet as an object worn around the neck to protect its wearer from a variety of afflictions. The first use of *amulētum* is usually attributed to Pliny's *Natural History*. The OED is uncertain whether Greek *telesm* might also have an Arabic origin. That telesm is related to *telos* (Emily Bagarawanath, personal communication), referring to an end, purpose, or goal, makes for a more interesting commensuration with jimat.

39 It is striking that this is the only time Veth mentions jimat in his four-volume work on Java. Calling Hajis "the most dangerous element in native society," he also claims they use magic (*toverkunsten*) to heal the sick (1875: vol. 1, 406).

40 Yet another indication that such locations need have nothing to do with undermining an oath.

41 Dictionaries define *wesi* (*besi* in modern Indonesian) *kuning* as "metal said to have magical power" (Echols and Shadily 1992) and "magical iron" (Stevens

and Schmidgall-Tellings 2004). According to Van Hien, it was made by forging together gold, silver, copper, tin, zinc, lead, and iron in equal proportions and weights, resulting in a metal that should look and sound like gold (1934: vol. 3, 39–40). Kruyt (1906: 162) notes that Javanese claim *tosan kuning* comes from a spirit called a *demit*, and carrying it renders someone invulnerable.

42   For kiyai, see chapter 1.

43   *Doa* usually is glossed as prayer. Poensen appears to equate *doa* with *rapal*.

44   The first thirteen appear to be organized by the way they are worn: ten necklaces followed by three rings. But more rings appear later in the list.

45   A fourth photo shows mostly manufactured metallic items: an old spearhead, a small iron bar masked as pencil lead, and a European angel (Meijer 1935: 111).

46   In presenting savages as materialists and Europeans as spiritual, Wilken echoes Hegel. Retaining but revaluing this dichotomy—and replacing "savage" with Oriental—formed another, now more familiar, stereotype.

47   Wilken's source is seventeenth-century naturalist Rumphius's *Ambonese Cabinet of Curiosity*, an apt title as bezoar not only interested Indonesians but found a place in the cabinets of curiosity (or wonders) popular among elite Europeans. The latter, like Indonesians, considered bezoar potent—for example, as antidotes to poisons— and sometimes set them in rings or necklaces.

48   For the concepts Kruyt develops, see chapter 3.

49   The *Encyclopaedie's* fetish recalls classic tropes: "Any object can be made into a fetish. This depends sometimes on the particular circumstances under which one finds such an object." As for jimat, a one-line entry explains it as a "corruption of the Arab. 'azimat, which means amulet, talisman." *Encyclopaedie van Nederlandsch-Indië*, 2nd ed., s.v. "djimat" and "fetis."

50   After serving as a second lieutenant in the Indies army, Spat taught Malay and Indies ethnology to aspiring officers at the Royal Military Academy at Breda. Later, at the University of Utrecht's ethnology department, he taught Malay language and literature as well as Islamic law, focusing on the Indies.

51   After all, the *matter* of jimat involved claims the Dutch found absurd: that slips of paper or strips of metal could make flesh impervious to bullets.

52   On coins, with their political heads and economic tails, see Hart (1986).

53   Probably, anyway. Just how "European" civil servants were when jimat became a matter of colonial concern cannot be taken for granted. At least some would have grown up in creolized households, or had Indonesian mothers or nursemaids (see chapter 4). Still, they wouldn't have been the ones discovering such items, and might not have recognized these uses.

54   One friend rattled off the names of several kinds of metal that could make skin impenetrable (*besi tawar*, *besi prungu*, *besi kerawan*, and the famous *besi kuning*); others mentioned *pragolan*, *ikat pingan* (worn around the waist), and *lungsir petak* (a neckpiece). They did not necessarily know what they actually looked like.

55   I found one online: http://cakepane.blogspot.com/2015/02/carcan-mirah-kecubung -dan-batu-permata.html, accessed September 1, 2019. Other Carcan address what certain animals (dogs, roosters, and especially doves) bring to one's home.

56 Wearing a jimat is not the only practice aiming at such an effect.

57 Indeed, on first encountering eyeglasses on the noses of Dutch envoys, some members of Bali's ruling class treated them as possible sources of power (Wiener 2014).

58 I leave aside problems with the concept *nonhuman*. Latour introduced it as infralanguage to avoid the concept of object.

59 I rely here especially on Stengers and Latour's (2015) introduction to the English translation, and to that form of instauration that yields "thinginess."

60 The exception is Poensen's brief account.

61 Wiener (2016); Fox (2016, 2018).

62 Wiener (2016); Fox (2016, 2018).

63 Jimat never appear as such in a manual written by Serrurier, director of the Royal Museum for Ethnology in Leiden, but surely counted among the fetishes, amulets, and grimoires (*toverboeken*, literally "books on magic or sorcery") he lists. His advice to travelers: "take everything that you can get" (1891: 158).

INTERLUDE 3. COORDINATING DEVICES

1 Feminist science studies highlight ways that generalized and standardized categories elide relevant differences (e.g., Keller 1983).

2 In *Primitive Culture* (1958 [1871]), Tylor addresses magic in one chapter, entitled "Survival in Culture."

3 Tylor speaks of the "universal diffusion of magical ideas among mankind, excepting only the limited class who have abandoned them through higher education" (1883: vol. 15, 205).

4 Having discredited magic, Tylor devotes his last paragraph to a small historical redemption as the cradle for science's infancy.

5 For the debate, see Stocking (1974: 1–3); Boas (1974) lays out his objections to Mason's position.

6 http://databases.prm.ox.ac.uk/fmi/webd/rethinking_volumes, accessed August 25, 2022.

7 Anthropologists still inform the *Britannica*'s magic; Africanist John Middleton coauthored the entry in the current online version. But he has two coauthors: a historian of medieval England and the author of a book on the Golden Dawn, a secret society that inspired movements such as Wicca.

CHAPTER 3. THINGS COLLECTIVE

Earlier versions of much of chapter 3 appeared in *Comparative Studies in Society and History* and *Social Anthropology*.

1 Since *kris* is an English word, I leave that spelling in quoting texts written in English.

2 I learned of the clash between curators and the Communication Department from Pieter ter Keurs (personal communication). Such disagreements are hardly unique; see McCracken (2005: 119–58).

3 Van Duuren focuses on Indonesia and Malaysia. Keris also are found in southern Thailand, the southern Philippines, Brunei, and Singapore.

4 Inside the Puri the Dutch found both guns and gunpowder. A correspondent noted that the gunpowder "bore the mark of English companies," indexing the arms trade forming the background to Conrad's "Karain" (*De Locomotief*, May 9, 1908, section 1, page 2).

5 Numbers calculated by the victors. For more about the event, see Wiener (1995).

6 According to the *Surabaiasch Handelblad*, April 25, 1908, and M. van Geuns's editorial (May 6, 1908).

7 Letter from Resident de Bruyn Kops to Governor-General van Heutsz, Missive No. 3141/2 Singaraja, May 24, 1908, and Letter from Governor-General van Heutsz to Resident de Bruyn Kops, June 5, 1908, both in V. January 13, 1909, no. 42, Ministry of Colonies archives in the National Archives in The Hague.

8 "Buit" in *Bijblad* (1908: 129). I am grateful to Joanneke Fleischauer for finding this document.

9 Perhaps to emphasize this, on June 29, 1908, De Bruyn Kops mentions another keris belonging to the Déwa Agung that had come into his hands after the shipment. During a trip to Lombok he offered it to the Déwa Agung's half-brothers, but they refused it. What happened to it then he does not say. He estimated its value at f500. His offer seems oddly contrary to the arguments he advanced just weeks earlier.

10 Extract from Government Resolution of November 14, 1908, no. 7, in Kolonien Resolutien na 1900, V. January 13, 1909, no. 42. I found a discrepancy between the list of ninety-three articles to be sent to the Netherlands appended to the resolution, and the number shipped. The additional materials included thirteen keris, other weapons, and a variety of further items. Judging from the custom house inventory of the shipment, some had been offered for sale; perhaps they did not find buyers. The same shipment included two boxes "of ethnographic interest" from a 1907 exploration of southern New Guinea. In 1985, I discovered from Leiden's museum records that over half of the ten keris from Klungkung were stolen in the 1960s.

11 Groot (2009). By comparison, an Asiatic Society was established in Calcutta in 1784, but the Royal Asiatic Society of Bengal wasn't founded until 1823 (Pargiter 1923: vii).

12 *De Locomotief*, no. 110, May 11, 1908.

13 Ultimately, stories blamed the Déwa Agung (Wiener 1995).

14 The ones sent do not match those *De Locomotief* mentioned. In particular, the pusaka that could cause earthquakes does not appear on De Bruyn Kops's list. According to Pedersen (2007), it had been brought to Karangasem centuries before.

15 Appendix 3 of Letter 3016/2 from Resident de Bruyn Kops to the governor-general, May 19, 1908, reproduced in *Beschrijving van eenige tijdens de Zuid-Bali Expedities 1906–1908 buitgemaakte vorstelijke poesaka-wapens*. Stevens and Schmidgall-Tellings (2004) define *wasiat* as last will and testament with the secondary meaning of heirloom, with *keris wasiat* as an example, glossing it as "hereditary kris having *sakti*, supernatural power." An older dictionary offers "magic power (of an ancient heirloom)" as *wasiat*'s second meaning (Echols and Shadily 1992). I see these glosses as evidence of the impact of Dutch discussions of keris.

16 Note that both spoke of "magical" rather than "supernatural" powers (as per the jimat laws). Perhaps "magical" seemed a better fit for things that could alter material conditions, and thus were hard to explain in psychological terms.

17 Letter from Resident de Bruyn Kops to the governor-general, June 20, 1908, in V. January 13, 1909, no. 42, Algemeen Rijksarchief, Ministry of Colonies, Kolonien Resolutien na 1900.

18 Lodewijk Willem Christiaan van den Berg wrote a dissertation on Islamic law at Leiden and then held legal and administrative positions in the Indies for nearly two decades. He was appointed the government's first adviser on Eastern languages and Muslim law in 1878. In 1887 he took up a professorship in Indology at Delft, specializing in the "religious laws, traditions, and customs of the Dutch East Indies" (Kuitenbrouwer 2014).

19 Not only Van den Berg but all Dutch scholars take Gowa and Bone in South Sulawesi as the prime example of rijkssieraden. Most of what they say of those realms, however, appears to be unique.

20 As Bali's oldest and most venerable polity, Klungkung possessed several famous keris. Tales concerning the acquisition of two appear in the *Babad Dalem*, a text chronicling the dynasty's founding and subsequent fortunes. The keris forwarded to Batavia also included one Gianyar's ruler surrendered to the Déwa Agung's father.

21 *Encyclopaedie van Nederlandsch-Indië*, 2nd ed., s.v. "wapens der Inlandsche bevolking."

22 Wilken only discusses Malacca, the Padang and Palembang highlands in Sumatra, the two semiautonomous Javanese principalities of Soerakarta and Yogyakarta, and Gowa and Bone. Van den Berg incorporates other portions of Sumatra, Banjarmasin in Kalimantan, and several realms in the "outer islands" to the east. All of those Wilken mentions serve as the primary examples in later accounts.

23 In his preface, he declares he hesitated to write about animism because it seemed arrogant to think he could improve on Wilken. Because Wilken's work no longer was readily available, and much new data had appeared, he had proceeded.

24 The model seems to be chemical elements such as oxygen or nitrogen, that in Dutch (and German) end in *stof*, material. Kruyt notes in a footnote he provisionally called it "life fluid" (*levensfluide*) until Chantepie de Saussaye, a theologian and Leiden professor of religion, suggested soulstuff. Wilken too wrote in dialogue with a Dutch theologian, his colleague Cornelius Petrus Tiele, professor of the history of religion at Leiden.

25 Semangat involves enthusiasm or liveliness. It is noteworthy that Skeat speaks of *magic*, as did Frazer, his contemporary.

26 While Kruyt is unusually explicit in acknowledging that his analysis is based on inference, he follows the familiar method of asserting that a practice originally must have worked otherwise to make it conform to his thesis (recall Wilken on amulets).

27 He does, however, mention Knebel's article at the start of his discussion of examples.

28 According to WorldCat, Kruyt's book on animism fared remarkably well, with eighteen editions (in three languages) between 1906 and 2010.

29 Kruyt actually mentions "magical powers" in passing, once in relation to iron and once to refer to particular rijkssieraden.

30 Alkema (1930), a former missionary appointed to teach Sundanese and missionary history at Utrecht, commented that the theories about magic the "men of science" had introduced also treated Christian sacraments as instances of similar mental processes rather than as products of revelation. He found being on the receiving end of modern critique far from enjoyable.

31 For Van Ossenbruggen's career, see De Josselin de Jong (1977: 8, 30–31).

32 As a follower of Wilken, it is not surprising that he too never mentions jimat but talks about amulets, basically understanding them as Wilken does. He does, however, address specific amulets in relation to specific substances and practices in elaborating how magic involves the association of (false) ideas.

33 He adds: "the smith then is also with all primitives the magician par excellence, the forge a kind of temple" (1916: 241).

34 See Van Duuren (2002) for references to discussions of forging in and around Banjarmasin in Kalimantan. Given the dates, the Banjarmasin War (1859–63) likely stoked that interest.

35 The VOC granted them the status of autonomous principalities as they were heirs to the former realm of Mataram; the Netherlands Indies considered them vassal states.

36 By way of contrast, Malinowski (1961 [1922]) compares kula valuables to Britain's crown jewels—and does not call them either fetishes or magical.

37 I owe my insights on this topic to Harm Stevens, who kindly gave me a guided tour through Delft's Leger Museum.

38 Kreps (2004) links pusaka to current understandings of museums as repositories of cultural heritage.

39 See also Latour (2005b). There are, of course, other ways to commensurate than by finding similarities with European practices. Marx went in the opposite direction (though calling commodities fetishes invokes the moderns' purifying impulse); along similar lines, Taussig argues about enchantment (see epilogue).

40 As Latour (1993) notes, this does not mean, as the National Rifle Association insists, that "guns don't kill people; people kill people." Neither guns on their own nor unarmed people have deadly force. It is the combination—plus ammunition and aiming—that kills.

41 Latour's factish (1999, 2010) is part of an argument about the construction of fetishes and scientific facts—either of which may be constructed well or badly.

42 For more on markets and museums vis-à-vis ethnographic artifacts, see Penny (2002). For the pertinence of this relationship for keris, see Van Duuren (2002), passim.

43 Keris named in the resident's report remained at the Batavian Society (*Gids* 1917), though one (belonging to a priest) returned to Bali.

44 Governor-General van Heutsz actually considered this, though I can no longer find my source.

45 For these expeditions and what they yielded, see Budiarti (2005, 2007), Ernawati (2005, 2007), and Stevens (2005, 2007).

46 In practice, this is not always possible. For example, the guidebook to the Batavian Society Museum's Treasure Room identifies things by name and describes them by appearance, putting together two separate forms of identification. It fails, however, to link them to the third, crucial one, listing them by the numbers they were given in the display case in which they were exhibited rather than by inventory numbers (*Gids* 1917, 1928). According to Brinkgreve and Stuart-Fox, the museum's curator, C. M. Pleyte, authored the first edition of the guide, in 1912. They also discovered in the museum's own copy of the latter that an unknown person had jotted the inventory numbers by hand (2007: 161–62).

47 Van Duuren (2002) includes, for example, a book for pawnshop employees.

48 The same term is used for rooms displaying valuable and rare objects in Dutch museums too. *Treasure Room* is a literal translation, which I prefer to the dictionary translation of *treasury*, although the latter is suggestive in connection to the market value of the items exhibited there. F. D. K. Bosch speaks of Batavia's "gold-chamber" (1937/38: 122).

49 Four cases contained Klungkung booty. Brinkgreve and Stuart-Fox (2007) offer an excellent discussion of the museum's Bali collection, especially objects taken during the 1906 expedition to Badung and Tabanan.

50 Bosch also noted that Sunday visits afforded a chance for "native" youths to see and be seen by friends and neighbors, or make a romantic attachment public.

51 Bone and Gowa's famous rijkssieraden arrived at the Batavian Society as war booty in 1905–6 (Budiarti 2007).

52 This visit is not mentioned in the documents. I learned of it from the daughter of the Klungkung visitor, a surviving half-brother of the Déwa Agung killed in 1908 and (as Grader's report confirms) the only man still alive who could recognize specific keris.

53 A Balinese interlocutor told me that I Durga Dingkul formed the "center" of the king's power, as Durga holds sway over all destructive forces.

54 I concur with Moll's clarification (and for the most part with his understanding of *pajenengan*). People in Klungkung in the 1980s told me, in fact, that a pajenengan guards the realm, which brings them in line with colonial accounts of rijkssieraden.

55 Unpublished document, "Concept-Nota," dated May 1938 and stamped Udayana Fakultas Sastra (provided to me by B. and G. Solyom). "*Geheim*" (secret) is typed in the upper left and below that the subject ("Rijkssieraden Zelfbestuurders in Bali"). I do not know if these documents actually were sent to the governor-general. The full correspondence may exist in Indonesia's National Archives, but I was unable to locate it.

56 The new Déwa Agung's uncle (see note 52) described I Durga Dingkul's blade for Grader as having an image of Betara Durga (the goddess Durga) on it. Several people in Klungkung told me it was in fact sent to Bali, but upon its arrival Gianyar's ruler (who had requested the return of a keris his ancestor had surrendered to Klungkung before 1908) insisted it was his. The dispute led officials to send it back to Batavia, and it was lost when a Japanese plane bombed the ship.

57 http://www.vikingsword.com/ethsword/.
58 An embedded history of Protestant iconoclasm appears in these references to African ancestor sculptures and Catholic saints. I find it suggestive that only artifacts from the Netherlands' major colony have provoked such active engagement.
59 Unlike Indonesian museums; see below.
60 https://en.wikipedia.org/wiki/De_Kris_Pusaka, accessed December 29, 2019. In 2007 an online discussion forum existed in which people reminisced about the series and wrote of their own experiences with keris and keris lore; it no longer exists, however.
61 https://www.thejakartapost.com/life/2017/08/10/jokowi-to-lend-own-keris -collection-to-surakarta-museum.html, accessed November 22, 2023.
62 That I Durga Dingkul could not be identified from the written material available to the curators may serve as a trace of a clash between what mattered when keris were accessioned and what mattered not only to Klungkung rulers but to colonial officials (their specificity and history). But see note 56.
63 For uncommoning, see Blaser and De la Cadena (2017) and Wiener (2017) (including more about this keris).
64 See https://ich.unesco.org/en/RL/indonesian-kris-00112, accessed November 6, 2019.

INTERLUDE 4. GETTING CAUGHT

1 His ambiguous phrasing raises the intriguing possibility that witches *might* exist, though not as Azande describe and deal with them.
2 Though Stoller and Olkes (1989) make ample use of Songhay titles such as *sorko* and *souhanci*, it is worth noting that Stoller feels comfortable routing those through *sorcery*. Similarly, West, while deploying numerous Shimakonde terms, does not hesitate to intersperse these with *sorcerer* and *sorcery*.
3 Use of protective words and things from field sites may be widespread. Also see Wiener (1999b) for an argument about multiply positioned individuals.

CHAPTER 4. DANGEROUS LIAISONS

This chapter develops materials previously published in *History and Anthropology*, *Colonial Collections Revisited*, and *Anthropologica*.

1 Geerken had no personal experience of guna-guna but repeats stories he has heard. In general, he uses the term as a synonym for what he finds inexplicable.
2 Some anthropologists may know Gorer as the author of a staid monograph on the Lepcha of Sikkim as well as studies of national character. At this time, however, he was an aspiring popular writer, with books on the Marquis de Sade and a trip to West Africa. After his return from Southeast Asia, a major in the Gurkha Rifles who had read his Africa book invited him to spend a year in Sikkim. To prepare, he briefly studied with Ruth Benedict and Margaret Mead (Gorer 1938).
3 See, for example, Hives and Lumley (1930).

4 A now commonplace insight (e.g., Bhabha 1994; Stoler 1995; Stoler and Cooper 1997).

5 See Stoler (1995).

6 See Van Marle (1951–52) for a good discussion.

7 Guna-guna occurred prior to this (e.g., Blussé 1986; Stockdale 1995 [1811]: 51), but was less remarkable when European endogamy was rare and witchcraft was deemed plausible.

8 While he lists Islamic entities, sacred places, and creation stories, he focuses on those he terms *tiang pasek*. Ironically, this is a derogatory name, bestowed by the growing Islamic reform movement: Ricklefs derives *pasek* from Arabic *fasiq*, for "godless, sinful" (2007: 90, n. 12). Tiang pasek also were becoming known as *abangan* (literally, "red ones"), as in Geertz (1960).

9 I suspect Van Hien belonged to a theosophical lodge, another possible arena for meeting Javanese (their members included aristocrats educated in colonial schools; see De Tollenaere 1996 and Sears 1996). Theosophical ideas, though, were readily available in books and journals. While Van Hien gives the impression that he is reporting what he learned from Javanese interlocutors, Peter Boomgaard (personal communication) claims that he drew on published materials without acknowledging them. Boomgaard also, however, notes that many of those publications are obscure, which raises the question of how Van Hien found them.

10 *Jaka* means young man or bachelor; *tua*, old. "Old bachelor" seems a suggestive name, though he may have misidentified the beetle (googling identifies *jaka tua* as a plant).

11 The same passages appear in the 1896 edition.

12 Did Van Hien mean to suggest that the word could be glossed as "uniting"? It is hard to understand why. *Guna-guna* derives from Sanskrit (Zoetmulder 1982: vol. 1, 553), for quality or characteristic, rooting it in exchanges and translations predating the Dutch. It passed into Old Javanese as *guna*, virtue, excellence, accomplishment, skill, as well as use. To *maguna* is to possess good qualities, be excellent, virtuous, talented, expert, capable, useful, and thus attractive to others.

13 *Guna-guna* appears in several archipelago languages, including Balinese and Indonesian, though not Javanese. Indonesian anthropologist Koentjaraningrat, however, uses *guna-guna* for "Javanese sorcery" or "love magic" in *Javanese Culture* (1985: 420).

14 Since Daum published before van Hien, it is possible some of van Hien's account of guna-guna was cribbed from the novelist.

15 Europeans weren't the only readers and writers of guna-guna tales. In 1896 an Indo named G. Francis published a work in Malay entitled *Njai Dasima*, in which a Muslim uses guna-guna to convince the eponymous nyai to leave her English lover. Siegel 1997 offers an insightful analysis, including a discussion of the popularity of a 1920s film based on the story among Indo and "native" audiences.

16 In the Indies such anxieties appear by the mid-nineteenth century (Stoler 1995: 104).

17 He is partly alluding to the "hidden forces" I address in chapter 5. Van Wulfften Palthe was the main authority; others cite and develop his ideas (e.g., Raptschinsky 1941; Winckel 1938). Hermans (1925) argues that nervous disorders mainly threatened those with a family history of such ailments. By contrast, Kohlbrugge

(1907) insists that incompatibility between European work culture and the tropical milieu rendered even Javanese civil servants susceptible to neurasthenia.

18 Apart from repatriation, physicians prescribed physical labor, sexual moderation, and a European family life, drawing on an emerging "bourgeois ethic of morality and work" (Stoler 1989: 646).

19 Such views may explain Snouck Hurgronje's scathing review of his book (1908). As a proponent of the Ethical Policy, Snouck could hardly have accepted Kohlbrugge's pessimistic claims about the tropics or his skepticism about the possibility or desirability of trying to turn Indonesians into modern, rational thinkers.

20 For example, Hermans (1925); for discussions, Locher-Scholten (1994), Stoler (1995). See Bastiaans (1970) for memories of such exposure and retrospective responses.

21 Martin and Tops (1991: 1360) define *toverij* as magic, sorcery (with connotations of necromancy and witchcraft), sympathetic magic, white magic, black magic, and a piece of magic (i.e., a trick or spell). *Hekserij* is sorcery, witchcraft, and magic (552). *Magie* (807) is defined as conjuring, sleight of hand, hocus-pocus, and enchantment or fascination. Magic in the sense of witchcraft or sorcery is included, though not as the first meaning, which emphasizes performance. This is not the anthropologists' *magie*. De Blécourt (1990: 22) emphasizes that *toverij* is the original Dutch term, and *hekserij* was introduced from German.

22 *Tovermiddelen* also refers to magic spells and potions; the Dutch does not distinguish substances from words.

23 No entries for guna-guna on its own appear in the *Encyclopaedie*; the 1917 edition mentions it under poisons (*vergiften*).

24 Spat found Mauss, who thinks magic through the concept of power, more inspiring.

25 His source for these is Skeat (1965 [1900]).

26 What Dutch authorities coded as sorcery or witchcraft (*toverij*) concerned officials only when it led to acts criminal by other criteria, such as killing the witch. The issue that then faced judges was whether "native belief" counted as a mitigating circumstance (and on this score courts were inconsistent). But what Indonesians claimed people the Dutch labeled witches were capable of doing, or what (if anything) such people had to do with dukun aroused little interest, at least before Lesquillier. Such indifference contrasted markedly with British Africa, where anti-witchcraft ordinances led to a host of conundrums (how to differentiate witches from those who healed the misfortunes they sent; how to differentiate colonizers from the witches they apparently were protecting), a contrast also noted by Ellen (1993). For more on "witchcraft" in specific legal cases, including Lesquillier's discussion of them, see Wiener 2015.

27 In one novel, for example, the totok main character, a lawyer exasperated by his superstitious Indies wife and mother-in-law, repeatedly reassures himself that suggestion can explain a number of peculiar events, reminding himself at the same time that, unlike even these beloved women, he is *nuchter*, levelheaded (Van Wermeskerken 1922).

28 Salverda (1994) provides a subtle sociolinguistic analysis of the novel, focusing on its use of Indies-Dutch. Kijdsmeir cribbed some of his plot from another Daum

novel (1997 [1893]). In the latter, the creole wife is killed not by guna-guna but by the feared "pill number eleven" that gave the book its title; a jilted nyai is responsible.

29 Educated Eurasians, all too aware that totoks associated magic with ignorant "natives," responded enthusiastically to Hitzka's articles, which appeared in *Onze Stem* (Our Voice). According to Van der Veur (1969: 77), this was the journal of the Eurasian League.

30 Similarly, in the novel *Rumah Angker* a totok lawyer hears rumors of guna-guna's use in witness tampering (Van Wermeskerken 1922).

31 The term *guna-guna* also became linked to Bali, due to a film of that title about witchcraft among Balinese. However, guna-guna stories mainly came from Java, which had the largest European and Eurasian populations and the most fraught relationships. In a novel set in Bali, a European who suspects his Balinese mistress of guna-guna grew up on Java (Fabricius 1948).

32 These substances also show up in Geerken (2010: 300).

33 Gorer presents himself as a neutral recorder. Once Muller begins his tale, for example, Gorer removes himself from the scene, bracketing Muller's remarks by quotation marks. But by letting Muller speak for himself, Gorer also establishes distance. While Muller assumes a sympathetic listener, Gorer's comments elsewhere show this to be false. Thus Gorer regrets he had little contact with Indonesians, noting that whenever possible he spoke at length to chauffeurs and servants, whom he found the most interesting people around. Moreover, the tale immediately follows Gorer's positive comments about Bali—and even the distinctions Gorer draws among archipelago populations make Muller's claims about "Malays" as a race suspect. Finally, Gorer is highly critical of the Nazis, whose racial attitudes resemble Muller's.

34 See chapter 5.

35 From Allen (2007), I learned to call practitioners of such arts *deceptionists*.

36 https://www.stedelijk.nl/en/news/open-call-municipal-art-acquisitions-2022, accessed May 13, 2022.

37 The name of one of them, Made Ngurah Amanda Pinatih, indicates a Balinese parent. The name of the other curator, Britte Sloothaak, is thoroughly Dutch.

INTERLUDE 5. THE MAGIC OF MAGIC

1 Which is not to say it is easy: "Consciousness is the most stubborn substance in the cosmos, and the most fluid. It can be rigid as concrete, and it can change in an instant. A song can change it, or a story, or a fragrance wafting by on the wind" (Starhawk 1993: 153).

2 Stocking (1971) includes both notes and an analysis.

3 In several séances the first spirits to turn up are female, non-white (commonly American Indian) children.

4 I borrow "ghostbusting" from Viveiros de Castro (2003).

5 See Nietzsche (1974 [1887]: 245–46) for a discussion of habit and error pertinent to anthropology.

CHAPTER 5. HIDDEN FORCES

1 Older theatergoers may have recalled a three-part mini-series on Dutch TV in 1974, released on DVD in the early 2000s.
2 https://tga.nl/voorstellingen/de-stille-kracht, accessed May 21, 2020.
3 Pignarre and Stengers (2011) speak of "infernal alternatives" in their analysis of capitalism.
4 Such payments, along with tribute and compulsory services, formed most of the VOC's income.
5 Initially, coffee paid so well that Sundanese planted it in droves, until oversupply led prices to fall. To avoid such fluctuations, the VOC initiated quotas. According to Furnivall, these deployed considerable mathematical sleight of hand in calculating pounds per pikol. Hence in shipping to the Netherlands, a pikol of coffee was measured at 126 pounds but in purchasing from suppliers, one pikol equaled 140 pounds. To offset losses during transportation to Batavia, however, the VOC demanded 160 pounds per pikol from regents, who in turn set a pikol at 240 to 270 pounds. Hence cultivators had to furnish 240–70 pounds for every 126 pounds shipped to the Netherlands, but only were paid for fourteen. Officials pocketed the difference at every step (1944: 40).
6 The road was built to defend Java against British incursions. Developments in France, both revolutionary and imperial, shaped Dutch history from the mid-1790s to 1815. In 1806 Napoleon appointed his brother Holland's king; the Post Road was built during this French "interregnum," which ended with Java's conquest by the British East India Company and Raffles's installation as lieutenant-governor. The Congress of Vienna led to the return of the Indies to the Netherlands, now a unified kingdom.
7 Land rent, ironically, was meant to replace the VOC's forced deliveries and tribute.
8 Historians debate whether the system impoverished peasants and led to famine (forcing some into wage labor) or benefited them. Local authorities profited, since all officials—from regents to village headman—received a percentage of the crops, though as positions once subject to competition and even war became hereditary statuses and bureaucratic offices with sinecures, they became dependent on the colonial state. For more detailed assessments of the Cultivation System, see Van Niel (1992).
9 For colonial careers and European residents of the Indies, I consulted the *Almanak en Naamregister van Nederlandsch Indië*, an annual report on the colony. Thomas Elliott pursued additional materials on my behalf.
10 "Audience hall" interprets his *passeerbaan* as a Dutchification of a local structure, the *paseban*. It literally, however, means "passing lane." Perhaps officials were responsible for hilly sections of the Post Road in Sumedang?
11 My inspiration is Gramsci (1971: 324).
12 In the seventeenth century, aristocracy mattered far less in Holland than in England, given the importance in the former of wealth from global commerce, which underwrote experimentation and paid great attention to what the eye could see (Alpers 1983).

13 Possibly also her race, though Dornseiff calls her European (1853: 185).

14 Van Hoëvell's obituary (1850) praised his military exploits but critiqued his governing abilities.

15 See Gerstäcker (1871) and Van Swieten (1872).

16 I return to Van Swieten below.

17 *Biang Lala* was a biyearly magazine aimed at providing a forum for convivial conversation. Founded in 1852, it discontinued publication after only four years. (*Encyclopaedie van Nederlandsch-Indië*, 2nd ed., s.v. "Tijdschriften en Periodieken.")

18 Michiels achieved fame among Indonesians too. Soldiers knew him as General Tiger (*Macan*), perhaps a tribute to his fierceness (Gerstäcker 1871). I encountered him long before learning about Sumedang, from Balinese interlocutors who called him "Mr. Seven Stars" (*I Bintang Tujuh*), an appellation that puzzled me until I saw his official portrait, with its star-shaped medals. That they recalled him at all marks the historical achievement of causing his death. During a night attack, Klungkung's ruler sent out a bullet animated by an other-than-human force, which unerringly struck Michiels, burrowing into his body and whizzing through vital organs to snuff out his life (Wiener 1995). Michiels apparently was plagued by entities Europeans did not acknowledge.

19 His memorialization may also have spurred an 1854 investigation into the Sumedang affair (see below).

20 See Van Hoëvell (1850) and Multatuli (1967 [1860]). Multatuli was the pen name of Eduard Douwes Dekker, who worked under him in Sumatra and authored another famous colonial novel, *Max Havelaar*. It portrays Michiels as a tyrant and lambasts him for allowing lust to lead to administrative improprieties. (This charge was picked up later in Bekeerde 1916: 716.) *Max Havelaar*'s depiction of aristocratic corruption and exploitation of peasants lent support to opponents of the Cultivation System, who sought to replace the government monopoly with the free market. The limits of the liberal position are well expressed by Van Hoëvell when he notes that despite his failures as an administrator, Michiels deserves a place among other heroes "who conquered or kept these beautiful possessions for the Netherlands" (1850: 376).

21 Van Hoëvell (1849), who visited Sumedang in 1847, says nothing about the stones.

22 Friends helped me to translate this from German after I discovered the published English translation significantly altered Pfeiffer's straightforward recounting of what she heard. For instance: not "people" but "the natives" claim the house is haunted; the stones don't rain but are thrown; and the government "proved more than a match" for the ghost, and "checkmated" him, a fitting representation of the imaginary of colonial regimes, victorious even over forces they consider fantasies.

23 Van Hoëvell and Buddingh served together in the church in Batavia. Van Hoëvell was a famous figure in Indies and Dutch politics and media. He is best known for his opposition to the Cultivation System and promotion of liberal reforms. After disagreements with the governor-general, he returned to the Netherlands, where he served as member of parliament and later on the Council of State. He founded the *Tijdschrift voor Nederlands-Indie* in 1838, editing it until 1862.

24 See Reid (1985) for the properties and history of the betel quid.

25 On her journey, Pfeiffer visited the United States, where she met Washington Irving, famed purveyor of spooky tales. Though she says nothing about spiritualism, it began as an American development and was spreading to Europe, especially Britain and France.

26 In describing Sufi rites as tricks, Dutch authors anticipate Robert-Houdin, the "father" of modern stage magic (Jones 2010).

27 Davidson and Duffin (2012) track what they term lithobalia much earlier; these events, though, again seem to involve rocks that hit people rather than avoiding them.

28 See chapter 4.

29 He claims not only Sundanese but also Javanese and Moluccans use this term, which provides a clue to his possible identity. Reference to Moluccans might allude to an old incident in Ambon (Ackers 2007: 23–32).

30 The timing supports my suspicion that what spurred interest were plans to build a monument to Michiels.

31 Either rumors the house had been demolished were wrong or he did not realize the assistant resident's house was not the one Von Kessinger had occupied.

32 The government's annual register identifies Dikhuis merely as a "European resident."

33 Gerstäcker may have met Gustav through Eduard L. W. Kinder, the government's German translator since 1838.

34 Hanover is listed as his birthplace in the Ministry of Colonies Register (*Stamboek*).

35 I suspect Albert was Gustav's kin but could not find confirmation.

36 Gerstäcker's friend also mentioned the report's disappearance, but claimed Baud took it to the Netherlands. He also included an anecdote about General von Gagern's meeting with Michiels, though it is far less flattering. According to him, when dining together Von Gagern insisted that Michiels tell him the story. Michiels at first refused and then relented, only to be met with Von Gagern's amused smile, which provoked him. Von Gagern finally had to apologize formally. Could Van Swieten's article also have aimed to challenge this story?

37 Did Baud receive it?

38 The pair were in high demand: during his London fieldwork. Tylor refers to them often but they did not turn up as planned at a séance he attended (Stocking 1971: 100).

39 Including Queen Sophie, King Willem III's estranged wife, who invited Scottish medium Daniel Home to hold séances in a palace in The Hague in 1858 (Ackers 2007: chapter 8; Britten 1884). Britten notes that those initially interested in spiritualism in The Hague were members of "the best society," and refers to people of "quality and standing" (1884: 328, 338).

40 According to Puhle (1999), the Zittau incident occurred in 1862.

41 The similarity of this word to *dabus* (and the substitutability of "w" and "b" in Indonesian languages) suggests he is referring to something like the Sufi rite Van Hoëvell and Buddingh described. But his brief description (involving binding and unbinding, and disappearing and reappearing) does not.

42 Metropolitan developments possibly informed Vorderman's unmasking practices. Mediums who produced manifestations triggered public confrontations, in which

both illusionists and men of science denounced them as tricksters; those accused adamantly denied the charge.

43 Wiselius's article overlaps with a piece on Javanese superstitions in Semarang (central Java) that the journal published a year earlier. It briefly refers to *gendruwo* as a garden ghost (*tuinspook*; Van Dissel 1870: 274); Javanese gardens contained trees.

44 Veth was a crucial player in both scholarly circles (apart from his Leiden chair, he edited the *Tijdschrift* and helped found the KITLV) and liberal politics (e.g., his review of *Max Havelaar* was decisive in shaping its impact; he was a pal of Van Hoëvell's). He supported policies that treated Indonesians as Dutchmen (e.g., individualizing land ownership) and favored assimilation (including education). See Van der Velde (2006).

45 Muecke (2021) led me to recognize this familiar move as a Harawayan god-trick.

46 Van Hien calls gendruwo tree-dwelling teases who enjoy frightening people not only by throwing stones and spitting sirih but also by taking terrifying shapes, blowing out lamps, and rattling doors and windows. He does not, notably, mention Sumedang.

47 The *stil* in stille kracht has different connotations than *hidden*. It means "quiet or silent," "mute," hushed," as well as "secret, concealed" (Martin and Tops 1991: 1281). English *hidden force* does its own useful work, however, invoking both occult movements and an intellectual tradition (e.g., Renaissance natural magic).

48 W. Bosch, "Wat is er van de Stille Kracht," *De Telegraaf*, December 21, 1900.

49 Papageno, "Indische Verborgenheden," *Java Bode* 50, no. 197 (August 29, 1901): 1–2; 50, no. 204 (September 7, 1901): 1–2: 50, no. 210 (September 14, 1901): 1–2.

50 Nieuwenhuys (1978: 256) cites a piece in the *Bataviaasch Nieuwsblad* (in 1921, during Couperus's last trip to the Indies) claiming that he drew on "secret dossiers" at Buitenzorg. That Couperus situates his most spectacular example of a hidden force manifestation in a bath house draws from his own uncanny experience: one evening when he went to take a bath, he saw a white specter (Heijne 1996). For speculations about his source, see, for example, Bastet (1987).

51 He may also have heard of more recent incidents. Ackers (2007) argues for events in 1892 involving Jan Jacob Bischoff, then assistant resident in Situbundo. Couperus could have read of these in a spiritualist publication or learned via word of mouth: during Couperus's visit, Valette's brother was Bischoff's (now resident of Batavia) secretary.

52 Another word with *goochel*– as root is *zinsbegoocheling*, hallucination. Van Oudijck vehemently rejects this, insisting "we saw it, we heard it, we felt it, it spat at us. . . . It is easy for people who didn't go through it to deny it" (Couperus 1985 [1900]: 226).

53 Here hidden force blends with guna-guna, an increasingly common trend. Jasper also reviewed the novel ("'n Critiekje," *Soerabaiasch Handelsblad*, February 27, 1901, and February 28, 1901). While admiring its descriptions of life in the Indies and the resident (although finding his fate implausible), he declared it excessively imaginative, terming "the hidden force" "fanaticism among natives."

54 One is recounted on April 20, 1893, in the newspaper *Mataram: Nieuws en Advertentie Blad van Djojka en Omstreken* (vol. 17, no. 32). Ackers (2007: chapter 7) elaborates on this and other incidents involving trees.

55 Malinowski (1948 [1925]) testified to such associations a century ago.

56 A supporter writes, "Stille Kracht . . . a real Indies expression! And because it is so genuinely Indies the Bertoen firm has assumed 'Stille Kracht' as motto" (Marcel 1920).

57 Both from the *Surabaiasch Handelsblad*, the latter on October 22, 1913, and the former on June 30, 1916.

58 Jan ten Brink, "Wat is er van de Stille Kracht?," *De Telegraaf*, December 8, 1900. In response, Willem Bosch, "Wat is er van de Stille Kracht," *De Telegraaf*, December 21, 1900.

59 For magician debunkers, see Jones (2017).

60 Such verbal reconstructions go back to Jean-Eugene Robert-Houdin, the "father of modern magic," who published reconstructions of how Algerian Sufis might produce the dramatic effects for which they were famed (Jones 2010, 2017). However, Schüttpelz and Voss (2020), who call them "substitution trials," trace them to a demonstration of magnetism by Mesmer that aimed to undermine a Bavarian exorcist and, with him, popular beliefs in demons.

61 Hitzka also addresses servants.

62 Few responded directly to Creusesol. Among those who did were Kalff (1925), who complains he ignores Von Kessinger's insistence that he tested the ceiling boards, and Baudisch (1926), who has no problem agreeing that some cases no doubt involved resentful servants, though not all. Both Kalff and Baudisch call Creusesol's suggestion that police dogs could locate perpetrators ridiculous.

63 Compare Geertz (1960: 16–18), who (like my Indonesian dictionary) speaks of *mamedi*, a class of spirits he calls "frighteners," which includes gendruwo. Van Hien treats gendruwo and medi as members of different categories: gendruwo as one of ninety-three "devils" (*duivels*, a translation of Malay *sétan*, a term taken from Islam) or nature spirits (*natuurgeesten*; 1934: vol. 1, 215); medi as a broad category for thirty-four "spooks" (*spoken*) and "hulls" (*schillen*), remnants of once living humans (1934: vol. 1, 249–56). Van Hien divides medi into human and nonhuman specters. The first are ghostly residues of deceased individuals; the second, elementaries. In addition to making use of them to throw stones or spit sirih, they may also be deployed to kill someone or make them ill, or, via guna-guna, lovesick (1934: vol. 2, 250).

64 I suspect *jin* might be the term reformist Muslims used for a variety of named entities.

65 Possibly learned from Javanese members of the Theosophical Society: theosophy became popular among a certain class of Javanese intellectuals (De Tollenaere 1996; Sears 1996). But as his use of categories from Dutch ethnology (e.g., animism) shows, he drew on European sources as well as Javanese interlocutors.

66 I was unable to discover Baudisch's first name or nationality. The preface states he wrote in German and an A. C. Christoffels translated his book. He appears to have been living on Java in Solo (1926: 1).

67 Both also highlight the girl to which the phenomenon seemed directed—Creusesol claims that someone (likely a "prominent native") had designs on her and sought to make the Von Kessingers willing to let her go; Baudisch identifies her as the (unconscious) physical medium responsible for the incident.

68 Baudisch labels the causal agent a poltergeist but treats poltergeists as creations of physical mediums rather than spirits.

69 Kalff may have introduced this (Papageno, "Indische Verborgenheden," *Java Bode*, August 17, 1901). Even Creusesol acknowledges it in passing (1916: 35).

70 Mostly Michiels, though Creusesol declares he knew people who knew the Von Kessingers.

71 *Soerabaiasch Nieuwsblad*, June 29, 1916. A reporter quoting this text even signed himself "Converted" (Bekeerde 1916).

72 What Taussig (2003) terms the "skilled revelation of skilled concealment" as a trick of deductive reason.

73 See Hasskarl (1842) for a description of a journey to the Sumedang region (with no mention of the stones).

74 Susi Johnston, personal communication.

75 Or of efforts by the force or entity to help the girl involved. Some dukun (also balian) chew and then spit substances onto afflicted body parts (Gobée and Adriaans 1959: 1226); perhaps this includes sirih.

INTERLUDE 6. THE MAGIC OF SCIENCE STUDIES

1 Texts like Evans-Pritchard's *Witchcraft* are events. But to flex their paper muscles they need allies: publishers, libraries, bookstores, digitization, citation, discussion, syllabi.

2 Hollis and Lukes (1982); Horton and Finnegan (1973); Wilson (1970). The second volume was devoted entirely to Evans-Pritchard's ethnography and included a contribution by Tambiah (who published a standalone book on magic, science, religion, and rationality in 1990).

3 Augé's African ethnographies have never been translated into English.

4 Part 2 of Latour (1988).

5 In a different modality, his familiarity with the standard anthropological (and modern) treatment of "primitives" inspires the symmetry shaping his concept of the factish.

6 Beautifully elaborated in Pignarre (2023).

7 Stengers explicitly notes that invoking neopagan magic is risky. That she seems to bring it up near the end of the pieces in which it occurs may be a less overt expression of this sentiment.

8 See Pignarre and Stengers (2011) and Stengers (2005a, 2005b, 2018a, 2018b).

EPILOGUE

1 While throughout this book I've referred to Euro-Americans, such habits, affects, and practices are equally prevalent in Australia.

2 Picard 2024 offers an excellent discussion.

3 What follows comes from Stevens and Schmidgall-Tellings (2004: 380–81).

4 Oddly, they render *ilmu sihir* as hypnosis or shamanism, although the same phrase appears under *sihir* as black magic.

5 The glosses for Indonesian are once again Stevens and Schmidgall-Tellings (2004). For English-Indonesian, Echols and Shadily (1975).

6 https://edgeeffects.net/haraway-tsing-plantationocene/, accessed July 28, 2023.

7 Indos and Indies people certainly tried to use the category to fend off sneers (chapter 4).

8 See also Stengers (2018a).

AFTERWORD

1 For instance, the very dubious IQ tests for the "objective" measure of intelligence, which were the object of protests: they would define intelligence through "competencies" privileged at school and resulting in socially unfair and discriminatory politics. Critiques got no help from STS. In 1996, Hilary Rose remembered how painful and politically catastrophic had been the attitude of STS researchers, who would deride the idea that a difference could be made between "good" and "bad" sciences. Their critique of science's authority admitted no such difference (Rose 1996). See also Gould (1981), as well as his defense of the need to recognize that the closure of some controversies cannot be reduced to a successfully negotiated treaty but acknowledged as a "victory of knowledge" (1990).

2 Latour (2010), but already in Latour (1999). Factishes quickly disappeared from Latour's lexicon, but they were a decisive step toward his magnum opus, *An Inquiry into Modes of Existence* (Latour 2013). The analogy between fetishes and factishes has experimental facts for its prototypical example, but this analogy can be extended wherever the modern critical call to "break the fetishes" resounds. Latour (2013) attempts a reparation, a (re)learning of how to honor and take care of the different kinds of "beings" their practices fabricate or "instaurate," beings that Moderns are proud of but systematically mistreat, turning them into war machines against others. It is not the same project as the comparative anthropology of Latour (1993), which reduced the difference between "us" and "them" to the "quantitative only" difference between long and short networks but also proposed to prohibit any opposition against whatever would interfere with the lengthening of networks, that is, the progressive "objectivization of Nature" and the simultaneous "subjectivization of Society" (140). In Latour (2013), the perspective has radically changed: Moderns now must learn to present themselves with what they care for if they want to become capable of *encountering* others in a worthy manner.

3 Even if we follow distinct thinking paths, Karen Barad and I are both indebted to Niels Bohr, the rare example of a physicist who never forgot that a definition presupposes the creation of a relation and cannot be disentangled from what this relation demands.

4 William James participated in this infection, as he played a leading role in the Society for Psychical Research. James knew very well that psychical researchers were at risk of being duped by clever crooks, but he maintained that the multitude

of testimonies about "irregular" facts could not be thrown in the bin, rejected as "impossible," all the more so since what they might imply, still to be explored, was worth the risk.

5   Such disenchanting methods of dismemberment were inaugurated in Paris when, in 1784, experimenters like Franklin and Lavoisier participated in a royal commission charged with the mission to investigate Anton Mesmer's "magnetic fluid," the existence of which explained spectacular cures but also came to be associated with political agitation (the queen and the most humble of her servants, it was said, are equally sensitive to the fluid). The cures were accepted as real, but was their cause "really real"? The commission turned its back on the cures and invented a protocol to test effects of the hypothetical fluids against the hypothesis that these effects could be produced by "imagination." It looks like experimentation, but it is not, because (just like the "placebo" in contemporary medicine) it gives no counter-interpretation to the cures and, as one dissenting member of the commission protested, unilaterally imposes an either-or alternative, excluding, for instance, that the fluid may need imagination in order to operate.

6   Of course, we should not forget another difference: the symbiotic alliance between labs and the growing industrial capitalist network. The "difference that matters" to experimental scientists is also liable to generate what will matter to others, industrial, military, or state powers. Mastering "nature" but also so-called primitive populations who trust "magical" weapons may be obtained without the help of Science.

7   For the distinction between these infrastructures, see the online *Feral Atlas: The More-than-Human Anthropocene,* as well as its complement, Tsing et al. (2024).

8   It was only in 2008 that I "made public" my debt to Starhawk (Stengers 2008). But my interest intensified when I realized that the neopagan witches had been much more than surviving during the hostile eighties and nineties. They were actively and inventively participating in the antiglobalizing movement starting in Seattle in 1999. In 2003, my accomplice Philippe Pignarre published a translation of *Dreaming the Dark*, with a postface I wrote. It was a flop but inspired some precious allies such as Émilie Hache, and the text was available for a reedition in 2015 by a new activist-feminist collection of the Éditions Cambourakis, called "Sorcières." This time it reached its target, and one year later Émilie Hache published in the same collection, under the title "Reclaim," a translation of texts by ecofeminists and by their contemptuous academic prosecutors, which powerfully reactivated a file that French feminists had accepted as closed without even opening it. In the meantime, in 2005, Pignarre and I had succeeded, in *La Sorcellerie capitaliste*, in creating some trouble in the judgment of Marxist readers, presenting neopagan rituals, and the Goddess they make real, in terms not of beliefs but of the pragmatic efficacy which Marx's categories had lost through the stratagems of capitalist sorcery. The fact that Marxists do not take sorcery as a real force meant for us that they had not been able to recognize and design protections against those stratagems, trusting analyses guided by what Wiener calls "reality politics." That those who use these stratagems recognize themselves as sorcerers feels like a moot point from this point of view. It does not make a real difference.

9 See especially appendix A, "The Burning Times: Notes on a Crucial Period of History."

10 See, for example, James (1996: 230–31).

11 For a field study of this magic and those wield it, see Salomonsen (2002).

12 Neopagan witches keep "gravitas" for their rituals when they "close the circle." When they relax, they love to make fun of their own sacred symbols (but "not of somebody else's"). See Starhawk (2002: 202).

References

ABBREVIATIONS

Bijdragen tot de Taal-, Land-, en Volkenkunde (BKI)
Het Recht in Nederlandsch-Indië (RNI)
Indisch weekblad van het recht (IWvhR)
Indische Gids (IG)
Overzicht van de Inheemsche en Chineesch-Maleische Pers (IPO)
Soerabaiasch Nieuwsblad (SN)
Tijdschrift voor Nederlandsch-Indië (TNI)

REFERENCES

A. T. 1912–13. "Het ontworpen Strafwetboek en de occulte delicten." *IWvhR* 42, no. 2520: 165–66.

Abram, David. 1997. *The Spell of the Sensuous: Perception and Language in a More-than-Human World*. New York: Vintage.

Ackers, Coen. 2007. *Het regent steenen: De spirituele erfenis van Nederlands-Indië*. Amsterdam: Bolongara.

Adelante. 1898. "Concubinaat bij the ambtenaren van het binnenlandsch bestuur in Nederlandsch-Indie." *TNI* 2: 304–14.

Alkema, B. 1930. "Iets over Magie." *De Macedoniër. Zendingstijdschrift* 34: 24–28, 65–78, 97–108, 129–36, 177–84, 225–34.

Allen, Jonathan. 2007. "Deceptionists at War." *Cabinet* 26: 65–72.

Alpers, Svetlana. 1983. *The Art of Describing: Dutch Art in the Seventeenth Century*. Chicago: University of Chicago Press.

Asad, Talal. 1973. "Introduction." In *Anthropology and the Colonial Encounter*, edited by Talal Asad, 9–19. New York: Humanities Press.

Asad, Talal. 1986. "The Concept of Cultural Translation in British Anthropology." In *Writing Culture: The Poetics and Politics of Ethnography*, edited by James Clifford and George Marcus, 141–64. Berkeley: University of California Press.

Asad, Talal. 1993. *Genealogies of Religion: Discipline and Reasons of Power in Christianity and Islam*. Baltimore: Johns Hopkins University Press.

Avé, J. B. 1980. "Ethnographical Museums in a Changing World." In *From Field-Case to Show-Case: Research, Acquisition, and Presentation in the Rijksmuseum voor Volken-kunde (National Museum of Ethnology), Leiden*, edited by W. R. van Gulik, H. S. van der Straaten, and G. D. van Wengen, 11–28. Amsterdam: Gieben.

Barad, Karen. 2003. "Posthumanist Performativity: Toward an Understanding of How Matter Comes to Matter." *Signs: Journal of Women in Culture and Society* 28, no. 3: 801–31.

Barad, Karen. 2007. *Meeting the Universe Halfway: Quantum Physics and the Entangle-ment of Matter and Meaning*. Durham, NC: Duke University Press.

Barber, C. Clyde. 1979. *A Balinese-English Dictionary*. 2 vols. Aberdeen: University of Aberdeen Library.

Bastet, Frédéric. 1987. *Louis Couperus: Een biografie*. Amsterdam: E. M. Querido.

Bastiaans, Ch. J. 1970. *"Sêram": Langs de grenzen van een andere wereld*. Groningen: Jacobs.

Baudisch, A. 1926. *Het probleem van de "stille kracht."* Weltevreden: G. Kolff.

Beekman, E. M. 1996. *Troubled Pleasures: Dutch Colonial Literature from the East Indies, 1600–1950*. Oxford: Clarendon.

Bekeerde. 1916. "Oostersche mysteriën." *De Reflector* 1, no. 30: 714–16.

Bekker, Balthasar. 1691–93. *De betoverde wereld*. Amsterdam: Daniel van den Dalen. https://www.dbnl.org/tekst/bekk001beto01_01/.

Benjamin, Walter. 1969. "The Task of the Translator." In *Illuminations*, edited by Han-nah Arendt, translated by Harry Zohn, 69–82. New York: Schocken.

Bennett, Tony. 1995. *The Birth of the Museum: History, Theory, Politics*. London: Routledge.

Berg, C. C. 1936. "Verfijnde vormen van tooverij in de Hindoe-Javaansche maatschap-pij." In *Hekserij in de missielanden. Nederlandsche verslagen der XIVe Missiologische week van Leuven*, 67–108. Brussels: Boekhandel-Uitgeverij Universum.

Berg, L. W. C. van den. 1901. "De Mohammedaansche vorsten in Nederlandsch-Indië." BKI 6, no. 9: 1–80.

Bezemer, T. J. 1908. *Onze Oost. II: Iets over den Inlander en zijn zieleleven*. Amsterdam: S. L. Van Looy.

Bhabha, Homi K. 1994. *The Location of Culture*. London: Routledge.

Bijblad op het Staatsblad van Nederlandsch-Indië. 1908. Part 41, no. 6565–740. Batavia: Landsdrukkerij.

Blaser, Mario, and Marisol de la Cadena. 2017. "The Uncommons: An Introduction." *Anthropologica* 59, no. 2: 185–93.

Blavatsky, Helena Petrovna. 1881. "Stone Showers." *The Theosophist* 2, no. 11: 232–33.

Blécourt, Willem de. 1989. "Heksengeloof: Toverij en religie in Nederland tussen 1890 en 1940." *Sociologische gids* 36: 245–66.

Blécourt, Willem de. 1990. *Termen van toverij: De veranderende betekenis van toverij in Noordoost-Nederland tussen de 16de en 20ste eeuw*. Nijmegen: SUN.

Blécourt, Willem de. 1991. "Four Centuries of Frisian Witchdoctors." In *Witchcraft in the Netherlands: From the Fourteenth to the Twentieth Century*, edited by Marijke Gijswijt-Hofstra and Willem Frijhoff, 157–66. Rotterdam: Universitaire Pers.

Bloembergen, Marieke. 2009. *De geschiedenis van de politie in Nederlands-Indië: Uit zorg en angst*. Amsterdam: Boom.

Bloor, David. 1976. *Knowledge and Social Imagery*. London: Routledge & Kegan Paul.

Blussé, Leonard. 1986. *Strange Company: Chinese Settlers, Mestizo Women, and the Dutch in VOC Batavia*. Dordrecht: Foris.

Boas, Franz. 1974. "The Principles of Ethnological Classification." In *The Shaping of American Anthropology, 1883–1911: A Franz Boas Reader*, edited by George W. Stocking Jr., 61–67. New York: Basic Books.

Boomgaard, Peter. 1995. "Sacred Trees and Haunted Forests in Indonesia, Particularly Java, Nineteenth and Twentieth Centuries." In *Asian Perceptions of Nature: A Critical Approach*, edited by Ole Bruun and Arne Kalland, 47–62. Chippenham, UK: Curzon.

Bosch, F. D. K. 1937/38. "The Royal Batavian Society of Arts and Sciences." *Bulletin of the Colonial Institute of Amsterdam* 1: 116–24.

Bowker, Geoffrey C., and Susan Leigh Star. 1999. *Sorting Things Out: Classification and Its Consequences*. Cambridge, MA: MIT Press.

Brantlinger, Patrick. 1988. *Rule of Darkness: British Literature and Imperialism, 1830–1914*. Ithaca, NY: Cornell University Press.

Brinkgreve, Francine, and David Stuart-Fox. 2007. "Collections after Colonial Conflict: Badung and Tabanan 1906–2006." In *Colonial Collections Revisited*, edited by Pieter ter Keurs, 145–85. Leiden: CNWS.

Britten, Emma Hardinge. 1884. *Nineteenth Century Miracles, or Spirits and Their Work in Every Country of the Earth*. New York: Lovell.

Brook, Timothy. 2008. *Vermeer's Hat: The Seventeenth Century and the Dawn of the Global World*. New York: Bloomsbury.

Bubandt, Nils. 2017. "Haunted Geologies: Spirits, Stones, and the Necropolitics of the Anthropocene." In *Arts of Living on a Damaged Planet: Ghosts*, edited by Anna Tsing, Heather Swanson, Elaine Gan, and Nils Bubandt, 121–41. Minneapolis: University of Minnesota Press.

Buck-Morss, Susan. 2000. "Hegel and Haiti." *Critical Inquiry* 26, no. 4: 821–65.

Buddingh, S. A. 1859. *Neêrlands-Oost-Indië: Reizen over Java*. Rotterdam: M. Wijt en Zonen.

Budiarti, Hari. 2005. "The Sulawesi Collections: Missionaries, Chiefs, and Military Expeditions." In *Indonesia: The Discovery of the Past*, edited by Endang Sri Hardiarti and Pieter ter Keurs, 160–71. Amsterdam: KIT.

Budiarti, Hari. 2007. "Taking and Returning Objects in a Colonial Context: Tracing the Collections Acquired during the Bone-Gowa Military Expeditions." In *Colonial Collections Revisited*, edited by Pieter ter Keurs, 123–44. Leiden: CNWS.

Buys, M. 1891. *Batavia, Buitenzorg, en de Preanger: Gids voor bezoekers en toeristen*. Batavia: G. Kolff.

Callon, Michel. 1986. "Some Elements of a Sociology of Translation: Domestication of the Scallops and the Fishermen of St. Brieuc Bay." In *Power, Action, and Belief: A New Sociology of Knowledge?*, edited by John Law, 196–223. London: Routledge.

Cannon, Walter B. 1942. "'Voodoo' Death." *American Anthropologist* 42, no. 2: 169–81.

Chakrabarty, Dipesh. 2000. *Provincializing Europe: Postcolonial Thought and Historical Difference*. Princeton, NJ: Princeton University Press.

Chamberlayne, Richard. 1698. *Lithobolia, or The Stone-Throwing Devil Being an Exact and True Account (by Way of Journal) of the Various Actions of Infernal Spirits, or (Devils Incarnate) Witches, or Both, and the Great Disturbance and Amazement They Gave to George Waltons Family, at a Place Call'd Great Island in the Province of New-Hantshire in New-England*. London: E. Whitlook. https://quod.lib.umich.edu/e/eebo/A31609.0001.001.

Childers, James Saxon. 1933. *From Siam to Suez*. London: D. Appleton.

Christ, Carol P. 1979. "Why Women Need the Goddess: Phenomenological, Psychological, and Political Reflections." In *Womanspirit Rising: A Feminist Reader in Religion*, edited by Carol P. Christ and Judith Plaskow, 273–87. San Francisco: Harper and Row.

Cohn, Bernard. 1987. *An Anthropologist among the Historians and Other Essays*. Oxford: Oxford University Press.

Connor, Linda. 1982. "The Unbounded Self: Balinese Therapy in Theory and Practice." In *Cultural Conceptions of Mental Health and Therapy*, edited by J. Marsella and Geoffrey M. White, 251–67. Dordrecht: D. Reidel.

Connor, Linda, Patsy Asch, and Timothy Asch. 1986. *Jero Tapakan: Balinese Healer: An Ethnographic Film Monograph*. Cambridge: Cambridge University Press.

Conrad, Joseph. 1977 [1898]. "Karain: A Memory." In *Tales of Unrest*, 13–56. New York: Penguin Books.

Couperus, Louis. 1924. *Eastward*. Translated by J. Menzies-Wilson and C. C. Crispin. London: Hurst and Blackett.

Couperus, Louis. 1985 [1900]. *The Hidden Force*. Translated by Alexander Teixeira de Mattos, and revised and edited by E. M. Beekman. Amherst: University of Massachusetts Press.

Couperus, Louis. 1996. *De stille kracht*. Huizen: Pandora Pockets.

Creusesol. 1916. *Bestaat de stille kracht?* Semarang: G. C. T. van Dorp.

Damsté, Henri T. 1924. "Balische splinters: 22: Nang Moekanis, de wonderdokter." *Koloniaal Tijdschrift* 13, no. 6: 650–55.

Daum, P. A. 1964 [1889]. *Goena-goena: Een geschiedenis van stille kracht*. Amsterdam: E. M. Querido.

Daum, P. A. 1997 [1893]. *Nummer Elf: Oorspronkelijke Indische roman*. 's-Gravenhage: Thomas & Eras.

Davidson, Jane P., and Christopher John Duffin. 2012. "Stones and Spirits." *Folklore* 123, no. 1: 99–109.

Davies, Owen. 2012. *Magic: A Very Short Introduction*. Oxford: Oxford University Press.

Davies, Owen, and Willem de Blécourt. 2004. "Introduction: Beyond the Witch Trials." In *Beyond the Witch Trials: Witchcraft and Magic in Enlightenment Europe*, edited by Owen Davies and Willem de Blécourt, 1–8. Manchester: Manchester University Press.

Debaise, Didier. 2017. *Nature as Event: The Lure of the Possible*. Translated by Michael Halewood. Durham, NC: Duke University Press.

De K. v. W. 1907. "Goena-Goena." *Het toekomstig leven* 11, no. 12: 192–95.

De la Cadena, Marisol. 2010. "Indigenous Cosmopolitics in the Andes: Conceptual Reflections beyond 'Politics.'" *Cultural Anthropology* 25, no. 2: 334–70.

De la Cadena, Marisol. 2015. *Earth-Beings: Ecologies of Practice across Andean Worlds.* Durham, NC: Duke University Press.

De la Cadena, Marisol. 2021. "Not Knowing: In the Presence of . . ." In *Experimenting with Ethnography: A Companion to Analysis,* edited by Andrea Ballestero and Brit Ross Winthereik, 246–56. Durham, NC: Duke University Press.

De Leeuw, Hendrik. 1931. *Crossroads of the Java Sea.* New York: Jonathan Cape & Harrison Smith.

Despret, Vinciane. 2004. "The Body We Care For: Figures of AnthropoZooGenesis." *Body & Society* 10, nos. 2–3: 111–34.

Dissel, J. A. van. 1870. "Eenige bijgeloovigheden en gewoonten der Javanen." *TNI* 4, no. 1: 270–79.

Doel, H. W. van den. 1994. *De stille macht: Het Europese binnenlands bestuur op Java en Madoera 1808–1942.* Amsterdam: Bert Bakker.

Dornseiff, J. J. 1853. "Een vreemd vooral te Sumadang, in de Preanger-regentschappen, geschied." *Biang-Lala* 2, no. 1: 183–86.

Du Perron, E. 1984 [1935]. *Country of Origin.* Translated by Francis Bulhoff and Elizabeth Daverman. Edited by E. M. Beekman. Amherst: University of Massachusetts Press.

During, Simon. 2004. *Modern Enchantments: The Cultural Power of Secular Magic.* Cambridge, MA: Harvard University Press.

Durkheim, Émile. 1995 [1912]. *The Elementary Forms of Religious Life.* Translated by Karen E. Fields. New York: Free Press.

Duuren, David van. 1998. *The Kris: An Earthly Approach to a Cosmic Symbol.* Wijk and Aalberg: Pictures.

Duuren, David van. 2002. *Krisses: A Critical Bibliography.* Wijk en Aalberg: Pictures.

Duuren, David van. 2009. "Introduction." In *The Javanese Kris,* by Isaäc Groneman, 13–38. Leiden: C. Zwartenkot.

Echols, John M., and Hassan Shadily. 1975. *Indonesian-English Dictionary.* Ithaca, NY: Cornell University Press.

Echols, John M., and Hassan Shadily. 1992. *Kamus Indonesia-Inggris,* 3rd ed. Jakarta: Gramedia.

Elias, Norbert. 1978. *The History of Table Manners.* New York: Pantheon.

Ellen, Roy F. 1976. "The Development of Anthropology and Colonial Policy in the Netherlands, 1800–1960." *Journal of the History of the Behavioural Sciences* 12: 303–24.

Ellen, Roy. 1993. "Introduction." In *Understanding Witchcraft and Sorcery in Southeast Asia,* edited by C. W. Watson and Roy Ellen, 1–26. Honolulu: University of Hawai'i Press.

Encyclopaedie van Nederlandsch-Indië. 1917–35. 2nd ed. 7 vols. 's-Gravenhage: Martinus Nijhoff.

Ernawati, Wahyu. 2005. "The Lombok Treasure." In *Indonesia: The Discovery of the Past,* edited by Endang Sri Hardiarti and Pieter ter Keurs, 146–59. Amsterdam: KIT.

Ernawati, Wahyu. 2007. "The Lombok Treasure." In *Colonial Collections Revisited,* edited by Pieter ter Keurs, 186–202. Leiden: CNWS.

Evans-Pritchard, Edward Evan. 1937. *Witchcraft, Oracles, and Magic among the Azande.* Oxford: Clarendon.

Fabian, Johannes. 1983. *Time and the Other: How Anthropology Makes Its Object.* New York: Columbia University Press.

Fabricius, Johann. 1948. *Eiland der demonen: Roman over Bali.* Amsterdam: De Muiderkring.

Farquhar, Judith. 1994. *Knowing Practice: The Clinical Encounter in Chinese Medicine.* Boulder, CO: Westview.

Fasseur, Ceez. 1993. *De Indologen: Ambtenaren voor de Oost 1825–1950.* Amsterdam: Bert Bakker.

Fasseur, Ceez. 1995. *De weg naar het paradijs en andere Indische geschiedenissen.* Amsterdam: Bert Bakker.

Favret-Saada, Jeanne. 1980. *Deadly Words: Witchcraft in the Bocage.* Cambridge: Cambridge University Press.

Favret-Saada, Jeanne. 2012. "Being Affected." *HAU* 2, no. 1: 435–45.

Ferzacca, Steve. 2001. *Healing the Modern in a Javanese City.* Durham, NC: Carolina Academic Press.

Fields, Karen E. 1982. "Political Contingencies of Witchcraft in Colonial Central Africa: Culture and the State in Marxist Theory." *Canadian Journal of African Studies* 16, no. 3: 567–93.

Fox, Richard. 2016. "The Meaning of Life, or How to Do Things with Letters." In *The Materiality and Efficacy of Balinese Letters*, edited by Richard Fox and Annette Hornbacher, 23–53. Leiden: Brill.

Fox, Richard. 2018. *More than Words: Transforming Script, Agency, and Collective Life in Bali.* Ithaca, NY: Cornell University Press.

Frazer, Sir James George. 1922. *The Golden Bough: A Study in Magic and Religion.* New York: Macmillan.

Furnivall, J. S. 1944. *Netherlands India: A Study of Plural Economy.* New York: Macmillan.

Fussell, Paul. 1980. *Abroad: British Literary Traveling between the Wars.* New York: Oxford University Press.

Geerken, Horst H. 2010. *A Gecko for Luck: 18 Years in Indonesia.* Norderstedt: Books on Demand.

Geertz, Clifford. 1960. *The Religion of Java.* Chicago: University of Chicago Press.

Geertz, Hildred. 1975. "An Anthropology of Religion and Magic, I." *Journal of Interdisciplinary History* 6, no. 1: 71–89.

Gerstäcker, Friedrich. 1853. *Narrative of a Journey Round the World: Comprising a Winter-Passage across the Andes to Chili: With a Visit to the Gold Regions of California and Australia, the South Sea Islands, Java, Etc.* New York: Harper.

Gerstäcker, Friedrich. 1855. "Javaansche schetsen." *BKI* 3, no. 4: 413–91.

Gerstäcker, Friedrich. 1871. "Das gespenstige Steinwerfen." *Die Gartenlaube* 24: 397–99.

Gids voor den bezoeker van de schatkamer. 1917. Batavia: Bataviaasch Genootschap van Kunsten en Wetenschappen.

Gids voor den bezoeker van de schatkammer. 1928. Batavia: Ruygrok.

Gijswijt-Hofstra, Marijke. 1991. "Six Centuries of Witchcraft in the Netherlands: Themes, Outlines, and Interpretations." In *Witchcraft in the Netherlands: From the Fourteenth to the Twentieth Century*, edited by M. Gijswijt-Hofstra and W. Frijhoff, 1–36. Rotterdam: Universitaire Pers.

Gijswijt-Hofstra, Marijke. 1999. "Witchcraft after the Witch-Trials." In *Witchcraft and Magic in Europe*, vol. 5: *The Eighteenth and Nineteenth Centuries*, edited by B. Ankarloo and S. Clark, 95–190. Philadelphia: University of Pennsylvania Press.

Gilbert, Elizabeth. 2006. *Eat, Pray, Love: One Woman's Search for Everything across Italy, India, and Indonesia*. New York: Viking.

Gluckman, Max. 1963. "The Magic of Despair." In *Order and Rebellion in Tribal Africa*, 137–45. London: Cohen & West.

Gobée, E., and C. Adriaans. 1957–65. *Ambtelijke adviezen van C. Snouck Hurgronje*. 3 vols. 's-Gravenhage: Martinus Nijhoff.

Gorer, Geoffrey. 1936. *Bali and Angkor, or Looking at Life and Death*. Boston: Little, Brown.

Gorer, Geoffrey. 1938. *Himalayan Village: An Account of the Lepchas of Sikkim*. London: M. Joseph.

Gould, Stephen J. 1981. *The Mismeasure of Man*. New York: W. W. Norton.

Gould, Stephen J. 1990. "The Power of Narrative." In *An Urchin in the Storm: Essays about Books and Ideas*, 75–92. New York: Penguin.

Gramsci, Antonio. 1971. *Selections from the Prison Notebooks*. New York: International Publishers.

Gray, Natasha. 2005. "Independent Spirits: The Politics of Policing Anti-Witchcraft Movements in Colonial Ghana, 1908–1927." *Journal of Religion in Africa* 35, no. 2: 139–58.

Groneman, Isaäc. 2009. *The Javanese Kris*. Leiden: C. Zwartenkot.

Groot, Hans. 2009. *Van Batavia naar Weltevreden: Het Bataviaasch Genootschap van Kunsten en Wetenschappen 1778–1867*. Leiden: KITLV.

Habbema, J. 1919. "Bestrijding van het bijgeloof in Indië." *Koloniaal Tijdschrift* 8, no. 1: 313–15.

Haraway, Donna. 1991. "Situated Knowledges: The Science Question in Feminism and the Privilege of Partial Perspective." In *Simians, Cyborgs, and Women: The Reinvention of Nature*, 183–201. New York: Routledge.

Haraway, Donna. 1997. "Modest_Witness@Second_Millennium." In *Modest_Witness@Second_Millennium.FemaleMan©_Meets_OncoMouse™*, 23–45. New York: Routledge.

Hardin, Terri, ed. 1995. *Supernatural Tales from around the World*. New York: Barnes and Noble Books.

Hart, Keith. 1986. "Heads or Tails? Two Sides of the Coin." *Man* 21, no. 4: 637–56.

Hasskarl, J. K. 1842. "Soemadang: Op de grenzen van het district Lebak, in de Residentie Bantam." *TNI* 4, no. 2: 126–31.

Hegel, Georg W. F. 1991. *The Philosophy of History*. Translated by J. Sibree. Buffalo, NY: Prometheus.

Heijne, Bas. 1996. "Angst en schoonheid: Over Louis Couperus en Indië." Leiden: Louis Couperus Genootschap.

Hekmeijer, F. C. 1918. *Wetboek van strafrecht voor Nederlandsche Indië*, 2nd ed. Batavia: G. Kolff.

Hekserij in de missielanden: Nederlandsche verslagen der XIVe Missiologische week van Leuven. 1937. Brussels: Boekhandel-Uitgeverij Universum.

Hermans, E. G. 1925. *Gezondheidsleer voor Nederlandsch-Indië: Een boek voor ieder die naar Indie gaat, of daar woont.* Amsterdam: J. M. Meulenhoff.

Hien, H. A. van. 1896. *De Javaansche geestenwereld.* Semarang: G. C. T. van Dorp.

Hien, H. A. van. 1924. *De formulieren voor de stille kracht.* Weltevreden: Boekhandel Visser.

Hien, H. A. van. 1934. *De Javaansche geestenwereld en die betrekking, die tusschen de geesten en de zinnelijke wereld bestaat,* 6th ed. 3 vols. Batavia: G. Kolff.

Hirsch, A. S. 1919. *Geschiedenis van het wetboek van strafrecht voor Nederlandsche-Indië.* Batavia: G. Kolff.

Hitzka. 1930. "Over de Magie in Indië." *Onze Stem* 11: 1073–76, 1097–100, 1114–17, 1139–42, 1161–64, 1210–13, 1229–32, 1258–62, 1282–85, 1301–4.

Hives, Frank, and Gascoigne Lumley. 1930. *Ju-Ju and Justice in Nigeria.* London: Bodley Head.

Hoare, Quintin, and Geoffrey Nowell Smith. 1971. "Preface." In *Selections from the Prison Notebooks of Antonio Gramsci,* edited and translated by Quintin Hoare and Geoffrey Nowell Smith, xi–xv. New York: International Publishers.

Hoekendijk, C. J. 1920. *De toovenaar der Soendalanden.* Hoenderloo: Stichting Hoenderloo.

Hoëvell, W. R. van. 1849. *Reis over Java, Madura en Bali in het midden van 1847,* vol. 1. Amsterdam: P. N. van Kampen.

Hoëvell, W. R. van. 1850. "Varia." *TNI* 12, no. 2: 374–76.

Hollis, Martin, and Steven Lukes, eds. 1982. *Rationality and Relativism.* Cambridge, MA: MIT Press.

Horton, Robin, and Ruth Finnegan, eds. 1973. *Modes of Thought: Essays on Thinking in Western and Non-Western Society.* London: Faber & Faber.

James, William. 1979. *The Will to Believe and Other Essays in Popular Philosophy.* Cambridge, MA: Harvard University Press.

James, William. 1996. *Some Problems of Philosophy: A Beginning of an Introduction to Philosophy.* Lincoln: University of Nebraska Press.

Jasper, J. E. 1904. "Godsdienst, bijgeloof en adat." *Weekblad voor Indië* 1, no. 11: 129–32.

Jasper, J. E. 1932. "Van doekoens." *Pharmaceutisch-Tijdschrift voor Nederlandsch-Indië* 9: 34–38.

Jasper, J. E., and Mas Pirngadie. 1912–30. *De Inlandsche kunstnijverheid in Nederlandsch-Indië* 's-Gravenhage: Mouton.

Johnson, Paul Christopher. 2011. "An Atlantic Genealogy of 'Spirit Possession.'" *Comparative Studies in Society and History* 53, no. 2: 393–425.

Johnson, Paul Christopher. 2014a. "Introduction: Spirits and Things in the Making of the Afro-Atlantic World." In *Spirited Things: The Work of "Possession" in Afro-Atlantic Religions,* edited by Paul Christopher Johnson, 1–22. Chicago: University of Chicago Press.

Johnson, Paul Christopher. 2014b. "Towards an Atlantic Genealogy of 'Spirit Possession.'" In *Spirited Things: The Work of "Possession" in Afro-Atlantic Religions,* edited by Paul Christopher Johnson, 23–46. Chicago: University of Chicago Press.

Jones, Graham M. 2010. "Modern Magic and the War on Miracles in French Colonial Culture." *Comparative Studies in Society and History* 52, no. 1: 66–99.

Jones, Graham M. 2017. *Magic's Reason: An Anthropology of Analogy*. Chicago: University of Chicago Press.

Juynboll, H. H. 1912. *Catalogus van 'sRijks Ethnographisch Museum*, vol. 7: *Bali en Lombok*. Leiden: E. J. Brill.

Kalff, Samuel. 1925. "Indisch Occultisme." *Vragen van den Dag* 40: 444–57.

Kam, Garrett. 2019. *Balinese Keris: Metal, Masculinity, Magic*. Leiden: C. Zwartenkot.

Karchmer, Eric I. 2022. *Prescriptions for Virtuosity: The Postcolonial Struggle of Chinese Medicine*. New York: Fordham University Press.

Keane, Webb. 2007. *Christian Moderns: Freedom and Fetish in the Mission Encounter*. Berkeley: University of California Press.

Keller, Evelyn Fox. 1983. *A Feeling for the Organism: The Life and Work of Barbara McClintock*. New York: Henry Holt.

Kenyatta, Jomo. 1956 [1938]. *Facing Mount Kenya: The Tribal Life of the Gikuyu*. London: Secker & Warburg.

Kerremans, W. 1923. "Over de psychische mutaties bij Europeanen in de tropen." *Vragen van den Dag* 38: 886–91.

Keurs, Pieter ter. 2009. "Collecting in the Colony." *Indonesia and the Malay World* 37, no. 108: 147–61.

Kijdsmeir, Caesar. 1930. *Goena Goena*. Batavia: D'Oriënt.

Kinderen, T. H. der. 1873. *De Algemeene politiestrafreglementen voor de Europeanen en voor de inlanders in Nederlandsch-Indië*. Batavia: Ogilvie.

Knebel, J. 1898a. "Amulettes Javanaise." *Tijdschrift voor Indische Taal-, Land-, en Volkenkunde* 40: 497–507.

Knebel, J. 1898b. "À propos d'armes et d'autre objets désignés par les javanais sous les noms de kjai, njai, poen et si, kaämpoehan et kasiat: Croyances populaires et traditions." *Tijdschrift van het Bataviaasch Genootschap* 40: 239–86.

Koentjaraningrat. 1985. *Javanese Culture*. Singapore: Oxford University Press.

Kohlbrugge, J. H. F. 1907. *Blikken in het zieleleven van den Javaan en zijner overheerschers*. Leiden: E. J. Brill.

Koopmans van Boekeren, R. 1872. "Het geheimzinnig steenen werpen." *Elk wat wils: Kennis en Kunst*, 46–47, 54–56.

Koot, W. D. 1905. *Het concubinaat*. Soerabaja: Thies & Umbgrove.

Kreemer, J. 1888. "Iets over djimat's." *Mededeelingen van wege het Nederlandsche Zendelinggenootschap* 32: 349–54.

Kreps, Christina. 2004. "The Idea of 'Pusaka' as an Indigenous Form of Cultural Heritage Preservation." In *Performing Objects: Museums, Material Culture and Performance in Southeast Asia*, edited by Fiona Kerlogue, 1–14. London: Horniman Museum.

Kruyt, Albertus C. 1906. *Het animisme in den Indischen archipel*. 's-Gravenhage: Martinus Nijhoff.

Kruyt, Albertus C. 1918. "Measa: Eene bijdrage tot het dynamisme der Bare'e-sprekende Toradja's en enkele omwonende volken." *BKI* 74, no. 1: 233–60.

Kuitenbrouwer, Maarten. 2014. *Dutch Scholarship in the Age of Empire and Beyond*. Leiden: Brill.

Kuriyama, Shigehisa. 2002. *The Expressiveness of the Body and the Divergence of Greek and Chinese Medicine.* New York: Zone.

Langwick, Stacey A. 2011. *Bodies, Politics, and African Healing: The Matter of Maladies in Tanzania.* Bloomington: Indiana University Press.

Latour, Bruno. 1987. *Science in Action: How to Follow Scientists and Engineers through Society.* Cambridge, MA: Harvard University Press.

Latour, Bruno. 1988. *The Pasteurization of France.* Translated by Alan Sheridan and John Law. Cambridge, MA: Harvard University Press.

Latour, Bruno. 1990. "Drawing Things Together." In *Representation in Scientific Practice,* edited by Michael Lynch and Steve Woolgar, 19–68. Cambridge, MA: MIT Press.

Latour, Bruno. 1993. *We Have Never Been Modern.* Translated by Catherine Porter. Cambridge, MA: Harvard University Press.

Latour, Bruno. 1999. *Pandora's Hope: Essays on the Reality of Science Studies.* Cambridge, MA: Harvard University Press.

Latour, Bruno. 2004. "How to Talk about the Body? The Normative Dimension of Science Studies." *Body and Society* 10, nos. 2–3: 205–29.

Latour, Bruno. 2005a. "From Realpolitik to Dingpolitik, or How to Make Things Public." In *Making Things Public: Atmospheres of Democracy,* edited by Bruno Latour and Peter Weibel, 14–43. Cambridge, MA: MIT Press.

Latour, Bruno. 2005b. *Reassembling the Social: An Introduction to Actor-Network-Theory.* Oxford: Oxford University Press.

Latour, Bruno. 2010. *On the Modern Cult of the Factish Gods.* First chapter translated by Catherine Porter and Heather MacLean. Durham, NC: Duke University Press.

Latour, Bruno. 2013. *An Inquiry into Modes of Existence: An Anthropology of the Moderns.* Translated by Catherine Porter. Cambridge, MA: Harvard University Press.

Latour, Bruno, and Peter Weibel. 2020. "Seven Objections against Landing on Earth." In *Critical Zones: The Science and Politics of Landing on Earth,* edited by Bruno Latour and Peter Weibel, 12–19. Cambridge, MA: MIT Press.

Latour, Bruno, and Steve Woolgar. 1986 [1979]. *Laboratory Life: The Construction of Scientific Facts.* Princeton, NJ: Princeton University Press.

Law, John. 2015. "What's Wrong with a One-World World?" *Distinktion: Journal of Social Theory* 16, no. 1: 126–39.

Leavitt, John. 2015. "Words and Worlds: Ethnography and Theories of Translation." In *Translating Worlds: The Epistemological Space of Translation,* edited by Carlo Severi and William F. Hanks, 259–94. Chicago: HAU Books.

Lemaire, W. L. G. 1934. *Het Wetboek van strafrecht voor Nederlandsch-Indië vergeleken met het Nederlandse Wetboek van strafrecht.* Batavia: Noordhoof-Kolff.

Lesquillier, Nicolaas Willem. 1934. *Het adatdelictenrecht in de magische wereldbeschouwing.* Leiden: Boek-en Steendrukkerij Eduard Ijdo.

Levack, Brian P. 1999. "The Decline and End of Witchcraft Prosecutions." In *Witchcraft and Magic in Europe,* vol. 5: *The Eighteenth and Nineteenth Centuries,* edited by Bengt Ankarloo and Stuart Clark, 1–91. Philadelphia: University of Pennsylvania Press.

Lévi-Strauss, Claude. 1963. "The Sorcerer and His Magic." Translated by Claire Jacobson and Brooke Grundfest Schoepf. In *Structural Anthropology*, 167–85. New York: Basic Books.

Lévi-Strauss, Claude. 1987 [1950]. *Introduction to the Work of Marcel Mauss*. Translated by Felicity Baker. London: Routledge & Kegan Paul.

Lloyd, Genevieve. 1993. *The Man of Reason: "Male" and "Female" in Western Philosophy*, 2nd ed. Minneapolis: University of Minnesota Press.

Locher-Scholten, Elsbeth. 1994. "Orientalism and the Rhetoric of the Family: Javanese Servants in European Household Manuals and Children's Fiction." *Indonesia* 58: 19–39.

Locher-Scholten, Elsbeth. 2002. "State Violence and the Police in Colonial Indonesia circa 1920." In *Roots of Violence in Indonesia: Contemporary Violence in Historical Perspective*, edited by F. Colombijn and J. T. Lindblad, 81–104. Leiden: KITLV.

Lovric, Barbara J. A. 1987. "Rhetoric and Reality: The Hidden Nightmare. Myth and Magic as Representations and Reverberations of Morbid Realities." PhD dissertation, University of Sydney.

Luongo. Katherine. 2011. *Witchcraft and Colonial Rule in Kenya, 1900–1955*. New York: Cambridge University Press.

Macknick, Stephen, and Susana Martinez-Conde, with Sandra Blakeslee. 2011. *Sleights of Mind: What the Neuroscience of Magic Reveals about Our Brains*. London: Profile.

Maijer, L. T. 1918. *De Javaan als doekoen: Een ethnografische bijdrage*. Weltevreden: G. Kolff.

Malinowski, Bronislaw. 1948 [1925]. "Magic, Science, and Religion." In *Magic, Science and Religion and Other Essays*, 1–71. New York: Free Press.

Malinowski, Bronislaw. 1956 [1938]. "Introduction." In *Facing Mount Kenya: The Tribal Life of the Gikuyu*, by Jomo Kenyatta, vii–xiv. London: Secker & Warburg.

Malinowski, Bronislaw. 1961 [1922]. *Argonauts of the Western Pacific*. New York: E. P. Dutton.

Marcel, Jacob. 1920. "Stille kracht." *De Reflector* 5, no. 1: 14–15.

Marees, Pieter de. 1912 [1602]. *Beschriyvinghe ende historische verhael van het Gout Koninckrijck van Gunea*. 's-Gravenhage: Martinus Nijhoff. https://www.dbnl.org/tekst/mare014besc02_01/.

Marees, Pieter de. 1987 [1602]. *Description and Historical Account of the Gold Kingdom of Guinea*. Oxford: Oxford University Press.

Marle, A. van. 1951–52. "De groep der Europeanen in Nederlands-Indië, iets over ontstaan en groei." *Indonesië* 5: 97–121, 314–41, 481–507.

Martin, W., and G. A. J. Tops. 1991. *Van Dale: Groot woordenboek Nederlands-Engels*. Utrecht: Van Dale Lexicografie.

Marx, Karl. 1973. *Grundrisse*. Translated by Martin Nicolaus. London: Penguin.

Mauss, Marcel. 1972. *A General Theory of Magic*. Translated by Robert Brain. New York: W. W. Norton.

McCracken, Grant. 2005. *Culture and Consumption II: Markets, Meaning, and Brand Management*. Bloomington: Indiana University Press.

Meijer, D. H. 1935. "Bijgeloof in dienst van de politie en de misdadigers." *Djawa* 15: 107–22.

Ming, Hanneke. 1983. "Barracks-Concubinage in the Indies, 1887–1920." *Indonesia* 35: 65–93.

Mitchell, W. J. T. 2005. *What Do Pictures Want? The Lives and Loves of Images.* Chicago: University of Chicago Press.

Moeran, Brian. 2017. "Fashion Magazines and Fashion as a System of Magic." *Anthropology Today* 33, no. 2: 3–9.

Mol, Annemarie. 1999. "Ontological Politics: A Word and Some Questions." *Sociological Review* 47, no. 1: 74–89.

Mol, Annemarie. 2002. *The Body Multiple: Ontology in Medical Practice.* Durham, NC: Duke University Press.

Montgomery, Scott. 2002. *Science in Translation.* Chicago: University of Chicago Press.

Moore, Jason W. 2010. "'Amsterdam Is Standing on Norway' Part II: The Global North Atlantic in the Ecological Revolution of the Long Seventeenth Century." *Journal of Agrarian Change* 10, no. 2: 118–227.

Muecke, Stephen. 2021. "Whitefella Magic: A 'Posthumanist' Take on the *Dark Emu* Debate." *Overland Magazine*, August 10.

Multatuli. 1967 [1860]. *Max Havelaar, or The Coffee Auctions of the Dutch Trading Company.* Translated by Roy Edwards. Amherst: University of Massachusetts Press.

Nietzsche, Friederich. 1974 [1887]. *The Gay Science.* Translated by Walter Kaufmann. New York: Random House.

Nietzsche, Friederich. 1979 [1873]. "On Truth and Lies in a Nonmoral Sense." In *Philosophy and Truth: Selections from Nietzsche's Notebooks of the Early 1870s*, edited and translated by Daniel Breazeale, 79–100. Amherst, NY: Humanity Books.

Nieuwenhuys, Rob. 1978. *Oost-Indische spiegel: Wat Nederlandsche schrijvers en dichters over Indonesië hebben geschreven, vanaf de eerste jaren der compagnie tot op heden.* Amsterdam: Querido.

Onghokham. 1978. "The Inscrutable and the Paranoid: An Investigation into the Sources of the Brotodiningrat Affair." In *Southeast Asian Transitions: Approaches through Social History*, edited by Ruth T. McVey, 112–57. New Haven, CT: Yale University Press.

Ooggetuige, Een. 1898. "Spiritisme onder de Javanen (Geschreven voor de Locomotief)." *Insulinde* 3, no. 31: 272–73.

Ossenbruggen, F. D. E. van. 1916. "Het primitieve denken zooals dit zich uit voornamelijk in pokkengebruiken op Java en elders." *BKI* 71: 1–370.

Ossenbruggen, F. D. E. van. 1926. "Het magisch denken van de Inlander." *IG* 48, no. 1: 289–303.

P. 1894."Talisman om den eed krachteloos te maken." *IWvhR* 32, no. 1592: 209.

Pargiter, Frederick Eden. 1923. *Centenary Volume of the Royal Asiatic Society of Great Britain and Ireland 1823–1923.* London: The Society.

Pedersen, Lene. 2007. "An Ancestral Keris, Balinese Kingship, and a Modern Presidency." In *What's the Use of Art? Functions, Movements, and Memories of Asian "Art Objects,"* edited by Jan Mrazek and Morgan Pitelka, 214–37. Honolulu: University of Hawai'i Press.

Pels, Peter. 1998. "The Magic of Africa: Reflections on a Western Commonplace." *African Studies Review* 41, no. 3: 193–209.

Pels, Peter. 2003. "Introduction." In *Magic and Modernity: Interfaces of Revelation and Concealment*, edited by Birgit Meyer and Peter Pels, 1–38. Stanford, CA: Stanford University Press.

Pels, Peter, and Oscar Salemink. 1994. "Introduction: Five Theses on Ethnography as Colonial Practice." *History and Anthropology* 8: 1–34.

Penny, H. Glenn. 2002. *Objects of Culture: Ethnology and Ethnographic Museums in Imperial Germany*. Chapel Hill: University of North Carolina Press.

Pfeiffer, Ida. 1856. *Meine zweite Weltreise*. Vienna: C. Gerold's Sohn.

Picard, Michel. 2024. *Kebalian: The Dialogic Construction of Balinese Identity*. Singapore: NUS Press.

Pietz, William. 2022. *The Problem of the Fetish*. Chicago: University of Chicago Press.

Pignarre, Philippe. 2023. *Latour-Stengers: An Entangled Flight*. Translated by Stephen Muecke. Cambridge: Polity.

Pignarre, Philippe, and Isabelle Stengers. 2011. *Capitalist Sorcery: Breaking the Spell*. Translated by Andrew Goffey. New York: Palgrave Macmillan.

Poensen, C. 1878. "Iets over Javaansche dieven." *Mededeelingen van Wege het Nederlandsche Zendelinggenootschap* 22: 99–146.

Poensen, C. 1879. "Djimat." *Mededeelingen van Wege het Nederlandsche Zendelinggenootschap* 23: 229–66.

Ponder, H. W. 1990 [1942]. *Javanese Panorama: More Impressions of the 1930s*. Singapore: Oxford University Press.

Porter, Roy. 1999. "Witchcraft and Magic in Enlightenment, Romantic, and Liberal Thought." In *Witchcraft and Magic in Europe*, vol. 5: *The Eighteenth and Nineteenth Centuries*, edited by Bengt Ankarloo and Stuart Clark, 191–282. Philadelphia: University of Pennsylvania Press.

Powell, Hickman. 1930. *The Last Paradise*. New York: Jonathan Cape and Harrison Smith.

Puhle, Annekatrin. 1999. "Ghosts, Apparitions, and Poltergeist Incidents in Germany between 1700 and 1900." *Journal of the Society for Psychical Research* 63, no. 857: 292–305.

Quijano, Anibal. 2000. "Coloniality of Power, Eurocentrism, and Latin America." *Nepantla: Views from the South* 1, no. 3: 533–80.

Raptschinsky, B. 1941. *Kolonisatie van blanken in de tropen*. Den Haag: H. P. Leopolds.

Reid, Anthony. 1985. "From Betel-Chewing to Tobacco Smoking in Indonesia." *Journal of Asian Studies* 44, no. 3: 529–47.

Ricklefs, M. C. 2007. *Polarizing Javanese Society: Islamic and Other Visions (c. 1830–1930)*. Honolulu: University of Hawai'i Press.

Rose, Hilary. 1996. "My Enemy's Enemy Is, Only Perhaps, My Friend." *Social Text* 46–47: 61–80.

Rush, James R. 1990. "Journeys to Java: Western Fiction about Indonesia 1600–1980." In *Asia in Western Fiction*, edited by Robert W. Winks and James R. Rush, 137–58. Honolulu: University of Hawai'i Press.

S. 1921. "Iets over djimat's en misdrijf." *De Nederlandsch-Indische Politiegids* 5, no. 2: 33–34.

Said, Edward. 1978. *Orientalism*. New York: Random House.

Salomonsen, Jone. 2002. *Enchanted Feminism: The Reclaiming Witches of San Francisco.* London: Routledge.

Salverda, Reinier. 1994. "Indisch-Nederlands in het Batavia van de jaren dertig: De roman Goena Goena van Caesar Kijdsmeir." *Indische Letteren* 9, no. 1: 29–43.

Sartono Kartodirdjo. 1966. *The Peasants' Revolt of Banten in 1888, Its Conditions, Course, and Sequel: A Case Study of Social Movements in Indonesia.* 's-Gravenhage: Martinus Nijhoff.

Sartono Kartodirdjo. 1972. "Agrarian Radicalism in Java: Its Setting and Development." In *Culture and Politics in Indonesia*, edited by C. Holt, 71–125. Ithaca, NY: Cornell University Press.

Sartono Kartodirdjo. 1973. *Protest Movements in Rural Java: A Study of Agrarian Unrest in the Nineteenth and Early Twentieth Centuries.* Singapore: Oxford University Press.

Schenkhuizen, Marguérite. 1993. *Memoirs of an Indo Woman: Twentieth-Century Life in the East Indies and Abroad.* Edited and translated by Lizelot Stout van Balgooy. Athens: Ohio University Center for International Studies.

Scheper-Hughes, Nancy, and Margaret M. Lock. 1987. "The Mindful Body: A Prolegomenon to Future Work in Medical Anthropology." *Medical Anthropology Quarterly* 1, no. 1: 6–41.

Schneider, David M. 1984. *A Critique of the Study of Kinship.* Ann Arbor: University of Michigan Press.

Schulte-Nordholt, Henk. 1986. *Bali: Colonial Conceptions and Political Change 1700– 1940.* Rotterdam: Comparative Asian Studies Programme, Erasmus University.

Schulte-Nordholt, Henk. 1991. "The Jago in the Shadow: Crime and 'Order' in the Colonial State in Java." *RIMA: Review of Indonesian and Malaysian Affairs* 25, no. 1: 74–91.

Schüttpelz, Erhard, and Ehler Voss. 2020. "Quite as Powerful: The Mediumistic Controversy in the 19th Century." In *Mediality on Trial: Testing and Contesting Trance and Other Media Techniques*, edited by Ehler Voss, 67–77. Berlin: De Gruyter.

Scidmore, Eliza Ruhamah. 1984 [1899]. *Java: The Garden of the East.* Singapore: Oxford University Press.

Sears, Laurie. 1996. *Shadows of Empire: Colonial Discourse and Javanese Tales.* Durham, NC: Duke University Press.

Serrurier, L. 1891. *De pionier: Handleiding voor het verzamelen en waarnemen op natuurkundig gebied.* Leiden: De Breuk & Smits.

Shapin, Steven. 1994. *A Social History of Truth: Civility and Science in Seventeenth-Century England.* Chicago: University of Chicago Press.

Shapin, Steven, and Simon Schaffer. 1985. *Leviathan and the Air Pump: Hobbes, Boyle, and the Experimental Life.* Princeton, NJ: Princeton University Press.

Shiraishi, Takashi. 1990. *An Age in Motion: Popular Radicalism in Java, 1912–1926.* Ithaca, NY: Cornell University Press.

Siegel, James T. 1997. *Fetish, Recognition, Revolution.* Princeton, NJ: Princeton University Press.

Silverstein, Michael. 2003. "Translation, Transduction, Transformation: Skating 'Glossando' on Thin Semiotic Ice." In *Translating Cultures: Perspectives on Translation and Anthropology*, edited by Paula G. Rubel and Abraham Rosman, 75–109. Oxford: Berg.

Skeat, Walter William. 1965 [1900]. *Malay Magic: An Introduction to the Folklore and Popular Religion of the Malay Peninsula*. London: Frank Cass.

Skemer, Don C. 2006. *Binding Words: Textual Amulets in the Middle Ages*. University Park: Pennsylvania State University Press.

Snouck Hurgronje, C. 1908. "Blikken in het zieleleven van den Javaan?" *De Gids* 26, no. 3: 422–47.

Soeriokoesoemo, R. M. S. 1919. "Het djimat in woelige tijden." *Wederopbouw* 2: 160–63.

Souriau, Étienne. 2015. *The Different Modes of Existence*. Translated by Erik Beranek and Tim Howles. Minneapolis: Univocal.

Spat, C. 1906. *Het heidendom bij de volken van den Indischen archipel*. Breda: De Koninklijke Militaire Academie.

S[pat], C[laas]. 1927. "Magie." In *Encyclopaedie van Nederlandsch-Indië*, edited by D. G. Stibbe and C. Spat, 263–71. 's-Gravenhage: Martinus Nijhoff.

Starhawk. 1987. *Truth or Dare: Encounters with Power, Authority, and Mystery*. New York: HarperCollins.

Starhawk. 1993. *The Fifth Sacred Thing*. New York: Bantam.

Starhawk. 1997. *Dreaming the Dark: Magic, Sex, and Politics*. Boston: Beacon.

Starhawk. 2002. *Webs of Power: Notes from the Global Uprising*. Gabriola Island, BC: New Society.

Stengers, Isabelle. 2000. *The Invention of Modern Science*. Translated by Daniel W. Smith. Minneapolis: University of Minnesota Press.

Stengers, Isabelle. 2003. "The Doctor and the Charlatan." *Cultural Studies Review* 9, no. 2: 11–36.

Stengers, Isabelle. 2005a. "The Cosmopolitical Proposal." In *Making Things Public: Atmospheres of Democracy*, edited by Bruno Latour and Peter Weibel, 994–1003. Cambridge, MA: MIT Press.

Stengers, Isabelle. 2005b. "Introductory Notes on an Ecology of Practices." *Cultural Studies Review* 11, no. 1: 183–96.

Stengers, Isabelle. 2008. "Experimenting with Refrains: Subjectivity and the Challenge of Escaping Modern Dualism." *Subjectivity* 22, no. 1: 38–59.

Stengers, Isabelle. 2011a. "Comparison as a Matter of Concern." *Common Knowledge* 17, no. 1: 48–63.

Stengers, Isabelle. 2011b. *Thinking with Whitehead: A Free and Wild Creation of Concepts*. Translated by Michael Chase. Cambridge, MA: Harvard University Press.

Stengers, Isabelle. 2018a. "The Challenge of Ontological Politics." In *A World of Many Worlds*, edited by Marisol de la Cadena and Mario Blaser, 83–111. Durham, NC: Duke University Press.

Stengers, Isabelle. 2018b. "Postlude." *SubStance* 47, no. 1: 146–55.

Stengers, Isabelle, and Bruno Latour. 2015. "The Sphinx of the Work." In *The Different Modes of Existence*, by Étienne Souriau, 11–94. Minneapolis: Univocal.

Stevens, Alan M., and A. E. Schmidgall-Tellings. 2004. *A Comprehensive Indonesian-English Dictionary*. Athens: Ohio University Press.

Stevens, Harm. 2005. "Collecting and 'The Rough Work of Subjugation': Van Daalen, Snouck Hurgronje, and the Ethnographic Exploitation of North Sumatra." In

Indonesia: The Discovery of the Past, edited by Endang Sri Hardiarti and Pieter ter Keurs, 76–84. Amsterdam: KIT.

Stevens, Harm. 2007. "G. C. E. van Daalen, Military Officer and Ethnological Field Agent: The Ethnological Exploration of Gayo and Alas, 1900–1905." In *Colonial Collections Revisited*, edited by Pieter ter Keurs, 115–22. Leiden: CNWS.

Stockdale, John Joseph. 1995 [1811]. *Island of Java*. Singapore: Periplus.

Stocking, George W., Jr. 1971. "Animism in Theory and Practice: E. B. Tylor's Unpublished 'Notes on "Spiritualism."' *Man* 6, no. 1: 88–104.

Stocking, George W., Jr. 1974. "Introduction: The Basic Assumptions of Boasian Anthropology." In *The Shaping of American Anthropology 1883–1911: A Franz Boas Reader*, edited by George W. Stocking Jr., 1–20. New York: Basic Books.

Stocking, George W., Jr. 1987. *Victorian Anthropology*. New York: Free Press.

Stoler, Ann L. 1989. "Making Empire Respectable: The Politics of Race and Sexual Morality in Twentieth-Century Colonial Cultures." *American Ethnologist* 16, no. 4: 634–60.

Stoler, Ann. 1992. "Sexual Affronts and Racial Frontiers: European Identities and the Cultural Politics of Exclusion in Colonial Southeast Asia." *Comparative Studies in Society and History* 34, no. 4: 514–51.

Stoler, Ann Laura. 1995. *Race and the Education of Desire*. Durham, NC: Duke University Press.

Stoler, Ann Laura. 2002. *Carnal Knowledge and Imperial Power: Race and the Intimate in Colonial Rule*. Berkeley: University of California Press.

Stoler, Ann Laura, and Frederick Cooper. 1997. "Between Metropole and Colony: Rethinking a Research Agenda." In *Tensions of Empire: Colonial Cultures in a Bourgeois World*, edited by Frederick Cooper and Ann Laura Stoler, 1–56. Berkeley: University of California Press.

Stoller, Paul, and Cheryl Olkes. 1989. *In Sorcery's Shadow: A Memoir of Apprenticeship among the Songhay of Niger*. Chicago: University of Chicago Press.

Stronks, G. J. 1991. "The Significance of Balthasar Bekker's *The Enchanted World*." In *Witchcraft in the Netherlands*, edited by Marijke Gijswijt-Hofstra and Willem Frijhoff, 149–56. Rotterdam: Universitaire Pers.

Stuart-Fox, David, with Ketut Liyer. 2015. *Pray, Magic, Heal: The Story of Bali's Famous Eat, Pray, Love Folk Healer*. New York: New Saraswati Press.

Styers, Randall. 2004. *Making Magic: Religion, Science, and Magic in the Modern World*. Oxford: Oxford University Press.

Suit, Natalia K. 2020. *Qur'anic Matters: Material Mediations and Religious Practice in Egypt*. London: Bloomsbury Academic.

Swieten, J. van. 1872. "Varia: Een zoek geraakt document over het gebeurde in 1831 te Soemedang." *TNI* 1, no. 2: 493–96.

Tambiah, Stanley Jeyaraja. 1984. *Buddhist Saints of the Forest and the Cult of Amulets*. Cambridge: Cambridge University Press.

Tambiah, Stanley Jeyaraja. 1990. *Magic, Science, Religion, and the Scope of Rationality*. Cambridge: Cambridge University Press.

Taussig, Michael. 1980. *The Devil and Commodity Fetishism*. Chapel Hill: University of North Carolina Press.

Taussig, Michael. 1987. *Shamanism, Colonialism, and the Wild Man*. Chicago: University of Chicago Press.

Taussig, Michael. 1993. *Mimesis and Alterity: A Particular History of the Senses*. New York: Routledge.

Taussig, Michael. 1997. *The Magic of the State*. New York: Routledge.

Taussig, Michael. 2003. "Viscerality, Faith, and Skepticism: Another Theory of Magic." In *Magic and Modernity: Interfaces of Revelation and Concealment*, edited by Birgit Meyer and Peter Pels, 272–306. Stanford, CA: Stanford University Press.

Taussig, Michael. 2020. *The Mastery of Non-Mastery in the Age of Meltdown*. Oxford: Oxford University Press.

Taylor, Jean Gelman. 1983. *The Social World of Batavia: European and Eurasian in Dutch Asia*. Madison: University of Wisconsin Press.

Termorshuizen, Gerard. 1988. *P. A. Daum: Journalist en romancier van tempo doeloe*. Amsterdam: Nijgh & Van Ditmar.

Thomas, Northcote Whitridge. 1905. "Javanese Poltergeists." *Occult Review* 2, no. 11: 223–28.

Thomas, Northcote Whitridge. 1911. "Magic." In *Encyclopaedia Britannica*, 11th ed., vol. 17, 304–15. London: The Encyclopaedia Britannica Company.

Till, Margreet van. 2011. *Banditry in West Java 1869–1942*. Translated by David McKay and Beverly Jackson. Singapore: NUS.

Tollenaere, Herman A. O. de. 1996. *The Politics of Divine Wisdom: Theosophy and Labour, National, and Women's Movements in Indonesia and South Asia 1875–1947*. Nijmegen: Katholieke Universiteit Nijmegen.

Trouillot, Michel-Rolph. 1995. "An Unthinkable History." In *Silencing the Past: Power and the Production of History*, 70–107. Boston: Beacon.

Tsing, Anna Lowenhaupt, Jennifer Deger, Alder Keleman Saxena, and Feifei Zhou. 2024. *Field Guide to the Patchy Anthropocene: The New Nature*. Stanford, CA: Stanford University Press.

Tylor, Edward Burnett. 1874. "Magic and Witchcraft." In *Notes and Queries on Anthropology: For the Use of Travelers and Residents in Uncivilized Lands*, 60–61. London: Edward Stanford.

Tylor, Edward Burnett. 1883. "Magic." *Encyclopaedia Britannica*, 9th ed., vol. 15, 199–206. New York: Charles Scribner's Sons.

Tylor, Edward Burnett. 1958 [1871]. *Primitive Culture*. 2 vols. New York: Harper & Brothers.

Van der Veer, Peter. 2014. *The Modern Spirit of Asia: The Spiritual and the Secular in China and India*. Princeton, NJ: Princeton University Press.

Van der Veur, Paul. 1955. "Introduction to a Socio-Political Study of the Eurasians of Indonesia." PhD dissertation, Cornell University.

Van der Veur, Paul. 1969. "Race and Color in Colonial Society: Biographical Sketches by a Eurasian Woman Concerning Pre-World War II Indonesia." *Indonesia* 6: 69–80.

Van Klinken, Gerry. 2007. "Return of the Sultans: The Communitarian Turn in Local Politics." In *The Revival of Tradition in Indonesian Politics*, edited by Jamie S. Davidson and David Henley, 149–69. London: Routledge.

Van Niel, Robert. 1992. *Java under the Cultivation System: Collected Writings*. Leiden: KITLV.

Velde, Paul van der. 2006. *A Life-Long Passion: P. J. Veth (1814–1895) and the Dutch East Indies*. Leiden: KITLV.

Venuti, Lawrence. 2002 [1995]. *The Translator's Invisibility: A History of Translation*, 2nd ed. London: Routledge.

Venuti, Lawrence, ed. 2012. *The Translation Studies Reader*, 3rd ed. London: Routledge.

Vermeulen, Han F. 2008. "Anthropology in the Netherlands: Past, Present, and Future." In *Other People's Anthropologies: Ethnographic Practice on the Margins*, edited by Alexandar Bošković, 44–69. New York: Berghahn.

Veth, P. J. 1875–82. *Java, geographisch, ethnologisch, historisch*. 4 vols. Haarlem: Erven F. Bohn.

Viveiros de Castro, Eduardo. 2003. "And." *Manchester Papers in Social Anthropology* 7.

Viveiros de Castro, Eduardo. 2004a. "Exchanging Perspectives: The Transformation of Objects into Subjects in Amerindian Ontologies." *Common Knowledge* 10, no. 3: 463–84.

Viveiros de Castro, Eduardo. 2004b. "Perspectival Anthropology and the Method of Controlled Equivocation." *Tipití: Journal of the Society for the Anthropology of Lowland South America* 2, no. 1: 1–22.

Vorderman, A. G. 1877. "Gandaroewa (onzichtbaar steenenwerpen) in de Preanger." *Natuurkundig Tijdschrift voor Nederlandsch Indië* 37: 55–66.

Vorderman, A. G. 1893. "Inlandsche vergiften." *Tijdschrift voor Inlandsche Geneeskundigen* 1, no. 6: 81–83.

Vredenbregt, J. 1973. "Dabus in West Java." *BKI* 129, nos. 2–3: 302–20.

W., K. v. 1907. "Toovermiddelen in Indië." *De Hollandsche Revue* 12: 408–11.

Waardt, Johannes Hendrik Marie de. 1991. "Toverij en samenleving. Holland 1500–1800." PhD dissertation, Erasmus University, Rotterdam.

Wagner, Roy. 1975. *The Invention of Culture*. Chicago: University of Chicago Press.

Watson, C. W. 1993. "Introduction." In *Understanding Witchcraft and Sorcery in Southeast Asia*, edited by C. W. Watson and Roy Ellen, 1–26. Honolulu: University of Hawai'i Press.

Wermeskerken, Henri van. 1922. *Roemah Angker: Roman van stille kracht en Indisch bijgeloof*. Haarlem: J. W. Boissevain.

West, Harry. 2007. *Ethnographic Sorcery*. Chicago: University of Chicago Press.

Whitehead, Alfred N. 1967. *Science and the Modern World*. New York: Free Press.

Whitehead, Alfred N. 1968. *Modes of Thought*. New York: Free Press.

Wiener, Margaret J. 1995. *Visible and Invisible Realms: Power, Magic, and Colonial Conquest in Bali*. Chicago: University of Chicago Press.

Wiener, Margaret J. 1999a. "Making Local History in New Order Bali: Public Culture and the Politics of the Past." In *Staying Local in the Global Village: Bali in the Twentieth Century*, edited by Raechelle Rubinstein and Linda H. Connor, 51–89. Honolulu: University of Hawai'i Press.

Wiener, Margaret. 1999b. "'Pay No Attention to the Man behind the Curtain': Irreverent Notes on Gender and Ethnography." *Anthropology and Humanism* 24, no. 2: 95–108.

Wiener, Margaret J. 2003. "Hidden Forces: Colonialism and the Politics of Magic in the Netherlands Indies." In *Magic and Modernity: Interfaces of Revelation and Concealment*, edited by Birgit Meyer and Peter Pels, 129–58. Stanford, CA: Stanford University Press.

Wiener, Margaret. 2014. "Optical Allusions: Looking at Looking, in Balinese-Dutch Encounters." *Heidelberg Ethnology*, Occasional Papers no. 2, 1–20.

Wiener, Margaret J. 2015. "Colonial Magic: The Dutch East Indies." In *The Cambridge History of Witchcraft and Magic*, edited by David Collins, 482–517. Cambridge: Cambridge University Press.

Wiener, Margaret J. 2016. "'The World Is Full of Letters': Graphic Ideologies, Graphic Technologies, and Transformative Practices in Bali." In *The Materiality and Efficacy of Balinese Letters: Situating Scriptural Practices*, edited by Richard Fox and Annette Hornbacher, 51–69. Leiden: Brill.

Wiener, Margaret J. 2017. "Things in (Un)Common: Two Reflections." *Anthropologica* 59, no. 2: 239–50.

Wilken, G. A. 1885. *Het animisme bij de volken van den Indischen Archipel*. Leiden: E. J. Brill.

Williams, Raymond. 1977. *Marxism and Literature*. Oxford: Oxford University Press.

Williams, Raymond. 1997. "Advertising: The Magic System." In *Problems in Materialism and Culture*, 170–95. London: Verso.

Wilson, Bryan, ed. 1970. *Rationality*. Oxford: Blackwell.

Winckel, C. W. F. 1938. "The Feasibility of White Settlements in the Tropics: A Medical Point of View." In *Comptes Rendus du Congrès International de Géographie Amsterdam*, vol. 10 : *Géographie Coloniale*, 345–56. Leiden: E. J. Brill.

Wiselius, J. A. B. 1872. "Iets over het geestendom en de geesten der Javanen." *TNI* 1, no. 2: 23–33.

Wiskerke, C. 1919. "Fetisisme in Nederlandsch-Indië." *Vragen van den Dag* 34: 853–63.

Wit, Augusta de. 1984 [1912]. *Java: Facts and Fancies*. Singapore: Oxford University Press.

Wittig, Monique. 1969. *Les guérillères*. Paris: Minuit.

Woodward, Mark R. 2011. "The Javanese Dukun: Healing and Moral Ambiguity." In *Java, Indonesia and Islam*, 69–119. Dordrecht: Springer.

Wulfften Palthe, P. M. van. 1936. "Het medisch aspect van blanke kolonisatie in de tropen." *Tijdschrift van het Koninklijk Nederlandsch Aardrijkskundig Genootschap Amsterdam* 53: 352–59.

Yeazell, Ruth Bernard. 2005. "Merry Companies." *London Review of Books* 27, no. 2: 23–25.

Zoetmulder, P. J. 1982. *Old Javanese-English Dictionary*. 2 vols. 's-Gravenhage: Martinus Nijhoff.

Index

development of, 15–17; as ghostbusting praxis, 190; god-tricks, 214, 223, 240; "going native," 153–54, 250; purification role of, 188; as queer science, 190; as "reformer's science," 188, 234; and Science, 229, 236; as study of the "primitive," 15–16; symmetrical, 12; tradition of theoretical analysis, 5–6. *See also* animism; ethnology

art, Dutch, 21, 22, 104; keris treated as, 117, 143; skilled practices as, 14, 217, 228–29, 232, 238, 41, 254

artifacts, 247

Asad, Talal, 8, 16, 18, 152

ascesis, 38, 47–48, 62

association of ideas, 113, 130–31, 239

Azande, 29, 55, 151–52, 229, 230, 273n1

babu, 162, 167

Bali, 11, 16, 26; Badung 146–147; centenary of colonial conquests, 146–48; Jembrana, 34–35, 40, 50, 52, 55–56, 60; Klungkung, 119–25; Puri Agung Klungkung, 120–21, 148, 269n4; reform movement in 1920s, 53–54; Tumpek Landep, 135

balian, 33–35, 40, 53–59, 62–65; ascesis as technology of, 38, 47–48, 62; *balian tatakson*, 53, 54, 56, 59, 63, 263n36; *balian usada*, 53, 58, 59, 62; as "traditional healer," 33, 60; fraud signaled by wealth of, 40; harm done by, 60; translations of, 33, 56, 60. *See also dukun*; Nang Mukanis

Barad, Karen, 12, 107

Batavia, 76, 194; Ommelanden, 76

Batavian Society for Arts and Sciences, 97, 123, 136, 137–38; Treasure Room, 139–40, 142, 145, 149, 272n46, 272n48. *See also* National Museum of Indonesia

Baud, Jan Chrétien, 198–99, 207, 209, 217

becoming, 61–62, 107

Bekker, Balthasar, 19–22, 70

belief, 24–25, 133, 185, 227, 232, 240, 247, 251,; anthropology and, 153; dismissal of, 2, 9–10, 19, 25–26, 34, 46, 48, 85, 99, 113, 118, 124, 190; "exotic systems" of, 10, 16; as false, 34, 99, 108, 118, 170, 171, 185, 234; and *guna-guna*, 170–72; as inferred, 73, 86, 149; *jimat* claimed be symbol of, 79–80, 86, 104; knowledge versus, 26, 99, 230; "naive belief in naive belief," 51, 64; not referred to, 133; "native," 79, 85, 135, 149, 155, 156, 175, 181, 183, 206, 223, 275n26; reason versus, 19, 46, 51; and scholars, 224; skepticism versus, 193; as "what makes entities 'available' to events," 64. See also *geloof*

Berg, Lodewijk Willem Christiaan van den, 126, 141, 270n18

bêtise, 251

betoverde,19–22, 219

betoveren, 168–69

bezoars, 100, 108, 267n47

bijgeloof, 46. *See* superstition

biomedicine, 3, 263n39; body of, 57; deviation from, 41–42, 44–45, 56–57; *dukun* tied to, 41–44, 56–57; and *guna-guna*, 170; hegemony of reinforced by translations, 60; tropical neurasthenia, diagnoses of, 171, 179–80

"black magic": *guna-guna* translated as, 18, 169; *pangiwa*, 55, 60; *zwarte kunst*, 175–76

Blavatsky, Madame, 15, 221

Bloor, David, 12, 229, 230

bodies, *badan balus*, 53; biomedical 57; multiplicity of, 57–58; "talented," 61–63, 205; techniques of, 220

Bone and Gowa, rijkssieraden of, 137, 141, 270n19, 270n22, 272n51

Bosch, Johannes van den, 194–95, 203

Bosman, William, 21–22, 69–70

boundary projects, 24, 26, 162–63, 174, 183

Brinkgreve, Francine, 146–48, 272n46, 272n49

125; of objects, 106–7, 119, 126; of uses (*guna wasiyatnya*), 125; of world, 243.

instauration, 73, 107–8, 129, 149, 227, 268n59, 283n2

interstices, 34, 213, 225, 227

intra-action, 73, 107–8

invention of culture, 7, 236

irrationality, attributions of, 22–23, 39, 46, 118, 152, 262n27

irreductions, 8; Latour, 230–31.

Islam: Hajis, 38, 204, 266n39; and *jimat*, 87, 94, 101; and *rijkssieraden*, 126; Sufi, 74–75

Jaka tua, 165, 170, 172, 274n10

James, William, 249–50, 253–54, 283–84n4; *jampi*, 85, 265n28

Jasper, J. E., 44, 47, 48, 50, 61, 132, 218, 226, 261n16, 261n17, 261n18

Java, 20, 26–27, 56; British control of, 123, 195; deforestation, 226; Great Post Road, 194, 195–96, 277n6, 277n10; Java War (1825–30), 38, 198, 209; rural insurrections, 75; sexual and racial politics in, 160–64; Surakarta, 132, 141, 146; mud volcano eruption, 71; Yogyakarta, 132, 141

jimat: ability to attract, 105–6; abstract qualities attributed to, 93–94, 100–102, 107, 109; as actors, 77; as amulets or talismans, 71–72, 80–81, 94–95, 97, 101; Balinese interlocutors, views of, 105; as both potent and impotent, 78, 82–83; cabochon as, 105–6; as colonial obsession, 75–80, 86, 267n53; criminality associated with, 83–93; criminalization of in law, 76, 78, 83–87; "developed native" critique of moral panic over, 78–80, 93; *dukun* associated with, 72, 124; as element of everyday life, 78–79, 106, 108; *élmu* linked with, 81, 83–86; fetish associated with, 72, 76, 96–97; forensic possibilities of, 86–88, 93; from formerly hidden materials, 108;

and Garut massacre, 74–77, 80–81, 86, 101, 102; grave dirt, 88–92, 96, 266n36; inscriptions in, 87, 94, 108, 266n33; and insurgency, 74–83; invulnerability attributed to, 75–83, 85–86, 127; and Islam, 87, 94, 101; Javanese and Sundanese identification of, 104–5; *keris* compared with, 118–19, 145, 149–50; materiality of elided, 73, 93–94, 101, 106–7, 267n49; media discussions of, 77–79; movement of as unpredictable, 149–50; in museum collections, 89–92, 109; and "occult offenses," 84, 86, 93, 102, 264n12; and perjury in courtroom, 86–88, 265n31, 266n34; photographs of, *89–92*; as practice, 106–8; as prostheses, 106, 268n57; reality politics of, 76–77, 83, 84; and rebellion, 72, 75–83, 85; similarities with Dutch practices, 80, 93; state's policing of, 72–73, 76, 81; as symbol of belief, 79–80, 86, 104; terms used to gloss, 71–72, 267n49; theft associated with, 72, 88–93, 92, 94; *tosan kuning*, 88; types, 93, 105, 265n22; uncertainty about, 82, 93–94, 105; as vanishing, 109

jin, 56, 221, 281n64

kecubung, 165, 169, 170

Kenyatta, Jomo, 153, 188

keris, 18, 25; as art, 143; ceremonial, 123, 138; "cleansing" and offering/feeding, 129, 135; collected by politicians, 145–46; as collectives, 119–20, 125, 139, 145, 149–50, 156; commensurations in translation, 133–36; as commodities, 136–40, 269n10; connections created by, 150; as Dutch family heirlooms, 142–43; Dutch superstition about, 143–44; dynastic lines of, 119; enchantment of, 120; European, 149; exiled, 125; I Ardawalika, 141, 146–49, *147*; I Bangawan Canggu, 135; I Baru Gnit, 146, 148; I Durga Dingkul, 120, 135, 141,

legal codes: *adatrecht*, 84, 131, 146, 175, 227; Code Napoléon, 84; different for "natives," 84, 109; "occult offenses," 84, 86, 93, 102, 176, 264n12; presumed universality of, 84, 109

Lévi-Strauss, Claude, 10, 30, 263n40

magic: analysis of as term, 233–34; animism linked with, 113; as the "art of changing consciousness at will," 187; as art of effects, 254; coordinating devices for, 111–15; defamiliarization of, 25, 59, 241; defined in opposition to other categories, 9; as defining feature of primitive society, 12, 15; "diasporic," 185; as distinction between rational Europeans and irrational natives, 23–24, 26; encyclopedia entries for, 111–12; as ethnological category, 101; as experimental, 232; fall of attributed to science, 113; as feature of increasingly connected worlds, 150; as floating signifier, 10; Indonesian terms for, 237–38; *jimat* translated into, 94; language of, 22, 25, 240, 242, 168–238; as lexical item, 14, 41; magic, science, and religion, trio of, 235–38; making of as category, 12–16; monetary value of "magical powers," 137; as monotonous practice, 190; move from matter to mentality, 73, 131–32; no standards for, 111; as (k)nots, 113–14, 236, 238; as "not science," 236; positive associations, 242, 246; practices diffracted through, 4, 11, 22–24, 25–26, 34, 73, 102, 106; as product of colonial relations and disciplinarity, 13; re-cognization of, 16; relegated to past, 1, 19; sympathetic, 239; as target of colonial governance, 23; as technology of empire, 13–14, 234–35; as tool of the Church, 14; *toverij*, 173, 177, 183, 234, 238, 266n38, 275n21; translating of as (k)not-work, 9, 23, 134; travels across time and space, 3–4, 112; treated as worldwide phenomenon, 5, 10, 13, 15–16; used as ideological weapon, 9–10, 239; of the word magic, 187–90. *See also* amulets; fetishism; hidden forces; illusionism; *hekserij*; *jimat*; witch, figure of; witch doctor, figure of

magical, as modifier, 71

"magical power," 149; attributed to *keris*, 117–18, 120, 124–25, 143–44, 150, 269n14, 269n15, 270n16; as translation of *sakti*, 5–6, 118, 140, 257–58n6; *tover-kracht,* 217–18

magical thinking, 173–74

"magical worldview," 175

magicians, 9, 29–33, 37, 214

"magic of the moderns," 184, 241–42

magie, 14, 172–74, 180, 186, 234, 275n21

Malinowski, Bronislaw, 153, 187–90, 236, 250, 271n36

market economics, 272n48; hidden forces in, 219, 281n56; *keris* in, 136–40, 146, 269n10

Marx, Karl, 67, 101, 104, 241, 271n39, 284n8

materiality: analytic slide from, 131; Catholic and Protestant conceptions of, 68, 263n37; of *guna-guna*,180; hardness and oddness, 129; matter and spirit, 99; of *jimat* elided, 73, 93–94, 101, 106–7, 267n49; matter of, 106–7; of stones, 193. *See also* objects

mediums, 189, 209–11, 221, 224, 279–80n42; *balian tatakson*, 53, 54, 56, 59, 63; Herne and Williams, 210–11, 279n38

Meijer, D. H., 88, 92, 93, 97, 104

Mesmer, Anton, 281n60, 284n5

Michiels, Andreas Victor, 121, 196, 197–201, *199*, 203, 217; in anecdotes, 207; credibility of questioned, 209, 211, 213, 224; death and memorialization of, 200–201, 209, 278n18, 278n19

missionaries, 18, 60–61, 94, 97–98, 128–30, 172, 271n30

Mitchell, W. J. T., 109

modernity, 2, 20, 77, 264n14

moderns, 19, 46, 106–7, 253; "anthropology of," 230–31; body as object of biomedicine for, 57; death of magic among, 235; disenchanted, 65, 70; as "having Science," 245; "horror of becoming a dupe," 249–50, 253–54; "magic of," 184, 241–42; as tricksters, 120

Mol, Annemarie, 57, 111, 258n10

more-than-humans, 13–14, 19, 136; associations between, 64; Ausangate, 240; connection with, 226–27; fanatic access to, 38–39; in fields of relations, 58–49; forces and Powers, 59, 64; mediators, destruction of, 51; oaths as, 197–98; and rebellion, 37–38; *taksu,* 63; translated as gods and spirits, 35. See also *guna-guna; jimat; keris;* nonhumans; spirits

museums, 30, 109, 114, 271n38; collectives in, 140, 142–43; guidebooks, 139, 272n46; Indonesian visitors to, 139–42, 262n50; Museum Keris Nusantara, 146; National Museum of Ethnology (Leiden), 117–18, 123, 141, 143, 268n63, 269n10; *keris* in, 117–19, 136–40, 146; National Museum of Indonesia, 145, 146; offerings made in, 140; Pitt Rivers Museum (Oxford), 111, 114, 189;; Stedelijk Museum (Amsterdam), 185–86; Surabaya Police Museum exhibits, 89–92. See also Batavian Society for Arts and Sciences

Nang Mukanis, 44; anonymous letter about, 35, 52–56; arrest of, 36, 39, 46, 51, 64, 75; *badan halus,* 53, 56; Balinese views of, 52, 55–56; as fanatic, 37–38, 260n8; as fraud, 40–41, 46, 52; identification of with supreme deity, 53–54; influence of, 61–64; material goods of destroyed, 36, 40, 50–51; as "mentally impaired" or crazy, 37, 39, 52–55; memories of, 55–56; as "pretend

dukun," 52–53, 55; as threat to colonial state, 36, 37–39, 51–52; vulnerability of, 51, 54, 64. See also *balian*

Napoleon, 20, 84, 277n6

nationalists, 17, 26, 75, 79, 140–41, 163

"natives": credulity attributed to, 23, 26, 31, 34, 37, 40–41, 45–47, 50; "developed," 78–80, 93; native physicians, concept of, 42, 56–57, 60, 260n14; "occult offenses" promulgated for, 84, 86, 93, 102, 176, 264n12. See also development; "primitive" society

nature, 70, 102, 193, 223; and causality, 113, 173; culture confused with, 23–24, 26, 113, 145; as divide between West and the rest, 24; human, 13, 257; as law-bound, 11, 13, 22, 193, 223, 250; as new category, 19; as pre-existent, 13; purifications of, 26, 44, 102, 109, 157, 170, 172, 235; ; as singular, 7, 11, 24, 183; as universal 172, 183

nature, bifurcation of, 24, 44, 63, 102, 106–7, 169–70, 227, 246, 248–52; alternative to, 254–55

naturecultures, 8, 27, 69; intranaturalcultural products, 67–68

neopagans, 10, 24, 190, 245, 252–54, 282n7, 285n12; activists, 187, 245, 251–52, 255, 284n8

Netherlands, 4; art, Dutch, 21, 22, 104; art of, 21, 22; colonialism of, 16–22; deficit of 1800s, 194–96; Dutch Golden Age, 20–21; Dutch language, 9, 22; explicit relation between anthropology and colonialism, 17–18; investitures of monarchs, 134; modern institutions developed by, 19; prosecution of witches ended in 1600s, 19; religious toleration in, 21; voyage literature, 19–20. See also capitalism; Ethical Policy

networks, 1–2, 8–9, 24, 112, 135, 183, 283n2; capitalist, 284n6; cut, 26, 34, 51, 64, 135; and translation, 8, 178. See also collectives; factishes

"power of suggestion," 34, 51, 60–61, 64–65, 261–62n26, 275–76n27; in biomedicine, 42; and *guna-guna*, 170, 172, 175

practices: authenticating, 197–98; biomedical, 41–45, 56–57; as delusion and manipulation, 70; diffracted through magic, 4, 11, 22–24, 25–26, 34, 73, 102, 106; of "drawing things together," 111, 114; embedded in socionatural ecologies, 152–53; of experimental science, 247–48; *jimat* as, 106–8; "magic" used to describe, 111, 113–14, 118–20; native physicians, concept of, 56–57, 260n14; obligations associated with, 236–37; plurality of scientific, 251; re-threading the balian/dukun through, 56–61. *See also* (k)not-work; *specific practices*

"Preanger System", 194–95

prestidigitation, 206, 210–14

"primitive" society: anthropology as study of, 15–16; magic as defining feature of, 12, 15; "primitive," figure of, 16; valuing of objects in, 98–99. *See also* "natives"

property, 53, 122, 253

Protestant Christianity, 68, 79, 235, 261n22

psychology, 15, 31, 47, 61, 62, 246

puputan, 120–21

Puri Agung (Klungkung), 120–21, 148, 269n4

purification, 104, 120; reversed, 59, 104; and translation, 8, 133, 169–70, 231

pusaka, 117, 127–30, 140, 227; commensurations with European monarchies, 133–34, 271n36;

racial politics, 23, 155; in colonial Java, 160–63; and *guna-guna* tales, 178; of *sirih*, 203; twilight zones, 184

Raffles, Thomas Stamford, 123, 132, 195

real-ing, 22, 24–25, 102

reality, 9–12, 13, 60, 64, 145, 190, 215, 217, 218, 235–236, 248; added to by sciences, 254–55; brain's reality-shaping force, 254; disenchantment (demagification) of, 19; good, 187; of guna-guna, 157, 174, 176–178, 182; Javanese, 48; and (k)notting of *keris* to magic, 125. *See also* one-world world

reality politics, 10, 15, 21, 103,; 258n10, 284n8; academic, 224; in anthropology, 120, 152, 154, 224; of colonial regime, 34–35, 46–48; 76, 83–85, 124, 193, 223; explaining away as technique of, 152; and *guna-guna*, 177, ; inquisitorial power of, 252–53; and *jimat*, 76–77, 83, 84; and moderns, 184, 245; and neopagans, 245; ongoing struggles, 234–35; and relativity, 224; and science, 245–46, 249–53, 255

really real, 22, 64, 152, 224, 234, 241, 284n5

reason, 10, 70; attributed to white men, 48–51, 168, 194, 213, 223; colonial legacy of, 183; *nuchter*, 22, 276n27; and relativism, 229–31. *See also* science; Science; science studies

rebellion, 23, 61, 265n25; "developed native" critique of, 79–80, 93; *élmu* blamed for, 85; as fanaticism, 37–38; Garut (Cimareme) massacre, 74–77, 80–81, 86, 101, 102; and *jimat*, 72, 75–83, 85; and power of *keris*, 135; uprisings in the 1860s and early 1870s, 75; use of *keris* in 1916 and 1917, 39

reclaiming, 232, 243, 245, 252–53

regalia, 126, 134–41, 145

"regression," 184–85

relations: aid and care of ancestors, 59; field of, 58–59; inattention to as cause of afflictions, 58

relativist claims (cultural relativism), 7, 11–12, 24, 144–45, 224, 230, 236 religion, 1, 9–10; Catholic Church, 14, 31, 68, 261n22, 263n37; Indonesian for, 237; missionaries, 18, 60–61, 94, 97–98, 128–30, 172, 271n30; place of magic in, 235–36; Protestant Christianity, 68, 79, 235, 261n22; trio with magic and science, 235–38

resography, 119

revenge, 166, 220, 261–62n26, 261n25

rijkssieraden, 126–30, 132, 134; 270n19; "ceremonial objects,"141; European symbols of office compared with, 134; as "family fetishes," 129–30, 141; as neologism, 134; taken by colonial state, 137, 272n51. See also *pusaka*

Robert-Houdin, Jean-Eugene, 262, 279n26, 281n60

rumor, 60, 82, 234; about stone incident, 201–5, 217; and *guna-guna* tales, 156, 164, 167, 169, 171, 276n30

sakti, 118, 140; *ilmu kasaktian*, 238; translations of, 5–6, 257–58n6

Sang Hyang Widhi Wasa, 53–55

Sarekat Islam, 74–75, 80–81; "Division B," 75, 81

Sartono Kartodirdjo, 75–76, 77, 104, 109

science: as abstraction, 229, 237, 249; biomedicine as science with a difference, 42; and capitalism, 284n6; common sense informed by, 7–8; experimental/empirical, 196, 239, 247–48, 255, 284n5; fall of magic attributed to, 113; Indonesian terms for, 237–38; *keris* in the work of, 127–33; learning from or with, not about, 255; magic, science, and religion, trio of, 235–38; magic contrasted to, 9; nonbifurcative approaches, 254–55; physicists, 222, 250, 283n3

Science, 1, 245–50; "advance," 247–48; and anthropologists, 229, 236; with capital S, 11; and horror of becoming a dupe, 249–50, 253–54; multiple

sciences versus, 12, 245–48, 250, 255, 283n1; objectivity or rationality claimed by, 247–48; provincialized as European by dukun, 157; "ready-made science" contrasted with "science in the making," 248; reality of strengthened by "magic," 3; sciences weaponized as, 245; "science wars," 250–51; sociotechnical assemblages required by, 248; translations of, 237–38, 283n4; universality attributed to, 26, 246; war against opinion, 247

science studies, 8, 11–12, 106, 111, 229, 241, 246; anthropology's magic linked to, 229–30; iconoclastic case studies, 246, 283n1; and "ontological turn," 246; ontology in, 254–55, 258n10; sociology of scientific knowledge, 229–30

séances, 15, 189, 210, 276n3

sexual politics, 160–63

Shapin, Steven, 196, 197–98, 230

sirih, 202–4, 214, 215, 217

slowing down, 3–4, 53, 193

Snouck Hurgronje, Christiaan, 16–17, 82–83, 85, 92, 130, 265n23, 275n19

social technologies, 197–98

socionatural ecology, 152–53

Soetatmo (Raden Mas Soetatmo Soeriokoesoemo), 79–80, 104

sorcery: capitalist, 232, 241, 242, 277n3, 284n8; *tovenaar*, 22, 40, 60, 69, 169; *toverij*, 173, 177, 183, 234, 238; *tover-*, 217–18

soul: and materiality, 68; soulstuff, 128–30, 133–34, 270n24

Souriau, Étienne, 73, 107

Spat, Claas, 101, 174, 267n50

"spirit," controversies of interpretation, 53–55, 59–60

spiritism, 73, 98, 128, 187, 188

"spirit possession": criminalization of, 85, 263n32; *karauhan*, 53, 263n32; *kemasukan*, 53, 263n32

witchcraft: in Africa, 16, 29, 72, 152,
275n26; anti-witchcraft legislation,
16, 29, 275n26; "black magic," 175–76;
exorcised with language, 152; field
experience of, 151–52; "getting caught"
by, 154; and *guna-guna*, 175; laws precipitated by, 72; reclaiming of, 232, 243,
245, 252–53; witch doctor as one who
counters, 29–30, 260n15; #witchtok,
242. *See also* neopagans; *toverij*

witch doctor, figure of: arrests by colonial state, 33–34; biomedical views of,
65; cartoon example, 1–3, 2, 12, 13, 19;
colonial genealogy of, 29; in Evans-
Pritchard, 29; as fraudulent, 30–31,
61; as one who counters witchcraft,
29–30, 260n15; as *toverdokter* or *won-*
derdokter, 40, 42–44, 52, 61, 260n15. See
also *balian*; *dukun*

witch hunts, 10, 19, 112, 252–53, 257n1; and
dispossession of property, 253; and
toverij as term, 173, 234

witnesses, 194–200, 206, 208; authenticating practices, 197–98; credibility,
criteria for, 197–98; modest, figure of,
196, 197

women: bourgeois European in Indies,
160, 163; *babu*, 162, 167; gender in
colonial texts, 48, 198, 261n20; and
guna-guna, 155; *nyai*, 160, *161*, 163, 170,
178, 217, 274n15

world-making, 9, 11, 64, 242; colonial, 14,
15, 234–35; Indonesian, 218, 233, 238;
modernity as, 20; plural, 251

www.ingramcontent.com/pod-product-compliance
Lightning Source LLC
Chambersburg PA
CBHW020823270326
41928CB00006B/423